from
Lynn
Christmas '79

W9-AZQ-103

The New York Times
AT THE
MOVIES

The New York Times
AT THE
MOVIES

Edited by
ARLEEN KEYLIN
and
CHRISTINE BENT

Introduction by
BOSLEY CROWTHER

ARNO PRESS
NEW YORK • 1979

A Note to the Reader

Original copies of The New York Times were not available to the publisher. This volume, therefore, was created from 35mm microfilm.

Copyright © 1915, 1917, 1920, 1921, 1922, 1923, 1925, 1927, 1930, 1931, 1932, 1933, 1934, 1935, 1937, 1938, 1939, 1940, 1941, 1942, 1944, 1945, 1946, 1947, 1948, 1949, 1950, 1951, 1952, 1953, 1954, 1955, 1956, 1957, 1958, 1959, 1960, 1961, 1962, 1963, 1964, 1966, 1967, 1968, 1969, 1970, 1971, 1972, 1973, 1974, 1975, 1976, 1977, 1978, 1979 by The New York Times Company.

Copyright © 1979 by The New York Times Company.
All Rights Reserved.

Library of Congress Cataloging in Publication Data

Main entry under title:

The New York times at the movies.

    Includes index.
    1. Moving-pictures—Reviews.   I. New York times.
II. Title: At the movies.
PN1995.N397   791.43'7   79-13948
ISBN 0-405-12415-5

Editorial Assistant: Jonathan Cohen

Manufactured in the United States of America.

CONTENTS

A

The African Queen.............................1
All About Eve.................................3
All Quiet On the Western Front................5
All the King's Men............................7
All the President's Men.......................9
American Graffiti............................10
An American In Paris.........................11
Anatomy of a Murder.........................12
Angels With Dirty Faces......................13
Annie Hall..................................15
The Apartment...............................16
Around the World in Eighty Days.............17

B

Baby Doll...................................18
Bad Day at Black Rock.......................19
Bananas.....................................20
Beau Geste..................................21
Ben Hur.....................................22
Ben Hur.....................................23
The Best Year of Our Lives..................25
The Big Heat................................26
Birth of a Nation...........................27
Blackboard Jungle...........................28
Blazing Saddles.............................29
Bonnie & Clyde..............................31
Born Yesterday..............................32
The Bride of Frankenstein...................33
The Bridge On the River Kwai................35
Butch Cassidy and the Sundance Kid..........37

C

Cabaret.....................................39
Caine Mutiny................................40
Camille.....................................42
Captain Blood...............................44
The Carpetbaggers...........................45
Casablanca..................................47
Catch-22....................................48
The Champ...................................49
Citizen Kane................................51
City Lights.................................52
Cleopatra...................................54
Cleopatra...................................55
Close Encounters of the Third Kind..........57
Come Back Little Sheba......................59

D

David and Lisa..............................60
Deer Hunter.................................61
Deliverance.................................63

Detective Story.............................65
Dr. Jeckyll & Mr. Hyde......................66
Dr. No......................................67
Dr. Strangelove.............................69
Dinner at Eight.............................71
Dog Day Afternoon...........................72
Dracula.....................................73

E

Easy Rider..................................74
Exodus......................................75
Exorcist....................................77

F

42nd Street.................................79
Frankenstein................................80
The French Connection.......................81
From Here to Eternity.......................83
The Front Page..............................85

G

Gentleman's Agreement.......................87
Gigi..88
The Godfather...............................89
Godspell....................................91
Gone With the Wind..........................92
Goodbye Girl................................94
The Graduate................................95
Grand Hotel.................................97
Grease......................................99
The Great Dictator.........................100
Guess Who's Coming to Dinner...............101
Guns of Navarone...........................103

H

A Hard Day's Night.........................105
High Noon..................................107
High Sierra................................108
Hound of the Baskervilles..................109
House of Wax...............................110
How to Marry a Millionaire.................111
The Hucksters..............................113
The Hunchback of Notre Dame................114

I

In the Heat of the Night...................115

J

Jailhouse Rock.............................117

Jaws 118
Jazz Singer 119

K

The King and I 121
King Kong 123
King Kong 124
The Last Picture Show 125

L

Little Caesar 126
Little Miss Marker 127
Lolita 128
Love Story 129

M

The Magnificent Seven 130
The Maltese Falcon 131
A Man For All Seasons 132
Manhattan 134
Marty 136
Mary Poppins 137
MASH 139
Midnight Cowboy 141
Mildred Pierce 143
The Misfits 144
Mr. Smith Goes to Washington 145
My Fair Lady 147
My Little Chickadee 149

N

Network 150
A Night at the Opera 151

O

Of Mice and Men 153
On the Beach 155
On the Waterfront 156
Orphans of the Storm 157

P

The Phantom of the Opera 158
Planet of the Apes 159
Psycho 160

R

Rebecca 161

Rebel Without a Cause 163
The Road to Morocco 165
The Robe 167
Rocky 169
Room at the Top 171

S

Saturday Night Fever 172
The Searchers 174
Sergeant York 176
The Seven Year Itch 177
Shaft 178
Shane 179
The Sheik 180
Snow White and the Seven Dwarfs 181
Some Like It Hot 183
Sounder 184
Stagecoach 185
A Star is Born 186
A Star is Born 188
Star Wars 189
The Sting 191
The Sun Also Rises 192
Sunset Boulevard 193
Superman 196
Sweet Bird of Youth 197

T

Taxi Driver 198
The Ten Commandments 199
That's Entertainment 200
The Three Faces of Eve 201
To Have and Have Not 203
Tom Jones 204
The Towering Inferno 206
Treasure Island 207
The Treasure of Sierra Madre 209
The Turning Point 210
2001—A Space Odyssey 211

U

An Unmarried Woman 212

W

West Side Story 213
White Christmas 214
The Wizard of Oz 215

INTRODUCTION

One can say without fear of contradiction that no circumscribed body of film criticism in the United States rivals, in extent and revelation, that which has appeared in the columns of *The New York Times.* Over a span of close onto a century, beginning as it properly should with a charmingly wonderstruck account of the first public showing of the Edison-Armat Vitascope at the Koster & Bial Music Hall in New York City on the night of April 23, 1896, *The Times* has been industriously "covering" and reviewing the quantity and quality of the work in this medium with an ever-expanding comprehension of its importance as an art form.

Millions of words of commendation and certainly many more millions of reproof, disapproval and even damnation of individual films have appeared, reflecting the judgments of critics trained and qualified to do their jobs. This body of criticism is now available in a thoroughly-indexed collection of *all The Times'* film reviews, 1913-1978, published by The New York Times/Arno Press. Further volumes will be added to this series. In my estimation, this collection constitutes a superb and indispensable treasury of motion picture criticism, erudition and assorted reportage that stands as a monumental archive in the literature of the art of cinema.

Now, as a lighter companion to that treasury, Arno Press is offering this sampler of selections from all those thousands of reviews—a sort of run-down on what it has been like to go to the movies with *The New York Times* over the years. It is not in any way intended as a designation of the "best"—a presumption which would be most audacious, if not reckless, as I should know! As the author of three volumes of what I called "great" or "memorable" films, seen again and re-reviewed in a perspective of how they appear to me today, I have discovered the passion with which readers can disagree, even on choices *not* presented as necessarily the absolute *crème de la crème.* So I am relieved that the editors at Arno do not claim these selections to mark the "best," either in the quality of the pictures or the literary distinction of the reviews. The most that is claimed is that these entries represent the judgments of a broad taste in picking films that have had artistic merit and have widely and successfully entertained.

One feature of this volume is of particular worth. That is the illustration of each selection with still photographs pertinent to that film, shots of key scenes and/or portraits of the stars. This provision in such profusion as it is exercised here is one that could not be afforded in the complete collection of *Times'* reviews because of the obvious strictures imposed by the limitations of space. And, indeed, it is one that is prohibited by the same limitations in the regular day-by-day coverage of films in *The Times*, so that what we have here is an addendum that is unique in the publication of these reviews.

How much it contributes in substance and enjoyment to the visual recall of the films is something that only a reader who has waded through files of old reviews hoping to reconstruct in the mind's eye how the old films looked can fully appreciate. Words are quite obviously essential to the transmission of the intellectual and dramatic content of old films, but words can only suggest their visual or pictorial appearances. Aside from actually seeing the old films again, which is usually difficult if not impossible, the best thing is to have still photographs which evoke the characteristics of the movies. Many thanks to the editors of Arno for being so generous with the stills!

I am thankful, too, for the instances in which they have presented the reviews of certain pictures in their original productions and then have placed these alongside the critiques of the remakes of these pictures years later—a juxtaposing which demonstrates not only enormous changes that have occurred in cinematic styles and techniques but also the changes and contrasts in the sophistications of critics and audiences.

It is startling to read, for instance, *The Times'* review of the original *King Kong*, that classic monster picture which was released in 1933, and then to read the review of the 1977 remake and perceive the reaction of the present-day critic to essentially the same material. What an epitaph to anthropomorphic monsters! What a comment on modern suspension of disbelief! Now, if King Kong had been found on a distant planet...Well, I will not go into that!

Also gratifying—at least, to me personally—is the juxtaposing of the reviews of the original silent film of *Cleopatra*, made in 1917 with the then popular vamp, Theda Bara, as star and the spectacular (and notorious!) sound film version released in 1963 with Elizabeth Taylor in the title role. How remote, both in physical production and in theatrical style, does one perceive the original to be from the tremendous, opulent, colorful talking film that became one of the most talked-about and controversial motion pictures of the modern day! How phenomenal had been the advancement within the time-span between these two reviews!

And this brings me to my estimation of the long-run coverage of films by *The Times.* It has, above all, been objective, reasonably temperate and conscientiously fair. To be sure, criticism is subjective insofar as it exposes the tastes and the perceptions of the individual doing the criticizing—and that is as it should be. The quality of the mind of the reviewer is one of the stimulating revelations of a good critique. But personal ostentation and self-promotion are tendencies to be abominated. These are tendencies which are not apparent in the great body of film reviews in *The Times*—and I think that I, who was a long-time film critic for that publication, am entitled to say it, with all due modesty. *Times'* critics have been picked and trained to be fair and reliable analysts.

That is why I repeat that this volume of selected *Times'* film reviews is as fine and dependable a cross-section of good journalistic criticism as one can find anywhere, and that reading this book should give one a keen sense of what it has been like to go to the movies with *The New York Times.*

Bosley Crowther

'The African Queen,' Starring Humphrey Bogart, Katharine Hepburn, at the Capitol

THE AFRICAN QUEEN, adapted for the screen by James Agee and John Huston, from the novel, "The African Queen," by C. S. Forester; directed by Mr. Huston; produced by S. P. Eagle. A Horizon-Romulus Production released by United Artists. At the Capitol.

Charlie Allnut............Humphrey Bogart
Rose Sayer..............Katharine Hepburn
Rev. Samuel Sayer............Robert Morley
Captain of the Louisa.............Peter Bull
First Officer of the Louisa.....Theodore Bikel
German Army Officer..........Peter Swanick

By BOSLEY CROWTHER

Whether C. S. Forester had his salty British tongue in his cheek when he wrote his extravagant story of romance and adventure, "The African Queen," we wouldn't be able to tell you. But it is obvious—to us, at least—that Director John Huston was larking when he turned the novel into a film.

His lively screen version of it, which came to the Capitol yesterday with Katharine Hepburn and Humphrey Bogart in its two predominant roles, is a slick job of movie hoodwinking with a thoroughly implausible romance, set in a frame of wild adventure that is as whopping as its tale of off-beat love. And the main tone and character of it are in the area of the well-disguised spoof.

This is not noted with disfavor. Considering the nature of the yarn, it is hard to conceive its presentation in any other way—that is in the realistic channels of the motion-picture screen. For Mr. Forester's fable of love suddenly taking bloom in the hearts of a lady missionary and a Cockney rumpot while they're trying to escape down a German East African river in a wheezy steam-launch during World War I is so personally preposterous and socially bizarre that it would take a 'ot of doing to be made convincing in the cold, clear light of day. In the brilliance of Technicolor and with adventure intruding at every turn, any attempt at serious portrayal would be not only incongruous but absurd.

And so Mr. Huston merits credit for putting this fantastic tale on a level of sly, polite kidding and generally keeping it there, while going about the happy business of engineering excitement and visual thrills. His lady, played by Miss Hepburn with her crisp flair for comedy, is a caricature of a prissy female in her high choke collar, linen duster and limp cloth hat. And his man, played by Mr. Bogart, is a virtual burlesque of the tropical tramp, just one cut—and that a very thin one—above the ripe meatiness of the clown. Not since Elsa Lanchester and Charles Laughton appeared in a very similar picture, "The Beachcomber," several years ago, have the incongruities of social station and manners been so pointedly and humorously portrayed.

"Mr. Allnut—dear—what's your first name?" the lady politely inquires of her companion the morning after she has apparently submitted to him, in what is perhaps the screen's least lustful and least likely seduction scene. "Charlie," he beams, with melting coyness. It is that anomalous and droll.

No, all of it, however, Mr. Huston and his writer, James Agee, who assisted him in the preparation of the deliberately wordy script, have let the yarn slide onto the mud flats of heavy drama that Mr. Forester laid down, and while it is in that situation, they have let it become soggy in plot and mood. After running impossible rapids, eluding a German fort and keeping the romance skipping nimbly on the surface of sly absurdity, they have grounded their picture on a barrier of sudden solemnity and sanded it in with emotions that are neither buoyant nor credible. No wonder the fantastic climax that is abruptly and sentimentally contrived appears the most fulsome melodrama, unworthy of Mr. Huston and this film.

However, while it is skipping—and that is most of the time — there is rollicking fun and gentle humor in this outlandish "African Queen." There's nothing subtle or moralistic, mind you, outside of the jesting display that nature's most formidable creature is a serene and self-righteous dame.

Without two accomplished players, Mr. Huston could never have achieved his highly audacious purpose of a virtually two-character film, but Miss Hepburn and Mr. Bogart are entirely up to their jobs, outside of their lack of resemblance to the nationals they're said to be. Robert Morley is briefly effective as the lady's missionary brother who conveniently dies, and Peter Bull struts and puffs for one sequence as the captain of a German gunboat on an African lake.

For the rest, there is beauty and excitement in the lush and colorful scenes of a broad and forbidding African river, its foaming white rapids and falls, and the various birds and animals that live on the banks and in the stream. Mr. Huston went right to Africa for this genuine atmosphere. While the hardships were said to be oppressive, he and his producer, S. P. Eagle, have been repaid. Their picture is doubly provided with the insurance of popularity.

As the lady missionary and the Cockney rumpot, Katherine Hepburn and Humphrey Bogart in *The African Queen*.

HUMPHREY **BOGART!** KATHARINE **HEPBURN!** AND **AFRICA!**

HERE IS FABULOUS ADVENTURE!

HORIZON PICTURES presents

YOU'LL NEVER FORGET: This throbbing, reckless love! They never dreamed of being in each other's arms, yet the mystic spell of the jungle swept them to primitive, hungry embrace!

"THE **AFRICAN QUEEN**" color by **TECHNICOLOR**

SO GREAT ...it has been nominated for "Best Actor", "Best Actress" and "Best Director" Academy Awards!

Actually Filmed in The Splendors and Dangers of The Belgian Congo!

WITH **ROBERT MORLEY**

and Peter Bull · Theodore Bikel · Walter Cotell · Peter Swanwick · Richard Marner · Director of Photography Jack Cardiff · Based on the novel "The African Queen" by C. S. FORESTER · Adapted for the screen by JAMES AGEE & JOHN HUSTON · A HORIZON-ROMULUS PRODUCTION · Released thru United Artists

Produced by **S. P. EAGLE**

Directed by **JOHN HUSTON**

STARTS **WEDNESDAY · CAPITOL** B'way & 51st St.

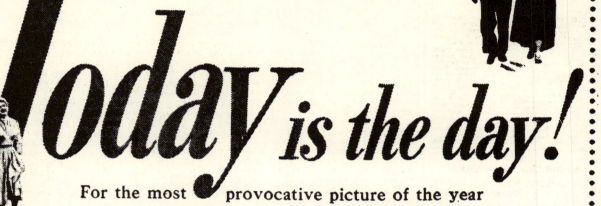

Today is the day!

For the most provocative picture of the year
from TWENTIETH CENTURY-FOX

CREATED BY THE WINNERS OF 8 ACADEMY AWARDS

BETTE DAVIS.......... *as Margo Channing*

ANNE BAXTER........ *as Eve Harrington*

GEORGE SANDERS .. *as Addison De Witt*

CELESTE HOLM........ *as Karen Richards*

Gary Merrill.............. *as Bill Simpson*

"all about eve"

ON STAGE
in person
MARTHA STEWART
The BLACKBURN TWINS

ON ICE!
"Deep Purple" starring
JOAN HYLDOFT
with the Roxy Skating
Blades and Belles
The Gae Foster Roxyettes
and Escorts and
H. Leopold Spitalny's,
Choral Ensemble

EXTRA!
PHIL ROMAYNE
TERRY BRENT

DARRYL F. ZANUCK .... *The Producer*

JOSEPH L. MANKIEWICZ .... *The Writer-Director*

**FOUR SCHEDULED
PERFORMANCES DAILY**

No Seating After Picture Starts!

All Tickets For All Performances On
Sale at Boxoffice or By Mail,
and Daily Before Each Performance.

1st Stage Show 10:45 A.M.   Picture 11:30 A.M.
2nd Stage Show · 2:00 P.M.   Picture · 2:45 P.M.
3rd Stage Show · 5:15 P.M.   Picture · 6:00 P.M.
4th Stage Show · 8:45 P.M.   Picture · 9:30 P.M.

There will be a half hour intermission between each show
All performances SAT & SUN approximately one hour later

NO INCREASE IN PRICES!

*It's all about women
—and their men!*

DOORS OPEN
10 A.M. **ROXY** 7th Avenue
and 50th St.

DOORS OPEN SATURDAY 11 A.M.

Bette Davis and Anne Baxter Star in 'All About Eve,' New Feature at Roxy Theatre

ALL ABOUT EVE, screen play by Joseph L. Mankiewicz, adapted from a short story and radio play by Mary Orr; directed by Mr. Mankiewicz; produced by Darryl F. Zanuck for Twentieth Century-Fox. At the Roxy.

Margo	Bette Davis
Eve	Anne Baxter
Addison De Witt	George Sanders
Karen	Celeste Holm
Bill Simpson	Gary Merrill
Lloyd Richards	Hugh Marlowe
Birdie	Thelma Ritter
Miss Casswell	Marilyn Monroe
Max Fabian	Gregory Ratoff
Phoebe	Barbara Bates
Aged Actor	Walter Hampden
Girl	Randy Stuart
Leading Man	Craig Hill
Doorman	Leland Harris
Autograph Seeker	Barbara White
Stage Manager	Eddie Fisher
Pianist	Claude Stroud

By BOSLEY CROWTHER

The good old legitimate theatre, the temple of Thespis and Art, which has dished out a lot of high derision of Hollywood in its time, had better be able to take it as well as dish it out, because the worm has finally turned with a venom and Hollywood is dishing it back. In "All About Eve," a withering satire—witty, mature and worldly-wise — which Twentieth Century-Fox and Joseph Mankiewicz delivered to the Roxy yesterday, the movies are letting Broadway have it with claws out and no holds barred. If Thespis doesn't want to take a beating, he'd better yell for George Kaufman and Moss Hart.

As a matter of fact, Mr. Kaufman and Mr. Hart might even find themselves outclassed by the dazzling and devastating mockery that is brilliantly packed into this film. For obviously Mr. Mankiewicz, who wrote and directed it, had been sharpening his wits and his talents a long, long time for just this go. Obviously, he had been observing the theatre and its charming folks for years with something less than an idolator's rosy illusions and zeal. And now, with the excellent assistance of Bette Davis and a truly sterling cast, he is wading into the theatre's middle with all claws slashing and settling a lot of scores.

If anything, Mr. Mankiewicz has been even too full of fight—too full of cutlass-edged derision of Broadway's theatrical tribe. Apparently his dormant dander and his creative zest were so aroused that he let himself go on this picture and didn't know when to stop. For two hours and eighteen minutes have been taken by him to achieve the ripping apart of an illusion which might have been comfortably done in an hour and a half.

It is not that his characters aren't full blown, that his incidents aren't brilliantly conceived and that his dialogue, pithy and pungent, is not as clever as any you will hear. In picturing the inside story of an ambitious actress' rise from glamour-struck girl in a theatre alley to flinty-eyed winner of the Siddons Prize, Mr. Mankiewicz has gathered up a saga of theatrical ambition and conceit, pride and deception and hypocrisy, that just about drains the subject dry.

Indeed, he has put so many characters — so many vivid Broadway types—through the flattening and decimating wringer of his unmerciful wit that the punishment which he gives them becomes painful when so lengthily drawn. And that's the one trouble with this picture. It beats the horse after it is dead.

But that said, the rest is boundless tribute to Mr. Mankiewicz and his cast for ranging a gallery of people that dazzle, horrify and fascinate. Although the title character — the self-seeking, ruthless Eve, who would make a black-widow spider look like a lady bug —is the motivating figure in the story and is played by Anne Baxter with icy calm, the focal figure and most intriguing character is the actress whom Bette Davis plays. This lady, an aging ,acid creature with a cankerous ego and a stinging tongue, is the end-all of Broadway disenchantment, and Miss Davis plays her to a fare-thee-well. Indeed, the superb illumination of the spirit and pathos of this dame which is a brilliant screen actress gives her merits an Academy award.

Of the men, George Sanders is walking wormwood, neatly wrapped in a mahogany veneer, as a vicious and powerful drama critic who has a licentious list towards pretty girls; Gary Merrill is warm and reassuring as a director with good sense and a heart, and Hugh Marlowe is brittle and boyish as a playwright with more glibness than brains. Celeste Holm is appealingly normal and naive as the latter's wife and Thelma Ritter is screamingly funny as a wised-up maid until she is summarily lopped off.

A fine Darryl Zanuck production, excellent music and an air of ultra-class complete this superior satire. The legitimate theatre had better look to its laurels.

On the stage at the Roxy are Martha Stewart and the Blackburn Twins and Joan Hyldoft, Phil Romayne and Terry Brent in an ice revue.

Bette Davis and Gary Merrill.

Bette Davis, Hugh Marlowe and Celeste Holm in a scene from *All About Eve*.

Lew Ayres

Young Germany in the War

By MORDAUNT HALL.

ALL QUIET ON THE WESTERN FRONT, with Louis Wolheim, Lewis Ayres, John Wray, Raymond Griffith, George Summerville, Russell Gleason, William Bakewell, Scott Kolk, Walter Browne Rogers, Ben Alexander, Owen Davis Jr., Beryl Mercer, Edwin Maxwell, Marion Clayton, Richard Alexander, Pat Collins, Yola D'Avril, Arnold Lucy, Bill Irving, Renee Damonde, Poupee Andriot, Edmund Breese, Heinie Conklin, Bertha Mann, Bodil Rosing, Joan Marsh and others, based on Erich Maria Remarque's book, directed by Lewis Milestone, with dialogue by Maxwell Anderson and George Abbott. At the Central Theatre.

From the pages of Erich Maria Remarque's widely read book of young Germany in the World War, "All Quiet on the Western Front," Carl Laemmle's Universal Pictures Corporation has produced a trenchant and imaginative audible picture, in which the producers adhere with remarkable fidelity to the spirit and events of the original stirring novel. It was presented last night at the Central Theatre before an audience that most of the time was held to silence by its realistic scenes. It is a notable achievement, sincere and earnest, with glimpses that are vivid and graphic. Like the original, it does not mince matters concerning the horrors of battle. It is a vocalized screen offering that is pulsating and harrowing, one in which the fighting flashes are photographed in an amazingly effective fashion.

Lewis Milestone, who has several good films to his credit, was entrusted with the direction of this production. And Mr. Laemmle had the foresight to employ those well-known playwrights, George Abbott and Maxwell Anderson, to make the adaptation and write the dialogue. Some of the scenes are not a little too long, and one might also say that a few members of the cast are not Teutonic in appearance; but this means but little when one considers the picture as a whole, for wherever possible, Mr. Milestone has used his fecund imagination, still clinging loyally to the incidents of the book. In fact, one is just as gripped by witnessing the picture as one was by reading the printed pages, and in most instances it seems as though the very impressions written in ink by Herr Remarque had become animated on the screen.

In nearly all the sequences, fulsomeness is avoided. Truth comes to the fore, when the young soldiers are elated at the idea of joining up, when they are disillusioned, when they are hungry, when they are killing rats in a dugout, when they are shaken with fear and when they, or one of them, becomes fed up with the conception of war held by the elderly man back home.

Often the scenes are of such excellence that if they were not audible one might believe that they were actual motion pictures of activities behind the lines, in the trenches and in No Man's Land. It is an expansive production with views that never appear to be cramped. In looking at a dugout one readily imagines a long line of such earthy abodes. When shells demolish these underground quarters, the shrieks of fear, coupled with the rat-tat-tat of machine guns, the bang-ziz of the trench mortars and the whining of shells, it tells the story of the terrors of fighting better than anything so far has done in animated photography coupled with the microphone.

There are heartrending glimpses in a hospital, where one youngster has had his leg amputated and still believes that he has a pain in his toes. Just as he complains of his, he remembers another soldier who had complained of the same pain in the identical words. He then realizes what has happened to him, and he shrieks and cries out that he does not want to go through life a cripple. There is the death room from which nobody is said to come out, and Paul, admirably acted by Lewis Ayres, is taken to this chamber shouting, as he is wheeled away, that he will come back. And he does. The agony in this hospital reflects that of the details given by Herr Remarque.

In an early sequence there is the introduction of the tyrant corporal, Himmelstoss, who has no end of ideas to keep young soldiers on the alert, sometimes amusing himself by making them crawl under tables and then, during the day, ordering them to fall on their faces in the mud. Just as by reading the book, one learns, while looking at this animated work, to hate Himmelstoss. And one occasion when the audience broke their wrapt stillness last night was with an outburst of laughter. This happened when Paul and his comrades lay in wait for the detested non-commissioned officer, and, after thrashing him, left him in a stagnant pool with a sack tied over his head.

Soldiers are perceived being taken like cattle to the firing line and then having to wait for food. There is the cook, who finds that he has enough rations for twice the number of the men left in the company, and when he hears that many have been killed and others wounded he still insists that these soldiers will only receive their ordinary rations. Here that amiable war veteran, Katczinsky, splendidly acted by Louis Wolheim, grabs the culinary expert by the throat and finally a sergeant intervenes and instructs the cook to give the company the full rations intended for the survivors and those who have either died or been wounded.

Now and again songs are heard, genuine melody that comes from the soldiers, and as time goes on Paul and his comrades begin to look upon the warfare with the same philosophic demeanor that Katczinsky reveals. But when the big guns begin to boom there are further terrors for the soldiers and in one of these Paul has his encounter with a Frenchman in a shell hole. Paul stabs the Frenchman to death and as he observes life ebbing from the man with whom he had struggled, he fetches water from the bottom of the shell hole and moistens the Frenchman's lips. It is to Paul a frightening and nerve-racking experience, especially when he eventually pulls from a pocket a photograph of the wife and child of the man he had slain.

Raymond Griffith, the erstwhile comedian who, years before acting in film comedies, lost his voice through shrieking in a stage melodrama, gives a marvelous performance as the dying Frenchman. It may be a little too long for one's peace of mind, but this does not detract from Mr. Griffith's sterling portrayal.

Another comedian, none other than George (Slim) Summerville, also distinguishes himself in a light but very telling rôle, that of Tjaden. It is he who talks about the Kaiser and himself both having no reason to go to war—the only difference, according to the soldier in the trenches, being that the Kaiser is at home. It is Tjaden who is left behind when the youngsters swim over to the farmhouse and visit the French girls.

Much has been made of the pair of boots and the soldier who wanted them and declared, when he got them from the man who passed on, that they would make fighting almost agreeable for anybody. Mr. Milestone has done wonders with this passage, showing the boots on the man and soon depicting that while they may have been comfortable and watertight, boots don't matter much when a shell with a man's name written on it comes his way.

The episodes are unfolded with excellent continuity and one of the outstanding ones is where Paul goes home and finds everything changed, including himself. He is asked by the same professor who had taught him, to talk to the new batch of pupils about the war. He remembers his enthusiasm for it when he enlisted in 1914 and he now knows how different are his impressions since he has been stringing barbed wire under the dangerous glare of Very lights in No Man's Land. He knows what a uniform means, and believes that there is no glory at the front; all he has to say to the boys is hard and terse. He tires of the gray heads who think that they know something about war and prefers to cut his leave short and go back to the fighting area rather than listen to the arguments of those who have not been disillusioned by shells, mud, rats and vermin.

During the intermission a curtain is lowered with "poppies, row on row," a glimpse of Flanders field. After that comes more grim battle episodes and more suffering of the men in the gray-green tunics.

All the players do capital work, but Beryl Mercer does not seem to be a good choice for the rôle of Paul's mother. This may be due, however, to having seen her relatively recently in the picturization of Sir James M. Barrie's playlet, "The Old Lady Shows Her Medals." Messrs. Milestone, Abbott and Anderson in this film have contributed a memorable piece of work to the screen.

Lew Ayres and Louis Wolheim in *All Quiet on the Western Front.*

and NOW the MOTION PICTURE!

"ALL QUIET on the WESTERN FRONT"

with Louis Wolheim, Lewis Ayres and John Wray. A Universal Picture

Presented by CARL LAEMMLE

OPENING TONIGHT AT 8:30

CENTRAL THEATRE, B'way and 47th St.

Twice Daily Thereafter, 2:45-8:45.

Seats now on sale for first four weeks

MATS.	$1.00, 75c, 50c		
NIGHTS	$2.00 $1.50 $1.00, 75c		
SAT. & SUN. MATS.	$1.50, $1.00, 75c		
SAT. & SUN. NIGHTS	$2.00, $1.50, $1.00		

"All Quiet on the Western Front" will NOT be shown elsewhere in Greater New York this season

THE PULITZER PRIZE WINNING NOVEL BECOMES A VITAL, VERY GREAT MOTION PICTURE

If he didn't own you, he'd buy you. And if you couldn't be bought, he'd ruin you!

COLUMBIA PICTURES
presents
ROBERT ROSSEN'S PRODUCTION
of

ALL THE KING'S MEN

Based upon the Pulitzer Prize Novel "All The King's Men" by Robert Penn Warren
with Broderick CRAWFORD · Joanne DRU · John IRELAND · John DEREK · Mercedes McCAMBRIDGE
Written for the Screen and Directed by ROBERT ROSSEN

'All the King's Men,' Columbia Film Based on the Novel by Warren, at Victoria

ALL THE KING'S MEN, screen play by Robert Rossen, based on the Robert Penn Warren novel of the same name; directed and produced by Mr. Rossen for Columbia Pictures. At the Victoria.

Willie Stark	Broderick Crawford
Anne Stanton	Joanne Dru
Jack Burden	John Ireland
Tom Stark	John Derek
Sadie Burke	Mercedes McCambridge
Adam Stanton	Shepperd Strudwick
Tiny Duffy	Ralph Dumke
Lucy Stark	Anne Seymour
Mrs. Burden	Katharine Warren
Judge Stanton	Raymond Greenleaf
Sugar Boy	Walter Burke
Dolph Pillsbury	Will Wright
Floyd McEvoy	Grandon Rhodes
Pa Stark	H. C. Miller
Hale	Richard Hale
Commissioner	William Bruce
Sheriff	A. C. Tillman
Madison	Houseley Stevenson
Minister	Truett Myers
Football Coach	Phil Tully
Helene Hale	Helene Stanley

By BOSLEY CROWTHER

Out of Robert Penn Warren's prize novel, "All the King's Men," which was obviously based on the familiar rise and fall of the late Huey Long, Robert Rossen has written and directed, as well as personally produced, a rip-roaring film of the same title. It opened at the Victoria yesterday.

We have carefully used that descriptive as the tag for this new Columbia film because a quality of turbulence and vitality is the one that it most fully demonstrates. In telling a complicated story of a self-made and self-styled "red-necked hick" who batters his way to political kingdom in an unspecified southern state, the picture bounces from raw-boned melodrama into dark psychological depths and thrashes around in those regions until it claws back to violences again. Consistency of dramatic structure—or of character revelation—is not in it. But it has a superb pictorialism which perpetually crackles and explodes.

And because of this rich pictorialism, which embraces a wide and fluid scene, it gathers a frightening comprehension of the potential of demagoguery in this land. From ugly illustrations of back-room spittoon politics to wild illuminations of howling political mobs, it catches the dim but dreadful aspect of ignorance and greed when played upon by theatrics, eloquence and bluff. It visions the vulgar spellbinders and political hypocrites for what they are and it looks on extreme provincialism with a candid and pessimistic eye.

In short, Mr. Rossen has assembled in this starkly unprettified film a piece of pictorial journalism that is remarkable for its brilliant parts. It clearly observes the beginnings of a Huey Long type of demagogue in an humble and honest lawyer fighting the "bosses" in a sleepy dirt-road town. It follows this disillusioned fellow as he gets the hang of politics and discovers the strange intoxication of his own unprincipled charm. And it wallows with him in egoism, corruption and dictatorial power until he is finally shot down by an assassin when his triumphs appear uncontrolled.

All of these things, Mr. Rossen, as director, has pictured stunningly. His final episode of personal violence and mob hysteria is superb for savagery. But in his parallel endeavors to transfer from Mr. Warren's book some real understanding of the character, he has met with much less success. In fact, the whole middle section of the film, which is deeply concerned with the brutal impact of the fellow upon his wife, son, mistress and friends, is a heavy confusion of dense dramatics that is saved from being downright dull only by the variety and vigor of pictorial detail.

And you may count as pictorial detail the performance which Broderick Crawford gives as the big, brawling, boisterous "hick" lawyer who makes himself a momentary "king." Mr. Crawford concentrates tremendous energy into every delineation he plays, whether it is the enthusiasm of a callow bumpkin or the virulence of a drunken demagogue. Although it is hard to know precisely why he gravitates and acts the way he does, he draws a compelling portrait, in two dimensions, of an egomaniac.

Less can be said for the other principal performers in the film—not because of their own shortcomings but because of the unresolved roles they play. Joanne Dru is a pretty, well-dressed cipher as the meaningless mistress of the man, and John Ireland is a loose-limbed, dead-panned puppet as a newspaper reporter who follows him around. Shepperd Strudwick fumbles vaguely with the passions of the doctor who assassinates the brute, and Mercedes McCambridge is picturesque but vagrant as a hard-boiled henchman in skirts. However, the various people who play cheap politicos, especially Will Wright and Ralph Dumke, are as genuine as pot-bellied stoves. As satellites to Mr. Crawford, in the raw, racy portions of the film, they help to bring color and excitement to this ironic "All the King's Men."

Broderick Crawford and Mercedes McCambridge in *All the King's Men.*

The Most Devastating Detective Story Of This Century.

REDFORD/HOFFMAN
"ALL THE PRESIDENT'S MEN"

ROBERT REDFORD/DUSTIN HOFFMAN "ALL THE PRESIDENT'S MEN"
Starring JACK WARDEN Special appearance by MARTIN BALSAM, HAL HOLBROOK and JASON ROBARDS as Ben Bradlee
Screenplay by WILLIAM GOLDMAN • Based on the book by CARL BERNSTEIN and BOB WOODWARD • Music by DAVID SHIRE
Produced by WALTER COBLENZ • Directed by ALAN J. PAKULA
A Wildwood Enterprises Production • A Robert Redford-Alan J. Pakula Film
Technicolor® From WARNER BROS
A WARNER COMMUNICATIONS COMPANY

WORLD PREMIERE ENGAGEMENT STARTS TOMORROW

— ON THE WEST SIDE —
LOEWS ASTOR PLAZA
B'way & 44th St — 869-8340
10:30, 1:00, 3:30, 6:00, 8:30, 11:00

— ON THE EAST SIDE —
LOEWS TOWER EAST
72nd St. & 3rd Ave. — 879-1313
12:30, 3:00, 5:30, 8:00, 10:30

— ON LONG ISLAND —
UA SYOSSET
Jericho Turnpike (516) 921-5810
1:45, 4:25, 7:15, 9:55

UA BELLEVUE
Upper Montclair — (201) 744-1455
1:45, 4:25, 7:15, 9:55

— IN NEW JERSEY —
General Cinema's
MENLO PARK
Rte. 1 at Parsonage Rd., Edison (201) LI 9-8787
2:00, 4:45, 7:30, 10:00

8

'President's Men', Spellbinding Film

By VINCENT CANBY

Newspapers and newspapermen have long been favorite subjects for movie makers—a surprising number of whom are former newspapermen, yet not until "All the President's Men," the riveting screen adaptation of the Watergate book by Carl Bernstein and Bob Woodward, has any film come remotely close to being an accurate picture of American journalism at its best.

"All The President's Men," directed by Alan J. Pakula, written by William Goldman and largely pushed into being by the continuing interest of one of its, stars, Robert Redford, is a lot of things all at once: a spellbinding detective story about the work of the two Washington Post reporters who helped break the Watergate scandal, a breathless adventure that recalls the triumphs of Frank and Joe Hardy in that long-ago series of boys' books, and vivid footnote to some contemporary American history that still boggles the mind.

●

The film, which opened yesterday at Loews Astor Plaza and Tower East Theaters, is an unequivocal smash-hit — the thinking man's "Jaws."

Much of the effectiveness of the movie, which could easily have become a mishmash of names, dates and events, is in its point of view, which remains that of its two, as yet unknown reporters. Carl Bernstein (Dustin Hoffman), highly competitive and a little more expe-

Jason Robards, newspaper editor, in *All the President's Men.*

The Cast

ALL THE PRESIDENT'S MEN, directed by Alan J. Pakula; screenplay by William Goldman, based on the book by Carl Bernstein and Bob Woodward; produced by Walter Coblenz; music, David Shire; director of photography, Gordon Willis; editor, Robert L. Wolfe; a Wildwood production, distributed by Warner Brothers. Running time: 136 minutes. At Loews Astor Plaza, 44th Street west of Broadway, and Loews Tower East, Third Avenue near 72d Street. This film has been rated PG.

Carl Bernstein	Dustin Hoffman
Bob Woodward	Robert Redford
Harry Rosenfeld	Jack Warden
Howard Simons	Martin Balsam
Deep Throat	Hal Holbrook
Ben Bradlee	Jason Robards
Bookkeeper	Jane Alexander
Debbie Sloan	Meredith Baxter
Dardis	Ned Beatty
Hugh Sloan, Jr.	Stephen Collins
Sally Aiken	Penny Fuller
Foreign Editor	John McMartin
Donald Segretti	Robert Walden
Frank Wills	Himself
Bachinski	David Arkin
Barker	Henry Calvert
Martinez	Dominic Chianese
Kay Eddy	Lindsay Ann Crouse
Miss Milland	Valerie Curtin
McCord	Richard Herd
Carolyn Abbot	Allyn Ann McLerie
Angry CRP woman	Neva Patterson
Al Lewis	Joshua Shelley

rienced than his partner, and Bob Woodward (Robert Redford), very ambitious and a dog for details.

It's through their eyes—skeptical, hungry, insatiably curious—that "All The President's Men" unfolds. It begins logically on the night of June 17, 1972, when five men were arrested in an apparent break-in at the headquarters of the Democratic National Committee in the Watergate complex in Washington, and continues through the spectacular series of revelations, accusations and admissions of guilt that eventually brought the Nixon Presidency to its conclusion.

Like Bernstein and Woodward in the course of their investigation, the film maintains bifocal vision, becoming thoroughly absorbed in the seemingly unimportant minutiae out of which major conspiracies can sometimes be reconstructed, yet never for long losing sight of the overall relevance of what's going on. Although "All The President's Men" is first and foremost a fascinating newspaper film, the dimensions and implications of the

Watergate story obviously give it an emotional punch that might be lacking if, say, Bernstein and Woodward had been exposing corruption in the Junior League.

●

Thus the necessity of the director's use of newsreel footage from time to time—the shots of President Nixon's helicopter making a night landing at the White House, which open the film; the television images of the President entering the House of Representatives, and of other familiar folk including former Attorney General John N. Mitchell, former Vice President Agnew, and, especially, Representative Gerald R. Ford announcing the nominination of President Nixon at the 1972 Republican National Convention.

Though the film will undoubtedly have some political impact, its strength is the virtually day-by-day record of the way Bernstein and Woodward conducted their investigations, always under the supervision of a kindly avuncular Ben Bradlee (Jason Robards), The Post's managing editor, who (in this film) gives out advice, cau-

tion and, occasionally, a "well-done," acting as Dr. Gillespie to their Dr. Kildares.

Mr. Redford and Mr. Hoffman play their roles with the low-keyed, understated efficiency required since they are, in effect, the straight men to the people and the events they are pursuing. The film stays out of their private lives but is full of unexpected, brief, moving glimpses into the private lives of their subjects, including a frightened bookkeeper (Jane Alexander) for the Committee to Re-elect the President, Donald Segretti (Robert Walden), the "dirty tricks" man, and Hugh Sloan Jr. (Stephen Collins), the committee treasurer, and his wife (Meredith Baxter).

The manners and methods of big-city newspapering, beautifully detailed, contribute as much to the momentum of the film as the mystery that's being uncovered. Maybe even more, since the real excitement of "All The President's Men" is in watching two comparatively inexperienced reporters stumble onto the story of their lives and develop it triumphantly, against all odds.

California Elegy

'American Graffiti' Has Premiere at Sutton

By ROGER GREENSPUN

At dusk the cars begin to congregate. The drivers, kids in their teens, meet and greet and happily insult one another. A few couples, going steady, may pair off. There is a high school dance, but there is also the lure of the main street to cruise up and down, exchanging pleasant-tries, looking for dates, for excitement, an impromptu race, even a little danger. Every radio in town is tuned in to Wolfman Jack with his line of eerie patter and all the latest hits — "Sixteen Candles," "The Book of Love" . . . It is early in the fall of 1962, somewhere in northern California.

●

Two of the boys, Curt Henderson and Steve Bolander, headed East to college, are uneasy at the prospect. John Milner, champion drag racer, is 22—old enough to know he's headed nowhere, except up to the neon-lighted circle of Mel's Drive-In and perhaps down to the stillness of the automobile graveyard at the edge of town. Those are roughly the perimeters of George Lucas's "American Graffiti," which examines that much of America as it lives for about 12 hours, from an evening to the following morning.

A lot happens. Steve (Ronny Howard) breaks up and makes up with Curt's sister Laurie (Cindy Williams). A younger boy, Terry, (Charlie Martin Smith) borrows Steve's Chevy, picks up a dizzy blonde (Candy Clark) for a night of horrendous misadventures, all greatly to her pleasure.

John (Paul Le Mat) enters the climactic drag race of his career. Curt (Richard Dreyfuss), the local intellectual, is almost inducted into the Pharaohs, the town gang. But Steve is following a vision, an elusive girl in a white Thunderbird who may have whispered "I love you." He never finds her. But when, in the morning, he takes off (via Magic Carpet Airlines), a white T-bird heads East on the road below. It is the only car we ever see leaving town. "American Graffiti" exists not so much in its individual stories as in its orchestration of many stories, its sense of time and place. Although it is full of the material of fashionable nostalgia, it never exploits nostalgia.

It is a very good movie, funny, tough, unsentimental. It is full of marvelous performances from actors (especially Candy Clark, Richard Dreyfuss and Cindy Williams) hardly known for previous screen credits. But for me its excitement comes at least partly from its indication of what may be a major new career.

George Lucas, 28 years old, has made one previous feature. It is a good science fiction film, "THX 1138," about a closed, tranquilized future society, controlled by mysterious broadcast voices, and from which there is almost no escape. For all its apparent differences, "American Graffiti" really presents the obverse of that world— now beneficent, familiar; but also closed, tuned in to mysterious voices, and offering almost no means of escape.

The Cast

AMERICAN GRAFFITI, directed by George Lucas; written by Mr. Lucas, Gloria Katz and Willard Huyck; editors, Verna Fields and Marcia Lucas; directors of photography, Ron Eveslage and Jan D'Alquen; music coordinator, Karin Green; produced by Francis Ford Coppola; released by Universal Pictures. At the Sutton Theater, Third Avenue and 57th Street. Running time: 110 minutes. This film has been classified PG.

Curt	Richard Dreyfuss
Steve	Ronny Howard
John	Paul Le Mat
Terry	Charlie Martin Smith
Laurie	Cindy Williams
Debbie	Candy Clark
Carol	Mackenzie Phillips
Disk Jockey	Wolfman Jack
Bob Falfa	Harrison Ford
The Pharaohs	Bo Hopkins, Manuel Padilla Jr., Beau Gentry

Bo Hopkins and Beau Gentry with Richard Dreyfuss in the nostalgic comedy, *American Graffiti.*

'An American in Paris,' Arrival at Music Hall, Has Gene Kelly and Leslie Caron in Leads

AN AMERICAN IN PARIS, screen play and story by Alan Jay Lerner; directed by Vincente Minnelli; produced by Arthur Freed for Metro-Goldwyn-Mayer. At the Radio City Music Hall.

Jerry Mulligan......................Gene Kelly
Lise Bourvier......................Leslie Caron
Adam Cook........................Oscar Levant
Henri Baurel....................Georges Guetary
Milo Roberts.........................Nina Foch
Georges Mattieu................Eugene Borden
Mathilde Mattieu............Martha Bamattre
Old Woman Dancer.............Mary Young

By BOSLEY CROWTHER

Count a bewitching French lassie by the name of Leslie Caron and a whoop-de-do ballet number, one of the finest ever put upon the screen, as the most commendable enchantments of the big, lavish musical film that Metro obligingly delivered to the Music Hall yesterday. "An American in Paris," which is the title of the picture, likewise the ballet, is spangled with pleasant little patches of amusement and George Gershwin tunes. It also is blessed with Gene Kelly, dancing and singing his way through a minor romantic complication in the usual gaudy Hollywood gay Paree. But it is the wondrously youthful Miss Caron and that grandly pictorial ballet that place the marks of distinction upon this lush Technicolored escapade.

Alongside this crisp and elfin youngster who plays the Parisian girl with whom the ebullient American of Mr. Kelly falls in love, the other extravagant characters of the romance seem standard and stale, and even the story seems wrinkled in the light of her freshness and charm. Mr. Kelly may skip about gaily, casting the favor of his smiles and the boon of the author's witticisms upon the whole of the Paris populace. Nina Foch may cut a svelte figure as a lady who wants to buy his love by buying his straight art-student paintings. And Oscar Levant may mutter wryly as a pal. But the picture takes on its glow of magic when Miss Caron is on the screen. When she isn't, it bumps along slowly as a patched-up, conventional musical show.

Why this should be is fairly obvious. Miss Caron is not a beauteous thing, in the sense of classic features, but she has a sweet face and a most delightful smile. Furthermore, she has winsomeness, expression and youthful dignity—and she can dance like a gossamer wood-sprite on the edge of a petal at dawn.

When she and Mr. Kelly first meet in a Paris cafe, the previous routine of "bon jours" and "voilas" and "mais ouis" is forgotten. Candor and charm invade the picture under Vincente Minnelli's helpful wand. And when they dance on a quai along the river, in hush of a Paris night, to "Our Love Is Here to Stay," the romance opens and unrepressed magic evolves. Then, in the final, bursting ballet, which is done to a brilliant score of Gershwin music orchestrated with his "American in Paris" suite, the little dancer and Mr. Kelly achieve a genuine emotional splurge. It is Mr. Kelly's ballet, but Miss Caron delivers the warmth and glow.

And a ballet it is, beyond question—a truly cinematic ballet—with dancers describing vivid patterns against changing colors, designs, costumes and scenes. The whole story of a poignant romance within a fanciful panorama of Paree is conceived and performed with taste and talent. It is the uncontested high point of the film.

Beside it such musical conniptions as Mr. Kelly and Mr. Levant giving out with "Tra-La-La," or Mr. Kelly doing a dance to "I Got Rhythm" with a bunch of kids, or Mr. Levant performing all the key jobs in a large symphonic rendition of Concerto in F are purely coincidental. And Georges Guetary's careful oozing of Gallic charm in "I'll Build a Stairway to Paradise" and "'S Wonderful" could well be done without. As a matter of fact, some of these numbers leave the uncomfortable impression that they were contrived just to fill out empty spaces in Alan Jay Lerner's glib but very thin script.

However, all things are forgiven when Miss Caron is on the screen. When she is on with Mr. Kelly and they are dancing, it is superb.

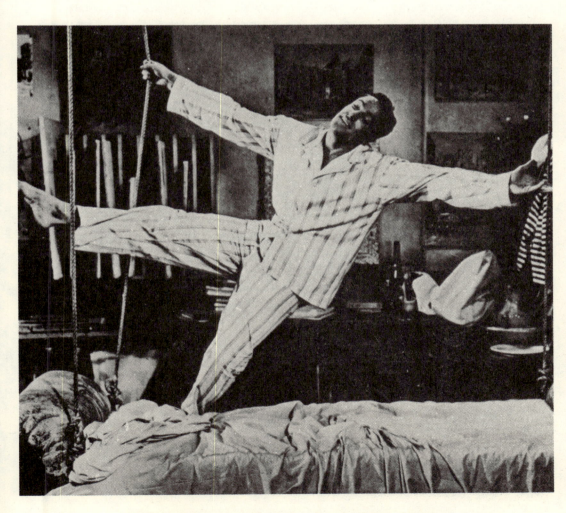

Gene Kelley in one of the dance scenes that earned him an "honorary Oscar" award for *An American in Paris*.

An American in Paris

TECHNICOLOR!
M-G-M!

NEXT ATTRACTION AT
RADIO CITY MUSIC HALL

Court Classic

By BOSLEY CROWTHER

AFTER watching an endless succession of courtroom melodramas that have more or less transgressed the bounds of human reason and the rules of advocacy, it is cheering and fascinating to see one that hews magnificently to a line of dramatic but reasonable behavior and proper procedure in a court. Such a one is "Anatomy of a Murder," which opened at the Criterion and the Plaza yesterday. It is the best courtroom melodrama this old judge has ever seen.

Perhaps "melodrama" is the wrong word. Perhaps it would be better to say this is really a potent character study of a group of people involved in a criminal trial. For Otto Preminger, who produced and directed it from a script adapted by Wendell Mayes from the highly successful novel of Robert Traver (Judge John D. Voelker), has as much fine illumination of the major personalities in this case as he has got strong suspense and pounding drama in the unfolding details of the trial.

Following the line of "Mr. Traver," even to the point of shooting all his film in the actual up-country of Michigan where the fictional murder case is set, Mr. Preminger has fittingly developed the sharp illusion of a realistic look, uninhibited and uncensored, at everything a small-town lawyer does to prepare and make a courtroom presentation of the defense of an accused murderer.

Neatly and with much local color, he finds the known facts in the case—that a moody young Army lieutenant has shot and killed a man, a tavern owner, whom the wife of the lieutenant says has raped her outside a trailer camp. Frankly, he drops the suspicion that the wife may be a bit on the shady side, that she may have been lying to the lieutenant and that he may be a mean, unstable type. And then, with this tempting information, he takes the case into court and achieves the succeeding revelation of character and conduct in that stringent atmosphere.

Actually, the major conflict and dramatic fascination from this point on is the battle of legal wits and personalities that is waged between the defense attorney and those of the prosecution, under the watchful eye of a shrewd, sardonic old judge. It is beautifully drawn and maneuvered battle, full of neat little triumphs on each side, leading to a most exciting climax and clear exposures of the principal characters.

The Cast

ANATOMY OF A MURDER, screen play by Wendell Mayes; based on the novel by Robert Traver; produced and directed by Otto Preminger; distributed by Columbia Pictures. At the Criterion, Broadway and Forty-fifth Street, and Plaza, Fifty-eighth Street, east of Madison Avenue. Running time 160 minutes.

Paul Biegler	James Stewart
Laura Manion	Lee Remick
Lieutenant Manion	Ben Gazzara
Parnell McCarthy	Arthur O'Connell
Judge Weaver	Joseph N. Welch
Maida	Eve Arden
Mary Pilant	Kathryn Grant
Claude Dancer	George C. Scott
Dr. Smith	Orson Bean
Mr. Lemon	Russ Brown
Paquette	Murray Hamilton
Mitch Lodwick	Brooks West
Sergeant Durgo	Ken Lynch
Sulo	John Qualen
Dr. Dompierre	Howard McNear
Dr. Raschid	Ned Wever
Madigan	Jimmy Conlin
Sheriff	Royal Beal
Mr. Burke	Joseph Kearns
Miller	Don Ross
Court Clerk	Lloyd Le Vasseur
Soldier	James Waters
Pie Eye	Duke Ellington

Most brilliantly revealed is the character of the lawyer for the defense, a part that is played by James Stewart in one of the finest performances of his career. Slowly and subtly, he presents us a warm, clever, adroit and complex man—and, most particularly, a portrait of a trial lawyer in action that will be difficult for anyone to surpass.

On the bench as the judge, Joseph N. Welch of Boston, the lawyer who distinguished himself in the Army-McCarthy hearings, does an unbelievably professional job. He is delightful and ever so convincing. Mr. Preminger scored a coup in getting him.

George C. Scott as a prosecuting attorney makes the courtroom battle a deadly duel by offering himself as a skillful and unrelenting antagonist, and Brooks West as his standard-brand associate adds to the personal variety. Lee Remick treads beautifully a fine line between never-resolved uncertainties as the wife of the lieutenant and Ben Gazzara makes the latter role one of the haughty and haunting mysteries and ironies of the film.

George C. Scott, Joseph N. Welch and Ben Gazzara starred in Otto Preminger's courtroom melodrama, *Anatomy of a Murder*.

Last year's No. 1 best-seller... This year's (we hope) No. 1 motion picture.

OTTO PREMINGER'S
ANATOMY OF A MURDER

STARRING
JAMES STEWART
LEE REMICK
BEN GAZZARA
ARTHUR O'CONNELL
EVE ARDEN
KATHRYN GRANT

and JOSEPH N. WELCH as Judge Weaver

WITH GEORGE C. SCOTT/ORSON BEAN/RUSS BROWN/MURRAY HAMILTON/BROOKS WEST screenplay by WENDELL MAYES from the best-seller by ROBERT TRAVER photography by SAM LEAVITT production designed by BORIS LEVEN produced and directed by OTTO PREMINGER/a Columbia release

► music by Duke Ellington ◄

'Angels With Dirty Faces,' Racy Guttersnipe Drama, With James Cagney, Comes to the Strand

ANGELS WITH DIRTY FACES, from a story by Rowland Brown; screen play by John Wexley and Warren Duff; directed by Michael Curtiz for Warner Brothers. At the Strand.

Rocky Sullivan...............James Cagney
Jerry Connolly...............Pat O'Brien
James Frazier..............Humphrey Bogart
Laury Ferguson.............Ann Sheridan
Mac Keefer................George Bancroft
Soapy.....................Billy Halop
Swing.....................Bobby Jordan
Bim......................Leo Gorcey
Pasty....................Gabriel Dell
Crab.....................Huntz Hall
Hunky...................Bernard Punsley
Steve....................Joe Downing
Edwards..................Edward Pawley
Blackie..................Adrian Morris
Rocky (As a boy).........Frankie Burke
Jerry (As a boy).........William Tracey
Laury (As a child).......Marilyn Knowlden
St. Brendan's Church Choir.

By FRANK S. NUGENT

The gutter is a rich breeding ground and its spawn matures with terrifying speed. In "Angels With Dirty Faces," new to the Strand yesterday, the Warners have focused their cameras sharply upon it, looking hard at the shabby tenements, the cellar hideout, the settlement house, a gang of growing hoodlums and two men—a criminal and a priest—whose roots were in that same East Side gutter, but who grew differently from it. They were friends once; they are friends still; but they are friends at war and one of them must be destroyed.

It is a savage melodrama Rowland Brown and his collaborators have written, a human story that James Cagney, Pat O'Brien and the Dead End boys have played, an engrossing and vivid motion picture that Michael Curtiz has directed. One of its greatest attributes is a realistic point of view. Father Connolly admits to tough Rocky Sullivan that crime appears to pay. He concedes that recklessness and a distorted kind of heroism tend to glorify the gangster, to make him a juvenile idol. The priest finally has to appeal to the gunman's courage to help him smash that idol by turning yellow in the death cell.

Cagney's Rocky Sullivan is Cagney at his best. Rocky is the swaggering little rowdy who returns to his old neighborhood and takes innocent delight in giving pointers in crime to Soapy, Bim, Crab, Hunky et al, a gang of kids who are the spitting images of Jerry Connolly and himself in their younger days. And when Jerry—who is Father Jerry now—remonstrates and says he wants the boys to grow up straight, Rocky just as obligingly rounds up the gang, shoves them onto the settlement house's basketball court and makes them play according to rules. He sees nothing incongruous in his coaching methods, either, although as a referee he is guilty of more personal fouls than e team lf.

The film proceeds racily, overcoming the familiarity of the ground it is covering by its surprising twists of plot and character, and it emerges as one of the most picturesque and dramatic of this year's crime studies. Besides Cagney, O'Brien and the Dead End hooligans, who are a crime wave in themselves, there are Humphrey Bogart, George Bancroft, Ann Sheridan and Frankie Burke (in an astonishing impersonation of Cagney the boy) in a panel of effective supplementary characterizations.

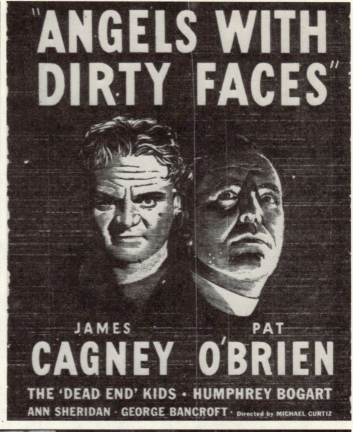

"ANGELS WITH DIRTY FACES"

JAMES **CAGNEY** PAT **O'BRIEN**

THE 'DEAD END' KIDS · HUMPHREY BOGART

ANN SHERIDAN · GEORGE BANCROFT · Directed by MICHAEL CURTIZ

James Cagney as the thug turned reformer with the Dead End Boys
in *Angels With Dirty Faces.*

STARTS TODAY

WOODY
ALLEN
DIANE
KEATON
TONY
ROBERTS
CAROL
KANE
PAUL
SIMON
SHELLEY
DUVALL
JANET
MARGOLIN
CHRISTOPHER
WALKEN
COLLEEN
DEWHURST

"ANNIE HALL"

A new comedy

The New York Times

THURSDAY, APRIL 21, 1977

Film: 'Annie Hall,' Allen at His Best

By VINCENT CANBY

ALVY SINGER (Woody Allen) stands in front of an orangey sort of backdrop and tells us, the movie audience, the joke about two women at a Catskill resort. "The food," says the first woman, "is terrible." "Yes," the second woman agrees, "and the portions are so small."

This, says Alvy Singer, is just about the way he feels about life. It's not great—in fact, it's pretty evenly divided between the horrible and the miserable—but as long as it's there, he wants more.

In this fashion, Woody Allen introduces us to the particular concerns of his fine new film, "Annie Hall," a comedy about urban love and incompatibility that finally establishes Woody as one of our most audacious film makers, as well as the only American film maker who is able to work seriously in the comic mode without being the least bit ponderous.

Because Mr. Allen has his roots as a writer of one-liners and was bred in television and nightclubs, standing up, it's taken us quite a while to recognize just how prodigiously talented he is, and how different he has always been from those colleagues who also make their livings as he once did, racing from Las Vegas to the Coast to Tahoe to San Juan, then back to Las Vegas. Among other things, he's the first major American film maker ever to come out of a saloon.

For all of Mr. Allen's growth as a writer, director and actor, "Annie Hall" is not terribly far removed from "Take the Money and Run," his first work as a triple-threat man, which is not to put down the new movie but to upgrade the earlier one. "Take the Money and Run" was a visualized nightclub monologue, as freely associated as an analysand's introspections on the couch.

This also is more or less the form of "Annie Hall," Alvy Singer's freewheeling, self-deprecating, funny and sorrowful search for the truth about his on-again, off-again affair with a beautiful young woman who is as emotionally bent as he is. The form of the two films is similar, but where the first was essentially a cartoon, "Annie Hall" has the humane sensibility of comedy.

●

It is, essentially, Woody's "Scenes From a Marriage," though there is no marriage, only an intense affair to which Alvy Singer never commits himself enough to allow Annie Hall (Diane Keaton) to give up her apartment and move in with him. Just why, we aren't told, though we can make guesses on the basis of the information furnished.

Alvy, who grew up as a poor Jewish boy in Brooklyn in a house under a

Somber Comedy

ANNIE HALL, directed by Woody Allen; screenplay by Mr. Allen and Marshall Brickman; produced by Charles H. Joffe, executive producer, Robert Greenhut; director of photography, Gordon Willis; editor, Ralph Rosenblum; distributed by United Artists. Running time: 94 minutes. At the Baronet Theater, Third Avenue near 59th Street; Little Carnegie Theater, 57th Street east of Seventh Avenue, and 34th Street East Theater, 34th Street near Second Avenue. This film has been rated PG.

Alvy Singer	Woody Allen
Annie Hall	Diane Keaton
Rob	Tony Roberts
Allison	Carol Kane
Tony Lacey	Paul Simon
Mom Hall	Colleen Dewhurst
Pam	Shelley Duvall
Robin	Janet Margolin
Duane Hall	Christopher Walken
Dad Hall	Donald Symington
Grammy Hall	Helen Ludlam
Alvy's Dad	Mordecai Lawner
Alvy's Mom	Joan Newman
Alvy, age 9	Jonathan Munk
Alvy's Aunt	Ruth Volner
Alvy's Uncle	Martin Rosenblatt
Joey Nichols	Hy Ansel
Aunt Tessie	Rashel Novikoff
Man in theater line	Russell Horton
Marshall McLuhan	Himself
Dorrie	Christine Jones
Miss Reed	Mary Boylan
Janet	Wendy Gerard
Coke Fiend	John Doumanian

Coney Island rollercoaster, is chronically suspicious and depressed. It may have started when he was 9 and first read about the expanding universe. What kind faith can you have if you know that in a couple of billion years everything's going to fly apart? With the firm conviction that the scheme is rotten, Alvy becomes a hugely successful television comedian somewhat on the scale of—you can guess Woody Allen.

Annie Hall is no less ambitious and mixed up, but for other reasons that, we must assume, have to do with the kind of WASPy, Middle Western household where Mom and Dad tend guilts as if they were prize delphiniums.

As Annie Hall, Miss Keaton emerges as Woody Allen's Liv Ullmann. His camera finds beauty and emotional re-

sources that somehow escape the notice of other directors. Her Annie Hall is a marvelous nut, a talented singer (which Woody demonstrates in a nightclub sequence that has the effect of a love scene), generous, shy, insecure and so uncertain about sex that she needs a stick of marijuana before going to bed.

Alvy, on the other hand, embraces sex as if it were something that wouldn't keep, even when it means going to bed with a dopey reporter from Rolling Stone (Shelley Duvall in a tiny role). The most Alvy can do to meet Annie's fears is to buy a red lightbulb for the bedroom lamp. He thinks it's sexy.

"Annie Hall" moves back and forth in time according to Alvy's recollections, from his meeting with Annie on a tennis court, to scenes of his childhood, to a disastrous visit with her family in Chippewa Falls, to trips to Hollywood and scenes of reconciliations and partings in New York. Throughout there are explosively comic set-pieces having to do with analysis, Hollywood, politics, you-name-it, but the mood, ultimately, is somber, thoughtful, reflective.

One of Mr. Allen's talents as a director is his casting, and "Annie Hall" contains more fine supporting performances than any other American film this year, with the possible exception of "The Late Show" and "Three Women." Most prominent are Paul Simon as a recording industry promoter, Carol Kane as Alvy's politically committed first wife, Tony Roberts as Alvy's actor-friend, Colleen Dewhurst as Annie Hall's mother, and Christopher Walken as Annie's quietly suicidal brother. That's to name only a few.

There will be discussion about what points in the film coincide with the lives of its two stars, but this, I think, is to detract from and trivialize the achievement of the film, which, at last, puts Woody in the league with the best directors we have.

●

"Annie Hall," which has been rated PG ("Parental Guidance Suggested"), contains some mildly explicit sex scenes, which, since sex is one of the things it's all about, could have been avoided only if it were a different film.

Diane Keaton with Woody Allen in *Annie Hall*.

'Apartment'

Jack Lemmon Scores in Billy Wilder Film

By BOSLEY CROWTHER

YOU might not think a movie about a fellow who lends his rooms to the married executives of his office as a place for their secret love affairs would make a particularly funny or morally presentable show, especially when the young fellow uses the means to get advanced in his job.

But under the clever supervision of Billy Wilder, who helped to write the script, then produced and directed "The Apartment," which opened at the Astor and the Plaza yesterday, the idea is run into a gleeful, tender and even sentimental film. And it is kept on the side of taste and humor by the grand performance of Jack Lemmon in the principal role.

This Mr. Lemmon, whose stock went zooming last year with "Some Like It Hot," takes precedence as our top comedian by virtue of his work in this film. As the innocent and amiable young bachelor who methodically passes around the key of his modest brownstone - front apartment among the sultans of the place where he is employed, he beautifully maintains the appearance of a lamb among ravening wolves. He has the air of a good-natured hermit who calls Grand Central Station his home.

The Cast

THE APARTMENT, from an original screen play by Billy Wilder and I. A. L. Diamond; directed and produced by Mr. Wilder for the Mirisch Company. A United Artists release. At the Astor Theatre. Broadway at Forty-fifth Street, and the Plaza Theatre, 42 East Fifty-eighth Street.

C. C. Baxter	Jack Lemmon
Fran Kubelik	Shirley MacLaine
J. D. Sheldrake	Fred MacMurray
Mr. Dobisch	Ray Walston
Mr. Kirkeby	David Lewis
Dr. Dreyfuss	Jack Kruschen
Sylvia	Joan Shawlee
Miss Olsen	Edie Adams
Margie MacDougall	Hope Holiday
Karl Matuschka	Johnny Seven
Mrs. Dreyfuss	Naomi Stevens
Mrs. Lieberman	Frances Weintraub Lax
The Blonde	Joyce Jameson

His character does not like what he's doing. He would much prefer to stay in his bed on a rainy night when a sozzled sales executive telephones and demands the key. But he turns out, in line of duty, when the hint of a promotion is flung, and he continued to oblige, confidentially, until the inevitably romantic trouble brews.

You can probably guess the reason. It is one of the elevator girls, for whom our fellow has worked up quite a fancy but whom he discovers is using the apartment with the head of personnel. Then he goes through an ordeal of worrying, especially after the girl has the rashness to choose the apartment for a suicide attempt on Christmas Eve. That makes for a sticky situation and a sharply ironic point of view on the perfidiousness of men with families playing around with the office girls.

Even in this dismal incident, Mr. Wilder and his co-author on the script, I. A. L. Diamond, have managed to keep the action and the dialogue tumbling with wit. In the midst of a grim operation to get a pill-poisoned girl to come awake, they relieve the graveyard tension with trenchant and credible gags. And they bring the sentiment to focus with a wistful remark from the girl. "When you're in love with a married man, you shouldn't wear mascara," she says.

Mr. Wilder has done more than write the film. His direction is ingenious and sure, sparkled by brilliant little touches and kept to a tight, sardonic line. In addition to Mr. Lemmon's, there's a splendid performance by Shirley MacLaine, as the daffy girl who gets into a lot of trouble, and a good one by Fred MacMurray, as the wicked boss. Jack Kruschen makes a funny doctor-neighbor who mistakes Mr. Lemmon for a ladies' man, and Ray Walston and David Lewis are amusing (and slightly sordid) wolves.

Adolph Deutsch has contributed a light, sentimental accompanying score, and Joseph LaShelle, the cinemaphotoger, has made the whole thing look quite stylish and metropolitan on the black-and-white large screen.

Movie-wise...

there has never been anything like

"THE APARTMENT"

love-wise,

laugh-wise

or otherwise-wise!

A MIRISCH COMPANY PRESENTATION STARRING

Jack Lemmon   Shirley MacLaine Fred MacMurray

Co-Starring Ray Walston   WITH JACK KRUSCHEN, DAVID LEWIS, JOAN SHAWLEE, NAOMI STEVENS,

HOPE HOLIDAY and Edie Adams   WRITTEN BY BILLY WILDER AND I. A. L. DIAMOND

DIRECTED BY BILLY WILDER   FILMED IN PANAVISION   RELEASED THRU UNITED ARTISTS

A BILLY WILDER "SOME LIKE IT HOT" PRODUCTION

Starts TODAY at Two Theatres!

DOORS OPEN 9:30 A.M. Late Film 11:45 P.M.

AIR CONDITIONED ASTOR B'way & 45th St.

AIR CONDITIONED PLAZA 58th near Madison

Feature at: 12:00, 2:05 4:10, 6:15, 8:20, 10:25

Jack Lemmon and Shirley MacLaine in *The Apartment*.

Mammoth Show

The Cast

AROUND THE WORLD IN 80 DAYS, screen play by S. J. Perelman; based on the Jules Verne novel; directed by Michael Anderson and produced by Michael Todd. At the Rivoli.

Phileas Fogg	David Niven
Passepartout	Cantinflas
Mr. Fix	Robert Newton
Princess Aouda	Shirley MacLaine
Members of the Reform Club	Robert Morley, Trevor Howard, Finlay Currie, Basil Sydney, Ronald Squires

and

Charles Boyer	Buster Keaton
Joe E. Brown	Evelyn Keyes
Martine Carol	Beatrice Lillie
John Carradine	Peter Lorre
Charles Coburn	Edmund Lowe
Ronald Colman	Victor McLaglen
Melville Cooper	Tim McCoy
Noel Coward	A. E. Matthews
Reginald Denny	Mike Mazurki
Andy Devine	John Mills
Marlene Dietrich	Alan Mowbray
Luis Miguel Dominguin	Edward R. Murrow
Fernandel	George Raft
Sir John Gielgud	Jack Oakie
Hermione Gingold	Gilbert Roland
Jose Greco	Cesar Romero
Sir Cedric Hardwicke	Frank Sinatra
Glynis Johns	Red Skelton
	Harcourt Williams

By BOSLEY CROWTHER

MICHAEL TODD, who has already shaken the foundations of the legitimate theatre with an onslaught of highly heterogeneous and untraditional musical shows, is apparently out to shatter the fundamental formation of the screen. That's the way it looks from his film version of "Around the World in 80 Days."

This mammoth and mad pictorial rendering of the famous old novel of Jules Verne, which was publicly unveiled last evening at the Rivoli, is a sprawling conglomeration of refined English comedy, giant-screen travel panoramics and slam-bang Keystone burlesque. It makes like a wild adventure picture and, with some forty famous actors in "bit" roles, it also takes on the characteristic of a running recognition game. It is noisy with sound effects and music. It is overwhelmingly large in the process known as Todd-AO. It runs for two hours fifty-five minutes (not counting an intermission). And it is, undeniably, quite a show.

•

Whether the cinema purists will immediately and gratefully concede that Mr. Todd has improved the breed of movies is something else again. The unities of content and method are not detectable in his splattered form. He and his people have commandeered the giant screen and stereophonic sound as though they were Olsen and Johnson (remember them?) turned loose in a cosmic cutting-room, with a pipe organ in one corner and all the movies ever made to toss around.

In a manner suspiciously imitative of the first Cinerama show (with which Mr. Todd had something inspirational to do), they open this film with Ed Murrow speaking a few well-chosen words and introducing a bit of the old Georges Melies silent fantasy "A Trip to the Moon." From this standard black-and-white primitive, they pull right to their wide and curved screen and a dazzling brilliant color picture of a guided missile being launched into the sky. This is explained by Mr. Murrow as an evidence of how the world does change—all of which is by way of pretty prologue to the nineteenth century fable of Mr. Verne.

The eccentric pattern, thus established, is continued expansively. There is naught but extravagant improvising in the subsequent adventures of Phileas Fogg. Once he and his comical valet, the non-decript Passepartout, are launched on their wagered endeavor to circumnavigate the globe in eighty days, the wraps are off. Anything can happen. And many varieties of things do.

In Paris, away from the Reform Club, the travelers embark in a balloon, which lifts them above a stunning layout of rural landscapes and bird's-eye-viewed chatteaux. They scoop some snow off an alp (a phony) to chill a bottle of champagne and, with fine geographical indifference, land their balloon in Spain.

This is a casual convenience which permits Mr. Todd to introduce José Greco and his troupe of Spanish dancers in some handsome flamenco stomps. It also allows the great Cantinflas, who plays the absurd Passepartout, to enact his famous burlesque of bullfighting, which he has often done in his nativae Mexican films. Thence the duo proceeds to a sun-drenched Suez, where they encounter the detective, Fix, who becomes the comical nemesis of their further journeys. And so it goes.

Time and a wish not to bore you do not permit us to catalogue the stops or the crazy variety of adventures of the travelers on their race around the world. They plunge through a studio jungle on an elephant. They behold a genuine Siamese royal barge, moving upon an ancient river. They ride ostriches through a back-lot Hong Kong. In America they fight whooping Indians from a colling and rocking Western train (a counterpart of Cinerama's roller coaster), and, while crossing the Atlantic in a ship, they strip the old tub down for firewood, in recollection of a Marx Brothers' film.

Let it be said for Michael Anderson, the director, that he has done a remarkable job in even keeping the picture going with so many "guests" in "bit" roles. Outside of Cantinflas and David Niven, who is excellent as the punctual Phileas Fogg. there are the late Robert Newton as Fix, the detective; Shirley MacLaine as Princess Aouda and an assortment of bit players ranging from Noel Coward as a British employment agent to Jack Oakie as the captain of the S. S. Henrietta. Even so, all and sundry play their roles honorably.

Is the whole thing too exhausting? It's a question of how much you can take. We not only took it but found it most amusing. Now—has it exhausted Mr. Todd?

Robert Newton, Shirley MacLaine, Cantinflas and David Niven in
Around the World in 80 Days.

OPENS WED. NIGHT OCT. 17th

The Big Show

MICHAEL TODD'S

Around the World in 80 days

in TODD-AO

ALL SEATS RESERVED

Seats now on sale at all Brokers and

RIVOLI

Broadway at 49th St., Circle 7-1633

Will Rogers Gala Benefit Performance, October 18th Tickets Available (Opening Night Sold Out)

--- MAIL ORDERS PROMPTLY FILLED ---

Herewith $ .... for .... seats

for the .... performance on

Alternates: Date .... Time .... Date .... Time

Name

Address

City .... Zone .... State

Streetcar on Tobacco Road

Williams-Kazan 'Baby Doll' Is at Victoria

The Cast

BABY DOLL, story and screen play by Tennessee Williams; directed by Elia Kazan; a Newtown Production presented by Warner Brothers. At the Victoria.

Archie.....................Karl Malden
Baby Doll..................Carroll Baker
Silva Vacarro..............Eli Wallach
Aunt Rose Comfort.....Mildred Dunnock
Rock.......................Lonny Chapman
Town Marshall..............Eades Hogue
Deputy.................Noah Williamson

By BOSLEY CROWTHER

IT looks as though the ghost of Tennessee Williams' "Streetcar Named Desire" has got bogged down in the mud of Erskine Caldwell's famous "Tobacco Road" in the screen play Mr. Williams has written for Elia Kazan's "Baby Doll."

For there is in this last picture, which opened at the Victoria last night with an elaborate benefit showing for the Actors Studio, a lot of the sort of personal conflict that occurred in Mr. Williams' former play taking place among characters in an environment in which Jeeter Lester would feel quite at home.

Mr. Williams again is writing tartly about decadence in the South in this film, which has drawn the condemnation of the Roman Catholic Church. His theme is the degeneration and inadequacy of old Southern stock, as opposed to the vital aggressiveness of intruding "foreigners." But where he was dealing with a woman of certain culture in "A Streetcar Named Desire," he is down to the level of pure "white trash" in this sardonic "Baby Doll."

This is the major shortcoming of Mr. Williams' and Mr. Kazan's film. Its people are virtually without character, content or consequence. Three of its four main people are morons or close to being same, and its fourth is a scheming opportunist who takes advantage of the others' lack of brains.

There is Archie Lee Meighan, the oafish owner of a broken-down country cotton gin, and his girl-wife, Baby Doll, an unmistakable victim of arrested development. Then there is Aunt Rose Comfort, an aged, pathetic simpleton, and there is wily Silva Vacarro, the "foreigner" who runs a rival cotton gin.

And what is the pertinent business with which the film is concerned? It is the uncovering by Vacarro that Archie Lee has set fire to his cotton gin. And how does he do this? By dallying unrestrainedly with Baby Doll, who has never submitted to her husband and is fair prey for Vacarro's game.

These are the people and the story, and unless they

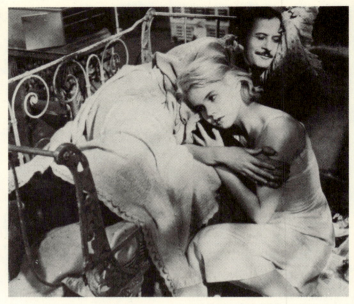

Carroll Baker and Eli Wallach in a scene from *Baby Doll*.

were shaped with utmost skill they would be something less than trifling; they would be unendurable. But no one can say that Mr. Williams is not a clever man with his pen. He has written his trashy, vicious people so that they are clinically interesting. And Karl Malden, Carroll Baker, Mildred Dunnock and Eli Wallach have acted them, under Mr. Kazan's superb direction, so that they nigh corrode the screen.

Archie Lee, played by Mr. Malden, is a man of immense stupidity, rendered the more offensive by his treachery and bigotry; and Baby Doll, played by Miss Baker, is a piteously flimsy little twist of juvenile greed, inhibitions, physical yearnings, common crudities and conceits. Vacarro, played by Mr. Wallach, is dynamic, arrogant and droll, and Aunt Rose Comfort, played by Miss Dunnock, is a pitifully patient, frightened freak.

baby doll

ELIA KAZAN'S PRODUCTION OF TENNESSEE WILLIAMS' "BABY DOLL"
NOW CAN BE SEEN AT THE VICTORIA THEATRE
BROADWAY AT 46th STREET
DOORS OPEN 9:30 A.M.
IT STARS KARL MALDEN AND CARROLL BAKER AND ELI WALLACH
STORY AND SCREEN PLAY BY TENNESSEE WILLIAMS • DIRECTED BY ELIA KAZAN • A NEWTOWN PROD.
PRESENTED BY WARNER BROS.

Spencer Tracy Seen in 'Bad Day at Black Rock'

BAD DAY AT BLACK ROCK, screen play by Millard Kaufman; adapted by Don McGuire from a story by Howard Breslin; directed by John Sturges; produced by Dore Schary for Metro-Goldwyn-Mayer. At the Rivoli.

John J. Macreedy	Spencer Tracy
Reno Smith	Robert Ryan
Liz Wirth	Anne Francis
Tim Horn	Dean Jagger
Doc Velie	Walter Brennan
Pete Wirth	John Ericson
Coley Trimble	Ernest Borgnine
Hector David	Lee Marvin
Mr. Hastings	Russell Collins
Sam	Walter Sande

By BOSLEY CROWTHER

MUCH the same sort of situation that prevailed in the memorable "High Noon" is apparent in "Bad Day at Black Rock," which came yesterday to the Rivoli. And a comparable regard for personal valor is involved in this Metro CinemaScope film.

A stranger drops off a streamliner at a California desert whistle-stop. The local characters view him with suspicion and treat him with cruel hostility. They're not accustomed to strangers in this lonely, flea-bitten town. The streamliner hasn't stopped in four years, and apparently few people ever pass through.

●

Especially are they wary of this stranger when they discover that he is interested in a certain Japanese farmer who they tell him left town a few years back. They wonder if he is a detective, seeing how he noses around. And he, in turn, wonders darkly why everyone is so hostile toward him.

Slowly, through a process of guarded discourse, which Director John Sturges has built up by patient, methodical pacing of his almost completely male cast, an eerie light begins to glimmer. The Japanese was actually slain, and most of the townsmen were in on it. That's why they're so wary and on edge. And the stranger, whose mission is simply to deliver a war medal of a hero son to the Japanese, comes to suspect that he is in the midst of a gang of arrogant murderers.

Why these small-time tyrants, dominated by a simpering Robert Ryan, should assume it necessary to murder the stranger, whom Spencer Tracy plays, is a point that the script of Millard Kaufman never makes reasonable. Thus a small doubt as to the logic of the drama is left in a close attendant's mind.

But the menace of these swaggering desert roughnecks is nonetheless creeping and cold. And the battle that Mr. Tracy puts up to save his hide is dramatically taut. When he comes out, it is obvious that not only valor but justice has prevailed.

Quite as interesting as the drama, which smacks of being contrived, are the types of masculine creatures paraded in this film. Mr. Tracy is sturdy and laconic as a war veteran with a lame arm (which does not hamper him, however, in fighting judo style). Mr. Ryan is angular and vicious as the uneasy king-pin of the town, and Walter Brennan is cryptic and caustic as the local mortician with a streak of spunk.

Ernest Borgnine as a pot-bellied bully (he was Fatso in "From Here to Eternity"), Dean Jagger as a rum-guzzling sheriff, Lee Marvin as a dim-witted tough, John Ericson as a nervous hotel clerk and Russell Collins as a station-master are all good, too. The only female in the film is Anne Francis.

She is more fetching than felicitous in this environment. Above all, the gritty, dry-hot feeling of a rough-plank desert town, lying bare beneath the sun and a mountain backdrop, is got in color on the Cinema-Scope screen. Dore Schary, who produced this film for Metro, strove for drama in the pictorial scene. And that, quite as much as the drama of personal conflict, is what "Bad Day at Black Rock" has.

Spencer Tracy and Ernest Borgnine in *Bad Day at Black Rock.*

M-G-M presents a suspenseful drama in
CINEMASCOPE and COLOR
SPENCER TRACY · ROBERT RYAN in
BAD DAY AT BLACK ROCK

TIME MAGAZINE says: "It starts M-G-M on the new year with its best footage forward! Spencer Tracy at his best!"

Co-Starring
ANNE FRANCIS · DEAN JAGGER · WALTER BRENNAN · JOHN ERICSON · ERNEST BORGNINE · LEE MARVIN
RUSSELL COLLINS · Screen Play by MILLARD KAUFMAN · Adaptation by DON McGUIRE · Based On a Story by HOWARD BRESLIN · Photographed in EASTMAN COLOR · Directed by JOHN STURGES · Produced by DORE SCHARY · AN M-G-M PICTURE

STARTS TODAY 9:30 A.M. RIVOLI
B'WAY at 49th St · CI 7-1633

Woody Allen Leads a 'Bananas' Revolution

BANANAS, directed by Woody Allen; written by Mr. Allen and Mickey Rose; director of photography, Andrew M. Costikyan; music by Marvin Hamlisch; produced by Jack Grossberg; released by United Artists Corporation. At the Coronet Theater, Third Avenue at 59th Street. Running time: 82 minutes. (The Motion Picture Association of America's Production Code and Rating Administration classifies this film: "GP—all ages admitted, parental guidance suggested.")

Fielding Mellish	Woody Allen
Nancy	Louise Lasser
Gen. Emilio M. Vargas	Carlos Montalban
Yolanda	Natividad Abascal
Esposito	Jacobo Morales
Luis	Miguel Suarez
Sanchez	David Ortiz
Diaz	Rene Enriquez
Arroyo	Jack Axelrod
Howard Cosell	Howard Cosell
Roger Grimsby	Roger Grimsby
Don Dunphy	Don Dunphy

By VINCENT CANBY

If you twist its arm (and anybody can—the movie is small), Woody Allen's new film, "Bananas," proclaims that all of life is raw material for a television game show. It opens with Howard Cosell and the staff of A.B.C.'s Wide World of Sports enthusiastically covering the Assassination of the Week, that of the President of the Latin-American republic of San Marcos, whose expiration, on cue, highlights the week of festivities begun with the sacking of the United States Embassy.

Some hallucinations later, the movie ends with Mr. Cosell hosting the on-camera consummation of a marriage, in the gold and white bridal suite of the Royal Manhattan Hotel, complete with instant replays and quarrelsome, post-encounter statements by the two principals.

●

Woody Allen is incurably, hopelessly sane, and "Bananas," which began yesterday at the Coronet Theater, is, without doubt the best Woody Allen comedy I've seen since his last film, "Take the Money and Run." It's also an indecently funny movie, on its own, and in spots— a qualification I add with some hesitation because I'm not sure that its unfunny spots are terribly important.

Thirty years ago, some very perceptive picture critics, including James Agee and Otis Ferguson, used to grow all sad and misty in print because W. C. Fields seldom made a movie that was as funny in its entirety as it was in its individual parts. Today, it doesn't make any difference. That was the sort of movie Fields made, and now we accept the rhythm of his comic genius, since it was an indispensable part of that genius.

The same may well be true of Woody Allen who, when he is good, is inspired. However, when he's bad, he's not rotten; rather, he's just not so hot.

"Bananas," which was directed and written by Allen (with Mickey Rose), had to do with Fielding Mellish (Allen) a frail, sly New York products tester, who accidentally becomes the dictator of San Marcos, and with Nancy (Louise Lasser), the sort of new school girl who breaks engagements to participate in dock strikes and yearns for relevance in her relationships.

Although it is cast in the comparatively classic, dumbslob-who-succeeds narrative form, nothing in the story is so important that it can't be interrupted or forgotten for a visual or verbal gag, a variation on an old joke, some satire that takes reality to its outer reaches, or just a nice, crazy reference to a film classic ("Potemkin") that has almost been loved to death.

●

Allen's view of the world is fraught with everything except pathos, and it's a view I happen to find very funny. Here is no little man surviving with a wan smile and a shrug, but a runty, wisemouthed guy whose initial impulses toward cowardice seem really heroic in the crazy order of the way things are. "New York Rifle Council Declares Death a Good Thing," reports a headline. The comic world of Allen's Fielding Mellish, however, is more fanciful than bleak or black. When Fielding, in a reverie, hears harp music, there is a logical explanation: there's a man playing a harp in Fielding's closet.

Allen is his own best actor, diffident and defensive, but I also like Miss Lasser (the former Mrs. Allen), who reminds me of a young Elaine May, and Carlos Montalban, as a Castro-like freedom fighter who, at his victory celebration, goes a little nuts and declares Swedish to be the official language.

Any movie that attempts to mix together love, Cuban revolution, the C.I.A., Jewish mothers, J. Edgar Hoover and a few other odds and ends (including a sequence in which someone orders 1,000 grilled cheese sandwiches) is bound to be a little weird— and most welcome.

A JACK ROLLINS-CHARLES H. JOFFE Production

woody allen's "bananas"

WITH LOUISE LASSER · Executive Producer CHARLES H. JOFFE · Produced by JACK GROSSBERG
Directed by WOODY ALLEN · Associate Producer and Editor RALPH ROSENBLUM, A.C.E. · COLOR by DeLuxe
Written by WOODY ALLEN and MICKEY ROSE · Music by MARVIN HAMLISCH · United Artists

GP ALL AGES ADMITTED

Remake of 'Beau Geste' With Gary Cooper Has Premiere at the Paramount

BEAU GESTE, screen play by Robert Carson based on the novel by Percival Christopher Wren; directed and produced by William A. Wellman for Paramount. At the Paramount.

Beau Geste ....Gary Cooper
John ....Ray Milland
Digby ....Robert Preston
Sgt. Markoff ....Brian Donlevy
Isobel Rivers ....Susan Hayward
Rasinoff ....J. Carrol Naish
Michael Geste (age 12)...Donald O'Connor
Major de Beaujolais......James Stevenson
Renoir ....Harry Woods
Dufour ....James Burke
Schwartz ....Albert Dekker
Hank Miller ....Broderick Crawford

Originals are always better than imitations, and in view of all the depressing copies of "Beau Geste" which the cinema has suffered during the last thirteen years (take any picture about the French Foreign Legion at random) the prototype of them all seems eminently worth repeating, for a change. It should also prove encouraging to persons with faith in the continuing validity of the screen's most gallant gestures to note that "Beau Geste," in the Paramount's current re-make, is still good cinema—that the absurd nobility, brotherly devotion and self-sacrifice of the Geste tribe are still unflagging ingredients for action melodrama.

On the other hand, the law of diminishing returns has got in its dirty work over the years: since 1926 the Foreign Legion motif has been so sadly overworked, so cruelly abused, that today the original may itself take on some of the irritatingly reminiscent quality of an imitation. In a sense, it is an imitation—an imitation in talk and sound effects of what was admittedly a classic in silence, and romantics with a too glowingly nostalgic recollection of Herbert Brenon's magnum opus may even be disappointed in the present exhibit. It must be acknowledged that the suspense and the timing are less torturing, less conducive to sweaty palms, than in the early epic, but then, it is now possible to hear the bugles and the wicked spatter of Arab gunfire, not to mention the shrieks of the poor devils beaten or maimed forever by that beast in human guise, Sergeant Markoff.

There is, of course, something a little nightmarish about the heroics of the Geste brothers, with their somewhat stagy, "Let me be the first to die" competition, something unreal about their eternal Britishness, which is not improved by the fact that "Beau" is now Gary Cooper, with unimpaired Texan accent, instead of Ronald Colman, that John, the survivor of all this touching fustian at last, is Ray Milland, and that Digby is the capable but curiously un-Anglican Robert Preston. These are niggling faults, but they mar what should be a poem of pure action, as do the children who play so stiffly the Geste brothers and Isobel Rivers in their chivalrous and storybook haunted youth.

On the whole, it is perhaps an unfortunate thing for Beau Geste the Second that Beau Geste the First was so distinguished, for Mr. Wellman's film seems dominated by the tremendous shadow of its predecessor. But it would be a mistake on that account to assume that the current generation will not find the current "Beau" a stirring piece of cinema, worth more than all the combined photostatic copies which followed the first and, alas! preceded the second. Those dead legionnaires, staring down from the gun embrasures of the desert fort, can still give one the creeps. The mystery of the disappearing bugler, of the two vanishing corpses, of the immense funeral pyre romantically burning in the desert, are still matters for shuddery speculation. Who stole that unparalleled sapphire, the "Blue Water"? The question is still a gripping one.

As for that earlier, perhaps blessedly silent, "Beau Geste"—what the present generation doesn't know, it will certainly never miss.

B. R. C.

Gary Cooper in Paramount's New "BEAU GESTE" IN PERSON ♪ PHIL SPITALNY AND HIS ALL-GIRL ORCHESTRA

Doors Open 8:00 A.M.

PARAMOUNT

Ray Milland, Gary Cooper and Robert Preston as the Geste brothers in *Beau Geste*.

A Stupendous Spectacle

BEN HUR, with Ramon Novarro, Francis X. Bushman, May McAvoy, Claire Mac-Dowell, Kathleen Key, Carmel Myers, Nigel de Brulier, Mitchell Lewis, Leo White, Frank Currier, Charles Belcher, Betty Bronson, Dale Fuller and Winter Hall, adapted from General Lew Wallace's drama, directed by Fred Niblo. Special music score by David Mendoza and William Axt. At the George M. Cohan Theatre.

The magnificent pictorial conception of "Ben Hur," on which no less than $3,000,000 has been lavished and which has taken nearly two years to produce, was presented last night at the George M. Cohan Theatre before an exceptionally brilliant gathering. As a film spectacle it is a masterpiece of study and patience, a photodrama which is filled with so much artistry that one would like to ponder over some of the scenes to glean all that is in them, instead of seeing just that passing flash. Ordinary conventional methods have for the most part been discarded by Fred Niblo, the director, who, while he has availed himself of every iota of photographic worth in the thrilling episodes, nevertheless finds it pleasant to get in trenchant streaks and positively sublime poetic touches. And when the march to Calvary is depicted it is done with such solemnity and quiet respect that one feels impelled to bow one's head.

On this production, which now is 12,000 feet in length, and which did not finish until after 11:30 last night, one must first comment upon the amazingly impressive structures, especially the Gate of Joppa, through which one perceives thousands of human beings forging their way, and the Antioch circus setting, which was built in Hollywood and where something like 9,000 persons were gathered as the audience for the chariot races. Although these episodes were filled with difficulty in the making, it is plain that the stupendous photographic feat was in reproducing the sea fight, which was filmed in the Mediterranean.

This comes in the first portion of the production and it is put forth with amazingly fine effect, particularly when two of the craft crash together and the fighting really begins. Here one perceives a half nude man slung over on the figure head of one of the wooden craft, and inside the vessels there are those hapless galley slaves who were doomed to row, year in and year out, pulling, in the half darkness, on a huge oar, while a fat Roman wields a mallet, beating time, according to what pace is wanted of the flesh and bone that propels the ship.

On one ship there are three decks of slaves, who are knouted when they become apathetic in their efforts, and just before the conflict occurs these sweaty, unkempt humans are shackled to their places. Mr. Niblo believes in numbers in everything. He shows it in this spectacle, and therefore when the vessel is about to sink there are scores of men's heads dotting the sea as they swim for the grinding cameras.

A most astounding performance happens in the initial chapter of this picture. It is that of a girl who was practically unknown on the screen eighteen months ago. She here delivers a portrayal of the Madonna that is gloriously beautiful. At first you may wonder who this young actress is, for her appearance is completely changed in the brief performance she gives here. She is none other than Betty Bronson, the girl who was selected to play the title rôle of "Peter Pan" a little more than a year ago, and who won further laurels by her impersonation of the slavey in Barrie's "A Kiss for Cinderella." In both those films she was a pert, lively, skittish little creature, fantastic, impudent or impish. In last night's presentation she is a creature of rare beauty, who herself seemed inspired in acting the rôle.

The famous chariot races have been depicted so thrillingly that this chapter evoked no little applause. Horses fell and piled up on each other. Chariots crashed and wheels went spinning or snapped in twain. There were Ben Hur's four white horses forging head, then losing ground, then coming up again, with the pugnacious Messala gazing at his adversary contemptuously, until the accident happens. The arena in which the race takes place is enormous, and from some of the camera "shots" the horses look like mere mice pulling on nutshells with a fly for a driver. About thirty horsemen could ride abreast in the narrowest section of this amphitheatre, and when the signal is waved for the race to start one can't help but be impressed by the space.

Some of the religious sequences are filmed in Technicolor, and by far the most successful of these episodes is Christ's ride into Jerusalem. In no place does Mr. Niblo show the Christus, the figure being concealed by palms as he rides on the ass. In the journey to Calvary bearing the cross, one sees merely a hand holding the cross and the other hand is extended occasionally to heal the sick who have faith, the lepers who are shunned by the populace.

The great decade (1915-1925) of the progression of Motion Picture Art reached its summit last night

at the GEO. M. COHAN THEATRE B'way, 42d St.

WHERE

BEN-HUR

was presented for the first time
Directed by FRED NIBLO
with RAMON NOVARRO, Betty Bronson, May McAvoy, Francis X. Bushman and Carmel Myers

Produced by Metro-Goldwyn-Mayer
in arrangement with
A. L. Erlanger, C. B. Dillingham & Florenz Ziegfeld, Jr.

TWICE DAILY (incl. Sunday), 2:30 and 8:30
Sunday and Holiday Matinees 3 P. M.

PRICES NIGHTS, SAT. & HOLIDAY MATS., 50c to $2.00
ALL OTHER MATS. (incl. Sun.), 50c to $1.00

All seats reserved
Tickets selling in advance for all performances

1st MATINEE TODAY at 2:30

TONIGHT at 8:30

Ramon Novarro, who plays the part of Ben-Hur, is a sturdy, handsome young chap, with an excellent figure. His performance is all that one could wish, for he is fervent and earnest throughout, and restrained in his display of affection for Esther, a rôle acted by May McAvoy. She is pretty, but her appearance would have been more effective in this part had she not donned a curly wig. Claire MacDowell is capital in the rôle of the Mother of Ben-Hur, and her performance in the episode wherein she and her daughter, Tirzah, are supposed to be lepers, is most stirring. Kathleen Key is clever as Tirzah.

Francis X. Bushman, a man of mighty muscle, well suited to the character of Messala, is effective in his acting. Last night he was among the audience and during the intermission one had the chance of looking upon Messala dressed in a dinner suit. One of his many friends approached him and asked:

"Well, Francis, how do you like yourself?"

He seemed to have been so interested in the wonderful spectacle that he was unable to give a ready reply.

And in one of the aisle seats sat Marcus Loew, head of Metro-Goldwyn-Mayer, the concern responsible for the photodrama. He was glowing with pleasure and he had every right to feel pride in this effort and others now on Broadway. He has "The Merry Widow" at the Embassy, and "The Big Parade" at the Astor, besides "His Secretary" at the Capitol. David Warfield, who sat with him, congratulated Mr. Loew on his firm's production of "Ben-Hur."

The chariot race—Novarro vs. Bushman in the original version of *Ben Hur*.

'Ben-Hur,' a Blockbuster

The Cast

BEN-HUR, screen play by Karl Tunberg, from the novel by Gen. Lew Wallace; directed by William Wyler; produced by Sam Zimbalist for Metro-Goldwyn-Mayer. At Loew's State Theatre, Broadway and Forty-fifth Street. Running time: 212 minutes.

Judah Ben-Hur	Charlton Heston
Quintus Arrius	Jack Hawkins
Messala	Stephen Boyd
Esther	Haya Harareet
Sheik Ilderim	Hugh Griffith
Miriam	Martha Scott
Simonides	Sam Jaffe
Tirzah	Cathy O'Donnell
Balthasar	Finlay Currie
Pilate	Frank Thring
Drusus	Terence Longden
Sextus	André Morell
Flavia	Marina Berti
Emperor Tiberius	George Relph
Amrah	Adi Berber
Malluch	Stella Vitelleschi
Mary	Jose Greci
Joseph	Laurence Payne
Jesus	Claude Heater

By BOSLEY CROWTHER

WITHIN the expansive format of the so-called "blockbuster" spectacle film, which generally provokes a sublimation of sensibility to action and pageantry, Metro-Goldwyn-Mayer and William Wyler have managed to engineer a remarkably intelligent and engrossing human drama in their new production of "Ben-Hur."

Without for one moment neglecting the tempting opportunities for thundering scenes of massive movement and mob excitement that are abundantly contained in the famous novel of Gen. Lew Wallace, upon which this picture is based, Mr. Wyler and his money-free producers have smartly and effectively laid stress on the powerful and meaningful personal conflicts that are strong in this old heroic tale.

As a consequence, their mammoth color movie, which opened at Loew's State last night, is by far the most stirring and respectable of the Bible-fiction pictures ever made.

This is not too surprising, when one considers that the drama in "Ben-Hur" has a peculiar relationship and relevance to political and social trends in the modern day. Its story of a prince of Judea who sets himself and the interests of his people against the subjugation and tyranny of the Roman master race, with all sorts of terrible consequences to himself and his family, is a story that has been repeated in grim and shameful contexts in our age. And where the parallels might be vague in the novel, which was first published, after all, away back in 1880, they can be made clearer in the film.

Significantly, they have been, both in Karl Tunberg's excellent screen play and in Mr. Wyler's largely personal and close-to direction design.

For, without stint, the interest is now focused on the character of Judah, son of Hur, and his emotional and spiritual development under the heavy shadows of tyranny, injustice and hate. And his final emergence from these oppressions imposed and aggravated by a slave state is achieved through his observation of the example and teachings of Jesus.

This pertinent theme of the story is appropriately and grippingly conveyed in some of the most forceful personal conflicts ever played in costume on the giant screen. Where the excitement of the picture may appear to be in the great scenes, such as those of the ancient sea battle in which Ben-Hur is involved as a galley slave or those of his final contention with Messala, the Roman tribune, in a mammoth chariot race, the area of fullest engrossment is the scenes of people meeting face to face —Ben-Hur verbally clashing with Messala, a Roman soldier suddenly looking upon Jesus.

Here is where the artistic quality and taste of Mr. Wyler have prevailed to make this a rich and glowing drama that far transcends the bounds of spectacle. His big scenes are brilliant and dramatic — that is unquestionable. There has seldom been anything in movies to compare with this picture's chariot race. It is a stunning complex of mighty setting, thrilling action by horses and men, panoramic observation and overwhelming dramatic use of sound.

But the scenes that truly reach you and convey the profound ideas are those that establish the sincerity and credibility of characters. Ben-Hur's encounters with his mother and his sister, who later become lepers during the time of their oppression, or his passing meetings with Jesus (who is, tactfully, never viewed in full face) are dignified and true. Likewise, the enactment of the Crucifixion is impressively personal, strong and real. It is not done in an aura of gauzy reverence but has the nature of a dark political deed.

For the performance of his characters, Mr. Wyler has a cast that impressively delivers the qualities essential to their roles. Charlton Heston is excellent as Ben-Hur— strong, aggressive, proud and warm — and Stephen Boyd plays his nemesis, Messala, with those same qualities, inverted ideologically.

Jack Hawkins as the Roman admiral who fatefully makes Ben-Hur his foster son, Haya Harareet as the Jewish maiden who tenderly falls in love with him, Hugh Griffith as the sheik who puts him into the chariot race and Sam Jaffe as his loyal agent— these also stand out in a very large cast.

Much more could be said in praise of the technical quality of this film, which vastly surpasses the silent version of the same story released back in 1926. Space does not permit it. Otherwise this review would run too long, which is the one thing this picture does distressingly. Three hours and thirty-two minutes of it, not counting intermission, is simply too much of a good thing. The stimulated soul may be willing but the tormented flesh is weak.

Same scene, same feeling, different actors; Charlton Heston and Stephen Boyd in the 1959 version of *Ben Hur*.

WORLD PREMIERE TONIGHT 8:00 P.M.

METRO-GOLDWYN-MAYER presents
A Tale of the Christ
by GENERAL LEW WALLACE

BEN HUR

DIRECTED BY
WILLIAM WYLER

STARRING
CHARLTON HESTON · JACK HAWKINS
HAYA HARAREET · STEPHEN BOYD
HUGH GRIFFITH · MARTHA SCOTT WITH CATHY O'DONNELL · SAM JAFFE

TECHNICOLOR®   SCREEN PLAY BY KARL TUNBERG · PRODUCED BY SAM ZIMBALIST   FILMED IN CAMERA 65

RESERVE YOUR SEATS NOW AT BOX-OFFICE OR BY MAIL!

THE NEW LOEW'S STATE

World Premiere Tonight at 8:30 o'clock

SAMUEL GOLDWYN'S
Greatest Production

MYRNA LOY

FREDRIC MARCH

"The BEST Years of Our Lives"

DANA ANDREWS

TERESA WRIGHT

VIRGINIA MAYO

Hoagy Carmichael

*The BEST Thing
That Ever Happened!*

Directed by   Screen Play by
WILLIAM WYLER · ROBERT E. SHERWOOD

from a novel by **MacKINLAY KANTOR** *and introducing* **Cathy O'Donnell**

with **Gladys George · Steve Cochran · Harold Russell · Roman Bohnen**
Released thru RKO Radio Pictures

*Gala Opening Tonight
for the benefit of*
THE LIGHTHOUSE
– all seats sold out

· ASTOR ·
BROADWAY & 45th STREET

*Continuous performances
starting Tomorrow*
6 shows daily
beginning at 9 A.M.

24

The New York Times

FRIDAY, NOVEMBER 22, 1946.

The Best Years of Our Lives

THE BEST YEARS OF OUR LIVES, screen play by Robert E. Sherwood, from the novel, "Glory For Me," by MacKinlay Kantor; directed by William Wyler and released through RKO. At the Astor.

Milly Stephenson	Myrna Loy
Al Stephenson	Frederic March
Fred Derry	Dana Andrews
Peggy Stephenson	Teresa Wright
Marie Derry	Virginia Mayo
Wilma Cameron	Cathy O'Donnell
Butch Engle	Hoagy Carmichael
Homer Parrish	Harold Russell
Hortense Derry	Gladys George
Pat Derry	Roman Bohnen
Mr. Milton	Ray Collins
Cliff	Steve Cochran
Mrs. Parrish	Minna Gombell
Mr. Parrish	Walter Baldwin
Mrs. Cameron	Dorothy Adams
Mr. Cameron	Don Beddoe
Bullard	Erskine Sanford
Luella Parrish	Marlene Aames
Rob Stephenson	Michael Hall

By BOSLEY CROWTHER

It is seldom that there comes a motion picture which can be wholly and enthusiastically endorsed not only as superlative entertainment but as food for quiet and humanizing thought. Yet such a one opened at the Astor last evening. It is "The Best Years of Our Lives." Having to do with a subject of large moment—the veteran home from war—and cut, as it were, from the heart-wood of contemporary American life, this film from the Samuel Goldwyn studio does a great deal more, even, than the above. It gives off a warm glow of affection for everyday, down-to-earth folks.

These are some fancy recommendations to be tossing boldly forth about a film which runs close to three hours and covers a lot of humanity in that time. Films of such bulky proportions usually turn out the other way. But this one is plainly a labor not only of understanding but of love from three men who put their hearts into it—and from several others who gave it their best work. William Wyler, who directed, was surely drawing upon the wells of his richest talent and experience with men of the Air Forces during the war. And Robert E. Sherwood, who wrote the screen play from a story by MacKinlay Kantor, called "Glory for Me," was certainly giving genuine reflection to his observations as a public pulse-feeler these past six years. Likewise, Mr. Goldwyn, who produced, must have seen this film to be the fulfillment of a high responsibility. All their efforts are rewarded eminently.

For "The Best Years of Our Lives" catches the drama of veterans returning home from war as no film—or play or novel that we've yet heard of—has managed to do. In telling the stories of three veterans who come back to the same home town—one a midde-aged sergeant, one an air officer and one a sailor who has lost both hands—it fully reflects the delicate tensions, the deep anxieties and the gnawing despairs that surely have been experienced by most such fellows who have been through the same routine. It visions the overflowing humors and the curious pathos of such returns, and it honestly and sensitively images the terrible loneliness of the man who has been hurt—hurt not only physically but in the recesses of his self-esteem.

Not alone in such accurate little touches as the first words of the sergeant's joyful wife when he arrives home unexpectedly, "I look terrible!" or the uncontrollable sob of the sailor's mother when she first sees her son's mechanical "hands" is this picture irresistibly affecting and eloquent of truth. It is in its broader and deeper understanding of the mutual embarrassment between the veteran and his well-intentioned loved ones that the film throws its real dramatic power.

Especially in the readjustments of the sailor who uses prosthetic "hooks" and of the airman who faces deflation from bombardier to soda-jerker is the drama intense. The middle-aged sergeant finds adjustment fairly simple, with a wife, two grown-up kids and a good job, but the younger and more disrupted fellows are the ones who really get it in the teeth. In working out their solutions Mr. Sherwood and Mr. Wyler have achieved some of the most beautiful and inspiring demonstrations of human fortitude that we have had in films.

And by demonstrating frankly and openly the psychological blocks and the physical realities that go with prosthetic devices they have done a noble public service of great need.

It is wholly impossible—and unnecessary—to single out any one of the performers for special mention. Fredric March is magnificent as the sergeant who breaks the ice with his family by taking his wife and daughter on a titanic binge. His humor is sweeping yet subtle, his irony is as keen as a knife and he is altogether genuine. This is the best acting job he has ever done. Dana Andrews is likewise incisive as the Air Forces captain who goes through a gruelling mill, and a newcomer, Harold Russell, is incredibly fine as the sailor who has lost his hands. Mr. Russell, who actually did lose his hands in the service and does use "hooks," has responded to the tactful and restrained direction of Mr. Wyler in a most sensitive style.

As the wife of the sergeant, Myrna Loy is charmingly reticent and Teresa Wright gives a lovely, quiet performance as their daughter who falls in love with the airman. Virginia Mayo is brassy and brutal as the latter's two-timing wife and Cathy O'Donnell, a new, young actress, plays the sailor's fiancée tenderly. Hoagy Carmichael, Roman Bohnen and Ray Collins will have to do with a warm nod. For everyone gives a "best" performance in this best film this year from Hollywood.

Harold Russell, Dana Andrews and Frederic March in *The Best Years of Our Lives.*

'The Big Heat' Has Premiere at the Criterion—'Grapes Are Ripe' Also Opens Here

THE BIG HEAT, screen play by Sydney Boehm, based on a story by William P. McGivern; directed by Fritz Lang; produced by Robert Arthur for Columbia. At the Criterion.

Dave Bannion	Glenn Ford
Debby Marsh	Gloria Grahame
Katie Bannion	Jocelyn Brando
Mike Lagana	Alexander Scourby
Vince Stone	Lee Marvin
Bertha Duncan	Jeanette Nolan
Tierney	Peter Whitney
Lieut. Wilkes	Willis Bouchey
Gus Burke	Robert Burton
Larry Gordon	Adam Williams
Commissioner Higgins	Howard Wendell
George Rose	Cris Alcalde
Hugo	Michael Granger
Lucy Chapman	Dorothy Green
Doris	Carolyn Jones

By BOSLEY CROWTHER

"Dice, Vice and Corruption"— those are the inducements advertised on the marquee of the Criterion Theatre, where "The Big Heat" opened yesterday. And dice, vice and corruption—especially corruption—are what you get a full share of in this Columbia crime melodrama, which has Glenn Ford as its taut, relentless star.

Say this for Fritz Lang, who directed, and Sidney Boehm, who wrote the script: They haven't insulted their players by putting them in a game of tiddlywinks. The business that occupies their hero in this tale of criminals and crooked politics is gambling, conspiracy, extortion, murder and a few other things. The police commissioner is the hireling of a steel-springed rackets boss. There are strata and sub-strata of underworldlings. Even the widow of a policeman is a bum.

In fact, it is in an endeavor to fathom the suicide of a seemingly honest policeman that Mr. Ford, as a detective, runs afoul of one or two little irregularities that cause his suspicions to hum. And the first thing you know, his nice detective, his home-loving family man, is mixed up in the stickiest lot of knavery since the Kefauver committee was on the air. His sweet wife, played by Jocelyn Brando, gets blown up outside his own home. He himself gets the air as a detective for yelling "murder!" And, indeed, he is all but killed. However, he cracks the crime ring and exposes the crooks and the thieves.

No matter about the implications of shady cops and political goons. The script is so vague in this department that no specific allusions may be found. The only concern of the film-makers is a tense and eventful crime show, and this they deliver in a fashion that keeps you tingling like a frequently struck gong. Thanks to Mr. Lang's vivid direction, you grunt when Mr. Ford throws a punch. You wince when a cretin-faced Lee Marvin flings scalding coffee into Gloria Grahame's eyes. It isn't a pretty picture. But for those who like violence, it's fun.

Miss Brando makes a briefly cosy housewife and Jeanette Nolan plays the widow viciously.

Glenn Ford, Lee Marvin and Howard Wendell from *The Big Heat*.

"THE BIG HEAT"

EXTRA IN PERSON! JOCELYN BRANDO star of "The Big Heat" will be in the Criterion lobby Today at 9:30 A.M. to meet her fans and to distribute autographed photos.

"The Way He Treats Women... Now I'm going to put the big heat on him the way he put it on those four girls!"

From The Saturday Evening Post Serial That Thrilled Millions!

starring
GLENN FORD · GLORIA GRAHAME · JOCELYN BRANDO

with Alexander Scourby · Lee Marvin · Jeanette Nolan · Screen Play by SYDNEY BOEHM
Based upon the SATURDAY EVENING POST serial by William P. McGivern · Produced by ROBERT ARTHUR · Directed by FRITZ LANG · A COLUMBIA PICTURE

STARTS 9:30 A.M. TODAY · ON THE GIANT SCREEN CRITERION B'way & 45th St.

'THE BIRTH OF A NATION.'

Film Version of Dixon's "The Clansman" Presented at the Liberty.

"The Birth of a Nation," an elaborate new motion picture taken on an ambitious scale, was presented for the first time last evening at the Liberty Theatre. With the addition of much preliminary historical matter, it is a film version of some of the melodramatic and inflammatory material contained in "The Clansman," by Thomas Dixon.

A great deal might be said concerning the spirit revealed in Mr. Dixon's review of the unhappy chapter of Reconstruction and concerning the sorry service rendered by its plucking at old wounds. But of the film as a film, it may be reported simply that it is an impressive new illustration of the scope of the motion picture camera.

An extraordinarily large number of people enter into this historical pageant, and some of the scenes are most effective. The civil war battle pictures, taken in panorama, represent enormous effort and achieve a striking degree of success. One interesting scene stages a reproduction of the auditorium of Ford's Theatre in Washington, and shows on the screen the murder of Lincoln. In terms of purely pictorial value the best work is done in those stretches of the film that follow the night riding of the men of the Ku-Klux Klan, who look like a company of avenging spectral crusaders sweeping along the moonlit roads.

The "Birth of a Nation," which was prepared for the screen under the direction of D. W. Griffith, takes a full evening for its unfolding and marks the advent of the two dollar movie. That is the price set for the more advantageous seats in the rear of the Liberty's auditorium.

It was at this same theatre that the stage version of "The Clansman" had a brief run a little more than nine years ago, as Mr. Dixon himself recalled in his curtain speech last evening in the interval between the two acts. Mr. Dixon also observed that he would have allowed none but the son of a Confederate soldier to direct the film version of "The Clansman."

One of the Civil War battles so vividly depicted in D.W. Griffith's *The Birth of A Nation*.

Lillian Gish and Henry B. Walthal in *The Birth of A Nation*.

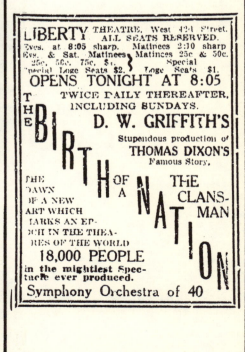

LIBERTY THEATRE, West 42d Street.
ALL SEATS RESERVED.
Eves. at 8:05 sharp.   Matinees 2:10 sharp
Eves. & Sat. Matinees   Matinees 25c & 50c.
25c, 50c, 75c, $1.   Special
Special Loge Seats $2.   Loge Seats $1.

OPENS TONIGHT AT 8:05

TWICE DAILY THEREAFTER,
INCLUDING SUNDAYS.

D. W. GRIFFITH'S

Stupendous production of
THOMAS DIXON'S
Famous Story,

THE
BIRTH OF A NATION
THE CLANSMAN

THE DAWN OF A NEW ART WHICH MARKS AN EPOCH IN THE THEATRES OF THE WORLD

18,000 PEOPLE

in the mightiest Spectacle ever produced.

Symphony Orchestra of 40

'Blackboard Jungle'

Delinquency Shown in Powerful Film

BLACKBOARD JUNGLE, screen play by Richard Brooks; based on the novel by Evan Hunter; directed by Mr. Brooks; produced by Pandro S. Berman for Metro-Goldwyn-Mayer. At Loew's State.

Richard Dadier	Glenn Ford
Anne Dadier	Anne Francis
Jim Murdock	Louis Calhern
Lois Judby Hammond	Margaret Hayes
Mr. Warneke	John Hoyt
Joshua Y. Edwards	Richard Kiley
Mr. Halloran	Emile Meyer
Dr. Bradley	Warner Anderson
Prof. A. R. Kraal	Basil Ruysdael
Gregory W. Miller	Sidney Poitier
Artie West	Vic Morrow
Belazi	Dan Terranova
Pete V. Morales	Rafael Campos
Emmanuel Stoker	Paul Mazursky
Detective	Horace McMahon
Santini	Jamee] Farah
De Lica	Danny Dennis

By BOSLEY CROWTHER

EVAN HUNTER'S "Blackboard Jungle," which tells a vicious and terrifying tale of rampant hoodlumism and criminality among the students in a large city vocational training school, was sensational and controversial when it appeared as a novel last fall. It is sure to be equally sensational and controversial, now that it is made into a film.

For this drama of juvenile delinquency in a high school, which Metro-Goldwyn-Mayer has made and which opened on Saturday at Loew's State, is no temperate or restrained report on a state of affairs that is disturbing to educators and social workers today. It is a full-throated, all-out testimonial to the lurid headlines that appear from time to time, reporting acts of terrorism and violence by uncontrolled urban youths. It gives a blood-curdling, nightmarish picture of monstrous disorder in a public school. And it leaves one wondering wildly whether such out-of-hand horrors can be.

In telling how one young teacher goes into a vocational school and pits himself against a classroom full of nothing less than hoarse and heartless "hoods," this picture begins with the feeling that the classroom is a bloody battleground, and then proceeds to present a series of episodes that bear out this grim anxiety.

From scenes that show the painful inability of the teacher to control his class, let alone interest his pupils and get something into their heads, to incidents of straight assault and battery, culminating with an attack upon the teacher by a kid with a knife, the emphasis is wholly upon impudence, rebellion and violence. To be sure, there is patiently developed a mutual respect and accord between the teacher and a Negro student, who happens to be able to sing and who finally comes to the aid of the teacher in the big showdown against the kid with the knife. But the manner in which the teacher eventually gains the respect of his whole class is simply by disarming the toughest hoodlum. This seems a bitter and superficial solution for the problem at hand.

As a straight melodrama of juvenile violence this is a vivid and hair-raising film. Except for some incidental romance, involving the teacher and his wife and a little business about the latter having a baby, it is as hard and penetrating as a nail. Richard Brooks, who wrote the screen play and directed, departs little from Mr. Hunter's book, and he puts his principal actors through paces that would seem to leave them permanently marred and scarred.

More than a question of entertainment is involved, however, in this film, since it treats of a contemporary subject that is social dynamite. And it is on the question of its faithfulness to over-all conditions that we suspect it may be challenged not only as responsible reporting but also as a desirable stimulant to spread before the young.

In a foreward it is carefully stated that "the scenes and incidents depicted here are fictional." So is the structure of the story.

THEY TURNED A SCHOOL INTO A JUNGLE!

This drama tells about the problem-kids in a big-city school . . . and the teacher who had to face them . . . and fight them! From the best-seller and famed magazine story that created a storm across the country! A fine film that everyone will want to see and should see!

M-G-M's
BLACKBOARD JUNGLE
A DRAMA OF TEEN-AGE TERROR!

Starring
GLENN FORD · ANNE FRANCIS · LOUIS CALHERN with MARGARET HAYES
Screen Play by RICHARD BROOKS · Based On the Novel by EVAN HUNTER · Directed by RICHARD BROOKS · Produced by PANDRO S. BERMAN · An M-G-M PICTURE

PREVIEW ALL DAY **TODAY** · **Loew's STATE** ON THE WIDE-VISION SCREEN WITH PERSPECTA STEREOPHONIC SOUND
DOORS OPEN 8 A.M. Plus last showings of "Timberjack"
Broadway & 45th St.

Screen: 'Blazing Saddles,' a Western in Burlesque

BLAZING SADDLES, directed by Mel Brooks; screenplay by Mr. Brooks, Norman Steinberg, Andrew Bergman, Richard Pryor and Alan Uger, based on a story by Mr. Bergman; produced by Michael Hertzberg; director of photography, Joseph Biroc; editors, John C. Howard and Danford Greene; music composed and conducted by John Morris; a Crossbow production, distributed by Warner Brothers. Running time: 93 minutes. At the Sutton Theater, 57th Street, east of Third Avenue. This film has been rated R.

Bart	Cleavon Little
Jim	Gene Wilder
Gov. Leeotomane	Mel Brooks
Indian Chief	
Hedley Lamarr	Harvey Korman
Lili von Shtupp	Madeline Kahn
Taggart	Slim Pickens
Olson Johnson	David Huddleston
Rev. Mr. Johnson	Liam Dunn
Mongo	Alex Karras
Buddy Bizarre	Dom DeLuise

By VINCENT CANBY

Some film comedies, like Jacques Tati's "Playtime" and Woody Allen's "Sleeper," stay with you after you've seen them. The humor, firmly rooted in the wilder contradictions of life, flourishes in the memory. Other comedies, like Mel Brooks's "Blazing Saddles," the best title of the year to date, are like Chinese food. A couple of hours later you wonder where it went. You wonder why you laughed as consistently as you did.

"Blazing Saddles," which opened yesterday at the Sutton Theater, is every Western you've ever seen turned upside down and inside out, braced with a lot of low burlesque, which is fine. In retrospect, however, one remembers along with the good gags the films desperate, bone-crushing efforts to be funny. One remembers exhaustion, perhaps because you kept wanting it to be funnier than it was. Much of the laughter Mr. Brooks inspires is hopeful, before-the-gag laughter, which can be terribly tiring.

●

In short takes Mr. Brooks's comedy has rewarding shock, especially when he's being insulting or rude or when he is going too far in areas usually thought to be in bad taste. Throughout the film, Madeline Kahn does a marvelously unkind take-off on Marlene Dietrich, playing a a dance-hall star named Lili von Shtupp who has a slight speech defect. When someone gives Lili a flower, she responds: "Oh, a wed wose! How womantic!" She also sings a song, "I'm Tired" (lyrics by Mr. Brooks), which lays waste for all time "Falling in Love Again."

The trouble is that "Blazing Saddles" has no real center of gravity. It has a story, something about a black sheriff (Cleavon Little) and his white sidekick (Gene Wilder) who save the town of Ridge Rock from land speculators, but as charming and funny as Mr. Little and Mr. Wilder are, the film's focus is split among the comic set pieces and the various eccentric supporting characters.

Some of these are very amusing in themselves: a bigoted preacher (Liam Dunn) who decries the fate of his town ("...our people scattered, our cattle raped...."; a lecherous, near-sighted governor (Mr. Brooks), and a huge, beagle-brained desperado (Alex Karras) who has a fist fight with a horse.

The result of the film's short attention span is to make the smaller roles more effective than the larger ones. Harvey Korman, a gifted comic actor who is so fine as Carol Burnett's television co-star, tries very hard to be funny as a crooked businessman and sometimes succeeds. But it's apparent that he's hard put to keep up with the movie's restless shifting from satire to parody to farce to blackout sketch.

●

Throughout "Blazing Saddles" I kept being reminded of 'Sleeper,' both films being the work of men who had their first real successes as gag writers. Both worked for Sid Caesar, and both still appreciate the need for getting a joke to the audience fast and then moving on. However, "Sleeper" builds momentum through the continuing character played by Mr. Allen himself, and gives the impression of having been pared down to comic essentials.

"Blazing Saddles" has no dominant personality, and it looks as if it includes every gag thought up in every story conference. Whether good, bad or mild, nothing was thrown out.

Mr. Allen's comedy, though very much a product of our Age of Analysis, recalls the wonder and discipline of people like Keaton and Laurel and Hardy. Mr. Brooks's sights are lower. His brashness is rare, but his use of anachronism and anarchy recalls not the great film comedies of the past, but the middling ones like the Hope-Crosby "Road" pictures. With his talent he should do much better than that.

Gene Wilder and Cleavon Little stumble onto the set of a musical in progress in Mel Brooks' hilarious *Blazing Saddles.*

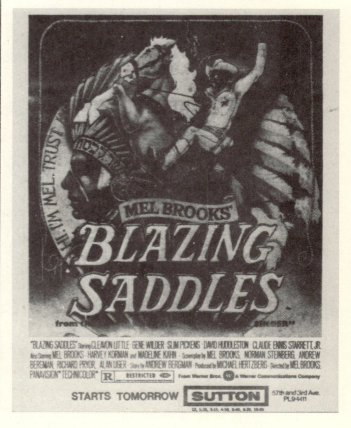

"IN MEL I TRUST."

MEL BROOKS'

BLAZING SADDLES

from ...

"BLAZING SADDLES" starring CLEAVON LITTLE · GENE WILDER · SLIM PICKENS · DAVID HUDDLESTON · CLAUDE ENNIS STARRETT, JR. Also starring MEL BROOKS, HARVEY KORMAN and MADELINE KAHN · Screenplay by MEL BROOKS, NORMAN STEINBERG, ANDREW BERGMAN, RICHARD PRYOR, ALAN UGER · Story by ANDREW BERGMAN · Produced by MICHAEL HERTZBERG · Directed by MEL BROOKS · PANAVISION® TECHNICOLOR® · R RESTRICTED · From Warner Bros. A Warner Communications Company

STARTS TOMORROW | SUTTON | 57th and 3rd Ave. PL 9-1411

12, 1:35, 3:15, 4:50, 6:40, 8:20, 10:05

WORLD PREMIERE
TODAY

WARREN
BEATTY
FAYE
DUNAWAY

MICHAEL J. POLLARD · GENE HACKMAN · ESTELLE PARSONS

BONNIE
AND CLYDE

They're young... they're in love

...and they kill people.

Written by DAVID NEWMAN and ROBERT BENTON · Music by Charles Strouse ·
Produced by WARREN BEATTY · Directed by ARTHUR PENN

TECHNICOLOR® · FROM WARNER BROS. / SEVEN ARTS, INC.

 THE COMPLETELY *New* FORUM 47th St. | **MURRAY HILL**
47th St. & Broadway PL 7-8320-1 | 34th East of Lexington Ave. MU 5-7652
12, 2, 4, 6, 8, 10, 12 | 12:30, 2:20, 4:20, 6:15, 8:15, 10:05

'Bonnie and Clyde' Arrives

Careers of Murderers Pictured as Farce

By BOSLEY CROWTHER

A RAW and unmitigated campaign of sheer press-agentry has been trying to put across the notion that Warner Brothers' "Bonnie and Clyde" is a faithful representation of the desperado careers of Clyde Barrow and Bonnie Parker, a notorious team of bank robbers and killers who roamed Texas and Oklahoma in the post-Depression years.

It is nothing of the sort. It is a cheap piece of bald-faced slapstick comedy that treats the hideous depredations of that sleazy, moronic pair as though they were as full of fun and frolic as the jazz-age cut-ups in "Thoroughly Modern Millie." And it puts forth Warren Beatty and Faye Dunaway in the leading roles, and Michael J. Pollard as their sidekick, a simpering, nose-picking rube, as though they were striving mightily to be the Beverly Hillbillies of next year.

It has Mr. Beatty clowning broadly as the killer who fondles various types of guns with as much nonchalance and dispassion as he airily twirls a big cigar, and it has Miss Dunaway squirming grossly as his thrill-seeking, sex-starved moll. It is loaded with farcical hold-ups, screaming chases in stolen getaway cars that have the antique appearance and speeded-up movement of the clumsy vehicles of the Keystone Cops, and indications of the impotence of Barrow, until Bonnie writes a poem about him to extol his prowess, that are as ludicrous as they are crude.

Such ridiculous, camp-tinctured travesties of the kind of people these desperados were and of the way people lived in the dusty Southwest back in those barren years might be passed off as candidly commercial movie comedy, nothing more, if the film weren't reddened with blotches of violence of the most grisly sort.

Arthur Penn, the aggressive director, has evidently gone out of his way to splash the comedy holdups with smears of vivid blood as astonished people are machine-gunned. And he has staged the terminal scene of the ambuscading and killing of Barrow and Bonnie by a posse of policemen with as much noise and gore as is in the climax of "The St. Valentine's Day Massacre."

This blending of farce with brutal killings is as pointless as it is lacking in taste, since it makes no valid commentary upon the already travestied truth. And it leaves an astonished critic wondering just what purpose Mr. Penn and Mr. Beatty think they serve with this strangely antique, sentimental claptrap, which opened yesterday at the Forum and the Murray Hill.

The Cast

BONNIE AND CLYDE; written by David Newman and Robert Benton; directed by Arthur Penn and produced by Warren Beatty; a Tatira-Hiller Production presented by Warner Bros.-Seven Arts. At the Forum Theater, Broadway at 47th Street, and the Murray Hill Theater, 34th Street east of Lexington Avenue. Running time: 111 minutes.

Clyde Barrow	Warren Beatty
Bonnie Parker	Faye Dunaway
C. W. Moss	Michael J. Pollard
Buck Barrow	Gene Hackman
Blanche	Estelle Parsons
Frank Hamer	Denver Pyle
Ivan Moss	Dub Taylor
Velma Davis	Evans Evans
Eugene Grizzard	Gene Wilder

Gene Hackman, Estelle Parsons, Warren Beatty, Faye Dunaway, and Michael J. Pollard in the gangster film, *Bonnie and Clyde.*

One of the many get-away scenes from *Bonnie and Clyde.*

'Born Yesterday' Is Reborn on Film in Columbia's Excellent Production at Victoria

BORN YESTERDAY, screen play by Albert Mannheimer, from the play by Garson Kanin; directed by George Cukor for Columbia Pictures. At the Victoria.

Billie Dawn	Judy Holliday
Paul Verrall	William Holden
Harry Brock	Broderick Crawford
Jim Devery	Howard St. John
Eddie	Frank Otto
Congressman Hedges	Larry Oliver
Mrs. Hedges	Barbara Brown
Sanborn	Grandon Rhodes
Helen	Claire Carleton

By BOSLEY CROWTHER

Just in time to make itself evident as one of the best pictures of this fading year is Columbia's trenchant screen version of the stage play, "Born Yesterday." More firm in its social implications than ever it was on the stage and blessed with a priceless performance by rocketing Judy Holliday, this beautifully integrated compound of character study and farce made a resounding entry at the Victoria yesterday.

On the strength of this one appearance, there is no doubt that Miss Holliday will leap into popularity as a leading American movie star—a spot to which she was predestined by her previous minor triumph in "Adam's Rib" as the tender young lady from Brooklyn who shot her husband (and stole the show) For there isn't the slightest question that Miss Holliday brings to the screen a talent for characterization that is as sweetly refreshing as it is rare.

Playing the wondrous ignoramus that she created on the stage—the lady to whom her crude companion rather lightly refers as a "dumb broad"—this marvelously clever young actress so richly conveys the attitudes and the vocal intonations of a native of the sidewalks of New York that it is art. More than that, she illuminates so brightly the elemental wit and honesty of her blankly unlettered young lady that she puts pathos and respect into the role.

But it must be said in the next breath that Miss Holliday doesn't steal this show—at least, not without a major tussle—for there is a lot of show here to steal. Not only has the original stage play of Garson Kanin been preserved by Screenwriter Albert Mannheimer in all of its flavorsome detail—and that, we might add, is a triumph of candor and real adapting skill—but George Cukor has directed with regard for both the humor and the moral. And Broderick Crawford has contributed a performance as the merchant of junk who would build himself up as a tycoon that fairly makes the hair stand on end.

Where this role was given some humor and even sympathy on the stage, in the memorable performance of Paul Douglas, Mr. Crawford endows it with such sting—such evident evil, corruption, cruelty and arrogance—that there is nothing amusing or appealing about this willful, brutish man. He is, indeed, a formidable symbol of the menace of acquisitive power and greed against which democratic peoples must always be alert. And that's why his thorough comeuppance, contrived by his newly enlightened "broad" amid the monuments of serene and beautiful Washington, is so winning and wonderful. In short, a more serious connotation has been given the role on the screen and Mr. Crawford plays it in a brilliantly cold and forceful style.

As the Washington correspondent hired to cultivate the junkman's girl—an enterprise which leads directly to her enlightenment and revolt—William Holden is tuned to perfection. He has dignity, diligence and reserve and gives a romantic demonstration of tolerance and amorous regard. It might be added in this connection that Miss Holliday, while frankly gotten up in the most absurdly tasteless outfits, is not a repulsive dish.

Howard St. John also gives a clean performance as the lawyer reduced to shady deals on the part of the horseback-riding braggart for fat and corrupting fees. Frank Otto is droll as a henchman and Larry Oliver injects a bit of gall into the somewhat reduced and denatured role of a Congressman.

With more room to move around in—meaning the City of Washington—and doing that in vivid fashion, "Born Yesterday" is reborn on the screen as a larger, stronger, more articulate and even more appealing prodigy.

Judy Holliday and William Holden in *Born Yesterday*.

WHO'S WHO in "BORN YESTERDAY"

William Holden as PAUL VERRALL
A boy with a nose for news, an ear to the ground, a foot in the door and an eye on a blonde!

Judy Holliday as BILLIE DAWN
Pretty, blonde, and pretty dumb. Has a weakness for nice things. Also has other weaknesses.

Broderick Crawford as HARRY BROCK
A tycoon who doesn't know what the word means. Has maybe the million bucks. Also has Billie Dawn —maybe.

COLUMBIA PICTURES presents

BROADWAY'S GREAT STAGE HIT...

BORN YESTERDAY

...Now a Perfectly Swell Motion Picture

starring

Judy HOLLIDAY · William HOLDEN · Broderick CRAWFORD

Screen Play by Albert Mannheimer · Produced by S. Sylvan Simon · Directed by George Cukor · Based on the Stage Play by Garson Kanin

STARTS **TODAY!**
CONTINUOUS PERFORMANCES

Victoria
B'WAY & 46th ST.

Doors Open 9:45 A.M.
LATE SHOWS NIGHTLY

The Monster Takes A Wife

At the Roxy.

THE BRIDE OF FRANKENSTEIN, suggested by the novel, "Frankenstein," by Mary Wollstonecraft Shelley; screen play by William Hurlbut and John L. Balderson; directed by James Whale; a Universal production.

The Monster	Boris Karloff
Henry Frankenstein	Colin Clive
Elizabeth	Valerie Hobson
The Mate	Elsa Lanchester
Mary Shelley	Elsa Lanchester
The Hermit	O. P. Heggie
Dr. Pretorious	Ernest Thesiger
Karl	Dwight Frye
Burgomaster	E. E. Clive
Minnie	Una O'Connor
Shepherdess	Anne Darling
Percy Shelley	Douglas Walton
Lord Byron	Gavin Gordon
Rudy	Neil Fitzgerald
Hans	Reginald Barlow
His Wife	Mary Gordon
Uncle Glutz	Gunnis Davis
Auntie Glutz	Tempe Piggott
Ludwig	Ted Billings
Butler	Lucien Prival

Not especially pleased with her mate, Boris Karloff, is Elsa Lanchester in *Bride of Frankenstein*.

Another astonishing chapter in the career of the Monster is being presented by Universal on the Roxy's screen. In "The Bride of Frankenstein," Boris Karloff comes again to terrify the children, frighten the women and play a jiggling tune upon masculine spines as the snarling, lumbering, pitiful Thing that a scientist formed from grave-snatched corpses and brought to life with the lightning.

So vividly are etched the memories of the Monster's first screen appearance that it seems scarcely possible that the original "Frankenstein" was shown on Broadway in December, 1931. Three and a half years was long to wait to learn whether the Monster died in the blazing tower where the end of "Frankenstein" left him. With this second chapter we know, of course, that he survived.

He had, one learns, taken refuge in the tower's water-filled cellar and now, in "Bride of Frankenstein," he clambers out, cuffs a few of the remaining villagers into oblivion and stalks once more through the moor, the graveyard and the hills, hated by man, gibbering at fire and—of all things—begging Frankenstein (Colin Clive, once more) to create a mate for him along the same general pattern.

In more ways than one, this is a changed Monster. At first, one must recall, he was pretty much of a thorough-going brute, a killer for the killing's sake. Now, possibly under the influence of Spring at Universal, he is slightly moon-struck, hungry for kindness and even—oh, perish the thought—for love. He learns to speak, to smoke cigars and drink wine. "Good," he says gluttonously, and points to the things he wants. "Bad!" he growls and shakes his square and metal-clipped head at fire. One will be amused at his softening, but it will be respectful amusement; one would not 'dare to laugh; he might snarl.

And so, driven by one force and another, poor Frankenstein and the wild-eyed Dr. Pretorious (who has experimented himself and created tiny humans which he keeps in small glass jars) go back into their laboratory, exhume more bodies, obtain a fresh human heart, harness again the power of the storms and convert Elsa Lanchester (Mrs. Charles Laughton in private life) into a bride for the Monster. It is rough on Miss Lanchester, but nothing to what happens to the lovelorn, calf-eyed Mr. Karloff.

The picture again ends with the apparent demise of the Monster—and his mate—but Mr. Karloff's best make-up should not be permitted to pass from the screen. The Monster should become an institution, like Charlie Chan.

Mr. Karloff is so splendid in the rôle that all one can say is "he is the Monster." Mr. Clive, Valerie Hobson, Elsa Lanchester, O. P. Heggie, Ernest Thesiger, E. E. Clive and Una O'Connor fit snugly into the human background before which Karloff moves. James Whale, who directed the earlier picture, has done another excellent job; the settings, photography and the make-up (contributed by Universal's expert, Jack Pierce) contribute their important elements to a first-rate horror film. F. S. N.

THE MONSTER DEMANDS A MATE!
Starts TODAY
DOORS OPEN 10:30 A.M.

The BRIDE of FRANKENSTEIN
A Universal Picture with
KARLOFF

★ BIG STAGE SHOW ★
TEDDY "BLUBBER" BERGMAN
JACK EDDY & CO.
THE GRETONAS
GAE FOSTER GIRLS

ROXY
25¢ ANY DAY ANY SEAT   35¢ ANY DAY ANY SEAT

SHOW VALUE OF THE NATION

Alec Guiness, William Holden and Jack Hawkins in *Bridge On the River Kwai*.

'The Bridge on the River Kwai' Opens

Memorable War Film Stars Alec Guinness

THE BRIDGE ON THE RIVER KWAI, screenplay by Pierre Boulle; based on his novel; directed by David Lean; produced by Sam Spiegel for Horizon Pictures; presented by Columbia. At the Palace. Running time: 161 minutes.
Shears .... William Holden
Colonel Nicholson .... Alec Guinness
Major Warden .... Jack Hawkins
Colonel Saito .... Sessue Hayakawa
Major Clipton .... James Donald
Lieutenant Joyce .... Geoffrey Horne
Colonel Green .... Andre Morell
Captain Reeves .... Peter Williams
Major Hughes .... John Boxer
Grogan .... Percy Herbert
Baker .... Harold Goodwin
Nurse .... Ann Sears
Captain Kanematsu .... Henry Okawa
Lieutenant Miura .... K. Katsumoto
Yai .... M. R. B. Chakrabandhu
Siamese Girls . Vilaiwan Seeboonreaung,
Ngamta Suphaphongs,
Javanart Punynchoti,
Kannikar Bowklee.

By BOSLEY CROWTHER

THERE are actually two motion picture dramas—two strong, suspenseful issues—embraced in Sam Spiegel's exceptional film production, "The Bridge on the River Kwai."

The first is a powerful personal drama of a conflict of wills between two military men, one the Japanese commander of a prisoner-of-war camp in the Burmese jungle and the other a British colonel brought there with a handful of his men. The second drama is a tingling action thriller that follows smoothly upon the resolution of the first. The crux of it is a bold maneuver to blow up a jungle railway bridge.

This mounting of drama upon drama in Mr. Spiegel's magnificent color film, which opened last night at the Palace for an extended two-a-day run, makes it more than a towering entertainment of rich variety and revelation of the ways of men. It makes it one of the niftiest bargains to be had on the screen this holiday.

•

Since both of the issues in this picture—the conflict of wills between two men and the subsequent contest to accomplish the destruction of the prisoner-built bridge—are loaded with mortal tension that holds the viewer in sweating suspense, it seems a shame that we have to give an inkling of the outcome of either one. But so much of the theme of the whole picture is conveyed in the resolution of the first that we have to tip you off to that one: the British colonel wins.

That is to say, he outfaces and outwits the camp commandant in compelling the latter's surrender on a military technicality. He refuses to permit himself or his officers to do manual labor on the building of the strategic bridge, as is brutally and illegally demanded by the snarling commandant. And for the first hour or so of the picture, he undergoes torture of a terrible, withering sort, until he catches his adversary in an ironic weakness and compels him to respect the military code.

He wins, but he wins at the expense of a shocking, significant compromise. He agrees to apply himself and officers as supervising engineers. He accepts the narrow technical victory with satisfaction and even pride, without regard for—or even apparent awareness of—the aid he will thus give the enemy. The building of the bridge for the one-track railway becomes the sole aim of this man with the one-track mind.

Here is the heart of this fine picture, here is its stark and potent theme: discipline and conformity are the obsession of the professional militarist. And upon this rising realization hinges all the subsequent drama and suspense as a small commando team inches into the jungle to destroy the colonel's precious bridge. Does the colonel actually stop his own countrymen? This one we will not reveal!

Brilliant is the word, and no other, to describe the quality of skills that have gone into the making of this picture, from the writing of the script out of a novel by the Frenchman Pierre Boulle, to direction, performance, photographing, editing and application of a musical score.

David Lean has directed it so smartly and so sensitively for image and effect that its two hours and forty-one minutes seem no more than a swift, absorbing hour. In addition to splendid performance, he has it brilliantly filled with atmosphere—the atmosphere of war's backwash and the jungle—touched startlingly with humor, heart and shock.

In the line of performance, Alec Guinness does a memorable—indeed, a classic—job in making the ramrod British colonel a profoundly ambiguous type. With a rigid, serene disposition, he displays the courage and tenacity of a lion, as well as the denseness and pomposity of a dangerously stupid, inbred snob. He shows, beneath the surface of a hero, the aspects of an inhuman fool. He gives one of the most devastating portraits of a militarist that we have ever seen.

As his Japanese opposite number, old Sessue Hayakawa is superb—brutal, stubborn, sluggish an equally grotesque fool. Jack Hawkins is droll and determined as the British major who leads the commando raid and William Holden is delightfully gallant as an American sailor mixed up in this strange affair. James Donald, Geoffrey Horne and Peter Williams are splendid as British army chaps, and a bunch of little Oriental females add spice as native porters on the raid.

A real bridge and natural settings in Ceylon have been exquisitely photographed by Jack Hildyard's color cameras.

Here is a film we guarantee you'll not forget.

IT'S HERE—TONIGHT!

COLUMBIA PICTURES presents A SAM SPIEGEL PRODUCTION

WILLIAM HOLDEN
ALEC GUINNESS   JACK HAWKINS

"THE BRIDGE ON THE RIVER KWAI"

TECHNICOLOR   CINEMASCOPE

with SESSUE HAYAKAWA · JAMES DONALD · ANN SEARS and introducing GEOFFREY HORNE
Directed by DAVID LEAN · Screenplay by PIERRE BOULLE, Based on his Novel

RESERVED SEATS ONLY
TICKETS NOW ON SALE FOR FIRST EIGHT WEEKS
at BOX-OFFICE or by MAIL
RKO PALACE
BROADWAY & 47th STREET · PL 7-2626
FIRST PUBLIC PERFORMANCE TONIGHT at 8:30
NIGHTLY at 8:30 — MATS. WED. SAT. & SUN. 2:30 — SPECIAL HOLIDAY MATS. DAILY DEC. 26 thru DEC. 31

PAUL NEWMAN IS BUTCH CASSIDY AND THE SUNDANCE KID IS ROBERT REDFORD™ KATHARINE ROSS IS ETTA PLACE.

Not that it matters, but most of it is true.

20th CENTURY-FOX PRESENTS

A GEORGE ROY HILL-PAUL MONASH PRODUCTION

CoStarring STROTHER MARTIN   JEFF COREY   HENRY JONES

Executive Producer: PAUL MONASH, Produced by JOHN FOREMAN

Directed by GEORGE ROY HILL, Written by WILLIAM GOLDMAN

Music Composed and Conducted by BURT BACHARACH,   A NEWMAN-FOREMAN PRESENTATION

PANAVISION® COLOR BY DELUXE   [Hear HAL DAVID and BURT BACHARACH'S "Raindrops Keep Fallin' On My Head" as sung by B.J. Thomas.]

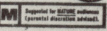

STARTS TODAY

NEW PENT HOUSE
B'way & 47th St.   757-5450
A PACIFIC EAST THEATRE
11. 1. 3. 5. 7. 9. 11

SUTTON
57th St. and 3rd Ave. • PL 9-1411
11. 1. 3. 5. 7. 9. 11

Slapstick and Drama Cross Paths in 'Butch Cassidy'

BUTCH CASSIDY AND THE SUNDANCE KID, written by William Goldman; directed by George Roy Hill; produced by John Foreman; released by 20th Century-Fox Film Corporation. At the Penthouse Theater, Broadway and 47th Street and the Sutton Theater, Third Avenue and 57th Street. Running time: 110 minutes. (The Motion Picture Association of America's Production Code and Rating Administration classifies this film; "M—suggested for mature audiences, parental discretion advised.")

Butch Cassidy	Paul Newman
The Sundance Kid	Robert Redford
Etta Place	Katharine Ross
Percy Garris	Strother Martin
Bike Salesman	Henry Jones
Sheriff Bledsoe	Jeff Corey
Woodcock	George Furth
Agnes	Cloris Leachman
Harvey Logan	Ted Cassidy

By VINCENT CANBY

"BUTCH Cassidy and the Sundance Kid" were real-life, turn-of-the-century outlaws who, in 1905, packed up their saddlebags, along with Sundance's mistress (a schoolteacher named Etta Place), and left the shrinking American West to start a new life, robbing banks in Bolivia.

According to the movie which opened yesterday at the Penthouse and Sutton Theaters, their decline and fall was the sort of alternately absurd and dreamy saga that might have been fantasized by Truffaut's Jules and Jim and Catherine—before they grew up.

Butch (Paul Newman) is so amiable that it's not until he gets to Bolivia, and is more or less forced to go straight, that he ever brings himself to shoot a man. Sundance (Robert Redford) behaves like the perpetual younger brother. Although confident of his own abilities, he always defers to Butch, whose schemes end in disaster more often that success. Etta (Katharine Ross) is the kind of total woman who can cook, keep house of sorts, seldom grumbles, and, if necessary, will act as third gun.

This is an attractive conceit and much of "Butch Cassidy and the Sundance Kid" is very funny in a strictly contemporary way—the last exuberant word on movies about the men of the mythic American West who have outlived their day. Butch and Sundance have the physical graces of classic Western heros, but all four feet are made of silly putty.

When they try to rob a train and blow open its safe, the dynamite charge destroys not only the safe but also the entire baggage car. When they can escape from a posse only by jumping from a high cliff into a raging rapids below, Sundance must admit ruefully that he doesn't know how to swim.

George Roy Hill ("Thoroughly Modern Millie," "Hawaii") who directed, and William Goldman, the novelist ("Boys and Girls Together") and occasional scenarist ("Harper"), who wrote the original screenplay, have consciously mixed their genres. Even though the result is not unpleasant, it is vaguely disturbing—you keep seeing signs of another, better film behind gags and effects that may remind you of everything from "Jules and Jim" to "Bonnie and Clyde" and "The Wild Bunch."

In the center of the movie is a lovely, five-minute montage—done in sepia still photographs of the period—showing Butch, Sundance and Etta having a brief fling in New York and making the steamer passage to South America. The stills tell you so much about the curious and sad relationship of the three people that it's with real reluctance that you allow yourself to be absorbed again into further slapstick adventures.

There is thus, at the heart of "Butch Cassidy," a gnawing emptiness that can't be satisfied by an awareness that Hill and Goldman probably knew exactly what they were doing—making a very slick movie. They play tricks on the audience, by turning a bit of melodrama into a comic blackout, and by taking short cuts to lyricism as when we get an extended sequence showing Butch clowning on a bicycle for the benefit of Etta backed by full orchestra playing Burt Bachrach's latest. I admire Bachrach but he simply is not Georges Delerue as Hill is not Truffaut; nor, for that matter, is Goldman.

There are some bothersome technical things about the movie (the camera is all zoom, zoom, zoom) but the over-all production is very handsome, and the performances fine, especially Newman, Redford and Miss Ross, who must be broadly funny and straight, almost simultaneously. They succeed even if the movie does not.

Paul Newman and Robert Redford as the likeable con men in *Butch Cassidy and the Sundance Kid.*

"CABARET" — Liza Minnelli, as the brash Sally Bowles, belts out a song while Joel Grey, the master of ceremonies at the sleazy Kit Kat Klub, looks on. Bob Fosse's film, based on the Broadway musical, about decadent doings in Berlin during the thirties, co-stars Michael York. Today, the Ziegfeld.

Liza Minnelli Stirs a Lively 'Cabaret'

CABARET, directed by Bob Fosse; screenplay by Jay Allen, based on the musical play "Cabaret" by Joe Masteroff, the play "I Am a Camera" by John Van Druten and the "Berlin Stories" of Christopher Isherwood; musical direction and orchestrations by Ralph Burns; music by John Kander; lyrics by Fred Ebb; photographed by Geoffrey Unsworth; edited by David Bretherton; produced by Cy Feuer; released by Allied Artists. At the Ziegfeld Theater, Avenue of the Americas and 54th Street. Running time: 118 minutes. (The Motion Picture Association of America's Production Code and Rating Administration classifies this film: "PG—parental guidance suggested, some material may not be suitable for pre-teen-agers.")

Sally Bowles	Liza Minnelli
Brian Roberts	Michael York
Maximilian von Heune	Helmut Griem
Master of Ceremonies	Joel Grey
Fritz Wendel	Fritz Wepper
Fraulein Schneider	
Elisabeth Neumann-Viertel	

By ROGER GREENSPUN

I doubt whether too many young women have had a fuller life in art than Christopher Isherwood's divinely decadent and infinitely appealing English girl adrift in Berlin in the early 1930's, Sally Bowles. She has gone from fiction to theater ("I Am a Camera") and thence to film, then back to theater, a Broadway musical, and now again to film.

And though I haven't seen everything that came between, I have seen enough and heard enough to guess that Sally has fared best at first, in Isherwood's lovely, minor "Berlin Stories," and at last, in Bob Fosse's new movie version of the musical "Cabaret," which opened yesterday at the Ziegfeld Theater.

A lot has happened to Sally and her friends in the process. She is now an American (Liza Minnelli), while her young man, Brian (Michael York), is now British. There is another girl, a Jewish Berlin department-store heiress (Marisa Berenson), and a man for her (Fritz Wepper). In the midst of everything there appears a handsome German baron (Helmut Griem), who seduces both Sally and Brian and then drops them. Brian's bisexuality now has as much as Sally's accidental pregnancy to do with moving the plot, and it connects as well with a general theme of sick sexual ambiguity that runs through the film as a kind of working motif.

The master of sexual ambiguity, and the master of motifs is again Joel Grey, master of ceremonies at the Kit Kat Klub, the cellar cabaret where Sally sings and dances, and where everything, even the rise of the Third Reich, is "beautiful."

"Cabaret" is not so much a movie musical as it is a movie with a lot of music in it. Several numbers from the Broadway show have been dropped, and some new, and better ones added—by John Kander and Fred Ebb, the original composer and lyricist—and all for Miss Minnelli. Most of the music is limited to performance at the Kit Kat Club, and Fosse's approach has been not to open up but rather to confine, on a small and well-defined stage, as much of "Cabaret" as means to be musical theater.

Thus the film has a musical part and a nonmusical part (except for Miss Minnelli, none of the major characters sings), and if you add this to the juxtaposition of private lives and public history inherent in the scheme of the "Berlin Stories," you come up with a structure of extraordinary mechanical complexity. Since everything has to do with everything else and the Cabaret is always commenting on the life outside it, the film sometimes looks like an essay in significant crosscutting, or associative montage. Occasionally this fails; more often it works.

Fosse makes mistakes, partly because his camera is a more potent instrument than he realizes, but he also makes discoveries — and "Cabaret" is one of those immensely gratifying imperfect works in which from beginning to end you can literally feel a movie coming to life.

The film gains a good deal from its willingness to isolate its musical stage—even to observe it from behind the heads of a shadowy audience in the foreground—so that every time we return to the girls and their leering master (by now, a superbly refined caricature) we return, as it were, to a sense of theater. And when at certain moments that theater is occupied only by Liza Minnelli, working in a space defined only by her gestures and a few colored lights, it becomes by the simplest means an evocation of both the power and fragility of movie performance so beautiful that I can think of nothing to do but give thanks.

Everybody in "Cabaret" is very fine, and meticulously chosen for type, down to the last weary transvestite and to the least of the bland, blond open-faced Nazis in the background. As for Miss Minnelli, she is sometimes wrong in the details of her role, but so magnificently right for the film as a whole that I should prefer not to imagine it without her.

With her expressive face and her wonderful (and wonderfully costumed) body she moves and sings with a strength, warmth, intelligence, and sensitivity to nuance that virtually transfixes the screen.

Joel Grey won best supporting actor for his role as Master of Ceremonies in *Cabaret*.

40

'Caine Mutiny' Arrives

Vibrant Depiction of Novel Is at Capitol

THE CAINE MUTINY, screen play by Stanley Roberts, from the novel by Herman Wouk; directed by Edward Dmytryk; produced by Stanley Kramer for Columbia Pictures. At the Capitol.

Captain Queeg	Humphrey Bogart
Lieut. Barney Greenwald	José Ferrer
Lieut. Steve Maryk	Van Johnson
Lieut. Tom Keefer	Fred MacMurray
Ensign Willie Keith	Robert Francis
May Wynn	May Wynn
Captain DeVriess	Tom Tully
Lieutenant Commander Challee	E. G. Marshall
Lieut. Paynter	Arthur Franz
Meatball	Lee Marvin
Captain Blakely	Warner Anderson
Horrible	Claude Akins
Mrs. Keith	Katharine Warren
Ensign Harding	Jerry Paris

By BOSLEY CROWTHER

THE job of compacting and containing Herman Wouk's "The Caine Mutiny" into two hours of color motion picture, with all the character and drama preserved, was one that compared in major aspects with the similar job on "From Here to Eternity." And we're glad to report that Columbia Pictures and Producer Stanley Kramer have achieved this extraordinarily difficult endeavor with clarity and vigor, on the whole.

This tale of the tensions and turmoils among the officers and crew of a Navy destroyer-minesweeper in the Pacific in World War II is a compound of several personal dramas and conflicts of male temperaments, all drawn to a fine, explosive crisis during a violent typhoon at sea. At the core of its swirling rotation are the bravery and cowardice of men. These are the elements that stand out sharply and gauntly in this film, which was greeted by swarming patrons at the Capitol yesterday.

•

Unfortunately, Screenwriter Stanley Roberts, in preparing the complicated script, endeavored to cram into the picture more of the novel than was required. He gave a great deal of attention to the completely extraneous love affair between Keith, a secondary junior officer, and the night club singer, May Wynn. This was both useless and artless. Whenever the love affair obtrudes, the genuine drama is side-tracked and the criss-crossing tensions are snapped.

Also, the structure of the story presented in Mr. Wouk's book was not entirely felicitous for the playing of a drama on the screen. Yet Mr. Roberts has endeavored to follow it faithfully. As a consequence, the naval court-martial that follows the howling typhoon, wherein the executive officer relieves the incompetent captain of command, becomes an anticlimax as it covers essentially the same ground and repeats the collapse of the captain that are visibly shown in the storm.

On the stage, this Caine mutiny court-martial is brilliant because it unfolds in the calm atmosphere of a courtroom the events that have gone before—events that are graphically enacted prior to the trial on the screen. The sole achievement of the trial in the picture is that of demonstrating the perfidy of one man—Lieut. Tom. Keefer. The audience already knows the captain's guilt.

This is a weakness of the picture that takes a lot of time, since more than twenty minutes are virtually wasted in building up to the thin theatrics at the end.

However, the body of the picture—the good, solid, masculine core—that has to do with the chafing of naval officers under a neurotic captain's command is salty, exciting and revealing. And it is smartly and stingingly played by a cast of able performers, with Edward Dmytryk calling the turns.

Van Johnson as the blunt executive officer who commits the so-called act of mutiny does an excellent job of revealing the distress and resolution of this man, and Fred MacMurray is likewise fascinating as the modern "sea lawyer" who eggs him on. Humphrey Bogart's twitchy performance of the "by-the-book" Captain Queeg is a bit in the usual Bogart manner but, by and large, it is sound. Robert Francis as the romancing ensign, Tom Tully as the sloppy captain who precedes Queeg and José Ferrer as the lawyer for the defendant in the court-martial are good. As it happens, the role of the lawyer has little body in the film.

Thanks to the help of the Navy, the shipboard business is on the beam, the blue-water shots of maneuvers are spanking and the atmosphere is keen.

"The Caine Mutiny," though somewhat garbled, is a vibrant film.

Fred MacMurray, Humphrey Bogart and Robert Francis in a scene from *The Caine Mutiny*.

THE HOMER DICKENS STILL COLLECTION

"You are so young...
where can you have
learned all you know
about women like me?"

Greta
GARBO
(The Lady of the Camelias)

Loves

Robert
TAYLOR

in

"CAMILLE"

with

LIONEL BARRYMORE

JESSIE RALPH · ELIZABETH ALLAN

LENORE ULRIC and others

Directed by George Cukor

A Metro-Goldwyn-Mayer Picture

•

Also Pete Smith Novelty

"WANTED: A MASTER"

•

Starts TODAY

DOORS OPEN 9:45 A. M.

CAPITOL

BROADWAY AND 51st STREET

Major Edward Bowes, Managing Director

'Camille,' With Greta Garbo and Robert Taylor, Opens At the Capitol

CAMILLE., as adapted by Zoe Akins, Frances Marion and James Hilton from Alexandre Dumas's "La Dame Aux Camelias"; directed by George Cukor; produced by Metro-Goldwyn-Mayer. At the Capitol.

Marguerite	Greta Garbo
Armand	Robert Taylor
Monsieur Duval	Lionel Barrymore
Nichette	Elizabeth Allan
Nanine	Jessie Ralph
Baron de Varville	Henry Daniell
Olympe	Lenore Ulric
Prudence	Laura Hope Crews
Gaston	Rex O'Malley
Gustave	Russell Hardie
Saint Gaudens	E. E. Clive
Henri	Douglas Walton
Corinne	Marion Ballou
Marie Jeanette	Joan Brodel
Louise	June Wilkins
Valentin	Fritz Leiber Jr.
Mme. Duval	Elsie Esmonds

By FRANK S. NUGENT

Having passed its fiftieth anniversary, "Camille" is less a play than an institution. Just as "Hamlet" is the measure of the great actor, so has the Dumas fils' classic become the ultimate test of the dramatic actress. Greta Garbo's performance in the new Metro-Goldwyn-Mayer version at the Capitol is in the finest tradition: eloquent, tragic, yet restrained. She is as incomparable in the rôle as legend tells us that Bernhardt was. Through the perfect artistry of her portrayal, a hackneyed theme is made new again, poignantly sad, hauntingly lovely.

George Cukor, the classicist of the Metro studios, has retained the full flavor of the period—France in the middle of the last century—without drenching his film with the cloying scent of a hothouse. "Camille," under his benign handling and the understanding adaptation by Zoe Akins, Frances Marion and James Hilton, is not the reverentially treated museum piece we half expected to see. Its speech has been modernized, but not jarringly; its characters, beneath the frill and ruffles of the Fifties, have the contemporary point of view; its tragedy is still compelling, for the Lady of the Camellias must eternally be a tragic figure.

Miss Garbo has interpreted Marguerite Gautier with the subtlety that has earned for her the title, "first lady of the screen." Even as the impish demi-mondaine of the early sequences, she has managed to convey the impression of maturity, of a certain etherealism and spiritual integrity which raise her above her surroundings and mark her as one apart. Her love for Armand, dictating her flight from Paris and the protection of the Baron de Varville, becomes, then, less a process of reformation and regeneration than it is the natural realization of her true character; less a variation of life than a discovery of life.

To appreciate her complete command of the rôle, one need only study her approach to the key scenes of the drama. Where the less sentient Camille bides her time until the moment comes for her to tear her passions and the scenery to tatters, Garbo waits and then understates. It is her dignity that gives strength to her scene with

M. Duval when he asks her to give up his son. It is because her emotions do not slip their leash—when you feel that any second they might—that saves her parting scene with Armand from being a cliché of renunciation. And, above all, it is her performance in the death scene—so simply, delicately and movingly played—which convinces me that Camille is Garbo's best performance.

Robert Taylor is surprisingly good as Armand, a bit on the juvenile side at times, perhaps, but certainly not guilty of the traditional sin of the many Armands of the past—callowness. As the Baron de Varville, Henry Daniell is suavely perfect. It is a matter for rejoicing that a character so clearly stamped for villainy, should receive, belatedly, some of the sympathy he deserved: Camille did, you know, treat him shamefully. From Jessie Ralph as Nanine, Lionel Barrymore as M. Duval, Lenore Ulric as Olympe, Laura Hope Crews as Prudence and Rex O'Malley as Gaston we have received what we had every right to expect—good, sound, supporting performances. That they should have been noted at all, in view of Miss Garbo's brilliant domination of the picture, is high praise indeed.

Robert Taylor and Greta Garbo in Camille's death scene.

Greta Garbo as *Camille.*

A Newcomer Named Errol Flynn in a Handsome Film Version of 'Captain Blood,' at the Strand.

CAPTAIN BLOOD, based on the novel by Rafael Sabatini; screen play by Casey Robinson; directed by Michael Curtiz; a Warner Brothers production. At the Strand.

Peter Blood	Errol Flynn
Arabella Bishop	Olivia de Havilland
Colonel Bishop	Lionel Atwill
Levasseur	Basil Rathbone
Jeremy Pitt	Ross Alexander
Hagthorpe	Guy Kibbee
Lord Willoughby	Henry Stephenson
Wolverstone	Robert Barrat
Dr. Bronson	Hobart Cavanaugh
Dr. Whacker	Donald Meek
Mrs. Barlow	Jessie Ralph
Honesty Nuttall	Forrester Harvey
Rev. Ogle	Frank McGlynn Sr.
Captain Gardner	Holmes Herbert
Andrew Baynes	David Torrence
Cahusac	J. Carroll Naish
Don Diego	Pedro de Cordoba
Governor Steed	George Hassell
Kent	Harry Cording
Baron Jeffreys	Leonard Mudie
Prosecutor	Ivan Simpson
Captain Hobart	Stuart Casey
Lord Gildoy	Dennis D. Auburn
Mrs. Steed	Mary Forbes
Clerk of the Court	E. E. Clive
Lord Chester Dyke	Colin Kenny
Mrs. Baynes	Maude Leslie
Slave	Gardner James
King James	Vernon Steele

By ANDRE SENNWALD.

The history of Dr. Peter Blood. Sabatini's gentleman corsair, is treated with visual beauty and a fine, swaggering arrogance in the new screen version of "Captain Blood" at the Strand Theatre. With a spirited and criminally good-looking Australian named Errol Flynn playing the genteel buccaneer to the hilt, the photoplay recaptures the air of high romantic adventure which is so essential to the tale. Providing a properly picturesque background for Dr. Blood's piratical career, the Warner Brothers skillfully reconstruct the England of the sanguinary Monmouth uprising, the West Indies of tortured slaves and savage masters, and the ships that sailed the Spanish Main flying the jolly roger.

Only yesterday Basil Rathbone was grinding the poor of Paris in "A Tale of Two Cities," and now, with equal skill if slightly increased likableness, he is quarreling with Captain Blood over the disposition of the handsome English captive, Miss Arabella Bishop. Mr. Rathbone has a habit of dying violently in his pictures, but his demise in this one, when Blood punctures him at the conclusion of a desperately waged duel, seems more lamentable than usual. Perhaps it is because he lacks the proper seasoning of villainy this time.

All Levasseur, the picturesque French freebooter, wanted was the girl, who was rightfully his by right of conquest. Somehow it seemed extravagantly prissy of the Englishman to fight him in abstract defense of the lady's honor instead of admitting candidly that he wanted Arabella for himself. Anyway, it is a brave bit of sword-play that these audacious fellows put on, up and down the Coast, while their rival crews look on.

You may recall that Dr. Blood was an amateur pirate, forced into the business because King James had shipped him off to the Indies with the other condemned Monmouth rebels. A physician by profession, his part in the uprising was innocent, but the king's court convicted him along with the rest. He scorned his masters and laughed when they flogged him, but Arabella saved him from a living death in her uncle's mines at Port Royal because she liked his courage and his face. Then he led the slaves in an uprising, stole a Spanish ship while its crew was looting the town and became the most celebrated corsair in the Caribbean.

Mr. Flynn has an effective cast at his back. Olivia de Havilland is a lady of rapturous loveliness and well worth fighting for. Lionel Atwill, as the cruel governor of Port Royal, is as thorough a knave as Peter Blood is a gentleman. Among the excellent group of players who people the smaller rôles you will discover E. E. Clive, the wonderful jurist of "A Tale of Two Cities," who is humorously effective if somewhat less spectacular as the clerk of the bloody assizes.

Errol Flynn in his first starring role— the swashbuckling, *Captain Blood.*

NOW!

A MILLION DOLLARS' WORTH OF ADVENTURE packed into this miracle of motion pictures!

CAPTAIN BLOOD

WITH ERROL FLYNN
OLIVIA DE HAVILLAND
LIONEL ATWILL · BASIL RATHBONE

STRAND · 25c

Midnite Shows—B'way & 47th — to 1 p.m.

A Cosmopolitan Production
A First National Picture
Presented by Warner Bros.

'The Carpetbaggers' Opens

By BOSLEY CROWTHER

JOSEPH E. LEVINE has completed the circle. He is back peddling "Hercules," or, at least, a curiously close resemblance to that overblown film and character with which he started his career as a distributor—and later producer—in 1959.

The film is "The Carpetbaggers," a sickly sour distillation of Harold Robbins's big-selling novel. And the character is Jonas Cord Jr., the novel's grotesque aviation and film tycoon who bulges with money instead of muscles but otherwise is quite similar to Hercules.

That is to say, he is an outright synthetic fabrication of a character designed to conform to a popular legend or myth. He is a thoroughly mechanical movie puppet, controlled by a script-writer's strings. Only instead of being a noble hero, the personification of a chivalrous myth, he is a contemptible hero, conforming to the myth of the heel.

In the last few minutes, however, the puppeteers, John Michael Hayes, who wrote the script from Mr. Robbins's novel, and Edward Dmytryk, who directed it, decide to pull the strings that will make him come out a repentant, humbled heel. They have him return to the wife he has abused through most of the film with as little motivation or justification as he had for marrying her.

They obviously don't need motivations for pulling this string or that in this film, which opened yesterday at the Paramount, the Festival,

The Cast

THE CARPETBAGGERS, screenplay by John Michael Hayes, adapted from the novel by Harold Robbins; directed by Edward Dmytryk; produced by Joseph E. Levine and presented by Paramount Pictures. At the Paramount Theater, Broadway and 43d Street; the Festival Theater, 57th Street west of Fifth Avenue and other theatres. Running time: 150 minutes.

Jonas Cord Jr.	George Peppard
Rina	Caroll Baker
Nevada Smith	Alan Ladd
Dan Pierce	Bob Cummings
Jennie Denton	Martha Hyer
Monica Winthrop	Elizabeth Ashley
McAllister	Lew Ayres
Bernard B. Norman	Martin Balsam
Buzz Dalton	Ralph Taeger
Jedediah	Archie Moore
Jonas Cord Sr.	Leif Erickson
Morrissey	Arthur Franz
Amos Winthrop	Tom Tully
The Prostitute	Audrey Totter
David Woolf	Tom Lowell

and 30 other theaters in the metropolitan area.

All they need is the gleaming inspiration of the knowledge that the events in the book were sufficiently sordid and sadistic to sell a claimed 5,000,000 copies. And so they have set about translating these events to film, with as much innuendo (without using the four letter words and the detailed boudoir descriptions) as the law and the Production Code will allow.

They have got their principal character, who is evidently meant to remind us of a noted eccentric aircraft builder and occasional producer of films, go through the seamy business of consolidating his father's financial interests after the old man has died, sticking pins in his father's widow, who was evidently one of his old girls. They have got him becoming famous, going to Hollywood hooking up with disreputable movie people and running the gamut in that community.

But each successive episode

it is unlikely that you will experience in a lifetime all that you will see in...

JOSEPH E. LEVINE presents THE CARPETBAGGERS

starring GEORGE PEPPARD ALAN LADD BOB CUMMINGS
MARTHA HYER ELIZABETH ASHLEY LEW AYRES
MARTIN BALSAM RALPH TAEGER ARCHIE MOORE
CARROLL BAKER as RINA

based on the novel "The Carpetbaggers" by
screenplay by JOHN MICHAEL HAYES HAROLD ROBBINS
TECHNICOLOR® PANAVISION®

music composed and conducted by ELMER BERNSTEIN

directed by EDWARD DMYTRYK

produced by JOSEPH E. LEVINE Paramount Release

THIS IS ADULT ENTERTAINMENT!

in this character's crude and cruel career is manufactured claptrap, superficial and two-dimensional. And George Peppard's acting of the character is expressionless, murky and dull. If that party he's made up to resemble wanted to sue the makers of this film, he shouldn't care about suing for libel, but just for making the

character so uninteresting.

Carroll Baker, at least, has some color and a sandpaper personality as the sex-loaded widow the stepson turns into a platinum-blonde star. And Elizabeth Ashley comes through as a fairly real person in the role of the flip-talking flapper he marries and then puts through the emotional mill.

Alan Ladd is stout and stuffy as Nevada Smith, the double-crossed old pal, and Robert Cummings smirks and glitters artificially as a Hollywood agent. Martha Hyer as a sullied starlet, Lew Ayres as a lawyer type and Martin Balsam as a harassed producer do well enough by these roles.

But they all lack exciting direction. Mr. Dmytryk has gone at this film, which might have been trenchant in the manner of "Citizen Kane," with a baseball bat. He has beaten it down to a square, flat surface, without cinematic lift or style. And, somehow, color makes it look more synthetic than it might look in black-and-white.

However, the drums have been beating for it, as they did for "Hercules." It will probably be seen by millions of people — and that should satisfy Mr. Levine.

Robert Cummings as a villain, Martha Hyer as a sullied starlet, from *The Carpetbaggers.*

'Casablanca,' With Humphrey Bogart and Ingrid Bergman, at Hollywood—'White Cargo' and 'Ravaged Earth' Open

CASABLANCA; screen play by Julius J. and Philip G. Epstein and Howard Koch; from a play by Murray Burnett and Joan Alison; directed by Michael Curtis; produced by Hal B. Wallis for Warner Brothers. At the Hollywood.

Rick	Humphrey Bogart
Ilsa Lund	Ingrid Bergman
Victor Laszlo	Paul Henreid
Capt. Louis Renault	Claude Rains
Major Strasser	Conrad Veidt
Senor Ferrari	Sydney Greenstreet
Ugarte	Peter Lorre
Carl	S. Z. Sakall
Yvonne	Madeleine LeBeau
Sam	Dooley Wilson
Annina Brandel	Joy Page
Berger	John Qualen
Sascha	Leonid Kinskey
Jan	Helmut Dantine
Dark European	Curt Bois
Croupier	Marcel Dalio
Singer	Corinna Mura
Mr. Leuchtag	Ludwig Stossel
Mrs. Leuchtag	Ilka Gruning
Senor Martinez	Charles La Torre
Arab Vendor	Frank Puglia
Abdul	Dan Seymour

By BOSLEY CROWTHER

Against the electric background of a sleek cafe in a North African port, through which swirls a backwash of connivers, crooks and fleeing European refugees, the Warner Brothers are telling a rich, suave, exciting and moving tale in their new film, "Casablanca," which came to the Hollywood yesterday. They are telling it in the high tradition of their hard-boiled romantic-adventure style. And to make it all the more tempting they have given it a top-notch thriller cast of Humphrey Bogart, Sydney Greenstreet, Peter Lorre, Conrad Veidt and even Claude Rains, and have capped it magnificently with Ingrid Bergman, Paul Henreid and a Negro "find" named Dooley Wilson.

Yes, indeed, the Warners here have a picture which makes the spine tingle and the heart take a leap. For once more, as in recent Bogart pictures, they have turned the incisive trick of draping a tender love story within the folds of a tight topical theme. They have used Mr. Bogart's personality, so well established in other brilliant films, to inject a cold point of tough resistance to evil forces afoot in Europe today. And they have so combined sentiment, humor and pathos with taut melodrama and bristling intrigue that the result is a highly entertaining and even inspiring film.

The story, as would be natural, has its devious convolutions of plot. But mainly it tells of a tough fellow named Rick who runs a Casablanca cafe and of what happens (or what happened last December) when there shows up in his joint one night a girl whom he had previously loved in Paris in company with a fugitive Czech patriot. The Nazis are tailing the young Czech; the Vichy officials offer only brief refuge—and Rick holds the only two sure passports which will guarantee his and the girl's escape. But Rick loves the girl very dearly, she is now married to this other man—and whenever his Negro pianist sits there in the dark and sings "As Time Goes By" that old, irresistible feeling consumes him in a choking, maddening wave.

Don't worry; we won't tell you how it all comes out. That would be rankest sabotage. But we will tell you that the urbane detail and the crackling dialogue which has been packed into this film by the scriptwriters, the Epstein brothers and Howard Koch, is of the best. We will tell you that Michael Curtiz has directed for slow suspense and that his camera is always conveying grim tension and uncertainty. Some of the significant incidents, too, are affecting—such as that in which the passionate Czech patriot rouses the customers in Rick's cafe to drown out a chorus of Nazis by singing the Marseillaise, or any moment in which Dooley Wilson is remembering past popular songs in a hushed room.

We will tell you also that the performances of the actors are all of the first order, but especially those of Mr. Bogart and Miss Bergman in the leading roles. Mr. Bogart is, as usual, the cool, cynical, efficient and super-wise guy who operates his business strictly for profit but has a core of sentiment and idealism inside. Conflict becomes his inner character, and he handles it credibly. Miss Bergman is surpassingly lovely, crisp and natural as the girl and lights the romantic passages with a warm and genuine glow.

Mr. Rains is properly slippery and crafty as a minion of Vichy perfidy, and Mr. Veidt plays again a Nazi officer with cold and implacable resolve. Very little is demanded of Mr. Greenstreet as a shrewd black-market trader, but that is good, and Mr. Henreid is forthright and simple as the imperiled Czech patriot. Mr. Wilson's performance as Rick's devoted friend, though rather brief, is filled with a sweetness and compassion which lend a helpful mood to the whole film, and other small roles are played ably by S. Z. Sakall, Joy Page, Leonid Kinskey and Mr. Lorre.

In short, we will say that "Casablanca" is one of the year's most exciting and trenchant films. It certainly won't make Vichy happy —but that's just another point for it.

The stars of the classic, *Casablanca*, Humphrey Bogart and Ingrid Bergman.

Nichols Captures Panic of 'Catch-22'

CATCH-22, directed by Mike Nichols; screenplay by Buck Henry, based on the novel by Joseph Heller; cinematographer, David Watkin; music supervised by John Hammell; produced by John Calley; released by Paramount Pictures. At the Paramount Theater at Columbus Circle and the Sutton Theater, Third Avenue and 57th Street. Running time; 129 minutes. (The Motion Picture Association of America's Production Code and Rating Administration classifies this film; "R—restricted, persons under 17 require accompanying parent or adult guardian.")

Captain Yossarian	Alan Arkin
Colonel Cathcart	Martin Balsam
Major Danby	Richard Benjamin
Captain Nately	Art Garfunkel
Dr. Daneeka	Jack Gilford
Major Major	Bob Newhart
Chaplain Tappman	Anthony Perkins
Nurse Duckett	Paula Prentiss
Lieutenant Dobbs	Martin Sheen
Milo Minderbinder	Jon Voight
General Dreedle	Orson Welles
Hungry Joe	Seth Allen
Captain Orr	Robert Balaban
Captain McWatt	Peter Bonerz
Aardvark	Chuck Grodin
Lieut. Col. Korn	Buck Henry
Colonel Moodus	Austin Pendleton
Nately's whore	Gina Rovere
Luciana	Olympia Carlisli
Old Man	Marcel Dalio

By VINCENT CANBY

Panic, like some higher forms of grief and joy, is such an exquisite emotion that nature denies its casual recollection to all except psychotics, a few artists and an occasional, pre-existential hero like Yossarian, the mad bombardier of Joseph Heller's World War II novel, "Catch-22."

Once experienced by the normal neurotic, panic is immediately and efficiently removed from reality, twice removed, in fact, transformed into a memory of a memory. But Yossarian is not your normal neurotic. At the United States Air Force base on the tiny Mediterranean island of Pianosa, which Heller describes as a defoliated, shrunken, surreal Corsica, Yossarian lives in a state of perpetual, epic panic. For Yossarian, a willing convert to paranoia, panic is a kind of Nirvana.

He is convinced that everyone wants him dead—the Germans, his fellow officers, Nurse Duckett, bartenders, bricklayers, landlords, tenants, patriots, traitors, lynchers and lackeys. If they don't get him, Yossarian is aware that there are lymph glands, kidneys, nerve sheaths, corpuscles, Ewing's tumors and, possibly, Wisconsin shingles that will.

Because mankind is conspiring in his death, and he wants to survive, Yossarian knows that the whole world is crazy—and he's absolutely right, almost, you might say, dead-on-target.

It's the special achievement of Heller's novel, as well as of Mike Nichols's screen version, that Yossarian's panic emerges as something so important, so reasonable, so moving and so funny. In the peculiar, perfectly ordered universe of Pianosa, where the system of rewards and punishments is perfectly disordered, panic is positive and fruitful, like love.

"Catch-22," which opened yesterday at the new Paramount Theater on Columbus Circle and at the Sutton Theater, is, quite simply, the best American film I've seen this year. It looks and sounds like a big-budget, commercial service comedy, but it comes as close to being an epic human comedy as Hollywood has ever made by employing the comic conventions of exaggeration, fantasy, shock, and the sort of insult and reverse logic that the late Lulu McConnell elevated to a fine, low art form on radio's "It Pays to Be Ignorant."

I do have some reservations about the film, the most prominent being that I'm not sure that anyone who has not read the novel will make complete sense out of the movie's narrative line that Nichols and his screenwriter, Buck Henry, have shaped in the form of flashbacks within an extended flashback. Missing, too, are some relevant characters (ex-Pfc. Wintergreen, the dispassionate, God-surrogate who actually rules Pianosa) and relevant sequences, as when Chaplain Tappman learns to lie and thus makes his accommodation with the system).

Great movies are complete in themselves. "Catch-22" isn't, but enough of the original remains so that the film becomes a series of brilliant mirror images of a Strobelit reality.

Nichols and Henry, whose senses of humor coincide with Heller's fondness for things like the manic repetition of words and phrases, have rearranged the novel without intruding on it. Most of the film is framed by Yossarian's delirium (after he has been stabbed by what appears to be a German P.O.W.) and is played in the form of funny and sad blackout sketches.

These involve, to name just a few, Colonel Cathcart (Martin Balsam), whose dearest desire is to be featured in The Saturday Evening Post; Captain Nately (Art Garfunkle), the rich Boston boy who is fated to love a mean Roman whore; Major (Bob Newhart), the timid squadron commander; General Dreedle (Orson Welles), who likes to say "Take him out and shoot him" when people behave stupidly; Captain Orr (Robert Balaban), who practices crashing in preparation for an escape to Sweden; Milo Minderbinder (Jon Voight), the squadron's mess officer, a sort of one-man, free-enterprise convulsion, and glum old Doc Daneeka (Jack Gilford).

Each one is marvelous, but it is Alan Arkin as Yossarian who provides the film with its continuity and dominant style. Alkin is not a comedian; he is a deadly serious actor, but because he projects intelligence with such monomanical intensity, he is both funny and heroic at the same time.

The film is Nichols's third ("Who's Afraid of Virginia Woolf?", "The Graduate") so it may be safe to say now that he's something more than lucky. "Catch-22" is a giant physical production, even by Hollywood's swollen standards, but the complexities of the physical production never neutralize the personal comedy, even when Nichols has a bomber crash in flames as the background to a bit of close-up dialogue.

"Catch-22" is so good that I hope it won't be confused with what is all too loosely referred to as black comedy, which usually means comedy bought cheaply at the expense of certain human values, so that, for example, murder is funny and assassination is hilarious. "Catch-22," like Yossarian, is almost beside itself with panic because it grieves for the human condition.

Father and Son

THE CHAMP, based on a story by Frances Marion; directed by King Vidor; produced by Metro-Goldwyn-Mayer. At the Astor Theatre.

Champ.....................Wallace Beery
Dink.......................Jackie Cooper
Linda........................Irene Rich
Sponge.......................Rosco Ates
Tim.......................Edward Brophy
Tony.......................Hale Hamilton
Jonah......................Jesse Scott
Mary Lou................Marcia Mae Jones

By MORDAUNT HALL.

Without much to lean on in the way of a story, the ponderous Wallace Beery and the diminutive Jackie Cooper, under King Vidor's expert direction, last night succeeded in stirring the emotions of an audience in the Astor in a film called "The Champ." This picture is a further example of clever acting saving the day, for there is little in this narrative of horse racing and pugilistic bouts that possesses much akin to originality, except possibly the loyalty of a boy to his father, an ex-prize-fighting champion, who is addicted to drinking and gambling.

Mr. Vidor, whose last production was "Street Scene," has tackled this venture in a restrained fashion, always permitting the performances of Master Cooper and Mr. Beery to hold up a sequence that might have been banal and trite without them. Sympathy is elicited for Dink (Jackie Cooper), when his father goes astray, and whatever one may think of the horse, known as Little Champ, the fact that this animal falls and loses the race is at least a little different from the average race track yarn.

One moment Champ, played by Mr. Beery, is winning at gambling and a little later he has not only lost all his cash but also the ownership to Little Champ. This causes one to become rather impatient with the Champ, particularly when after promising Dink not to drink any more, he steers straight for a saloon. Dink always forgives his father, no matter what happens and the Champ eventually wins a fight, but he taxes his heart to such an extent that he goes the way of all flesh.

In the course of this adventure Dink discovers that Linda, played by Irene Rich, is his mother. She has divorced the Champ—a fact that is not surprising—and has married again. Her husband, Tony, acted by Hale Hamilton, is only too willing to have Dink come and live with Linda and himself, but, after trying this out, the boy becomes tired of the respectable existence and forthwith leaves to find his father, who is released from jail through Tony's influence.

There are several sequences with Dink and the Champ that are not without effect. One sees them going to sleep at night, with the father wrapping all the covers around him. In the morning, however, Dink has stolen the sheet and blankets from his father. All this sort of thing aroused laughter, but one nevertheless wondered why Mr. Vidor had undertaken the direction of this picture and also why this type of screen chronicle had been selected to succeed that grand production, "The Guardsman."

In the last reel there is the prize fight between the Champ and a belligerent and nimble Mexican. This is quite well staged, with all the inevitable counts and the Champ being saved by the bell. He is determined not to go down in defeat at the hands of the Mexican and therefore with one last effort he succeeds in delivering the blow that knocks his opponent unconscious. Instead of the usual sweetheart watching at the ring side, there is little Dink, whose bright eyes urge on his father, until he is afraid that the Mexican is one too many for him. Then the boy wants to throw in the towel, for which the Champ rebukes him good-naturedly immediately after the encounter.

Frances Marion, the author of this story, has written one of those tried and trusted affairs that were all very well in the days of old silent pictures, but something more novel and subtle is needed now.

Wallace Beery and Jackie Cooper in *The Champ*.

READ WHAT THE REVIEWERS SAY ABOUT IT TODAY!

The CHAMP

New York Cheers Them!
Wallace BEERY
Jackie COOPER

King Vidor's Superb Direction!
Metro-Goldwyn-Mayer's
Greatest Talkie of 1931

FIRST MATINEE TODAY 2:40—TONIGHT 8:40

ASTOR

BROADWAY & 45th ST. Twice Daily, 2:40—8:40. Three Times Sundays and Holidays, 3—6—8:50. Mats. (exc. Sat.) 50c to $1.00. Eves. 50c to $2.00. All Seats Reserved.

Orson Wells as Charles Foster Kane, gubenatorial candidate, in *Citizen Kane.*

Orson Welles's Controversial 'Citizen Kane' Proves a Sensational Film at Palace

CITIZEN KANE; original screen play by Orson Welles and Herman J. Mankiewicz; produced and directed by Orson Welles; photography by Gregg Toland; music composed and conducted by Bernard Herrmann; released through RKO-Radio. At the Palace.

Charles Foster Kane	Orson Welles
Kane, aged 8	Buddy Swan
Kane 3d	Sonny Bupp
Kane's Father	Harry Shannon
Jedediah Leland	Joseph Cotten
Susan Alexander	Dorothy Comingore
Mr. Bernstein	Everett Sloane
James W. Gettys	Ray Collins
Walter Parks Thatcher	George Coulouris
Kane's Mother	Agnes Moorehead
Raymond	Paul Stewart
Emily Norton	Ruth Warrick
Herbert Carter	Erskine Sanford
Thompson	William Alland
Miss Anderson	Georgia Backus
Mr. Rawlston	Philip Van Zandt
Headwaiter	Gus Schilling
Signor Matiste	Fortunio Bonanova

By BOSLEY CROWTHER

Within the withering spotlight as no other film has ever been before, Orson Welles's "Citizen Kane" had its world première at the Palace last evening. And now that the wraps are off, the mystery has been exposed and Mr. Welles and the RKO directors have taken the much-debated leap, it can be safely stated that suppression of this film would have been a crime. For, in spite of some disconcerting lapses and strange ambiguities in the creation of the principal character, "Citizen Kane" is far and away the most surprising and cinematically exciting motion picture to be seen here in many a moon. As a matter of fact, it comes close to being the most sensational film ever made in Hollywood.

Count on Mr. Welles; he doesn't do things by halves. Being a mercurial fellow, with a frightening theatrical flair, he moved right into the movies, grabbed the medium by the ears and began to toss it around with the dexterity of a seasoned veteran. Fact is, he handled it with more verve and inspired ingenuity than any of the elder craftsmen have exhibited in years. With the able assistance of Gregg Toland, whose services should not be overlooked, he found in the camera the perfect instrument to encompass his dramatic energies and absorb his prolific ideas. Upon the screen he discovered an area large enough for his expansive whims to have free play. And the consequence is that he has made a picture of tremendous and overpowering scope, not in physical extent so much as in its rapid and graphic rotation of thoughts. Mr. Welles has put upon the screen a motion picture that really moves.

As for the story which he tells—and which has provoked such an uncommon fuss—this corner frankly holds considerable reservation. Naturally we wouldn't know how closely—if at all—it parallels the life of an eminent publisher, as has been somewhat cryptically alleged. But that is beside the point in a rigidly critical appraisal. The blamable circumstance is that it fails to provide a clear picture of the character and motives behind the man about whom the whole thing revolves.

As the picture opens, Charles Kane lies dying in the fabulous castle he has built—the castle called Xanadu, in which he has surrounded himself with vast treasures. And as death closes his eyes his heavy lips murmur one word, "Rosebud." Suddenly the death scene is broken; the screen becomes alive with a staccato March-of-Time-like news feature recounting the career of the dead man—how, as a poor boy, he came into great wealth, how he became a newspaper publisher as a young man, how he aspired to political office, was defeated because of a personal scandal, devoted himself to material acquisition and finally died.

But the editor of the news feature is not satisfied; he wants to know the secret of Kane's strange nature and especially what he meant by "Rosebud." So a reporter is dispatched to find out, and the remainder of the picture is devoted to an absorbing visualization of Kane's phenomenal career as told by his boyhood guardian, two of his closest newspaper associates and his mistress. Each is agreed on one thing—that Kane was a titanic egomaniac. It is also clearly revealed that the man was in some way consumed by his own terrifying selfishness. But just exactly what it is that eats upon him, why it is there and, for that matter, whether Kane is really a villain, a social parasite, is never clearly revealed. And the final, poignant identification of "Rosebud" sheds little more than a vague, sentimental light upon his character. At the end Kubla Kane is still an enigma—a very confusing one.

But check that off to the absorption of Mr. Welles in more visible details. Like the novelist, Thomas Wolfe, his abundance of imagery is so great that it sometimes gets in the way of his logic. And the less critical will probably be content with an undefined Kane, anyhow. After all, nobody understood him. Why should Mr. Welles? Isn't it enough that he presents a theatrical character with consummate theatricality?

We would, indeed, like to say as many nice things as possible about everything else in this film—about the excellent direction of Mr. Welles, about the sure and penetrating performances of literally every member of the cast and about the stunning manner in which the music of Bernard Herrmann has been used. Space, unfortunately, is short. All we can say, in conclusion, is that you shouldn't miss this film. It is cynical, ironic, sometimes oppressive and as realistic as a slap. But it has more vitality than fifteen other films we could name. And, although it may not give a thoroughly clear answer, at least it brings to mind one deeply moral thought: For what shall it profit a man if he shall gain the whole world and lose his own soul? See "Citizen Kane" for further details.

Orson Wells with Dorothy Comingore as Susan Alexander, Kane's mistress.

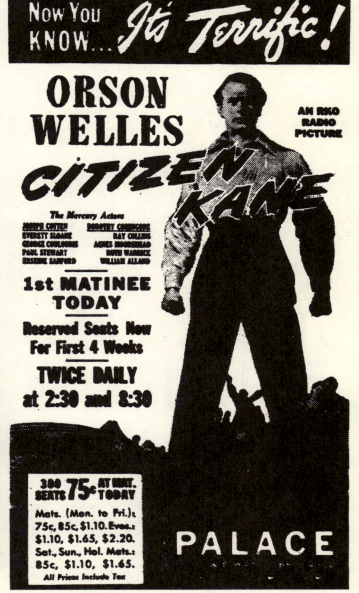

Now You Know... *It's Terrific!*

ORSON WELLES

AN RKO RADIO PICTURE

CITIZEN KANE

The Mercury Actors

JOSEPH COTTEN	DOROTHY COMINGORE
EVERETT SLOANE	RAY COLLINS
GEORGE COULOURIS	AGNES MOOREHEAD
PAUL STEWART	RUTH WARRICK
ERSKINE SANFORD	WILLIAM ALLAND

1st MATINEE TODAY

Reserved Seats Now For First 4 Weeks

TWICE DAILY at 2:30 and 8:30

300 SEATS 75c AT MAT. TODAY

Mats. (Mon. to Fri.): 75c, 85c, $1.10. Eves.: $1.10, $1.65, $2.20. Sat., Sun., Hol. Mats.: 85c, $1.10, $1.65. All Prices Include Tax

PALACE

CHAPLIN HILARIOUS IN HIS 'CITY LIGHTS'

Tramp's Antics in Non-Dialogue Film Bring Roars of Laughter at Cohan Theatre.

TAKES FLING AT "TALKIES"

Pathos Is Mingled With Mirth in a Production of Admirable Artistry.

By MORDAUNT HALL.

CITY LIGHTS, with Charlie Chaplin, Virginia Cherrill, Florence Lee, Harry Myers, Allar Garcia, Hank Mann and others, written and directed by Mr. Chaplin. At the George M. Cohan Theatre.

Charlie Chaplin, master of screen mirth and pathos, presented at the George M. Cohan last night before a brilliant gathering his long-awaited non-dialogue picture, "City Lights," and proved so far as he is concerned the eloquence of silence. Many of the spectators either rocking in their seats with mirth, mumbling as their sides ached, "Oh, dear, oh, dear," or they were stilled with sighs and furtive tears. And during a closing episode, when the Little Tramp sees through the window of a flower shop the girl who has recovered her sight through his persistence, one woman could not restrain a cry.

Mr. Chaplin arrived in the theatre with a police guard, and after greeting some of his many friends in the house he took an aisle seat beside Miss Constance Collier. When the picture came to an end he went to the stage and thanked those present for the enthusiasm with which they had received his work.

It is a film worked out with admirable artistry, and while Chaplin stoops to conquer, as he has invariably done, he achieves success. Although the Little Tramp in this "City Lights" in some sequences is more respectable than usual, owing to circumstances in the story, he begins and ends with the same old clothes, looking, in fact, a trifle more bedraggled in the last scene than in most others of his comedies. He has the same antics, the same flip of the heel, the same little cane, mustache, derby hat and baggy trousers.

Here one comes to the conclusion that Chaplin is in many respects the O. Henry of the screen, for he has twists to his sequences that are just as unexpected as those of the famous short story writer.

This tale happens in any city. It seems to be a mixture of Philadelphia, London, New York and Hollywood. And in the beginning the comedian takes a fling at the talking pictures, revealing by incoherent sounds that one can understand what is meant and also that these sounds are quite unnecessary. He wastes no time in getting down to comedy, for right at the outset is the episode wherein the Little Tramp is discovered in the arms of a central figure of a group of statuary that has just been unveiled.

Not long after that he meets the flower girl and with gentle suggestion it is conveyed to the spectator that she is sightless. This girl is impersonated by Virginia Cherrill, who by accident one night before the comedian had cast his picture sat next to him at a pugilistic encounter in Hollywood. Under Chaplin's unfailing guidance, Miss Cherrill gives a charmingly impressive performance.

Then there is the meeting of the Little Tramp and the Eccentric Millionaire, played by Harry Myers, who did so well in the old picture of Mark Twain's "Connecticut Yankee at the Court of King Arthur."

(continued)

The "Little Tramp" in *City Lights*.

BEGINNING TODAY
CONTINUOUS
DAILY FROM 9 A.M.
POPULAR PRICES
50 C and $1.00

CHARLIE CHAPLIN
in
"CITY LIGHTS"
A Comedy Romance in Pantomime

MIDNIGHT PERFORMANCE EVERY NIGHT BUT SUNDAY

GEO. M. COHAN THEATRE
Broadway • Between 42nd and 43rd Sts.

This Millionaire loves the Little Tramp as a brother when he is in his cups, but when he is sober he does not recognize him, which naturally makes it most awkward at times for the Tramp, whose one aim in life is to get enough money together to pay a specialist to perform an operation on the blind girl's eyes.

The first meeting between the Millionaire and the Tramp is when the Millionaire goes to a river embankment, bent on suicide, with a stone and a noosed rope in a suit case. The Tramp endeavors to persuade the Millionaire to abandon the idea of taking his life and the chapter of accidents ends in the Little Tramp being hurled into the water with the noose around his neck and the Millionaire having to officiate as the rescuer.

Perhaps the stretch that caused most merriment is where the Little Tramp finds himself in the prize ring facing a real pugilist. He darts about, always keeping, so far as is possible, behind the referee, and during some of the scenes the Tramp separates the referee and his antagonist. In any ordinary comedy the Tramp would have won the contest, but Chaplin wills otherwise.

The Millionaire gives the Tramp his expensive car. Thus the little fellow discovers himself thrown out of the house by the sober Millionaire, but he has a glistening car. Without a penny in his pocket and eager for a smoke he drives the automobile slowly along the curb and observes a man throw away a half-smoked cigar. Quick as a flash the Tramp leaps out of the car and, as he does so another tatterdemalion stoops to pick up the cigar. The Little Tramp, however, pushes the other man aside, looks at him as much as to say, "I saw it first," then he picks up the butt and enters his lovely runabout.

After the Millionaire has taken back his automobile, the Tramp, in his efforts to get money for the blind girl, has his worries as a street cleaner. Then he has the great satisfaction of again falling into the arms of the Millionaire, happily intoxicated. The Tramp unfolds the pathetic story of the blind girl and the Millionaire in a most generous mood peels off more than a thousand dollars in bills. Burglars are in the house and in the course of the excitement the Millionaire sobers up, with the consequence that the Little Tramp has to scoot away. He succeeds in giving the flower girl the money, but

cannot evade spending a few months in prison.

At the film's end is a beautifully poetic bit, with the little fellow peering in at the window of a flower shop and recognizing the hitherto blind girl who has recovered her sight and does not, of course, know him. She laughs at him, and through another masculine figure, well dressed, one realizes that she imagines that her hero must look like this individual. A touch of the hand, however, reveals that the humble, little chap with the torn trousers and odd mustache, is her benefactor.

The synchronized music score helps the movement of this comedy. It was composed by Chaplin and arranged by Arthur Johnston. There are times when the notes serve almost for words and so far as sound effects go, Chaplin won gales of laughter last night when the Tramp swallows a whistle and every time he breathes he whistles. This sound interlude was made the most of, for the whistle calls cabs and dogs and angers a host of people.

It was a joyous evening. Mr. Chaplin's shadow has grown no less.

The Tramp and the Millionaire, Harry Myers.

The Tramp and his flower girl, Virginia Cherrill.

THEDA BARA AS CLEOPATRA.

With Much Rolling of Eyes She Portrays "the Siren of All Ages."

Cleopatra of Egypt was among the earliest of the vampires of history, if not the earliest, and it was therefore but a matter of time until the siren Theda Bara should duly attend to the transfer of that temptress to the movie screen. The result is "Cleopatra," an uncommonly fine picture which was unreeled for the first time at the Lyric Theatre last night before as audience which included the dazzling Miss Bara herself. The star, by dint of much rolling of eyes and many other manoeuvres, contributes a thoroughly successful portrait of "the serpent of the Nile, the siren of the ages, and the eternal feminine," in the words of the screen, and thus does the ill-starred Queen of Egypt become the well-starred queen of movies.

The story of Cleopatra's many loves needs but the slightest elaboration to make it the finest sort of film fare, and movie fans are certain to flock to it. From a scenic standpoint, also, it is quite a triumph for the director. The Sphinx, the pyramids and a goodly section of Rome are duly duplicated, and the larger scenes are handled in a way that suggests D. W. Griffith. The naval battle at Actium is made most impressive, and the handling of the chariots also furnishes many a thrilling moment.

Miss Bara, to quote the program, "wears fifty distinctively different costumes," many of which are so thoroughly in attune with the period that they are likely to cause not a little comment. In addition to the star, the film enlists the services of Fritz Leiber as Caesar, Thurston Hall as Antony, and Henri de Vries, the Dutch actor, as Octavius. The picture was photographed in California during last Summer.

At the Strand Theatre Billie Burke was seen for the first time yesterday afternoon in "Arms and the Girl," and "The Co-respondent," with Elaine Hammerstein in the leading rôle, began an engagement at the Broadway. Charles Ray, in "The Son of His Father," is the new attraction at the Rialto, and Alice Brady, in "A Maid of Belgium," opened at the Park on Saturday.

William Fox Presents THEDA BARA in
CLEOPATRA

OPINIONS OF OTHER JUDGES ON CLEOPATRA.

¶ "Living every day of her life in the passion of love, hate, jealousy and ambition, wielding her dominion over men or dying in the attempt", says Mahaffy, celebrated English student of the ancient world.

¶ "One of the tragic figures of history," says the great Italian historian Ferrero.

¶ "Her grace and finished manners concealed a ruthless ferocity," says Josephus, scholar of antiquity.

¶ "Of surpassing beauty, brilliant to look upon and to listen to, ambitous for renown and most scornfully bold," says Dio, Roman source of modern savants.

¶ "Cleopatra is among the ten great women of all time," say the historians.

¶ "The beautiful and clever Cleopatra," Mommsen, great researcher, calls her.

WHAT WILL BE YOUR VERDICT after you see THEDA BARA'S portrayal of the passions and pageants of Egypt's vampire queen? ? ? ? ?

Produced at an approximate cost of $500,-000 and with a cast of about thirty thousand men and women, this photodrama resurrects the life and love of Cleopatra, Antony and Caesar and in striking fidelity to antiquity shows how one woman changed the destinies of the world.

LYRIC Theatre
42nd St., W. of Broadway
Mat. 2:30. Eve. 8:30   All Seats Reserved 25c—$1.00

Theda Bara as *Cleopatra*, 1917.

'Cleopatra' Has Premiere at Rivoli

4-Hour Epic Is Tribute to Its Artists' Skills

By BOSLEY CROWTHER

FORGET the fantastic sum that "Cleopatra" is reported to have cost. Forget the length of time it took to make it and all the tattle of troubles they had, including the behavior of two of its spot-lighted stars. The memorable thing about this picture, which opened last night at the Rivoli, is that it is a surpassing entertainment, one of the great epic films of our day.

This may come as surprising information to those who have blindly assumed that any film of such mammoth proportions (it runs a few minutes more than four hours, excluding the intermission) and which has gone through so much storm and strife could not possibly be a cohesive, intelligent piece of work. But the slip-up in this assumption was that it didn't make due allowance for the tremendous potential of the story and the proven skill of the artists who did the job.

After all, what we know from history of the ancient Egyptian queen, who cast her spell over the two great Roman generals Julius Caesar and Mark Antony and, by her relations with them, affected the destiny of the world, is fraught with imperishable romance, adventure and tragedy. It is history of mighty dimensions, human drama on a grand and noble scale, which has fired the imaginations of poets and playwrights from Shakespeare to Shaw.

Why, then, shouldn't this tremendous story be envisioned supremely on the screen, which has the facilities for showing the true magnitude of great events, as well as the close, emotional contacts of strong personalities? There is no reason why it shouldn't. And the bright news this morning is that, thanks to the aptness of the medium, to fine photography in color and Todd-AO, and to the skill of many fine artists, it has been envisoned handsomely.

In this exciting achievement, Joseph L. Mankiewicz, as the screen playwright and director, has played the most influential role. For it is his fabrication of characters of colorfulness and depth, who stand forth as thinking, throbbing people against a background of splendid spectacle, that gives vitality to this picture and is the key to its success.

These are not obvious actors in geegaw costumes who march around in a fake world staked out by Cecil B. DeMille. (You may remember he did a "Cleopatra" —a lulu—back in 1934.) These are plausible people, maturely conceived and turned loose in a realm of political intrigues, conflicts and thrusts for personal power. They are moved by considerable forces, emboldened by well-defined desires, and they speak literate words that crackle with sophisticated imagery and wit.

Elizabeth Taylor's Cleopatra is a woman of force and dignity, fired by a fierce ambition to conquer and rule the world—at least, the world of the Mediterranean basin—through the union of Egypt and Rome. In her is impressively compacted the arrogance and pride of an ancient queen.

But she is not an ancient queen, mind you, in the quality of her thought—nor, indeed, in the modified high style of her exceedingly low-cut gowns. Mr. Mankiewicz has wisely not attempted to present us with historical copies. He and the writers who have helped him have drawn their major dramatic episodes from Plutarch, Suetonius and others. But the minds of their characters work along lines more in accord with contemporary thought, just as do those of the characters in the plays of Shakespeare and Shaw.

Thus Miss Taylor's sultry sovereign is a temptress who also can tag Alexander the Great's ambition to rule the world as a "grand design";

The Cast

CLEOPATRA, screenplay by Joseph L. Mankiewicz, Ranald MacDougall and Sidney Buchman. Based upon histories by Plutarch, Suetonius, Appian, other ancient sources and "The Life and Times of Cleopatra," by C. M. Franzero. Directed by Mr. Mankiewicz and produced by Walter Wanger for 20th Century-Fox in Todd-AO. At the Rivoli Theater, Broadway and 49th Street. Running time: 243 minutes.

Cleopatra	Elizabeth Taylor
Mark Antony	Richard Burton
Julius Caesar	Rex Harrison
High Priestess	Pamela Brown
Flavius	George Cole
Sosigenes	Hume Cronyn
Apollodorus	Cesare Danova
Brutus	Kenneth Haigh
Agrippa	Andrew Keir
Rufio	Martin Landau
Octavian	Roddy McDowall
Germanicus	Robert Stephens
Eiras	Francesca Annis
Pothinos	Gregoire Aslan
Ramos	Martin Benson
Theodotos	Herbert Berghof
Phoebus	John Cairney
Lotos	Jacqui Chan
Charmian	Isabelle Cooley
Achillas	John Doucette
Canidius	Andrew Faulds
Cimber	Michael Gwynn
Cicero	Michael Hordern
Cassius	John Hoyt
Euphranor	Marne Maitland
Casca	Carroll O'Connor
Ptolemy	Richard O'Sullivan
Calpurnia	Gwen Watford
Decimus	Douglas Wilmer
Queen at Tarsus	Marina Berti
High Priest	John Karlsen
Caesarion (age 4)	Loris Loddi
Octavia	Jean Marsh
Marcellus	Gin Mart
Mithridates	Furio Meniconi
Caesarion (age 7)	Del Russell
Caesarion (age 12)	Kenneth Nash
Valvus	John Valva

who can urge the visiting Caesar with this ambition in familiar "one-word" terms and who can dare, when the great Roman general is solemnly placing her on her throne, to note sotto voce that his knees are bony or, when they meet later in Rome, throw a wink at him.

She is likewise clever and passionate, able to lure Caesar to her bed with chic and voluptuous seductions and with the promise of a son. Yet she is powerless to avoid a howling tantrum when she is deserted temporarily by Antony. It is her varied dispositions and approaches to these two men - respectful and confident towards Caesar, domineering and adoring towards Antony - that mark the dramatic pattern and bulge the emotional bounds.

Caesar is no fustian tyrant. Played stunningly by Rex Harrison, he is a statesman of manifest wisdom, shrewdness and magnanimity. And he is also a fascinating study in political ambiguities. He is torn by loyalty, ambition and wishes for his son. Mr. Harrison's faceted performance is the best in the film.

But Richard Burton is nonetheless exciting as the arrogant Antony - a man the very opposite of Caesar, whom he would so much like to be. He is the stubborn professional soldier, aspiring to statesmanlike deeds, but lacking the brains, the self-assurance, everything but the raw vitality. The tragedy lies in his incompetence to accomplish Cleopatra's bold design, while being inevitably locked to her - and she to him - by the bonds of love.

TONIGHT AT 8 P.M.
THE WORLD PREMIERE OF THE MOTION PICTURE THE WORLD HAS BEEN WAITING FOR TAKES PLACE AT THE
RIVOLI THEATRE
49TH STREET & BROADWAY

...th Century-Fox presents ELIZABETH TAYLOR in Joseph L. Mankiewicz' "CLEOPATRA" starring ...CHARD BURTON as MARK ANTONY · REX HARRISON as JULIUS CAESAR · Also starring Pamela Brown · George ...le · Hume Cronyn · Cesare Danova · Kenneth Haigh · Roddy McDowall · Produced by Walter Wanger ...ected by Joseph L Mankiewicz · Screenplay by Joseph L Mankiewicz, Ranald MacDougall and ...ney Buchman · Music by Alex North   Color by DeLuxe · In TODD-AO

TWO PERFORMANCES DAILY STARTING TOMORROW

Elizabeth Taylor as *Cleopatra*, Queen of the Nile, enters Imperial Rome in style.

An Out of This World Encounter

By VINCENT CANBY

IN THE 1950'S, the decade in which we fought the Korean War, witnessed the rise and fall of Senator Joseph R. McCarthy and fretted (along with Mort Sahl) about the atomic bomb's falling into the hands of Princess Grace, and Prince Rainier, science-fiction films enjoyed a new, lively popularity largely by feeding on our wildest nightmares. We watched movies in which planets fought wars with each other, worlds threatened to collide and a huge malignant carrot, a vegetable with a higher form of intelligence, landed at the North Pole.

A favorite theme was the invasion of earth by alien creatures who, 9 times out of 10, were up to no good. The unholy immigrants in "The Invasion of the Body Snatchers" attempted to usurp earth by catching the souls of the incumbents in giant peapods, receptacles that suggested the work of an early Jasper Johns.

Sometimes the visitors were motivated by a territorial imperative—they were running out of air back home or there were no more materials for beer cans. Often the creatures were simply making mischief, though occasionally they expressed benign intentions. From Krypton came Superman to play the role of a supercharged savior whose work would never be done.

Klaatu, the impeccably space-suited, English-accented visitor in "The Day the Earth Stood Still," wanted earthlings to stop fooling around and live in peace. The implied threat of Klaatu's "Or else . . ." might have struck some of us as galactic neo-fascism, but that was to read the film deeper than it was meant to go.

Steven Spielberg's giant, spectacular "Close Encounters of the Third Kind," which opened at the Ziegfeld Theater yesterday, is the best—the most elaborate—1950's science fiction movie ever made, a work that borrows its narrative shape and its concerns from those earlier films, but enhances them with what looks like the latest developments in movie and space technology. If, indeed, we are not alone, it would be fun to believe that the creatures who may one day visit us are of the order that Mr Spielberg has conceived—with, I should add, a certain amount of courage and an entirely straight face.

Mr. Spielberg's tongue is not in his cheek, as was George Lucas's when he made "Star Wars," the funniest, farthest-out kid-trip of this decade to date. "Star Wars" is virtually an anthology of all sorts of children's literature. "Close Encounters" is science fiction that means us to say, "this is the way it could be," though we don't for a minute forget that we're watching a movie almost entirely related to other movies—the ones that Mr. Spielberg, who's just 30 years old, grew up with, rather than a movie with its own poetic vision, like Stanley Kubrick's "2001."

As he has demonstrated in "The Sugarland Express" and especially in "Jaws," Mr. Spielberg is at his best as a movie craftsman, someone who seems to know by instinct (and after millions of hours of movie-watching) how best to put together any two pieces of film for maximum effect. He's serious about this—sensation as an end in itself, an interest that defines better than anything else his generation as moviegoers, music lovers and moviemakers.

"Close Encounters" is most stunning when it is dealing in visual and aural sensations that might be described as being in the 70's Disco Style. The unidentified flying objects that both terrorize and enchant the citizens of Muncie, Ind., early in the film, when the night sky is suddenly filled with blinking lights and several brilliantly colored shapes, each of which looks like a Portuguese man-of-war, make up an extraordinary psychedelic light show.

The disco manner is further suggested in the movie's use of sound, an almost nonstop confusion of voices, languages, technical jargon, weather, vehicles and (I sometimes suspect) gibberish, often so noisy that you can't hear yourself think.

Though "Close Encounters" is strictly a product of the 70's in its dress and manners, its heart is in the 50's. This is apparent from the first scene, when a squadron of World War II fighter planes, missing on a training mission more than 30 years earlier, suddenly turn up intact, as good as new, in the Mexican desert. In classic sci-fi manner, Mr. Spielberg's screenplay then cuts from this general introduction to the "mystery" to encounters with the mystery by individual folks in Muncie, homespun types like you and me who draw us into the adventure.

Mr. Spielberg's homespun types are mostly serviceable characters like Roy Neary, a blue-collar worker whose life is changed the night he spots the U.F.O.'s over Muncie. As do many of the others who shared his experience, Roy is obsessed by the memory, though his wife and three children think he is nuts. Another person similarly obsessed is a young mother, played by Melinda Dillon, whose 4-year-old son appears to be in some kind of psychic connection with the U.F.O's.

Following this initial, quite magnificent display of the movie technicians' special-effects wizardry, "Close Encounters" settles down to cross-cutting between scenes of Roy's seemingly lunatic efforts to find the U.F.O.s again, and the efforts being made by an international team of scientists who are preparing themselves for the second coming (of the U.F.O.s.)

The final 30 to 40 minutes of the film, however, are what it's all about—and they are breathtaking: the close encounter of the third kind in which the earthlings and the alien creatures come together on a secret landing field in Wyoming. This sequence, as beautiful as anything I've seen since "2001," has been deliberately designed to suggest a religious experience of the first kind. Whether or not you believe it, this climax involves the imagination in surprising, moving ways. This is a day in which the earth might have stood still.

Shades of 1950's

CLOSE ENCOUNTERS OF THE THIRD KIND, directed and written by Steven Spielberg; produced by Julia Phillips and Michael Phillips; music, John Williams; director of photography, Vilmos Zsigmond; visual effects coordinator, Douglas Trumbull; editor, Mike Kahn; distributed by Columbia Pictures. Running time: 137 minutes. At the Ziegfeld Theater, 54th Street west of the Avenue of the Americas. This film has been rated PG.

Roy Neary	Richard Dreyfuss
Claude Lacombe	Francois Truffaut
Ronnie Neary	Teri Garr
Jillian Guiler	Melinda Dillon
Barry Guiler	Cary Guffey
David Laughlin	Bob Balaban
Robert	Lance Hendriksen
Wild Bill	Warren Kemmerling
Farmer	Roberts Blossom
Jean Claude	Phillip Dodds
Brad Neary	Shawn Bishop
Sylvia Neary	Adrienne Campbell
Toby Neary	Justin Dreyfuss
Team Leader	Merrill Connally
Major Benchley	George Dicenzo

Richard Dreyfuss begins to understand his fantastic obsession in a scene from *Close Encounters of the Third Kind*.

THAT GIRL IN THEIR HOUSE SPELLED TROUBLE!

Hal Wallis'
PRODUCTION OF

Come Back, Little Sheba

FROM THE SENSATIONAL
THEATRE GUILD PLAY

Are you sorry
you had to
marry me, Doc?

STARRING
BURT LANCASTER
...as "DOC"

In an utterly different, utterly realistic
role...as a man driven to violence
by the two women in his house.

Co-starring TERRY MOORE
with RICHARD JAECKEL · Directed by DANIEL MANN
Screenplay by KETTI FRINGS

"If Doc gets her out of running his hand
through my hair...what's the harm?"

SHIRLEY BOOTH
...as "LOLA"

"...Likely to win an Oscar as the
year's best movie actress."
—LIFE Magazine

Based on the original play by William Inge
Produced on the stage by the Theatre Guild

A PARAMOUNT PICTURE

STARTS TODAY   *Victoria*   **DOORS OPEN 9:45 A.M.**
B'WAY & 46th ST.

Shirley Booth, Burt Lancaster Team Up in 'Come Back, Little Sheba,' at the Victoria

COME BACK, LITTLE SHEBA, screen play by Ketti Frings, based on the play by William Inge; directed by Daniel Mann; produced by Hal B. Wallis. A Hal Wallis Production, presented by Paramount Pictures. At the Victoria.

Doc' Delaney	Burt Lancaster
Lola Delaney	Shirley Booth
Marie Buckholder	Terry Moore
Turk Fisher	Richard Jaeckel
Ed Anderson	Philip Ober
Mrs. Coffman	Liza Golm
Bruce	Walter Kelley

By BOSLEY CROWTHER

Thanks to Producer Hal Wallis and Director Daniel Mann, who had the good sense not to tamper too much with the original play of William Inge, the screen version of "Come Back, Little Sheba," which opened at the Victoria last night, makes as poignant and haunting a drama as was brought forth upon the stage. For this we may also be grateful to Burt Lancaster and Shirley Booth, who contribute two sterling performances in the picture's leading roles.

Kept pretty much within the four walls of the commonplace, middle-class home of the middle-aged, childless couple of whose wistful lives the drama treats, the film nonetheless succeeds in seeming to move a great deal and say a lot about the small and pathetic human frailty with which it is concerned.

Actually, the crux of the drama is nothing more than a crisis that occurs in the drab and monotonous relations of this uninspired husband and wife. Stirred into passion and rebellion by the proximity of amorous youth, represented by a young lady boarder and her callow, college-boy beau, the husband kicks over the traces of rigid temperance he has patiently held, abuses his wife for being a slattern and takes a knife to her. Then, after this violent outburst, he docilely returns to his home, and the wife, badly shaken by the call-down, appears to make an effort to improve.

That is the substance of the drama, but around it there graphically turns a vastly suggestive panorama of two pathetically cramped and wasted lives. There is the wife, a dull and bulky shadow of a Nineteen Twenties vamp, and the husband, a washed-out relic of a hopeful medical student gone to pot. And it is in the subdued illumination of these two characters through the amiable progress of the picture that its theatrical validity lies.

Enough cannot be said for the excellence of the performance Miss Booth gives in this, her first screen appearance—which, in itself, is something of a surprise. Her skillful and knowing creation of a depressingly common type—the immature, mawkish, lazy housewife —is visualization at its best. And the excellence of Mr. Lancaster as the frustrated, inarticulate spouse, weak-willed and sweetly passive, should not be overlooked. As on the stage, it is the tandem of these two performances that makes the show.

As the pretty and hot-blooded boarder, Terry Moore strikes precisely the right note of timeless and endless animalism and Richard Jaeckel is good as the boy who carnally pursues her. Philip Ober also does a first-rate job as a pillar of Alcoholics Anonymous who is the steady and reliable friend in need. One of the few excursions of the camera away from the home to look in on an A. A. meeting is one of the nicer bits of Americana in the film.

"Come Back, Little Sheba" may not go down in the books as a great American movie, but it is one of which all may be proud.

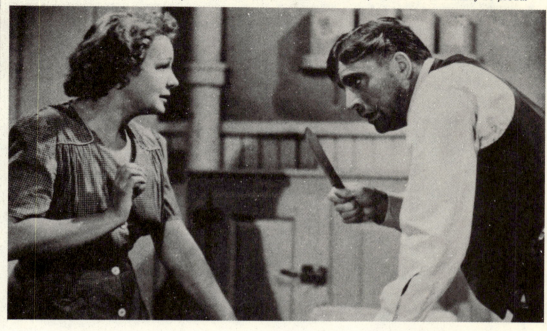

Shirley Booth and Burt Lancaster as the mismatched couple in *Come Back Little Sheba*.

'David and Lisa'

Odd Romance Involves Mentally Ill Children

By BOSLEY CROWTHER
Special to The New York Times.

NEW YORK.

An odd little boy-meets-girl romance is rather crudely but courageously played in the picture called "David and Lisa," now at the Plaza Theater. It is the strange tenderness that develops between a psychoneurotic youth and a schizoid girl who are thrown together as lonely patients in a private psychiatric school.

The nature of mental illness is always hard to define one the screen, as witness the current film, "Freud." And this problem of definition is one of the stumbling blocks in this film.

All it is able to tell us about the lad, played by hand-

The Cast

"DAVID AND LISA," screen play by Eleanor Perry, based on a fictionalized case history by Dr. Theodore Isaac Rubin; directed by Frank Perry and produced by Paul M. Heller. A Continental Distributing Release. At the Plaza Theater, East 58th Street. Running time: 94 minutes.

David	Keir Dullea
Lisa	Janet Margolin
Dr. Swinford	Howard Da Silva
Mrs. Clemens	Neva Patterson
John	Clifton James
Mr. Clemens	Richard McMurray
Maureen	Nancy Nutter
Simon	Mathew Anden
Carlos	Jaime Sanchez

some Keir Dullea, is that he is extremely, resistant to forming friendships and has a phobia about being touched. He hates his mother, distrusts his father, is antagonistic toward the head of the school, and repulses the other patients—except this girl.

She, a plainly demented little creature who talks crazily in rhymes, is treated by him with mild compassion and then with deep concern. Unwittingly they help each other by having someone for whom to care. Whatever it is that is her trouble, it is presumably modified by him.

As we say, the psychiatric definitions are vague and elusive in this film, and, therefore, the whole situation of conflict must be taken on verbal trust. But the visual aspects of mental patients are strongly presented by Mr. Dullea and by dark-haired Janet Margolin, who plays the schizoid girl. Their growing curiosity and attachment in the midst of a cheerless institute is specifically and touchingly presented by them—and that's the sum and substance of the film.

Howard Da Silva does a good, straight job of shaping the basic outlines of the head of the school, and Neva Patterson is hard and two-dimensional as the mother of the boy. Richard McMurray as the father and Matthew Anden as another patient in the notably permissive institution catch glints of characters in their brief roles.

"David and Lisa" was produced by Paul M. Heller and directed by Frank Perry, who has done a simple, commendable, sympathetic semi-documentary.

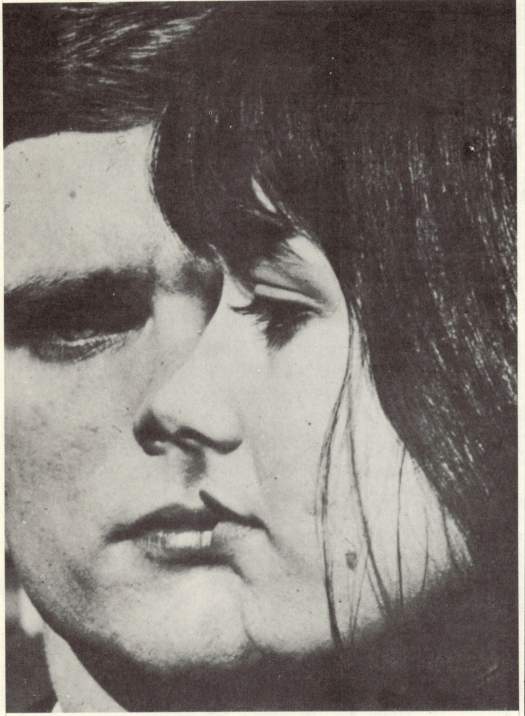

Keir Dullea and Janet Margolin in an unusual film about the mentally ill, *David and Lisa.*

NOMINATED FOR 2 ACADEMY AWARDS!

DAVID & LISA

AN UNUSUAL LOVE STORY!

A Continental Distributing Corp. Release - Affiliate of the Walter Reade Sterling Group

PLAZA
58th St. E of Madison · EL 5-3320

Feature at: 12 40, 2 30, 4 25, 6 15, 8 05, 10 00

Blue-Collar Epic

THE DEER HUNTER, directed by Michael Cimino; screenplay by Deric Washburn; story by Michael Cimino, Deric Washburn, Louis Garfinkle, and Quinn K. Redeker; director of photography, Vilmos Zsigmond; production consultant, Joann Carelli; art directors, Ron Hobs and Kim Swados; editor, Peter Zinner; music by Stanley Myers; produced by Barry Spikings, Michael Deeley, Michael Cimino, and John Peverall; released by Universal Studios. At the Coronet Theater, 59th Street and Third Avenue. Running time: 183 minutes. This film is rated R.

Michael	Robert DeNiro
Stan	John Cazale
Steven	John Savage
Nick	Christopher Walken
Linda	Meryl Streep
John	George Dzundza
Axel	Chuck Aspegren

By VINCENT CANBY

MICHAEL CIMINO's "The Deer Hunter" is a big, awkward, crazily ambitious, sometimes breathtaking motion picture that comes as close to being a popular epic as any movie about this country since "The Godfather." Though he has written a number of screenplays, Mr. Cimino has only directed one other movie (the 1974 box-office hit, "Thunderbolt and Lightfoot"), which makes his present achievement even more impressive. Maybe he just didn't know enough to stop. Instead, he's tried to create a film that is nothing less than an appraisal of American life in the second half of the 20th century.

I don't mean to make "The Deer Hunter" sound like "War and Peace" or even "Gone With the Wind." Its view is limited and its narrative at times sketchy. It's about three young men who have been raised together in a Pennsylvania steel town, work together in its mill, drink, bowl and raise hell together, and then, for no better reason than that the war is there, they go off to fight in Vietnam.

"The Deer Hunter," which opens today at the Coronet, is an update on the national dream, long after World War I!, when America's self-confidence peaked, after the Marshall Plan, after Korea, dealing with people who've grown up in the television age and matured in the decade of assassinations and disbelief.

●

The three friends, all of Russian extraction, are Mike (Robert DeNiro), Nick (Christopher Walken) and Steve (John Savage). Mike is the one who calls the tune for his friends. To the extent that any one of them has an interior life, it is Mike, a man who makes a big thing about hunting, about bringing down a deer with one shot. More than one shot apparently isn't fair. As codes go this one is not great, but it is his own.

Nick goes along with Mike, sometimes suspecting that Mike is eccentric, but respecting his eccentricities. Steve is the conventional one, whose marriage (a Russian Orthodox ceremony, followed by a huge, hysterical reception) occupies most of the film's first hour and sets out in rich detail what I take to be one of the movie's principal concerns — what happens to

Americans when their rituals have become only quaint reminders of the past rather than life-ordering rules of the present.

Mr. Cimino has described his treatment of the three friends' war experiences as surreal, which is another way of saying that a lot of recent history is elipsized or shaped to fit the needs of the film. What is not surreal is the brutality of the war and its brutalizing effects, scenes that haunt "The Deer Hunter" and give point to the film even as it slips into the wildest sort of melodrama, which Mr. Cimino plays out against the background of the collapse of Saigon and the American withdrawal from Southeast Asia. It's Armageddon with helicopters.

Most particular and most savage is the film's use of Russian roulette as a metaphor for war's waste. It's introduced when the three friends, prisoners of war of the North Vietnamese, are forced by their captors to play Russian roulette with one another. The game crops up again in Saigon where, according to this film, it was played in back-street arenas rather like cockfighting pits, for high-dollar stakes. These sequences are as explicitly bloody as anything you're likely to see in a commercial film. They are so rough, in fact, that they raise the question of whether such vivid portrayals don't become dehumanizing themselves.

More terrifying than the violence — certainly more provocative and moving — is the way each of the soldiers reacts to his war experiences. Not once does anyone question the war or his participation in it. This passivity may be the real horror at the center of American life, and more significant than any number of hope-filled tales about raised political consciousnesses. What are these veterans left with? Feelings of contained befuddlement, a desire to make do and, perhaps, a more profound appreciation for love, friendship and community. The big answers elude them, as do the big questions.

●

Deric Washburn's screenplay, which takes its time in the way of a big novel, provides fine roles for Mr. DeNiro, Mr. Walken and Mr. Savage, each of whom does some of his best work to date. Meryl Streep, who has long been recognized for her fine performances on the New York stage, gives a smashing film performance as the young woman, who, by tacit agreement among the friends, becomes Nick's girl but who stays around long enough to assert herself. In the splendid supporting cast are George Dzundza, Chuck Aspegren, Shirley Stoler and Rutanya Alda. The late John Cazale makes his last film appearance a memorable one as the kind of barroom neurotic who might at any moment go seriously off his rocker.

"De Niro's acting is perhaps his purest yet, you sense a power in him. 'The Deer Hunter' places director Michael Cimino right at the center of film culture. The film dares to say that things have come down to life versus death, and it's time someone said this big and strong without fear."
— NEWSWEEK, Jack Kroll

"So real, you can feel it in your bones. DeNiro has accomplished an amazing characterization and the others make you see a world you've never known. Director Cimino has made a picture that resounds and echoes with a true American voice."
— N.Y. POST, Archer Winsten

"Directed by Michael Cimino, written by Deric Washburn, 'The Deer Hunter' has qualities that we almost never see any more — range and power and breadth of experience. What really counts is authenticity, which this movie has by the ton...An epic."
— NEW YORK, David Denby

"A big awkward, crazily ambitious motion picture that comes as close to being a popular epic as any movie about this country since 'The Godfather.' Its vision is that of an original, major new filmmaker."
— N.Y. TIMES, Vincent Canby

"'THE DEER HUNTER' IS A MONUMENTAL ACHIEVEMENT IN AN ENSEMBLE OF TRIUMPHANT PERFORMANCES. IT IS REMARKABLE FOR ITS SENSITIVITY AND IS ALMOST ELEMENTAL IN ITS FORCE. IT IS A FILM THAT I WILL NOT FORGET."
—WNBC-TV, Gene Shalit

"Christopher Walken gives a devastating performance — one deserving of an Oscar nod."
— ABC-TV, Rona Barrett

"Robert De Niro reclaims his title as our finest young dramatic male star."
— LIFE MAGAZINE

"★★★★! An emotionally stirring movie that demonstrates real originality. Cimino emerges as one of the most exciting directing talents of the decade."
— N.Y. DAILY NEWS, Kathleen Carroll

"An extraordinary new film — a shattering experience. 'The Deer Hunter' has affected me more profoundly than any film I have seen in years. From start to finish this three-hour film is made with consummate skill. Cimino joins his contemporaries Coppola and Scorcese as a major force in American filmmaking. Robert De Niro is superb. The most suspenseful, terrifying sequence of men at war ever commited to celluloid. The images are worthy of Goya. Even now Cimino may not realize that he has made the greatest anti-war movie since 'Grand Illusion.' It's thrilling to see ensemble playing of this quality in an American film. John Savage gives an electrifying performance. He captures naked, animal fear with more shocking intensity than I have ever seen on the screen."
— NEW WEST, Stephen Farber

"I hope that this blockbuster of a film wins the Academy Award for Best Picture of 1978. It fully deserves it."
— AFTER DARK, Norma McLain Stoop

ROBERT DE NIRO
A MICHAEL CIMINO FILM

THE DEER HUNTER

UNIVERSAL PICTURES and EMI FILMS present "THE DEER HUNTER"
Co-starring JOHN CAZALE · JOHN SAVAGE · MERYL STREEP · CHRISTOPHER WALKEN · Screenplay by DERIC WASHBURN · Story by MICHAEL CIMINO & DERIC WASHBURN and LOUIS GARFINKLE & QUINN K. REDEKER · Production Consultant JOANN CARELLI · Associate Producers MARION ROSENBERG and JOANN CARELLI · Music by STANLEY MYERS · Produced by BARRY SPIKINGS, MICHAEL DEELEY, MICHAEL CIMINO and JOHN PEVERALL · Director of Photography VILMOS ZSIGMOND ASC · Directed by MICHAEL CIMINO · A UNIVERSAL RELEASE · Now a JOVE Book · RESTRICTED
RECORDED IN DOLBY STEREO
WARNING
Due to the nature of this film, under 17 requires accompanying Parent or Adult Guardian (There will be strict adherence to this policy)

Robert De Niro and Meryl Streep in *The Deer Hunter*.

The Screen: James Dickey's 'Deliverance' Arrives

Voight and Reynolds Star in Poet's Film

Weekend Canoe Trip of 4 Men Is Shown

By VINCENT CANBY

James Dickey, who won the 1965 National Book Award for poetry and published his first novel, "Deliverance," in 1970, has been described as a poet "concerned primarily with the direct impact of experience."

In "Deliverance," he attempts to describe the direct impact of the experience of four Atlanta suburbanites—three of whom are less fit for hiking across a steep cornfield than for watching televised football—when they go on a weekend canoe trip that turns into a nightmare of the machismo mind.

Survival, says one of the characters helpfully (at least helpfully for those of us who suffer genetic deficiencies), is the name of the game. Together the members of the party shoot the white water and, individually, are assaulted by a couple of sodomy-inclined hillbillies, scale sheer cliffs using nothing more than what seem to be prehensile fingernails and fight

The Cast

DELIVERANCE, directed by John Boorman; screenplay by James Dickey, based on his novel; director of photography, Vilmos Zsigmond; editor, Tom Priestley; produced by Mr. Boorman; distributed by Warner Brothers. Running time: 109 minutes. At Loew's Tower East Theater, Third Avenue near 72d Street. This firm has been rated R.

Ed	Jon Voight
Lewis	Burt Reynolds
Bobby	Ned Beaty
Drew	Ronny Cox
Mountain Man	Billy McKinney
Toothless Man	Herbert (Cowboy) Coward
Sheriff Bullard	James Dickey
Old Man	Ed Ramey
Lonny	Billy Redden

death duels armed with bow-and-arrow before eventually finding their—well—deliverance.

The problem with the novel is that the perfectly legitimate excitement of the tall story is neutralized by a kind of prose that only Irving Wallace might envy (i.e. "She had great hands; they knew me"). Ordinarily, a film is much better suited than a novel for communicating the direct impact of experience, if only because the experience is immediate and unintellectualized, and you don't have to climb over picturesque semicolons to get from one statement of fact to another.

However, so many of Dickey's lumpy narrative ideas remain in his screenplay that John Boorman's screen version becomes a lot less interesting than it has any right to be. "Deliver-

ance," which opened yesterday at Loew's Tower East, is an action melodrama that doesn't trust its action to speak louder than words on the order of: "Sometimes you gotta lose yourself to find something." If anybody said that to me — seriously — in the course of a canoe trip I think I'd get out and wade.

This is a disappointment because the film contains some good things, including the look of the production, which was photographed by Vilmos Zsigmond, who did "McCabe and Mrs. Miller," entirely on locations in rural Georgia in a kind of bleached color that denies any thoughts of romantic sentimentality. The white water sequences are smashingly vivid and untricky, as is Boorman's treatment of his characters who, much of the time, are kept in a middle distance

—one that precludes a phony intimacy with them — until crucial moments when close-ups are necessary.

Best of all are the performances—by Jon Voight, as the thoughtful, self-satisfied businessman who rather surprisingly meets the challenge of the wilderness; Burt Reynolds, as the Hemingway hero who fails, through no real fault of his own, and Ned Beatty and Ronny Cox, as their two city friends whose total unsuitability for such a weekend venture is just one of a number of unbelievable and unexplained points in the Dickey screenplay. I wouldn't get into a Central Park rowboat with either one, but then Dickey's story is schematic, and to make his points about the nature of man he had to deny the very realism that the film pretends to deal in.

Burt Reynolds in *Deliverance*.

"I was so rigid in my seat from dread, tension and the sheer physical exhaustion of their ordeals that my adrenal gland is still over-active. Jon Voight brings depth to Dickey's insightful story, Burt Reynolds is superb."
—LIZ SMITH, Cosmopolitan

"Under John Boorman's clean-cut direction, Dickey's acclaimed novel emerges as a multileveled movie, a breathbating outdoor adventure story and a devastating comment on man's attempt to return to the primitive."
—JUDITH CRIST, New York Magazine

"Truly a wonder film in which direction, photography, acting and screenplay are in delicate and perfect balance. 'Deliverance' is absolutely everything that a movie should be."
—NORMA McLAIN STOOP, After Dark

Deliverance

A JOHN BOORMAN Film Starring
JON VOIGHT · BURT REYNOLDS in "DELIVERANCE" · Co-Starring NED BEATY · RONNY COX
Screenplay by James Dickey Based on his novel · Produced and Directed by John Boorman · PANAVISION® TECHNICOLOR®
From Warner Bros., A Warner Communications Company R RESTRICTED

LOEWS TOWER EAST
72ND STREET AND 3RD AVE.
12.00 2.00 4.00 6.00 8.00 10.00

Detective Story...

The love story of a man whose wife was more woman than angel!

"How many others were there, Mary?"

"BETTER THAN THE PLAY!"
—Time Magazine

KIRK **DOUGLAS**
ELEANOR **PARKER**
WILLIAM **BENDIX**
in
WILLIAM **WYLER'S**
PRODUCTION OF
SIDNEY KINGSLEY'S

also starring
CATHY O'DONNELL
and featuring
three members
of the original
Broadway cast
HORACE McMAHON
LEE GRANT
JOSEPH WISEMAN
MICHAEL STRONG
JAMES MALONEY

Detective Story
FROM THE SMASH STAGE SUCCESS!

Produced and Directed by **WILLIAM WYLER**
Screenplay by **PHILIP YORDAN** and **ROBERT WYLER**
Based on the play by **SIDNEY KINGSLEY** · A Paramount Picture

STARTS
Tomorrow
8:30 A.M.
ELECTION DAY

BRANDT'S
Mayfair
7th Ave. & 47th St.

EXTRA! TODAY ONLY! Special advance showings of a thrilling outdoor adventure story in Technicolor plus last times "THE DAY THE EARTH STOOD STILL".

'Detective Story,' Film Based on Sidney Kingsley Drama, Arrives at Mayfair

DETECTIVE STORY, screen play by Philip Yordan and Robert Wyler, based on the play by Sidney Kingsley; directed and produced by William Wyler for Paramount Pictures. At the Mayfair.

Detective James McLeod	Kirk Douglas
Mary McLeod	Eleanor Parker
Lieutenant Monaghan	Horace McMahon
Detective Lou Brody	William Bendix
A Shoplifter	Lee Grant
Arthur Kindred	Craig Hill
Susan Carmichael	Cathy O'Donnell
Detective Dakis	Bert Freed
Detective Gallagher	Frank Faylen
Detective Callahan	William Phillips
Detective O'Brien	Grandon Rhodes
Joe Feinson	Luis Van Rooten
Lawyer	Warner Anderson
Karl Schneider	George Macready
Charles Gennini	Joseph Wiseman
Lewis Abbot	Michael Strong
Patrolman Barnes	Russell Evans
Patrolman Keogh	Howard Joslyn
Miss Hatch	Gladys George
Willy, The Janitor	Burt Mustin
Mr. Pritchett	James Maloney
Tami Giacoppetti	Gerald Mohr

By BOSLEY CROWTHER

Sidney Kingsley's play, "Detective Story," has been made into a brisk, absorbing film by Producer-Director William Wyler, with the help of a fine, responsive cast. Long on graphic demonstration of the sort of raffish traffic that flows through a squadroom of plain-clothes detectives in a New York police station-house and considerably short on penetration into the lives of anyone on display, it shapes up as an impeccable mosaic of minor melodrama on the Mayfair's screen.

That should define the entertainment. Mr. Kingsley's talents were applied to a task of elaborate documentation of a busy squad-room in a theatrical frame, shaping into a fluid pattern myriad details of the baroque locale and the knocked-about personalities of the permanent residents and the riff-raff that goes through. And that is the pulsing panorama that Mr. Wyler has got upon the screen in as crisp and dynamic a handling of the material as could well be conceived.

Within what amounts to a matter of no more than six or eight hours in the cluttered and crowded headquarters of the Twenty-first Squad Detectives, a half dozen or so human crises are suddenly developed and passed and at least that many more vignettes of freakish human nature are exposed. There is the pathetic young fellow who has stolen for a fast-stepping doll, at last brought to sober realization of the nice girl who loved him all the time. There are the two rattle-brained burglars, an unredeemable pair, one of whom is a fourth offender and a definite man to watch. There is, too, the little shoplifter, a serio-comic girl; there's the "bull" who still grieves for a lost son, and many, many more.

But most particularly there is the detective who has a bitterness toward the world that drives him to go after criminals with a relentless and overpowering zeal—a man whose fixation on convictions brooks no pity or compromise. And it is the accumulation and revelation of a crisis in this man's life that make for the major interest and dramatic cohesion in the film.

To put it quite baldly and bluntly, which the picture commendably does, he discovers that his wife was once a patient of an illegal practitioner whom he has spent more than a year of careful sleuthing to bring to unassailable book. Thus his own wife becomes the challenge by which his capacity for pity is tried.

Do not search too hopefully for plausibility in this case. Neither Mr. Kingsley, the scriptwriters nor Mr. Wyler have—and that is the one shortcoming and disappointment of the film. The fact that the hero is a fanatic is merely stated, never explained; thus his violent and mingled reactions toward his wife have no solid, convincing grounds. And the consequent clashing and slashing of their tangled emotions that go on make for nothing more penetrating than a good superficial show. Toward its end, which is grisly and fatal, this observer was still wondering why.

However, as we say, that complication is but the arbitrary prop for the display and is no deeper than necessary to anchor the support for a story line. It is the complex of business in the squadroom, staged so snugly and naturally therein that Mr. Wyler hasn't even used mood music, that makes for interest in this film.

In the performance of this business, every member of the cast rates a hand, with the possible exception of Eleanor Parker as the hero's wife, and she is really not to blame. Kirk Douglas is so forceful and aggressive as the detective with a kink in his brain that the sweet and conventional distractions of Miss Parker as his wife appear quite tame. In the role of the mate of such a tiger—and of a woman who has had the troubled past that is harshly revealed in this picture—Mr. Wyler might have cast a sharper dame.

However, that is the one weak link. Mr. Douglas is, detective-wise, superb — and Horace McMahon runs him a close second as the keen-witted boss of the squad. William Bendix, Bert Freed and Frank Faylen are fine as assorted "bulls," while Lee Grant, Craig Hill and Joseph Wiseman stand out among the characters they run in. To toss off more plaudits for the acting would mean to go down the whole list.

"Detective Story" is a hard-grained entertainment, not revealing but bruisingly real.

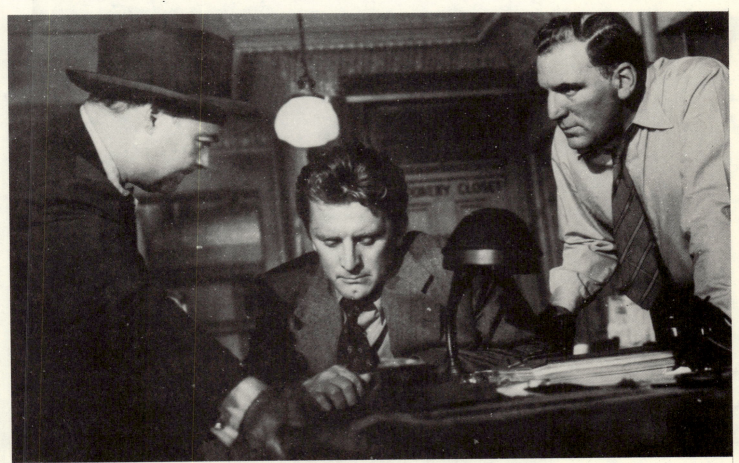

Luis Van Rooten, Kirk Douglas and William Bendix in *The Detective Story.*

Dr. Jekyll and Mr. Hyde

John Barrymore as Dr. Jekyll and Mr. Hyde came to the screen of the Rivoli yesterday afternoon.

This statement must be the outstanding and joyfully heralded feature of any report on the motion picture version of the story that Robert Louis Stevenson wrote and the play in which Richard Mansfield appeared—for the excellence of the photoplay, everything that distinguishes it from the pictures that come and go from day to day marks it as something special and extraordinary—is centered in Mr. Barrymore's flawless performance. He receives some aid from the camera, of course, but those who go to the Rivoli this week will be impressed more by his independence of cinematic trickery than by the skilful and wholly legitimate use he makes of it. Those who expect the photoplay to be good because "it's just the thing for the movies" will find that it is good because it's just the thing for John Barrymore. It is true that the screen lends itself peculiarly to the story, but it can be only a sufficient medium for Mr. Barrymore's unique ability. It is what Mr. Barrymore himself does that makes the dual character of Jekyll and Hyde tremendous. His performance is one of pure motion-picture pantomime on as high a level as has ever been attained by anyone. In a story that was written as a "shocker" and a play that is always a melodrama, he creates such a genuinely beautiful Jekyll and completely hideous Hyde, and emphasizes the contrast between the two with such a sure eye for essentials, that one must believe in both while he sees them and afterwards admire a work of art.

But all of this may seem trivial to some. While Mr. Barrymore is achieving greatness as Richard III on the stage, anything he does in "the movies" must be totally unimportant to many, and serious applause of his effort on the screen will probably be put on a par with lauding the idle limericks of a great poet. But there is no real support for such an attitude. Even if one waive the contention that Mr. Barrymore's Dr. Jekyll and Mr. Hyde is not reduced to present insignificance by his contemporary Richard III, he may fall back on the fact that a great many more people will see the former than the latter, and have through it their only opportunity of knowing anything about what Mr. Barrymore can do. This is true for today and more importantly true for the future. Coming generations—there's H. 3d, for example—will hear of John Barrymore's Richard III, and, only hearing, may be skeptical or indifferent, as are many today of reports about Booth and Garrick, but they may see Dr. Jekyll and Mr. Hyde and, in addition to enjoying something of Mr. Barrymore's art, they will receive a personal impression of the actor that will enable them to know and appreciate him as his predecessors are not now known and appreciated. And, anyhow, it is contended that Dr. Jekyll and Mr. Hyde is a work well worth while in itself for all time. So no apologies are offered for consideration of it.

High praise of the photoplay, however, must be limited to what Mr. Barrymore does in it. The production, aside from his performance, is uninspired. It is usual. The story has been movie-molded almost to the obliteration of its individual character, and those who were led to hope that it would escape the moral monger will be disappointed. It bears the unmistakable stamp of the motion-picture mill.

John Barrymore's acting, though, more than offsets everything else. It places the picture high up among screen accomplishments.

Also at the Rivoli is a frisky little comedy, entitled "Uneasy Feet," in which pantomimic legs and feet amusingly tell a story without the aid of words. It is a most agreeable departure from prevalent slapstick and horseplay.

Anita Stewart, as herself, with whatever power she has to charm and entertain, is at the Strand this week in "The Fighting Shepherdess," a photoplay of life as it was, or is imagined to have been, in Wyoming when sheepherders and cattle men were at war and primitive people lived rudely. The shepherdess would be helpless in a hostile environment, but she is a fighter and also has the good fortune to come under the protection of two strong men who are also noble. In the end, of course, she overcomes all obstacles and enemies, and triumphantly marries the hero from the East. The best characterizations of the picture are by Walter Long and Eugenie Besserer as the evil ones who threaten to destroy the heroine, and by Noah Beery and Gibson Gowland as the strong men who protect her. The chief merit of the picture is in the scenes composed by the director, Edward José, who, except for too many meaningless close-ups too long held, made all of his moving pictures with cinematic skill and an eye for beauty.

RIVOLI — BROADWAY at 49th ST.
Hugo Riesenfeld Director
ALL THIS WEEK

ADOLPH ZUKOR presents

JOHN BARRYMORE
IN
"Dr. JEKYLL and Mr HYDE"

A Paramount Artcraft Picture

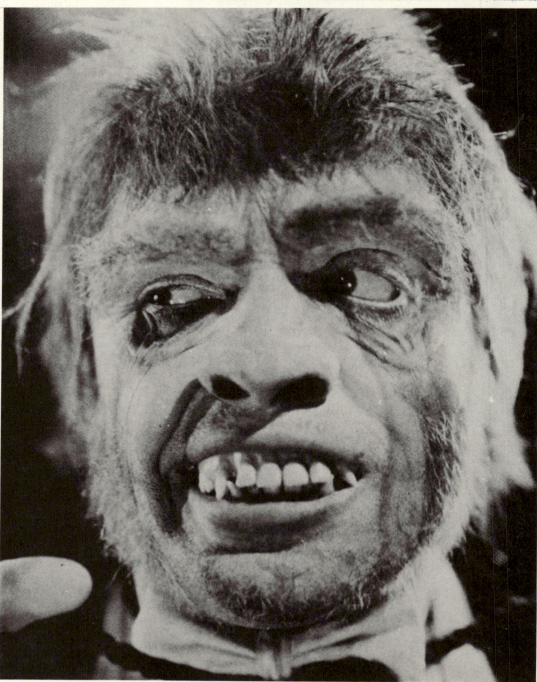

John Barrymore as the Mr. Hyde part of *Dr. Jeckyll and Mr. Hyde.*

'Dr. No,' Mystery Spoof

Film Is First Made of Ian Fleming Novels

By BOSLEY CROWTHER

IF you haven't yet made the acquaintance of Ian Fleming's suave detective, James Bond, in the author's fertile series of mystery thrillers akin to the yarns of Mickey Spillane, here's your chance to correct that misfortune in one quick and painless stroke. It's by seeing this first motion picture made from a Fleming novel, "Dr. No."

This lively, amusing picture, which opened yesterday at the Astor, the Murray Hill and other theaters in the "premiere showcase" group, is not to be taken seriously as realistic fiction or even art, any more than the works of Mr. Fleming are to be taken as long-hair literature. It is strictly a tinseled action-thriller, spiked with a mystery of a sort. And, if you are clever, you will see it as a spoof of science-fiction and sex.

For the crime-detecting adventure that Mr. Bond is engaged in here is so wildly exaggerated, so patently contrived, that it is obviously silly and not to be believed. It is a perilous task of discovering who is operating a device on the tropical island of Jamaica that "massively interferes" with the critical rocket launchings from Cape Canaveral.

Nonsense, you say. Of course, it's nonsense—pure, escapist bunk, with Bond, an elegant fellow, played by Sean Connery, doing everything (and everybody) that an idle day-dreamer might like to do. Called from a gambling club in London to pick up his orders and his gun and hop on a plane for Jamaica before a tawny temptress leads him astray, old "Double Oh Seven" (that's his code name) is in there being natty from the start. And he keeps on being natty, naughty and nifty to the end.

It's not the mystery that entertains you, it's the things that happen along the way—the attempted kidnapping at the Jamaica airport, the tarantula dropped onto Bond's bed, the seduction of the Oriental beauty, the encounter with the beautiful blond bikini-clad Ursula Andress on the beach of Crab Key. And it's all of these things happening so smoothly in the lovely Jamaica locale, looking real and tempting in color, that recommend this playful British film.

The ending, which finds Joseph Wiseman being frankly James Masonish in an undersea laboratory that looks like something inspired by

Sean Connery Stars as Agent James Bond

The Cast

DR. NO, screenplay by Richard Maibaum, Johanna Harwood and Berkley Mather, from the novel by Ian Fleming. Directed by Terence Young and produced by Harry Saltzman and Albert R. Broccoli. Released by United Artists. At the Astor Theater, Broadway and 45th Street, the Murray Hill Theater, 34th Street, east of Lexington Avenue, and other metropolitan area theaters. Running time: 105 minutes.

James Bond	Sean Connery
Honey	Ursula Andress
Dr. No	Joseph Wiseman
Felix Leiter	Jack Lord
M	Bernard Lee
Prof. Dent	Anthony Dawson
Quarrel	John Kitzmiller
Miss Taro	Zena Marshall
Sylvia	Eunice Gavson
Miss Moneypenny	Lois Maxwell
Puss-Feller	Lester Prendergast
Strangways	Tim Moxon

Oak Ridge, is a bit too extravagant and silly, and likewise too frantic and long. But something outrageous had to be found with which to end the reckless goings-on.

Ursula Andress in *Dr. No,* the first of the Ian Fleming novels to be made into a film.

'Dr. Strangelove,' a Shattering Sick Joke

Kubrick Film Presents Sellers in 3 Roles

DR. STRANGELOVE OR: HOW I LEARNED TO STOP WORRYING AND LOVE THE BOMB, screenplay by Stanley Kubrick, Terry Southern and Peter George, based on the book "Two Hours to Doom," by Mr. George; produced and directed by Mr. Kubrick. Presented by Columbia Pictures Corporation. At the Victoria Theater, Broadway and 46th Street, and the Baronet Theater, Third Avenue and 59th Street. Runnnig time: 93 minutes.

Group Captain Lionel Mandrake,
President Muffley,
Dr. Stangelove..................Peter Sellers
Gen. Buck Turgidson....George C. Scott
Gen. Jack D. Ripper......Sterling Hayden
Col. Bat Guana............Keenan Wynn
Maj. T. J. King Kong.......Slim Pickens
Ambassador de Sadesky......Peter Bull
Miss Scott....................Tracy Reed
Lieut. Lothar Zogg......James Earl Jones
Staines......................Jack Creley
Lieut. H. R. Dietrich......Frank Berry
Lieut. W. D. Kivel..........Glenn Beck
Capt. G. A. (Ace) Owens).Shane Rimmer
Lieut. B. Goldberg..........Paul Tamarin
General Faceman..........Gordon Tanner
Admiral Randolph.......Robert O'Neil
Frank.......................Roy Stephens

By BOSLEY CROWTHER

STANLEY KUBRICK'S new film, called "Dr. Strangelove or: How I Learned to Stop Worrying and Love the Bomb," is beyond any question the most shattering sick joke I've ever come across. And I say that with full recollection of some of the grim ones I've heard from Mort Sahl, some of the cartoons I've seen by Charles Addams and some of the stuff i've read in Mad Magazine.

For this brazenly jesting speculation of what might happen within the Pentagon and within the most responsible council of the President of the United States if some maniac Air Force general should suddenly order a nuclear attack on the Soviet Union is at the same time one of the cleverest and most incisive satiric thrusts at the awkwardness and folly of the military that have ever been on the screen. It opened yesterday at the Victoria and the Baronet.

My reaction to it is quite divided, because there is so much about it that is grand, so much that is brilliant and amusing, and much that is grave and dangerous.

On the one hand, it cuts right to the soft pulp of the kind of military mind that is lost from all sense of reality in a maze of technical talk, and it shows up this type of mentality for the foolish and frightening thing it is.

In a top-level Air Force general, played by George C. Scott with a snarling and rasping volubility that makes your blood run cold, Mr. Kubrick presents us with a joker whose thinking is so involved with programs and cautions

Peter Sellers as Group Captain Lionel Mandrake, one of the three roles he plays in *Dr. Strangelove.*

and suspicions that he is practically tied in knots.

It is he who is most completely baffled, bewildered and paralyzed when word comes through to Washington that a general in the Strategic Air Command has sent a wing of bombers off to drop bombs and that the planes cannot be recalled. It is he who has to answer to the President for this awesome "accident" when the President gathers his council in the War Room at the Pentagon. And it is he who looks the most unstable and dubious in the causes of peace when it begins to appear that the Russians have a retaliatory "doomsday device."

Some of the conversations in that War Room are hilarious, shooting bright shafts of satire through mounds of ineptitude. There is, best of all, a conversation between the President and an unseen Soviet Premier at the other end of a telephone line that is a titanic garble of nuttiness and platitudes.

Funny, too, in a mad way, is the behavior of the crew in one of the planes of the airborne alert force ordered to drop the bomb. The commander is a Texan who puts on a cowboy hat when he knows the mission is committed. Slim Pickens plays this role. He and Keenan Wynn as a foggy colonel are the funniest individuals in the film.

As I say, there are parts of this satire that are almost beyond compare.

On the other hand, I am

Slim Pickens preparing to ride the Bomb of Destiny in *Dr. Strangelove.*

troubled by the feeling, which runs all through the film, of discredit and even contempt for our whole defense establishment, up to and even including the hypothetical Commander in Chief.

It is all right to show the general who starts this wild foray as a Communist-hating madman, convinced that a "Red conspiracy" is fluoridating our water in order to pollute our precious body fluids. That is pointed satire, and Sterling Hayden plays the role with just a right blend of wackiness and meanness to give the character significance.

But when virtually everybody turns up stupid or insane —or, what is worse, psychopathic—I want to know what this picture proves. The President, played by Peter Sellers with a shiny bald head, is a dolt, whining and unavailing with the nation in a life-or-death spot. But worse yet, his technical expert, Dr. Strangelove, whom Mr. Sellers also plays, is a devious and noxious ex-German whose mechanical arm insists on making the Nazi salute.

And, oddly enough, the only character who seems to have much common sense is a British flying officer, whom Mr. Sellers—yes, he again—plays.

The ultimate touch of goulish humor is when we see the bomb actually going off, dropped on some point in Russia, and a jazzy sound track comes in with a cheerful melodic rendition of "We'll Meet Again Some Sunny Day." Somehow, to me, it isn't funny. It is malefic and sick.

Jean Harlow as Kitty Packard in *Dinner at Eight*.

Many Stars of the Metro-Goldwyn-Mayer Firmament In the Film Version of "Dinner at Eight."

DINNER AT EIGHT, an adaptation of the play by George S. Kaufman and Edna Ferber; directed by George Cukor; a Metro-Goldwyn-Mayer production. At the Astor.

Carlotta Vance	Marie Dressler
Larry Renault	John Barrymore
Dan Packard	Wallace Beery
Kitty Packard	Jean Harlow
Oliver Jordan	Lionel Barrymore
Max Kane	Lee Tracy
Dr. Wayne Talbot	Edmund Lowe
Mrs. Oliver Jordan	Billie Burke
Paula Jordan	Madge Evans
Jo Stengel	Jean Harsholt
Mrs. Wayne Talbot	Karen Morley
Hattie Loomis	Louise Closser Hale
Ernest DeGraff	Phillips Holmes
Mrs. Wendel	May Robson
Ed Loomis	Grant Mitchell
Miss Alden	Phoebe Foster
Miss Copeland	Elizabeth Patterson
Tina	Hilda Vaughn
Fosdick	Harry Beresford
Mr. Fitch	Edwin Maxwell
Mr. Hatfield	John Davidson
Eddie	Edward Woods
Gustave	George Baxter
The Waiter	Herman Bing
Dora	Anna Duncan

By MORDAUNT HALL.

Marie Dressler.

With its remarkable array of histrionic talent and with George Cukor at the helm, the film adaption of the play, "Dinner at Eight," which was offered last night by Metro-Goldwyn-Mayer at the Astor, could scarcely help being successful. And it lives up to every expectation, even though a few of the unforgettable lines penned by George S. Kaufman and Edna Ferber have been lost in the general shuffle. The picture clings as closely as possible to the original, and the many opportunities along cinematic lines have been fully appreciated by Mr. Cukor and others responsible for the offering.

This "Dinner at Eight" has a cast of twenty-five, and among the players are most of the stellar lights of the Metro-Goldwyn-Mayer studios, besides a few borrowed from other companies. It is one of those rare pictures which keeps you in your seat until the final fade-out, for nobody wants to miss one of the scintillating lines.

It is a fast-moving narrative with its humor and tragedy, one that offers a greater variety of characterizations than have been witnessed in any other picture. Some are polished and others decidedly rough and ready. They range from Mrs. Oliver Jordan, the snobbish hostess, who is wrapped up in the dinner she is giving for Lord and Lady Ferncliffe and his wife, Kitty, who in the play was said to talk "pure spearmint." But there is a reason in all cases for inviting the guests.

A strong line of drama courses through the story notwithstanding the flip dialogue. The picture runs along with a steady flow of unusually well knit incidents, which are woven together most expertly toward the end. This is owing to the fine writing of Mr. Kaufman and Miss Ferber, and it might easily be said that the wonder would be that anybody could go askew in turning such a play into pictorial form.

Veteran players of the stage, who have since been won over to talk-ing pictures, are the principal assets in this film. It is a great pleasure to behold Marie Dressler away from her usual rôles, dressed in the height of fashion and given lines that aroused gales of mirth from the first-night audience.

Miss Dressler acts Carlotta Vance, the stage beauty of the mauve decade. Carlotta is a woman of much common sense who has a retort for every quip made to her. When one woman, obviously well on in years, hints that she was a child when she first saw Carlotta, the former actress ends the conversation by suggesting that they talk about the Civil War. Carlotta has her Pekingese dogs, one of which boasts of the name of Tarzan.

Another stage favorite of old is Billie Burke, who appears as the handsome Mrs. Oliver Jordan. A week before the dinner in honor of the Ferncliffes, she is worrying about the affair, making sure that there will not be the slightest hitch. An orchestra is ordered, extra servants hired and, when the morning of the dinner comes around, an aspic in the form of a lion is made. Little does Mrs. Jordan think that her dinner is going to be a memorable fiasco.

Lionel Barrymore fills the part of Mr. Jordan, whose mind is more concerned about money matters and his steamship line than his wife's dinner. His brother John is cast as Larry Renauld, the motion picture actor who brags of having earned $8,000 a week at one time, while he has only 7 cents to his name.

The scenes depicting Dan Packard, played by Wallace Beery, and Kitty, his ash-blonde wife, acted by Jean Harlow, are filled with gruff fun. There is hardly a moment while they are at home when the air is not filled with acrimonious accusations and retorts. Kitty rather likes the idea of blossoming out in society, while Dan's heart is set on being a big gun in politics. Edmund Lowe impersonates Dr. Wayne Talbot, who is infatuated with Kitty, one of his patients.

Mrs. Jordan's state of mind can well be imagined when she hears over the telephone that the Ferncliffes are unable to attend the dinner as they are on their way to Florida. Added to this are other troubles, including the tragic end of Larry Renault, who, unknown to Mrs. Jordan, had had an affair with her daughter, Paula.

Miss Dressler is splendid as the wise Carlotta. Miss Burke's contribution to the story is all one could wish. She is the personification of an anxious hostess at one moment and subsequently a deeply disappointed woman. John Barry-more tackles his rôle with his usual artistry. His acting during Larry's last moments is most effective. Mr. Beery fits into the rôle of Dan Packard as though it were written especially for him and Miss Harlow makes the most of the part of Kitty. Lionel Barrymore is suave and sympathetic. Edmund Lowe does quite well as Dr. Talbot.

It was a grand evening, an entertainment that caused one to forget about the deluge outside.

Jean Harlow and Wallace Beery.

NRA — WE DO OUR PART

And...
THEY *do*
THEIR PARTS
magnificently..

MARIE DRESSLER ★
JOHN BARRYMORE ★
WALLACE BEERY ★
JEAN HARLOW ★
Lionel BARRYMORE ★
LEE TRACY ••••
EDMUND LOWE ★
BILLIE BURKE ★
★ Madge EVANS   Karen MORLEY ★
★ Jean HERSHOLT   Phillips HOLMES ★

Triumphant in last night's
WORLD PREMIERE of
DINNER at 8

From the Sam H. Harris stage play by GEORGE
S. KAUFMAN & EDNA FERBER

Now Playing
ASTOR
45th STREET & BROADWAY

Twice daily 2:50—8:50
Three times Sat., Sun.,
Hols. 2:50 5:50 8:50
Sat. Mid. Show. Mats.
50c to $1.00. Eves.
50c to $2.00.

Screen play by Frances Marion
and Herman J. Mankiewicz.
Produced by DAVID O.
SELZNICK. Directed by
GEORGE CUKOR.

Lumet's 'Dog Day Afternoon'

By VINCENT CANBY

"Dog Day Afternoon," which opened yesterday at the Cinema 1, is Sidney Lumet's most accurate, most flamboyant New York movie

‑‑that consistently vital and energetic Lumet genre that includes "The Pawnbroker" and "Serpico" and exists entirely surrounded by (but always separate from) the rest

of his work. Mr. Lumet's New York movies are as much aspects of the city's life as they are stories of the city's life.

"Dog Day Afternoon" is a melodrama, based on fact, about a disastrously ill-planned Brooklyn bank robbery, and it's beautifully

DOG DAY AFTERNOON, directed by Sidney Lumet; screenplay by Frank Pierson, based on a magazine article by P. F. Kluge and Thomas Moore; produced by Martin Bregman and Martin Elfand; editor, Dede Allen; director of photography, Victor J. Kemper; an Artists Entertainment Complex, Inc., production, distributed by Warner Brothers. Running time: 130 minutes. At the Cinema 1 Theater, Third Avenue near 60th Street. This film has been rated R.

Sonny	Al Pacino
Sal	John Cazale
Sheldon	James Broderick
Moretti	Charles Durning
Sylvia	Penny Allen
Mulvaney	Sully Boyar
Margaret	Beulah Garrick
Jenny	Carol Kane
Deborah	Sandra Kazan
Miriam	Marcia Jean Kurtz
Maria	Amy Levitt
Howard	John Marriott
Edna	Estelle Omens
Vi	Judith Malina
Angie	Susan Peretz
Leon	Chris Sarandon
Bobby	Gary Springer

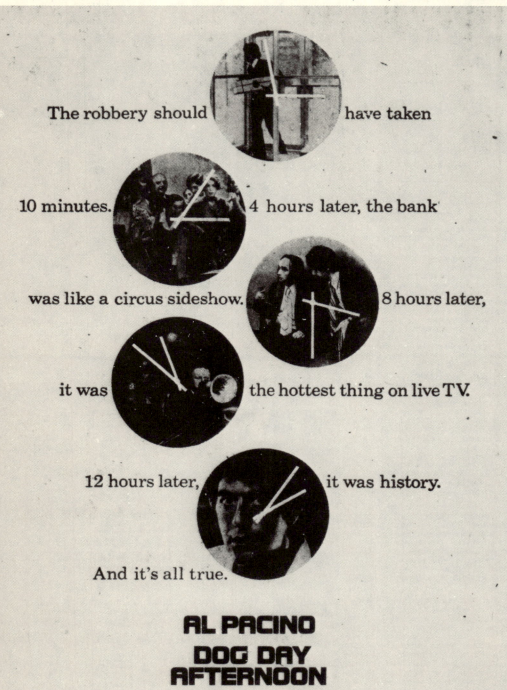

The robbery should have taken 10 minutes. 4 hours later, the bank was like a circus sideshow. 8 hours later, it was the hottest thing on live TV. 12 hours later, it was history. And it's all true.

AL PACINO DOG DAY AFTERNOON

An Artists Entertainment Complex Inc. Production

Also Starring JOHN CAZALE · JAMES BRODERICK and CHARLES DURNING as Moretti · Screenplay by FRANK PIERSON · Produced by MARTIN BREGMAN and MARTIN ELFAND

R RESTRICTED Under 17 requires accompanying Parent or Adult Guardian   Directed by SIDNEY LUMET · Film Editor DEDE ALLEN · TECHNICOLOR® From WARNER BROS. A WARNER COMMUNICATIONS COMPANY

acted by performers who appear to have grown up on the city's sidewalks in the heat and hopelessness of an endless midsummer.

If you can let yourself laugh at desperation that has turned seriously lunatic, the film is funny, but mostly it's reportorially efficient and vivid, in the understated way of news writing that avoids easy speculation.

Each of the several principal lives it touches has been grotesquely bent out of shape. The director and Frank Pierson, who wrote the fine screenplay, don't attempt to supply reasons. The movie says only that this is what happened. No more. This severely limits the film's emotional impact, though not its seriousness or its fascination. "Dog Day Afternoon" is a gaudy street-carnival of a movie that rudely invites laughs at inappropriate moments, which is in keeping with the city's concrete sensibility.

The incident on which the film is based was the attempt to rob a branch of the Chase Manhattan Bank on Aug. 22, 1972. The two bandits, one of whom was seeking money for a sex-change operation for a boyfriend, failed miserably, after they held the bank's employes hostage for 14 hours, appeared live on television, became the center of an impromptu neighborhood Mardi Gras, and negotiated for a jet plane to fly them out of the country.

●

Mr. Lumet's film is exclusively concerned with the robbery attempt and the time it occupied. Only briefly does the film move out of the bank and away from the lower-middle-class neighborhood of apartments over pizza parlors, barber shops and barrooms.

Bram Stoker's Human Vampire

By MORDAUNT HALL.

DRACULA, with Bela Lugosi, Helen Chandler, David Manners, Dwight Frye, Edward Van Sloan, Herbert Bunston, Frances Dade, Charles Gerrard, Joan Standing, Moon Carroll and Josephine Velez, based on Bram Stoker's novel, directed by Tod Browning; overture, "Rhapsody in Blue"; Movietone news reel; "Hello, New York!" with Santry and Norton and others, including Leonide Massine and the Roxyettes. At the Roxy.

Count Dracula, Bram Stoker's human vampire, who has chilled the spines of book readers and playgoers, is now to be seen at the Roxy in a talking film directed by Tod Browning, who delights in such blood-curdling stories. It is a production that evidently had the desired effect upon many in the audience yesterday afternoon, for there was a general outburst of applause when Dr. Van Helsing produced a little cross that caused the dreaded Dracula to fling his cloak over his head and make himself scarce.

But Dracula's evil work is not ended until Dr. Van Helsing hammers a stake through the Count's heart as he lies in his native earth in a box.

Mr. Browning is fortunate in having in the leading rôle in this eerie work, Bela Lugosi, who played the same part on the stage when it was presented here in October, 1927. What with Mr. Browning's imaginative direction and Mr. Lugosi's make-up and weird gestures, this picture succeeds to some extent in its grand guignol intentions.

As the scenes flash by there are all sorts of queer noises, such as the cries of wolves and the hooting of owls, not to say anything of the screams of Dracula's feminine victims, who are found with twin red marks on their white throats.

The Count is able to change himself into a vampire that flies in through the window and in this guise he is supposed to be able to talk to his victims, who are either driven insane or are so thoroughly terrified that they would sooner do his bidding that pay heed to those who have their welfare at heart. Martin, the keeper in the sanitarium in which an unfortunate individual named Renfield is under supervision, fires at the big bat with a shot gun, but, of course, misses.

To enhance the supernatural effect of this film there is a fog in many of the scenes. The first glimpses are of ordinary humans, but so soon as Renfield goes to the Transylvania castle of the Count, who lives on for centuries by his vampirish actions, there are bony hands protruding from boxes, rats and other animals fleeing, and corridors that are thick with cobwebs and here and there a hungry spider.

Most of the excitement takes place in Carfax Abbey and other places in England, the Count having traveled there to accomplish his blood-thirsty intentions. To start the grim work he causes all the ship's crew to go insane and commit suicide, but his subsequent activities are not as fruitful as he anticipates.

Helen Chandler gives an excellent performance as one of the girls who is attacked by the "undead" Count. David Manners contributes good work. Dwight Frye does fairly well as Renfield. Herbert Bunston is a most convincing personality. Charles Gerrard affords a few laughs as Martin.

This picture can at least boast of being the best of the many mystery films.

Begins TODAY
*The Strangest Passion
The World Has Ever Known*
Has held two generations in fascination and suspense

"DRACULA"
TOD BROWNING'S greatest production

First a best-selling book—then a sensational play — now, still greater as a talking picture!

with BELA LUGOSI
creator of the original stage rôle

HELEN CHANDLER
DAVID MANNERS
A UNIVERSAL PICTURE

50th St.—7th Ave.
Direction
S. L. ROTHAFEL
(ROXY)

ROXY

THE SMARTEST STAGE SHOW IN TOWN
"HELLO NEW YORK"
in seven scenes with a tremendous cast of principals, including Roxy Ballet—Chorus—Roxyettes in a riot of color, dance and song.
Vivian Hart—Hal Young—Snake Hips
Leonide Massine—Male Dancers
ROXY SYMPHONY
ORCHESTRA of 125
ERNO RAPEE Conducting
"RHAPSODY IN BLUE"
with Harry Ferrella

Count Dracula (Bela Lugosi) attacks sanitarium patient, Renfield (Dwight Frye).

A publicity still from *Dracula* featuring Bela Lugosi and Helen Chandler.

The New York Times

TUESDAY, JULY 15, 1969

'Easy Rider': A Statement on Film

EASY RIDER, written by Peter Fonda, Dennis Hopper and Terry Southern; directed by Mr. Hopper; produced by Mr. Fonda; presented by the Pando Company in association with Raybert Productions; released by Columbia Pictures. At the Beekman Theater, 65th Street at Second Avenue. Running time 94 minutes. (The Motion Picture Association of America's Production Code and Rating Administration classifies this film: "R—Restricted—persons under 16 not admitted, unless accompanied by parent or adult guardian.")

Wyatt	Peter Fonda
Billy	Dennis Hopper
George Hanson	Jack Nicholson
Rancher	Warren Finnerty
Stranger on Highway	Luke Askew
Lisa	Luana Anders
Karen	Karen Black

By VINCENT CANBY

"EASY RIDER," which opened yesterday at the Beekman, is a motorcycle drama with decidedly superior airs about it. How else are we to approach a movie that advertises itself: "A man went looking for America. And couldn't find it anywhere"? Right away you know that something superior is up, that somebody is making a statement, and you can bet your boots (cowboy, black leather) that it's going to put down the whole rotten scene. What scene? Whose? Why? Man, I can't tell you if you don't know. What I mean to say is, if you don't groove, you don't groove. You might as well split.

•

I felt this way during the first half-hour of "Easy Rider," and then, almost reluctantly, fell into the rhythm of the determinedly inarticulate piece. Two not-so-young cyclists, Wyatt (Peter Fonda) who affects soft leather breeches and a Capt. America jacket, and Billy (Dennis Hopper), who looks like a perpetually stoned Buffalo Bill, are heading east from California toward New Orleans.

They don't communicate with us, or each other, but after a while, it doesn't seem to matter. They simply exist —they are bizarre comic strip characters with occasional balloons over their heads reading: "Like you're doing your thing," or some such. We accept them in their moving isolation, against the magnificent Southwestern landscapes of beige and green and pale blue.

They roll down macadam highways that look like black velvet ribbons, under skies of incredible purity, and the soundtrack rocks with oddly counterpointed emotions of Steppenwolf, the Byrds, the Electric Prunes — dark and smoky cries for liberation.

Periodically, like a group taking a break, the cyclists stop (and so does the music) for quiet encounters—with a toothless rancher and his huge, happy family or with a commune of thin hippies, whose idyll seems ringed with unacknowledged desperation.

Suddenly, however, a strange thing happens. There comes on the scene a very real character and everything that has been accepted earlier as a sort of lyrical sense impression suddenly looks flat and foolish.

•

Wyatt and Billy are in a small Southern town—in jail for having disturbed the peace of a local parade—when they meet fellow-inmate George Hanson (Jack Nicholson), a handsome, alcoholic young lawyer of good family and genially bad habits, a man whose only defense against life is a cheerful but not abject acceptance of it. As played by Nicholson, George Hanson is a marvelously realized character, who talks in a high, squeaky Southern accent and uses a phrase like "Lord have mercy!" the way another man might use a four-letter word.

Hanson gets the cyclists sprung from jail and then promptly joins them. He looks decidedly foolish, sitting on the back of Wyatt's bike, wearing a seersucker jacket and his old football helmet, but he is completely happy and, ironically, the only person in the movie who seems to have a sense of what liberation and freedom are. There is joy and humor and sweetness when he smokes grass for the first time and expounds an elaborate theory as to how the Venutians have already conquered the world.

•

Nicholson is so good, in fact, that "Easy Rider" never quite recovers from his loss, even though he has had the rather thankless job of spelling out what I take to be the film's statement (upper case). This has to do with the threat that people like the nonconforming Wyatt and Billy represent to the ordinary, self-righteous, inhibited folk that are the Real America. Wyatt and Billy, says the lawyer, represent freedom; ergo, says the film, they must be destroyed.

If there is any irony in this supposition, I was unable to detect it in the screenplay written by Fonda, Hopper and Terry Southern. Wyatt and Billy don't seem particularly free, not if the only way they can face the world is through a grass curtain. As written and played, they are lumps of gentle clay, vacuous, romantic symbols, dressed in cycle drag.

"Easy Rider," the first film to be directed by Dennis Hopper, won a special prize at this year's Cannes festival as the best picture by a new director (there was only one other picture competing in that category).

With the exception of Nicholson, its good things are familiar things — the rock score, the lovely, sometimes impressionistic photography by Laszlo Kovacs, the faces of small-town America. These things not only are continually compelling but occasionally they dazzle the senses, if not the mind. Hopper, Fonda and their friends went out into America looking for a movie and found instead a small, pious statement (upper case) about our society (upper case), which is sick (upper case). It's pretty but lower case cinema.

Dennis Hopper, Peter Fonda and Jack Nicholson in *Easy Rider*.

A man went looking for America.
And couldn't find it anywhere...

(CANNES FILM FESTIVAL WINNER
"Best Film By a New Director")

EASY RIDER   PETER FONDA · DENNIS HOPPER · JACK NICHOLSON

The New York Times

FRIDAY, DECEMBER 16, 1960.

Long 'Exodus'

3½-Hour Film Based on Uris' Novel Opens

By BOSLEY CROWTHER

THE gingerly awaited film version of Leon Uris' novel, "Exodus," which its producer-director, Otto Preminger, unveiled at the Warner Theatre last night, turns out to be a massive, overlong, episodic, involved and generally inconclusive "cinemarama" of historical and fictional events connected with the liberation of the State of Israel in 1947-1948.

It also turns out to be a dazzling, eye-filling, nerve-tingling display of a wide variety of individual and mass reactions to awesome challenges and, in some of its sharpest personal details, a fine reflection of experience that rips the heart.

•

If this rapid-fire estimation of Mr. Preminger's effort to pack the guts of Mr. Uris' corpulent novel into a three-hour-and-thirty-two-minute film seems ambiguous and perhaps indecisive, it is because the film itself is an ambiguous piece of work, and the decisions that might have rendered it more cohesive and dramatically compelling were not made by the people who should have made them—namely, Mr. Preminger and Dalton Trumbo, who wrote the script.

Obviously, these two craftsmen, in all sincerity, wanted to embrace as much as they could of the three main phases of the popular novel. That is to say, they wanted to tell, first, the important story of the truly Odyssean transport of a shipload of European Jews from British blockaded Cyprus to forbidden Palestine. That is a full-scale social drama and a saga of resolution in itself, with its many vignettes of individual courage weaving into a large—well, mosaic is the word.

Then they wanted to continue the threads of several parallel plots involving an assortment of major characters through the subsequent conflicts and strains that occur vis-à-vis the powerful British prior to the United Nations' partition of Palestine. And, finally, they wished to tell something of the post-partition fight of the Jews against the displaced Arabs, with respect to the major characters that remain.

Opting to fill such a canvas, which was a critical decision in itself, Mr. Preminger and

The Cast

EXODUS, screen play by Dalton Trumbo, from the novel by Leon Uris; directed and produced by Otto Preminger; distributed by United Artists. At the Warner Theatre, Broadway and Forty-seventh Street. Running time: 212 minutes.

Ari Ben Canaan	Paul Newman
Kitty Fremont	Eva Marie Saint
General Sutherland	Ralph Richardson
Major Caldwell	Peter Lawford
Barak Ben Canaan	Lee J. Cobb
Dov Landau	Sal Mineo
Taha	John Derek
Mandria	Hugh Griffith
Lakavitch	Gregory Ratoff
Dr. Lieberman	Felix Aylmer
Akiva	David Opatoshu
Karen	Jill Haworth
Von Storch	Marius Goring
Jordana	Alexandra Stewart
David	Michael Wager
Reuben	Paul Stevens
Sarah	Betty Walker
Dr. Odenheim	Martin Miller
Sergeant	Victor Maddern

Mr. Trumbo took a long chance on tangling and losing some threads. With so many characters—at least seven—to be picked up and engineered through a maze of separate tensions, some of a political nature and some of a purely personal sort, and to be got through emotional situations and explosive civil war incidents, they ran the risk of being superficial and losing momentum in sequential stops and starts.

They were not able to escape it entirely. The principal weakness of their film is that it has so much churning around in it that no deep or solid stream of interest evolves—save a vague rooting interest in the survival of all the nice people involved.

•

Furthermore, Mr. Preminger has captured within the scope of his color cameras a continuously varied and vivid panorama of Cyprus and Palestine. He shot his picture in those places—most of it in the present Israel—and has spared no expense in reproducing historic events much as they occurred. The famous liberation of Jewish prisoners from the old fortress at Acre is excit-

ingly done, and other scenes of Haganah and Irgun actions against the British and Arabs are sharp and tough.

It is notable, incidentally, that Mr. Trumbo and Mr. Preminger have considerably temporized in exposing the adversaries. They have more tension between Haganah and Irgun than between Jews and British, and the Arabs seem mainly inspired to resist the partition by villainous former Nazi provocateurs.

In the end, one should take from this picture a shaken feeling of having been through a lot of harsh and ennobling experiences. There is a colorful musical score by Ernest Gold.

WORLD PREMIERE
TOMORROW 8 P.M. SHARP

EXODUS

MATINEES AT 2 P.M. EVENINGS AT 8 P.M.

Price scale: EVENINGS (Mon. thru Thurs.)—Orch. or Loge $3.00; Balcony $2.00
EVENINGS (Fri., Sat., Sun. & Holidays)—Orch. or Loge $3.50; Balcony $2.50
MATINEES (Monday thru Friday)—Orchestra or Loge $2.50; Balcony $1.50
MATINEES (Saturday, Sunday & Holidays)—Orch. or Loge $2.75; Balcony $1.50

SEATS NOW AVAILABLE THROUGH DECEMBER 1961. ALL SEATS RESERVED. HOLIDAY PRICES DURING CHRISTMAS AND EASTER WEEKS. ALL PRICES TAX INCLUDED. MAIL ORDERS ARE BEING ACCEPTED NOW.

Send Stamped Self-Addressed Envelope. Enclose Check or Money Order. State Preferences and Time of Performance. Make Checks Payable to Warner Theatre.

THE WARNER THEATRE B'way & 47 St. • CO 5-5710

Paul Newman masquerading as an Arab in a scene from *Exodus*.

WILLIAM PETER BLATTY'S

THE EXORCIST

Directed by WILLIAM FRIEDKIN

ELLEN BURSTYN · MAX VON SYDOW · LEE J. COBB
KITTY WINN · JACK MacGOWRAN   JASON MILLER as Father Karras
LINDA BLAIR as Regan · Produced by WILLIAM PETER BLATTY
Executive Producer NOEL MARSHALL · Screenplay by WILLIAM PETER BLATTY based on his novel
From Warner Bros. A Warner Communications Company   R RESTRICTED Under 17 requires accompanying Parent or Adult Guardian

WORLD PREMIERE WEDNESDAY **CINEMA I** 3rd Ave. at 60th St
                                                       PL 3·6022

Blatty's 'The Exorcist' Comes to the Screen

THE EXORCIST, directed by William Friedkin; produced and written by William Peter Blatty, based on his novel; executive producer, Noel Marshall; director of photography, Owen Roizman (Iraq sequences, Billy Williams); supervising film editor, J. J. Leondopoulos; editors, Evan Lottman, Norman Gay; distributed by Warner Brothers. Running time: 121 minutes. At the Cinema I Theater, Third Avenue near 60th Street. This film has been classified R.

Chris MacNeil	Ellen Burstyn
Father Merrin	Max von Sydow
Lt. Kinderman	Lee J. Cobb
Sharon	Kitty Winn
Burke Dennings	Jack MacGowran
Father Karras	Jason Miller
Regan	Linda Blair
Father Dyer	Rev. William O'Malley
President of University	Rev. T. Bermingham

By VINCENT CANBY

The Georgetown dinner party being given by Chris MacNeil (Ellen Burstyn), a Hollywood movie actress making a film in Washington, is going beautifully, with diplomats, astronauts, Senators and show people carrying on in high style. A movie director gets drunk and tries to beat up the butler while a swinging Jesuit priest plays the piano for a sing-along.

Everything is as it should be until Regan (Linda Blair), Chris's 12-year-old daughter, appears in the middle of the drawing room in her nightdress. As Chris watches appalled, Regan fixes her eyes on the astronaut, urinates on the floor and says:

"You're going to die up there."

That's more or less the first big scene in William Friedkin's film version of "The Exorcist," a chunk of elegant occultist claptrap that opened yesterday at the Cinema I. However, lots of other peculiar things have gone on before. A statue in the Catholic church down the street has been desecrated. Little Regan's bed has been bouncing around so antically she's been unable to sleep at night, and there have been unexplained noises in the attic of Chris's Georgetown mansion.

The devil, it seems, for all his supposed powers, can't break and enter without sounding like Laurel and Hardy trying to move a piano.

"The Exorcist," the story of the attempts to save the life of the demonically possessed Regan, is a practically impossible film to sit through, but not necessarily because it treats diabolism with the kind of dumb piety movie makers once lavished on the stories of saints.

It establishes a new low for grotesque special effects, all of which, I assume, have some sort of religious approval since two Jesuit priests, who are listed as among the film's technical advisers, also appear in the film as actors.

Among the sights to which the audience is treated are Regan, her face contorted and parched by the devil inside, vomiting what looks to be condensed split-pea soup onto an exorcising priest, and her paroxysms of fury as she jabs a crucifix into herself and shoves her mother's head down under her bloodied nightgown. In the context of this kind of spectacular nonsense, a carefully detailed sequence showing the child undergoing an encephalogram is almost therapeutic.

William Peter Blatty, who produced the film and adapted his best-selling novel for the screen, has succeeded in leaving out very few of the kind of ridiculous details that, I suspect, would have earned a less expensive, more skeptical film an X rating instead of the R rating that mysteriously has been achieved.

"The Exorcist" is not an unintelligently put-together film, which makes one all the more impatient with it.

The producer and the director have gone whole hog on (and over) their budget, which included the financing of a location trip to Iraq to shoot a lovely, eerie prefatory sequence at an archeological dig that is, as far as I can see, not especially essential to the business that comes after.

The cast is made up of some excellent actors: Ellen Burstyn (who is becoming America's answer to Glenda Jackson), Max von Sydow as the old Catholic priest who also functions as chief exorcist, the late Jack MacGowran as the director of the film within, Jason Miller as the priest who attains success through imitation of Jesus, and Lee J. Cobb as a kindly Jewish detective.

The care that Mr. Friedkin and Mr. Blatty have taken with the physical production, and with the rhythm of the narrative, which achieves a certain momentum through a lot of fancy, splintery cross-cutting, is obviously intended to persuade us to, suspend belief. But to what end? To marvel at the extent to which audiences will go to escape boredom by shock and insult.

According to trade reports, "The Exorcist" cost about $10-million. The money could have been better spent subsidizing a couple of beds at the Paine-Whitney Clinic.

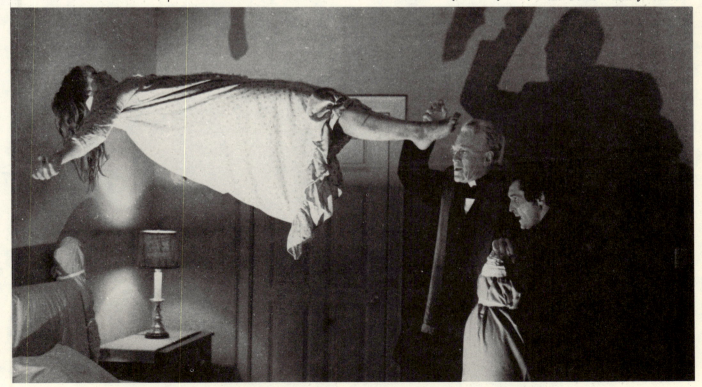

Max von Sydow and Jason Miller attempting to expel the devil from Linda Blair in a scene from *The Exorcist*.

Ruby Keeler makes her motion picture debut in Busby Berkeley's *42d Street*.

"42d Street."

Putting On a Show.

42D STREET, based on a novel by Bradford Ropes; directed by Lloyd Bacon; songs by Hal Dubin and Harry Warren; a Warner Brothers production. At the Strand.

Julian Marsh	Warner Baxter
Dorothy Brock	Bebe Daniels
Pat Denning	George Brent
Lorraine Fleming	Una Merkel
Peggy Sawyer	Ruby Keeler
Abner Dillon	Guy Kibbee
Barry	Ned Sparks
Billy Lawler	Dick Powell
Ann	Ginger Rogers
MacElroy	Allen Jenkins
The actor	Henry B. Walthall
Terry	Edward J. Nugent
Jerry	Harry Akst
Leading man	Clarence Nordstrom
Jones	Robert McWade
Andy Lee	George E. Stone
Song writer	Al Dubin
Song writer	Harry Warren

The liveliest and one of the most tuneful screen musical comedies that has come out of Hollywood was presented last night by the Warner Brothers at the Strand. It is known as "42d Street," the story being an adaptation of Bradford Ropes's novel of the same name, and the songs having been contributed by Al Dubin and Harry Warren. Although it has its artfully serious moments, it is for the most part a merry affair and in it Ruby Keeler (Mrs. Al Jolson) makes her motion picture début. Her ingratiating personality, coupled with her dances and songs adds to the zest of this offering. It is a film which reveals the forward strides made in this particular medium since the first screen musical features came to Broadway.

Although it has its boisterous moments, "42nd Street" is invariably entertaining. Part of the action is backstage training for a music show titled "Pretty Lady," and part is the first performance of the stage production, with Miss Keeler as Peggy Sawyer. Peggy substitutes with marked success for the original star, Dorothy Brock, who on the previous night fractured her ankle.

This feature begins cleverly and ends without the usual hugging and kissing scene, for which one can be thankful. Warner Baxter delivers one of the outstanding portrayals of his screen career as Julian Marsh, the stage director of "Pretty Lady." Mr. Baxter actually gives the impression of a very tired man, exhausted with rehearsals and dissatisfaction with the dancers and others in the show. Bebe Daniels appears as Dorothy Brock, in which rôle she is heard singing from time to time during the preparation of the musical comedy. Una Merkel impersonates a saucy chorus girl who is always ready with a smart retort for any impertinent young man.

The show within the story is imaginatively staged, with clever groupings of dancers and fine photography. In the course of this offering one bears such catchy musical compositions as "You're Getting to Be a Habit With Me," "I'm Young and Healthy," "Shuffle Off to Buffalo" and "Forty-second Street." One of the best of these pieces of music is "Shuffle Off to Buffalo," the action during the singing of it occurring on a train bound for Niagara Falls. It is an excellent example of stagecraft.

The wisecracks are delivered with the necessary flare, and the throng that packed the theatre last night laughed heartily over the misfortunes of Abner Dillon (Guy Kibbee) and the pert comments of various persons. Mr. Dillon is a man of means, who has put some $70,000 into the show, chiefly because he is most of the time greatly interested in Dorothy Brock. This young woman happens to be infatuated with Pat Denning, played by George Brent, and after more wine than is good for her she utters some stinging truths. And it is during this sequence that she falls and fractures her ankle.

Imagine Marsh's feelings, when, after being anxious over the outcome of the show and really only sure of Miss Brock's capabilities, he hears that she has suffered the accident! Then Peggy is elected to fill the principal rôle, and although she does not seem very promising at first, she scores a hit when the time comes. And Marsh at the stage entrance of the theatre hears his name mentioned as one of those who "gets all the breaks."

There was a time when spectators were satiated with backstage stuff, but here it is pictured brightly and with a degree of authenticity that makes it diverting. There are the familiar types who appear during rehearsals and also the assistant stage manager, the sleepy pianist, the dance director and so forth.

Mr. Kibbee is thoroughly believable as the old soak with more dollars than he ought to be trusted with. Ned Sparks, who is seen too rarely in pictures nowadays, does good work as a cigar-chewing theatrical expert. In fact, all those in the cast do very well.

After a most interesting short subject dealing with sharks and other fish, some of the Warner players were called to the stage. They included Tom Mix, Joe E. Brown, Bette Davis, Glenda Farrell, Preston Foster, Lyle Talbot, Eleanor Holm and Laura La Plante.

M. H.

Bebe Daniels and Dick Powell "rehearsing" one of their dance scenes in *42d Street*.

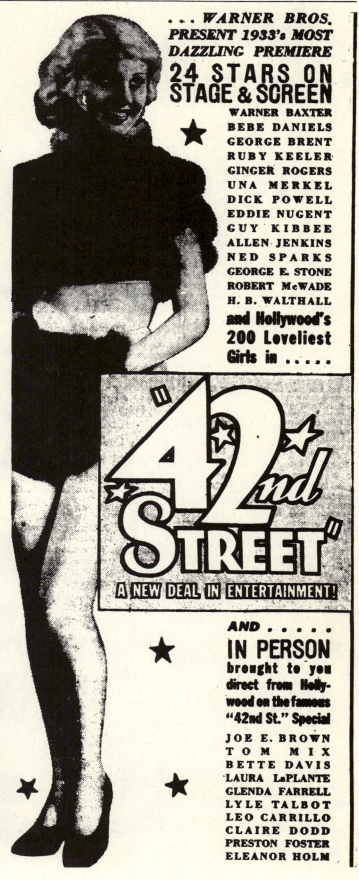

... WARNER BROS. PRESENT 1933's MOST DAZZLING PREMIERE

24 STARS ON STAGE & SCREEN

WARNER BAXTER
BEBE DANIELS
GEORGE BRENT
RUBY KEELER
GINGER ROGERS
UNA MERKEL
DICK POWELL
EDDIE NUGENT
GUY KIBBEE
ALLEN JENKINS
NED SPARKS
GEORGE E. STONE
ROBERT McWADE
H. B. WALTHALL
and Hollywood's 200 Loveliest Girls in .....

"42nd STREET"

A NEW DEAL IN ENTERTAINMENT!

AND .....

IN PERSON

brought to you direct from Hollywood on the famous "42nd St." Special

JOE E. BROWN
TOM MIX
BETTE DAVIS
LAURA LaPLANTE
GLENDA FARRELL
LYLE TALBOT
LEO CARRILLO
CLAIRE DODD
PRESTON FOSTER
ELEANOR HOLM

A Man-Made Monster in Grand Guignol Film Story

FRANKENSTEIN, based on Mary Wollstonecroft Shelley's book and adapted from John L. Balderston's play; directed by James Whale; a Universal production. At the Mayfair.

Frankenstein	Colin Clive
Elizabeth	Mae Clarke
Victor	John Boles
The Monster	Boris Karloff
Dr. Waldman	Edward Van Sloan
The Dwarf	Dwight Frye
The Baron	Frederick Kerr
The Burgomaster	Lionel Belmore
Peasant Father	Michael Mark
Mary the Child	Marilyn Harris

By MORDAUNT HALL.

Out of John L. Balderston's stage conception of the Mary Shelley classic, "Frankenstein," James Whale, producer of "Journey's End" as a play and as a film, has wrought a stirring grand-guignol type of picture, one that aroused so much excitement at the Mayfair yesterday that many in the audience laughed to cover their true feelings.

It is an artistically conceived work in which Colin Clive, the Captain Stanhope of the London stage production of the R. C. Sherriff play, was brought from England to act the rôle of Frankenstein, the man who fashions a monster that walks and thinks. It is naturally a morbid, gruesome affair, but it is something to keep the spectator awake, for during its most spine-chilling periods it exacts attention. It was Carl Laemmle, head of Universal, the firm responsible for this current picture, who presented Lon Chaney in "The Hunchback of Notre Dame," and while, as everybody knows, Quasimodo was a repellent sight, he was a creature for sympathy compared to the hideous monster in this "Frankenstein." Boris Karloff undertakes the Frankenstein creature and his make-up can be said to suit anybody's demands. He does not portray a robot but a monster made out of human bodies, and the reason given here for his murderous onslaughts is that Frankenstein's Man Friday stole an abnormal brain after he had broken the glass bowl containing the normal one. This Frankenstein does not know.

No matter what one may say about the melodramatic ideas here, there is no denying that it is far and away the most effective thing of its kind. Beside it "Dracula" is tame and, incidentally, "Dracula" was produced by the same firm, which is also to issue in film form Poe's "Murders in the Rue Morgue."

There are scenes in Frankenstein's laboratory in an old windmill, somewhere in Germany, where, during a severe electric storm, the young scientist finally perceives life showing in the object on an operating table. It is not long after that the monster walks, uttering a sound like the mooing of a cow. And then ensues the idea that while Frankenstein is proud of the creature he has made and boasts loudly about his achievement, he soon has reason to fear the brute, and in course of time it attacks Frankenstein's faithful servant, a bowed and bent little man, and kills him.

The scenes swing here and there to the Baron, Frankenstein's father, efficiently acted by Frederick Kerr, to those of a friend named Victor, played by John Boles, and to Elizabeth, Frankenstein's fiancée, portrayed by Mae Clarke. This is a relief, but they are all anxious about what Frankenstein is doing. They learn at the psychological moment, and have then still greater anxiety for Frankenstein.

Imagine the monster, with black eyes, heavy eyelids, a square head, huge feet that are covered with matting, long arms protruding from the sleeves of a coat, walking like an automaton, and then think of the fear in a village, and especially of the scientist, when it is learned that the monster has escaped from the windmill. It is beheld parading through the woods, sitting down playing with a little girl, and finally being pursued by a mob with flaming torches, for apparently fire is the only thing that causes the monster to hesitate.

The sounds of the cries of the pursuers and the strange noises made by the monster add to the disturbing nature of the scenes, and in a penultimate episode there is the struggle between the monster and Frankenstein. As a concession to the motion picture audience, Frankenstein is not killed, but he is badly injured. Two endings were made for this production, and at the eleventh hour it was decided to put in the one in which Frankenstein lives, because it was explained that sympathy is elicited for the young scientist and that the spectators would leave disappointed if the author's last chapter was adhered to.

As for the monster, he is burned when the villagers set fire to the windmill. From the screen comes the sound of the crackling of the blazing woodwork, the hue and cry of the frightened populace and the queer sounds of the dying monster.

Mr. Clive adds another fine performance to his list. He succeeds in impressing upon one the earnestness and also the sanity of the scientist, in spite of Frankenstein's gruesome exploits. Lionel Belmore gives an easy performance as the town burgomaster. Miss Clarke, Edward Van Sloan and Dwight Frye also serve well.

Boris Karloff as the Monster, *Frankenstein*.

THE MAN WHO MADE A MONSTER!

FRANKENSTEIN

A MONSTER...CREATED WITH A DIABOLICAL CUNNING... BY A MAD SCIENTIST...

A creature — half man — half fiend — a soulless wretch with a mechanical brain — knowing every human sensation except the love of woman.

To have seen "Frankenstein" is to wear a badge of courage.

No one seated during final reel!

A UNIVERSAL PICTURE

COLIN CLIVE
MAE CLARKE
JOHN BOLES
BORIS KARLOFF

No Thriller Ever Made Can Begin to Touch It!

Also Pathé News

RKO MAYFAIR
BROADWAY AT 47th · BRyant 9-6851-6892

STARTS TODAY
All Seats
10 A.M. til 1 P.M. 35¢

The creator, Dr. Frankenstein (Colin Clive), meets his creation, the Monster (Boris Karloff).

'The French Connection'

By VINCENT CANBY

The ads say that the time is just right for an out and out thriller like this, and I guess that you are supposed to think that a good old kind of movie has none too soon come around again. But "The French Connection," which opened yesterday at Loew's State 2 and Loew's Orpheum, is in fact a very good new kind of movie, and that in spite of its being composed of such ancient material as cops and crooks, with thrills and chases, and lots of shoot 'em up.

It concerns a very large shipment of unusually pure heroin that has been hidden somewhere in a late model Lincoln Continental for transport from Marseilles to New York City. Once in New York, it must, of course, be sold. And the point of sale becomes the point of ulti-

THE FRENCH CONNECTION, directed by William Friedkin, screenplay by Ernest Tidyman, based on the book by Robin Moore; director of photography, Owen Roizman; music by Don Ellis; produced by Philip D'Antoni for release by 20th Century-Fox. At Loew's State 2, Broadway at 45th Street, and Loew's Orpheum, Third Avenue and 86th Street. Running time: 104 minutes. (The Motion Picture Association of America's Production Code and Rating Administration classifies this film: "R—restricted, under 17 requires accompanying parent or adult guardian.")

Jimmy Doyle	Gene Hackman
Alain Charnier	Fernando Rey
Buddy Russo	Roy Scheider
Sal Boca	Tony LoBianco
Pierre Nicoli	Marcel Bozzuffi

mate encounter between the shipment's proprietor, a suave, civilized, elusive Frenchman (Fernando Rey), and a narcotics squad detective (Gene Hackman) who knows that a big deal is in the works and means to make a kill.

The Hackman characterization, one of the most successful in his career, and the only one that is allowed to emerge in much detail, virtually defines the attitude of "The French Connection." Hard-nosed, pork-pie-hatted, vulgar, a tough cop in the latest measure of a fine tradition, he exists neither to rise nor to fall, to excite neither pity nor terror—but to function. To function in New York City is its own heroism, and the film recognizes that, but it is not the heroism of conventional gesture, and so even the most conventional excitements of "The French Connection" carry with them a built-in air of fatigue.

I don't mean that they are not exciting. "The French Connection" is a film of almost incredible suspense, and it includes, among a great many chilling delights, the most brilliantly executed chase sequence I have ever

seen. But the conditions for the suspense (indeed, the conditions of the chase—to intercept a hijacked elevated train) carry with them the potential for failure not of this particular action, but of all action in the great doomed city that is the film's real subject. From the moment, very early on, when Hackman first pistol-whips a black pusher, you know that the world is cursed and that everybody playing out his allotted role is cursed along with it.

●

In a more pretentious and less perceptive film, destinies might have turned tragic. In "The French Connection" they become all but invisible.

The whole movie has slightly the look of being background material, or maybe excellent pre-credit material, for another movie. It moves at magnificent speed, and exhausts itself in movement. The central characters repeatedly appear as if out of the city's mass and then disappear into it again — a superb conception for an action of difficult pursuit, but one that never allows the luxury of personal identification.

That is why only Gene Hackman surfaces as a character, although there are the fragments of many good performance — seen as if across the street, outside the window, or at the other end of the subway platform.

There are also faults: a murder too many, some shaky motivation among the bad guys, a degree of coldness that perhaps even exceeds the requirements of the cold intelligence that controls the film.

But "The French Connection" is mostly a credit to everyone who helped shape it. This would include Ernest Tidyman, who wrote the screenplay and who also wrote "Shaft," Owen Roizman, the cinematographer, and William Friedkin, a director whose previous work ("The Birthday Party," "The Night They raided Minsky's... etc.) may not have prepared anyone for the excellence of this.

"There was one thing he wouldn't do... even for a woman!"

"Prew was a hardhead, ...the tougher it got, the better he liked it!"

BURT LANCASTER · MONTGOMERY CLIFT

"Looks colder'n an iceberg, but she knows the score. And I know the guy who taught her."

"He's such a comical little runt. He makes me want to cry while I'm laughin' at him."

DEBORAH KERR · FRANK SINATRA · DONNA REED

ON THE GIANT PANORAMIC SCREEN WITH STEREOPHONIC SOUND!

"Sure I'm nice to you. We're nice to all the boys."

Screen Play by DANIEL TARADASH · Based upon the novel by JAMES JONES · Produced by BUDDY ADLER · Directed by FRED ZINNEMANN · A COLUMBIA PICTURE

EXTRA! STARS IN PERSON! Meet the glamorous stars of "FROM HERE TO ETERNITY" TODAY in the Capitol lobby! DONNA REED from 10 to 11 A.M., and DEBORAH KERR, from 8:30 to 9:30 P.M., will greet their fans and distribute signed photos!

WORLD PREMIERE TODAY 10 A.M. · **COOL CAPITOL** B'way at 51st St.

"From Here to Eternity' Bows at Capitol With Huge Cast, Five Starring Roles

FROM HERE TO ETERNITY, screen play by Daniel Taradash; based on the novel by James Jones; directed by Fred Zinnemann; produced by Buddy Adler for Columbia. At the Capitol.

Sgt. Milton Warden	Burt Lancaster
Robert E. Lee Prewitt	Montgomery Clift
Karen Holmes	Deborah Kerr
Angelo Maggio	Frank Sinatra
Alma (Lorene)	Donna Reed
Capt. Dana Holmes	Philip Ober
Sgt. Leva	Mickey Shaughnessy
Mazzioli	Harry Bellaver
Sgt. "Fatso" Judson	Ernest Borgnine
Sgt. Maylon Stark	George Reeves
Sgt. Ike Galovitch	John Dennis
Sgt. Pete Karelsen	Tim Ryan
Mrs. Kipfer	Barbara Morrison
Georgette	Kristine Miller
Annette	Jean Willes
Sal Anderson	Merle Travis
Treadwell	Arthur Keegan
Sgt. Baldy Thom	Claude Akins
Sgt. Turp Thornhill	Robert Karnes
Sgt. Henderson	Robert Wilke
Cpl. Champ Wilson	Douglas Henderson
Friday Clark	Don Dubbins
Cpl. Paluso	John Cason
Capt. Ross	John Bryant

Out of "From Here to Eternity," a novel whose anger and compassion stirred a post-war reading public as few such works have, Columbia and a company of sensitive hands have forged a film almost as towering and persuasive as its source. Although it naturally lacks the depth and fullness of the 430,000 words and 850 pages of the book, this dramatization of phases of the military life in a peacetime army, which was unveiled at the Capitol yesterday, captures the essential spirit of the James Jones study. And, as a job of editing, emending, re-arranging and purifying a volume bristling with brutality and obscenities, "From Here to Eternity" stands as a shining example of truly professional moviemaking.

As may be surmised, credit for this metamorphosis cannot be localized. The team of scenarist, director, producer and cast has managed to transfer convincingly the muscularity of the basically male society with which the book dealt; the poignance and futility of the love lives of the professional soldiers involved, as well as the indictment of commanding officers whose selfishness can break men devoted to soldiering. They are trapped in a world they made and one that defeats them. Above all, it is a portrait etched in truth and without the stigma of calculated viciousness.

Cleaves To Author's Thesis

Although the incisive script fashioned by Daniel Taradash sidesteps such matters as the shocking "Stockade" chapters of the book, it fundamentally cleaves to the author's thesis. Set in Schofield Barracks in Oahu, Hawaii, in the months preceding the attack on Pearl Harbor, it is the tragic story of the youthful Pvt. Robert E. Lee Prewitt, hard-headed Kentuckian whose convictions are strong enough to force him to forego his passionate devotion to both the bugle and prize fighting despite the knowledge that his superior officer, Capt. Dana Holmes, and his crew of athletes will give him "The Treatment."

Frank Sinatra as Angelo Maggio and Montgomery Clift.

Cast Plays Roles Well

Fortunately the cast members measure up to their assignments. In Burt Lancaster, the producer has got a top kick to the manner born, a man whose capabilities are obvious and whose code is hard and strange but never questionable. He is a "thirty-year man" respected by his superiors and the G. I.'s with whom he fights and plays. His view of officers leaves him only with hatred of the caste although he could easily achieve rank, which would solve his romantic problem. But he is honest enough to eschew it and lose the only love he has known.

Montgomery Clift adds another sensitive portrait to an already imposing gallery with his portrayal of Prewitt. Since he has blinded a man in the ring, no carefully planned scheme of harassment will get him in again. And, since he considers it a slight when he has been passed over as a bugler who once played taps at Arlington National Cemetery, he deems it his right to be "busted" from corporal to conform to his credo that "if a man don't go his own way, he's nothin'."

Although it is a deviation from the norm, Frank Sinatra is excellent in the non-singing role of Angelo Maggio, a characterization rich in comic vitality and genuine pathos. Deborah Kerr, heretofore the genteel lady in films, contributes a completely tender stint as the passionate Karen Holmes, defeated by a callous mate and a fruitless marriage, who clings to a doomed love.

While Donna Reed is not precisely the picture of a lady of the evening, her delineation of Lorene, wracked between a desire to be "proper" and her anomalous affair with Prewitt, is polished and professional. Although Philip Ober's weak captain is a comparatively slight and shallow role, the company of G. I.'s and the Schofield Barracks, where some of the film was shot, gave the drama and the authenticity required.

"From Here to Eternity" is being shown on a wide screen and with Stereophonic sound. It does not need these enhancements. It has scope, power and impact without them.   A. W.

It is the story, also, of First Sgt. Milton Warden, top kick of the company, a rough-hewn pillar of strength whose know-how guides and supports the pompous and philandering captain and the admiring contingent of G. I.'s in his command. It is the tale of sinewy Angelo Maggio, enlisted man from the sidewalks of New York whose brave revolt against the confinements of the Army system ends in tragedy. And it is the account of the ill-fated affair between Karen Holmes, the captain's wife, and Sergeant Warden, as well as the romance of Private Prewitt and Lorene, whose charms were purveyed in Mrs. Kipfer's New Congress Club.

Credit Fred Zinnemann with an expert directorial achievement in maintaining these various involvements on equal and lucid levels. While each yarn is pertinent and commands attention, the conflicts of its principals are fayed neatly into a compact whole. And the climactic strafing of Schofield Barracks is a fittingly explosive finish to the two hours of uncluttered drama culled from an immense and sometimes sprawling work of fiction.

Montgomery Clift as Robert E. Lee Prewitt.

Burt Lancaster as Sergeant Warden and Deborah Kerr as Karen Holmes, the Captain's wife.

Adolphe Menjou and Pat O'Brien are the dedicated newspapermen while Mary Brian just looks on in a scene from *The Front Page.*

Newspaper Melodrama

THE FRONT PAGE, based on the play by Ben Hecht and Charles MacArthur; directed by Lewis Milestone; produced by Howard Hughes. At the Rivoli Theatre.

Walter Burns	Adolphe Menjou
Hildy Johnson	Pat O'Brien
Peggy	Mary Brian
Bensinger	Edward Everett Horton
Murphy	Walter Catlett
Earl Williams	George E. Stone
Molly	Mae Clarke
Pincus	Slim Summerville
Kruger	Matt Moore
McCue	Frank McHugh
Sheriff Hartman	Clarence H. Wilson
Schwartz	Fred Howard
Wilson	Phil Tead
Endicott	Eugene Strong
Woodenshoes	Spencer Charters
Diamond Louie	Maurice Black
Mrs. Grant	Effie Ellsler
The Mayor	James Gordon
Jacobi	Dick Alexander

By MORDAUNT HALL.

A witty and virile talking picture has been wrought from "The Front Page," the play of Chicago newspaper life by Ben Hecht and Charles MacArthur. This film, which is now at the Rivoli, differs but little in construction from the parent work. It is a fast-paced entertainment and, while its humor is frequently harsh, it assuredly won favor with the audience yesterday afternoon.

Adolphe Menjou, who has hitherto confined himself to the impersonation of suave philanderers, steps outside those bounds and portrays Walter Burns, the keen managing editor of a Chicago daily, a rôle that was acted on the stage by Osgood Perkins. Under the direction of Lewis Milestone, producer of "All Quiet on the Western Front," Mr. Menjou does excellent work. He may be a little too gentle occasionally, but in most of his scenes he is true to the character, even to digging his hands in his trouser pockets, raving about news leads and spouting expletives.

Pat O'Brien, a newcomer to the screen, is entrusted with the impersonation of Hildy Johnson, played on the stage by Lee Tracy. Mr. O'Brien gives quite a good account of himself as the reporter who, when he is about to abandon newspaper work, harkens to the call of a good story.

Although some of the minor characters are not quite as effective as they were on the stage, there is as good an impression of them as film footage permits. They indulge in their argot and have their own interpretations of the news of a story, this being set forth chiefly by the descriptions used by them in telephoning their news bulletins from the press room of the Criminal Courts Building in the Windy City.

In the course of this sturdy melodrama, Earle Williams, a convict who was to be executed, escapes, and general excitement reigns in the Criminal Courts Building. Sheriff Hartman is thoroughly humiliated, for the prisoner got away through having borrowed Hartman's pistol while demonstrating where he (Williams) stood during the moment of the crime of which he was convicted. Politics is mixed with newspaper activities when the Mayor and Hartman try to bribe a messenger who brings word of Williams's reprieve by the Governor.

It is emphatically humorous when Williams is hidden in a roll-top desk in the press room by Johnson and Burns, whose sole desire is to have a news scoop. And eventually there comes Hartman's discovery of the prisoner and the handcuffing of Johnson and Burns for helping a criminal to escape.

In a clever manner the producers have succeeded in retaining many more of the lines of the play than was anticipated. The censor is in more than one instance virtually defied through ingenious ideas.

Edward Everett Horton plays the dreamy, poetic reporter, Bensinger, in which rôle he is quite successful. Mary Brian is Peggy. Clarence H. Wilson gives a sterling performance as Hartman. Matt Moore, Slim Summerville, Spencer Charters and Walter Catlett do their share to make this a rousing entertainment.

IT'S DYNAMITE!

Explosive Drama!

T.N.T. Entertainment!

It'll blow the town apart!

The biggest picture scoop Broadway has witnessed in years — A great play now greater as a talkie!

From Ben Hecht's and Charles MacArthur's Famous Stage Success!

"The FRONT PAGE"

A United Artists Picture

Made by Howard Hughes who produced "Hell's Angels."

Directed by the director of "All Quiet On The Western Front"

with

ADOLPHE MENJOU   MARY BRIAN   PAT O'BRIEN   MATT MOORE
GEORGE STONE   MAE CLARKE   WALTER CATLETT
EDWARD EVERETT HORTON   SLIM SUMMERVILLE

What happens when a man has to choose between two loves — His work — His sweetheart. How he solves it tells the most electrifying rapid-fire dramatic story you have ever seen.

WORLD PREMIERE TODAY at 9 A. M.

Broadway at 49th

RIVOLI

Popular Prices · Continuous Performances

The Front Page with Adolphe Manjou and Pat O'Brien.

Darryl F. Zanuck
PRESENTS

GREGORY PECK
DOROTHY McGUIRE
JOHN GARFIELD

in Laura Z. Hobson's

Gentleman's Agreement

20th century-fox

with

Celeste HOLM · Anne REVERE · June HAVOC · Albert DEKKER · Jane WYATT · Dean STOCKWELL

Produced by DARRYL F. ZANUCK   Screen Play by MOSS HART   Directed by ELIA KAZAN

STARTS
TODAY   BRANDT'S
MAYFAIR   DOORS
OPEN 8:30 A.M.
EXTRA LATE SHOW NIGHTLY

7th Avenue & 47th Street

'Gentleman's Agreement,' Study of Anti-Semitism, Is Feature at Mayfair — Gregory Peck Plays Writer Acting as Jew

GENTLEMAN'S AGREEMENT, based on the novel by Laura Z. Hobson; screen play by Moss Hart; directed by Elia Kazan; produced by Darryl F. Zanuck for Twentieth Century-Fox Pictures. At the Mayfair.

Phil Green.....................Gregory Peck
Kathy........................Dorothy McGuire
Dave..........................John Garfield
Anne.........................Celeste Holm
Mrs. Green....................Anne Revere
Miss Wales....................June Havoc
John Minify...................Albert Dekker
Jane..........................Jane Wyatt
Tommy.........................Dean Stockwell
Dr. Craigie...................Nicholas Joy
Professor Lieberman...........Sam Jaffe
Personnel Manager.............Harold Vermilyea
Bill Payson...................Ransom M. Sherman
Hotel Manager.................Roy Roberts
Mrs. Minify...................Kathleen Lockhart
Bert McAnny...................Curt Conway
Bill..........................John Newland
Weisman.......................Robert Warwick
Miss Miller...................Louise Lorimer
Tingler.......................Howard Negley
Apartment Superintendent......Victor Kilian
Harry.........................Frank Wilcox
Receptionist..................Marlyn Monk
Maitre D......................Wilton Graff
Clerk.........................Morgan Farley

By BOSLEY CROWTHER

The shabby cruelties of anti-Semitism which were sharply and effectively revealed within the restricted observation of Laura Z. Hobson's "Gentleman's Agreement" have now been exposed with equal candor and even greater dramatic forcefulness in the motion-picture version of the novel which came to the Mayfair yesterday. In fact, every point about prejudice which Miss Hobson had to make in her book has been made with superior illustration and more graphic demonstration in the film, so that the sweep of her moral indignation is not only widened but intensified thereby.

Essentially, Miss Hobson's was a story of the emotional disturbance that occurs within a man who elects, for the sake of getting a magazine article, to tell people that he is a Jew and who experiences first-hand, as a consequence, the shock and pain of discriminations and social snubs. And it was the story of this same man's parallel romance with a supposedly unbigoted girl who, for all her intellectual convictions, can't quite shake the vicious prejudices of her particular group.

Shaped by Moss Hart into a screen play of notable nimbleness and drive, the bewilderments of Miss Hobson's hero become absorbing and vital issues on the screen and the eventual outcome of his romance becomes a matter of serious concern. For such aspects of anti-Semitism as professional bias against Jews, discrimination by swanky hotels and even the calling of ugly names have been frankly and clearly demonstrated for the inhuman failings that they are and the peril of a normal and happy union being wrecked on the ragged edges of prejudice is affectingly raised.

Indeed, on the grounds of the original, every good and courageous thing has been done by Twentieth Century-Fox, the producer, to make "Gentleman's Agreement" a sizzling film. A fine cast, brilliant direction by Elia Kazan and intrepidity in citing such names as Bilbo, Rankin and Gerald L. K. Smith give it realism and authenticity. To millions of people throughout the country, it should bring an ugly and disturbing issue to light.

But the weaknesses of the original are also apparent in the film —the most obvious of which is the limited and specialized area observed. Although the hero of the story is apparently assigned to write a definitive article on anti-Semitism in the United States, it is evident that his explorations are narrowly confined to the upper-class social and professional level to which he is immediately exposed. And his discoveries are chiefly in the nature of petty bourgeois rebuffs, with no inquiry into the devious cultural mores from which they spring.

Likewise it is amazing that the writer who undertakes this probe should be so astonished to discover that anti-Semitism is cruel. Assuming that he is a journalist of some perception and scope, his imagination should have fathomed most of these sudden shocks long since. And although the role is crisply and agreeably played by Gregory Peck, it is, in a careful analysis, an extraordinarily naive role.

Also the role of his young lady, which Dorothy McGuire affectingly plays, is written to link in a disquieting little touch of "snob appeal." Maybe the image of the actress in conjunction with the "station-wagon set" is a bit reminiscent of "Claudia" and her juvenile attitudes. But the suggestion of social aspiration—and accomplishment—confuses the issues very much.

It is likewise this reviewer's opinion that John Garfield's performance of a young Jew, lifelong friend of the hero, is a bit too mechanical and that a scene with Sam Jaffe as a Jewish scientist introduces a false note of low comedy. However, June Havoc, Albert Dekker, Celeste Holm and Anne Revere are variously brittle and competent as other characters, so we'll settle for a draw.

The film still has abundant meaning and should be fully and widely enjoyed.

Celeste Holm and Gregory Peck in *Gentlemen's Agreement*.

'Gigi,' Fair Lady of Filmdom

The Cast

GIGI, screenplay by Alan Jay Lerner; based on the novel by Colette; songs with lyrics by Mr. Lerner and music by Frederick Loewe; directed by Vincente Minnelli; produced by Arthur Freed; presented by Metro-Goldwyn-Mayer. At the Royale Theatre (Forty-fifth Street, West of Broadway). Running time: 116 minutes.

Gigi	Leslie Caron
Honore Lachaille	Maurice Chevalier
Gaston Lachaille	Louis Jourdan
Mme. Alvarez	Hermione Gingold
Liane D'Exelmans	Eva Gabor
Sandomir	Jacques Bergerac
Aunt Alicia	Isabel Jeans
Manuel	John Abbott

By BOSLEY CROWTHER

THERE won't be much point in anybody trying to produce a film of "My Fair Lady" for awhile, because Arthur Freed has virtually done it with "Gigi," which had a grand première at the Royale last night.

On an obviously blank-check commission from Metro-Goldwyn-Mayer, which has long had the notion that money is just something you spend on musical films, he has taken a popular Colette novel, already done as a French movie and a Broadway play, and placed it coyly in the hands of two wizards, Alan Jay Lerner and Frederick Loewe. Maybe Mr. Freed didn't realize it, but they just happen to be the gentlemen who wrote the book, lyrics and music for "My Fair Lady," now in its third year on Broadway.

Also, by possible coincidence, he had Cecil Beaton do the production design, costumes and scenery, for presentation in color and CinemaScope. Mr. Beaton just happens to be the gentleman who designed the "My Fair Lady" costumes.

And what do you think they've come up with? Well, you will probably be amazed —as we're sure Mr. Freed was—to discover they've come up with a musical film that bears such a basic resemblance to "My Fair Lady" that the authors may want to sue themselves.

We began to perceive it faintly almost at the start with the colorful introduction of the lively heroine. She's a bright little teen-age tomboy living in Paris at the century's turn and highly resistant to the notion, insisted upon by her grandmother and great-aunt, that she should grow up.

Particularly is she resistant to their intention that she should learn all the graces and qualities of a lady so that she may become an accomplished courtesan. The idea of love repels her. She even sings a little song indicating her disgust with Parisians.

Does this remind you of anyone?

Then, as the picture continues and the hero is clearly built up as an elegant, blasé young bachelor with an amiable indifference toward the child, it is plain that he's being set for dazzling when the butterfly bursts from the cocoon. It does and he is— all in the spirit of good, racy, romantic fun. And to clinch it, he sings a song called "Gigi," which let's it be generally known that he's grown accustomed to her face and other allurements. It is a strikingly reminiscent tune.

But don't think this point of resemblance is made in criticism of the film, for "Gigi" is a charming entertainment that can stand on its own two legs. It is not only a charming comprehension of the spicy confection of Colette, but it is also a lovely and lyrical enlargement upon that story's flavored mood and atmosphere.

Mr. Beaton's designs are terrific—a splurge of elegance and whim, offering fin-de-siècle Paris in an endless parade of plushy places and costumes. And within this fine frame of swanky settings, Vincente Minnelli has marshaled a cast to give a set of performances that, for quality and harmony, are superb.

Leslie Caron, the little lady who helped to make "Lili" a memorable film, gets something of the same sort of magic of youthful rapture as the heroine in this. Louis Jourdan is suave as the hero who holds out against her blossoming charms, and Maurice Chevalier is wonderfully easy as a mellowing boulevardier.

As the grandmother and great-aunt, Hermione Gingold and Isabel Jeans give elaborately humorous exhibitions of the airs and attitudes of ancient dames; Eva Gabor is posh as a passing mistress and John Abbott is droll as a valet.

Of Mr. Loewe's musical numbers, "Gigi" is probably the best, though M. Chevalier makes something quite beguiling of "Thank Heaven for Little Girls." He also imbues with cheerful poignance "I'm Glad I'm Not Young Anymore," and he and Miss Gingold sing a duet of wit and wisdom to "I Remember It Well." You will also find reminiscent the vastly colorful "Waltz at Maxim's."

Perhaps Messrs. Lerner, Loewe and Beaton have stolen "Gigi" from themselves, but they have no reason to regret or disguise it. They've left their "Lady" fingerprints for all to see.

Leslie Caron as the tomboy turned sophisticated Parisian in *Gigi*.

PREMIERE
TONIGHT 8:30 P.M.

OPENING NIGHT
SOLD OUT

The New Screen
Musical by
the Composers of
"My Fair Lady"

Gigi

M·G·M

AIR-CONDITIONED
ROYALE THEATRE
45th St. West of B'way

SEATS ON SALE 10 WEEKS IN ADVANCE

Moving and Brutal 'Godfather' Bows

By VINCENT CANBY

Taking a best-selling novel of more drive than genius (Mario Puzo's "The Godfather"), about a subject of something less than common experience (the Mafia), involving an isolated portion of one very particular ethnic group (first-generation and second-generation Italian-Americans), Francis Ford Coppola has made one of the most brutal and moving chronicles of American life ever designed within the limits of popular entertainment.

"The Godfather," which opened at five theaters here yesterday, is a superb Hollywood movie that was photographed mostly in New York (with locations in Las Vegas, Sicily and Hollywood). It's the gangster melodrama come-of-age, truly sorrowful and truly exciting, without the false piety of the films that flourished 40 years ago, scaring the delighted hell out of us while cautioning that crime doesn't (or, at least, shouldn't) pay.

●

It still doesn't, but the punishments suffered by the members of the Corleone Family aren't limited to sudden ambushes on street corners or to the more elaborately choreographed assassinations on thruways. They also include life-long sentences of ostracism in terrible, bourgeois confinement, of money and power but of not much more glory than can be obtained by the ability to purchase expensive bedroom suites, the kind that include everything from the rug on the floor to the pictures on the wall with, perhaps, a horrible satin bedspread thrown in.

Yet "The Godfather" is not quite that simple. It was Mr. Puzo's point, which has been made somehow more ambiguous and more interesting in the film, that the experience of the Corleone Family, as particular as it is, may be the mid-20th-century equivalent of the oil and lumber and railroad barons of 19th-century America. In the course of the 10 years of intra-Mafia gang wars (1945-1955) dramatized by the film, the Corleones are, in fact, inching toward social and financial respectability.

For the Corleones, the land of opportunity is America the Ugly, in which almost everyone who is not Sicilian or, more narrowly, not a Corleone, is a potential enemy. Mr. Coppola captures this feeling of remoteness

The Cast

THE GODFATHER, directed by Francis Ford Coppola; screenplay by Mario Puzo and Mr. Coppola, based on the novel by Mr. Puzo; director of photography, Gordon Willis; editors, William Reynolds and Peter Zinner; music composed by Nino Rota; produced by Albert S. Ruddy; distributed by Paramount Pictures. Running time: 175 minutes. At Loew's State I and II, Broadway at 45th Street; Loew's Orpheum and Cine Theaters, Third Avenue and 86th Street; and Loew's Tower East, Third Avenue, near 72d Street. The Motion Picture Association of America's Production Code and Rating Administration classifies this film "R—restricted, persons under 17 not admitted unless accompanied by a parent or adult guardian.")

Don Vito Corleone	Marlon Brando
Michael Corleone	Al Pacino
Sonny Corleone	James Caan
Clemenza	Richard Castellano
Tom Hagen	Robert Duvall
McCluskey	Sterling Hayden
Jack Woltz	John Marley
Barzini	Richard Conte
Kay Adams	Diane Keaton
Sollozzo	Al Lettieri
Tessio	Abe Vigoda
Connie Rizzi	Talia Shire
Carlo Rizzi	Gianni Russo
Fredo Corleone	John Cazale
Cuneo	Rudy Bond
Johnny Fontane	Al Martino
Mama Corleone	Morgana King

through the physical look of place and period, and through the narrative's point of view. "The Godfather" seems to take place entirely inside a huge smoky plastic dome, through which the Corleones see our real world only dimly.

Thus, at the crucial meeting of Mafia families, when the decision is made to take over the hard drug market, one old don argues in favor, saying he would keep the trade confined to blacks — "they are animals anyway."

This is all the more terrifying because, within their isolation, there is such a sense of love and honor, no matter how bizarre.

The film is affecting for many reasons, including the return of Marlon Brando, who has been away only in spirit, as Don Vito Corleone, the magnificent, shrewd, old Corleone patriarch. It's not a large role, but he is the key to the film, and to the contributions of all of the other performers, so many actors that it is impossible to give everyone his due.

Some, however, must be cited, especially Al Pacino, as the college-educated son who takes over the family business and becomes, in the process, an actor worthy to have Brando as his father; as well as James Caan, Richard Castellano, Robert Duvall, Al Lettieri, Abe Vigoda, Gianni Russo, Al Martino and Morgana King. Mr. Coppola has not denied the characters' Italian heritage (as can be gathered by a quick reading of the cast), and by emphasizing it, he has made a movie that transcends its

immediate milieu and genre.

"The Godfather" plays havoc with the emotions as the sweet things of life — marriages, baptisms, family feasts — become an inextricable part of the background for explicitly depicted murders by shotgun, garrote, machine gun and booby-trapped automobile. The film is about an empire run from a dark, suburban Tudor palace where people, in siege, eat out of cardboard containers while babies cry and get under foot. It is also more than a little disturbing to realize that characters, who are so moving one minute, are likely, in the next scene, to be blowing out the brains of a competitor over a white tablecloth. It's nothing personal, just their way of doing business as usual.

Marlon Brando and Al Pacino in *The Godfather*.

The Gospel According to 'Godspell' Comes to Screen

By VINCENT CANBY

In filling in some of the narrative gaps in the Gospel according to St. Mark, St. Matthew took pains with the chronology, which, if you read him closely, makes it seem as if Jesus, on the day after He delivered the Sermon on the Mount and effected three healings, was in such good form that He made two lake crossings, healed five more people and held several lengthy discussions.

It is this quality of nonstop busyness that is one of the chief assets of "Godspell," both of the Off Broadway musical (still running at the Promenade Theater on upper Broadway) and of the film adaptation that opened yesterday at the Columbia 2 Theater. Especially of the film.

•

This update of—and variation on—the Gospel according to St. Matthew is less a celebration of the life and teachings of Christ than it is a celebration of theater, music, youthful high spirits, New York City locations and the zoom lens. The movie amounts to one long, breathless production number (some of whose parts are considerably less effective than others), as well as a demonstrations that, in films, what is said is often less important than how it's said.

"Godspell" pretty much reduces the story of Jesus to conform to a kind of flower-child paranoia that was probably more popular three or four years ago than it is today: the only way to survive in this world is to drop out of it, which, if you think about it, effectively reverses Jesus' instructions to the disciples.

That, however, is to mistake what I, at least, understand "Godspell" to be all about. It's not about religion or philosophy but show business, and its frame—the life and death of Jesus re-enacted in contemporary Manhattan and environs — is hardly more than a gimmick to allow the show's authors to help themselves to some lovely original material never protected by copyright.

At its worst, "Godspell" exalts a kind of simplicity and sweetness that are often the disguises of fierce anti-intellectualism. Luckily, the film constantly betrays itself through its highly sophisticated show-biz manners. Jesus is not simply the androgynous circus clown He looks to be. As played by Victor Garber, He's a tireless hoofer and a most engaging

The Cast

GODSPELL, directed by David Greene; associate director, John-Michael Tebelak; screenplay by Mr. Greene and Mr. Tebelak, based on the stage production as conceived and directed by Mr. Tebelak; music and lyrics by Stephen Schwartz; director of photography, Richard G. Heimann; editor, Alan Heim; produced by Edgar Lansbury; released by Columbia Pictures. Running time: 103 minutes. At the Columbia 2 Theater, Second Avenue at 64th Street. This film has been classified G.

Jesus	Victor Garber
John, Judas	David Haskell
Jerry	Jerry Sroka
Lynne	Lynne Thigpen
Katie	Katie Hanley
Robin	Robin Lamont
Gilmer	Gilmer McCormick
Joanne	Joanne Jonas
Merrell	Merrell Jackson
Jeffrey	Jeffrey Mylett

minstrel man. One of the finest production numbers I've seen in years is the exuberant and ironic "All for the Best," which Jesus and John the Baptist (David Haskell) sing and dance all over New York, highlighted by a marvelous soft-shoe done in front of the Bulova Watch sign overlooking Times Square.

After a certain point, all of Stephen Schwartz's music begins to sound the same, but there is a momentum in its pacing that carries us over the monotony. Almost every member of the cast has his or her moment of glory at screen center. I think particularly of Robin Lamont, a beautiful honey blonde, who sings "Day by Day," and of several hugely funny parables acted out by virtually the entire company.

John-Michael Tebelak, who is credited with having "conceived and staged" the Off Broadway show, is credited as associate director of the film, and David Greene as its director. I have no idea who

GODSPELL
The Gospel According to Today

Wednesday, the extraordinary musical entertainment that has been enveloping stage audiences the world over with the happy communion of its love and enthusiasm will be spreading its joys to the New York screen.

COLUMBIA PICTURES PRESENTS A LANSBURY/DUNCAN/BERUH PRODUCTION • GODSPELL • SCREENPLAY BY DAVID GREENE and JOHN-MICHAEL TEBELAK • MUSIC AND LYRICS BY STEPHEN SCHWARTZ • PRODUCED BY EDGAR LANSBURY • DIRECTED BY DAVID GREENE

Continuous performances of Godspell start Wednesday, March 21

Columbia II
2nd Ave. at 64th St.
Tel. 832-2720
Boxoffice opens at noon daily

Tickets for advance sales for individuals or groups may be purchased at boxoffice.

did what, but the movie has the look of something shot by Richard Lester in an evangelical frame of mind. Ordinarily, this sort of fractured style is something I can easily resist, but it is the only way, I suspect, that "Godspell" could be made to work on film.

A contemporary version of the Gospels is acted out in song and dance by this zaney cast from *Godspell*.

David Selznick's 'Gone With the Wind' Has Its Long-Awaited Premiere at Astor and Capitol, Recalling Civil War and Plantation Days of South—Seen as Treating Book With Great Fidelity

GONE WITH THE WIND, as adapted by the late Sidney Howard from Margaret Mitchell's novel; directed by Victor Fleming, musical score by Max Steiner; production designer, William Cameron Menzies; special effects by Jack Cosgrove; fire scenes staged by Lee Zavitz; costumes designed by Walter Plunkett; photography by Ernest Haller, supervised for Technicolor Company by Natalie Kalmus; technical advisers, Susan Myrick and Will Price; historian, Wilbur G. Kurtz; produced by David O. Selznick and released by Metro-Goldwyn-Mayer. At the Capitol and Astor Theatres.

Scarlett O'Hara	Vivien Leigh
Rhett Butler	Clark Gable
Ashley Wilkes	Leslie Howard
Melanie Hamilton	Olivia de Havilland
Mammy	Hattie McDaniel
Gerald O'Hara	Thomas Mitchell
Ellen O'Hara	Barbara O'Neil
Frank Kennedy	Caroll Nye
Aunt Pittypat Hamilton	Laura Hope Crews
Doctor Meade	Harry Davenport
Charles Hamilton	Rand Brooks
Belle Watling	Ona Munson
Carreen O'Hara	Ann Rutherford
Brent Tarleton	George Reeves
Stuart Tarleton	Fred Crane
Pork	Oscar Polk
Prissy	Butterfly McQueen
Suellen O'Hara	Evelyn Keyes
Mrs. Merriwether	Jane Darwell
Mrs. Meade	Leona Roberts
Big Sam	Everett Brown
Uncle Peter	Eddie Anderson
Tom, a Yankee Captain	Ward Bond
Bonnie Blue Butler	Cammie King
Johnny Gallegher	J. M. Kerrigan
Emmy Slattery	Isabel Jewell
India Wilkes	Alicia Rhett
Jonas Wilkerson	Victor Jory
John Wilkes	Howard Hickman
Maybelle Merriwether	Mary Anderson
A Yankee Looter	Paul Hurst
Cathleen Calvert	Marcella Martin
Beau Wilkes	Mickey Kuhn
Bonnie's Nurse	Lillian Kemble Cooper
Reminiscent Soldier	Cliff Edwards
Elijah	Zack Williams

By FRANK S. NUGENT

Understatement has its uses too, so this morning's report on the event of last night will begin with the casual notation that it was a great show. It ran, and will continue to run, for about 3 hours and 45 minutes, which still is a few days and hours less than its reading time and is a period the spine may protest sooner than the eye or ear. It is pure narrative, as the novel was, rather than great drama, as the novel was not. By that we would imply you will leave it, not with the feeling you have undergone a profound emotional experience, but with the warm and grateful remembrance of an interesting story beautifully told. Is it the greatest motion picture ever made? Probably not, although it is the greatest motion mural we have seen and the most ambitious film-making venture in Hollywood's spectacular history.

It—as you must be aware—is "Gone With the Wind," the gargantuan Selznick edition of the Margaret Mitchell novel which swept the country like Charlie McCarthy, the "Music Goes 'Round" and similar inexplicable phenomena; which created the national emergency over the selection of a Scarlett O'Hara and which, ultimately, led to the $4,000,000 production that faced the New York public on two Times Square fronts last night, the Astor and the Capitol. It is the picture for which Mr. Gallup's American Institute of Public Opinion has reported a palpitantly waiting audience of 56,500,000 persons, a few of whom may find encouragement in our opinion that they won't be disappointed in Vivien Leigh's Scarlett, Clark Gable's Rhett Butler or, for that matter, in Mr. Selznick's Miss Mitchell.

For, by any and all standards, Mr. Selznick's film is a handsome, scrupulous and unstinting version of the 1,037-page novel, matching it almost scene for scene with a literalness that not even Shakespeare or Dickens were accorded in Hollywood, casting it so brilliantly one would have to know the history of the production not to suspect that Miss Mitchell had written her story just to provide a vehicle for the stars already assembled under Mr. Selznick's hospitable roof. To have treated so long a book with such astonishing fidelity required courage—the courage of a producer's convictions and of his pocketbook, and yet, so great a hold has Miss Mitchell on her public, it might have taken more courage still to have changed a line or scene of it.

But if Selznick has made a virtue of necessity, it does not follow, of necessity, that his transcription be expertly made as well. And yet, on the whole, it has been. Through stunning design, costume and peopling, his film has skillfully and absorbingly recreated Miss Mitchell's mural of the South in that bitter decade when secession, civil war and reconstruction ripped wide the graceful fabric of the plantation age and confronted the men and women who had adorned it with the stern alternative of meeting the new era or dying with the old. It was a large panel she painted, with sections devoted to plantation life, to the siege and the burning of Atlanta, to carpetbaggers and the Ku Klux Klan and, of course, to the Scarlett O'Hara about whom all this changing world was spinning and to whom nothing was important except as it affected her.

Some parts of this extended account have suffered a little in their screen telling, just as others have profited by it. Mr. Selznick's picture-postcard Tara and Twelve Oaks, with a few-score actors posturing on the premises, is scarcely our notion of doing complete justice to an age that had "a glamour to it, a perfection, a symmetry like Grecian art." The siege of Atlanta was splendid and the fire that followed magnificently pyrotechnic, but we do not endorse the superimposed melodramatics of the crates of explosives scorching in the fugitives' path; and we felt cheated, so ungrateful are we, when the battles outside Atlanta were dismissed in a subtitle and Sherman's march to the sea was summed up in a montage shot. We grin understandingly over Mr. Selznick's romantic omission of Scarlett's first two "birthings," and we regret more comic capital was not made of Rhett's scampish trick on the Old Guard of Atlanta when the army men were rounding up the Klansmen.

But if there are faults, they do not extend to the cast. Miss Leigh's Scarlett has vindicated the absurd talent quest that indirectly turned her up. She is so perfectly designed for the part by art and nature that any other actress in the role would be inconceivable. Technicolor finds her beautiful, but Sidney Howard, who wrote the script, and Victor Fleming, who directed it, have found in her something more: the very embodiment of the selfish, hoydenish, slant-eyed miss who tackled life with both claws and a creamy complexion, asked no odds of any one or anything—least of all her conscience—and faced at last a defeat which, by her very unconquerability, neither she nor we can recognize as final.

Miss Leigh's Scarlett is the pivot

(continued)

Another reason for the greatness of

GONE WITH THE WIND

REMEMBER YOUR FIRST INTRODUCTION TO SCARLETT O'HARA!

Margaret Mitchell describes her this way on page one of the book.

" Scarlett O'Hara was not beautiful, but men seldom realized it when caught by her charm . . . Her eyes were pale green without a touch of hazel, starred with bristly black lashes and slightly tilted at the ends. "

A tantalizing, provocative description of a woman in a thousand! Actually one woman in fourteen hundred! For to capture and portray that elusive charm and fire on the screen 1400 actresses were screen-tested—149,000 feet of black and white film and 13,000 feet of Technicolor film were exposed at a cost of $92,000.00! Only then was the selection of Vivien Leigh announced, whose green eyes, graceful 17-inch waist and tip-tilted nose proclaimed her a Scarlett every bit as alluring and teasing and lovely as the heroine of the book!

DAVID O. SELZNICK'S *production of*
MARGARET MITCHELL'S
Story of the Old South

GONE WITH THE WIND

in TECHNICOLOR *starring*

CLARK GABLE
as Rhett Butler

LESLIE · OLIVIA
HOWARD · De HAVILLAND
and presenting
VIVIEN LEIGH
as Scarlett O'Hara

A SELZNICK INTERNATIONAL PICTURE
Directed by VICTOR FLEMING
Screen Play by SIDNEY HOWARD • Music by Max Steiner
A Metro-Goldwyn-Mayer Release

Starts TUESDAY, December 19th—8:30 P. M.

ASTOR — B'WAY at 45th—ALL SEATS RESERVED
Twice Daily 2:15, 8:15 P. M. Mats. (exc. Sun., Hol.) 75c to $1.10. Eves. $1.10 to $2.20. Saturday, Sunday and Holiday Matinees 75c to $1.65.

CAPITOL — B'WAY at 51st—NO RESERVED SEATS
3 Cont. Shows Daily 11:30 A.M., 4:15 & 9:00 P.M. Before 5 P.M. (3 P.M. Sat., Sun., & Hol.) 75c, Loges $1.10. After 5 P.M. (3 P.M. Sat., Sun., & Hol.) $1.10. Loges $1.65.

(All Prices Include Tax)

"GONE WITH THE WIND" will not be shown except at advanced prices at least until 1941

of the picture, as she was of the novel, and it is a column of strength in a film that is part history, part spectacle and all biography. Yet there are performances around her fully as valid, for all their lesser prominence. Olivia de Havilland's Melanie is a gracious, dignified, tender gem of characterization. Mr. Gable's Rhett Butler (although there is the fine flavor of the smokehouse in a scene or two) is almost as perfect as the grandstand quarterbacks thought he would be. Leslie Howard's Ashley Wilkes is anything but a pallid characterization of a pallid character. Best of all, perhaps, next to Miss Leigh, is Hattie McDaniel's Mammy, who must be personally absolved of responsibility for that most "unfittin'" scene in which she scolds Scarlett from an upstairs window. She played even that one right, however wrong it was.

We haven't time or space for the others, beyond to wave an approving hand at Butterfly McQueen as Prissy, Thomas Mitchell as Gerald, Ona Munson as Belle Watling, Alicia Rhett as India Wilkes, Rand Brooks as Charles Hamilton, Harry Davenport as Doctor Meade, Carroll Nye as Frank Kennedy.

Clark Gable as Rhett Butler and Vivien Leigh as the stormy Scarlett O'Hara.

Hattie McDaniel as Mammy in *Gone With the Wind*.

Leslie Howard played Scarlett's rather pallid "lover", Ashley Wilkes.

Film: 'Goodbye Girl' Full of Wisecracks

By VINCENT CANBY

IF ONE COULD ENTER the mind of Neil Simon, I have the feeling it would be like attending a convention of standup comedians—everyone busy topping everyone else, not really listening to anything that's being said except to identify the key word that will be the springboard into the next snappy retort, then the next and the next. Exhausting without being much fun.

Which is more or less the way I feel about Mr. Simon's newest work, the original screenplay for "The Goodbye Girl," a movie that has the form of a romantic comedy but which is so relentlessly wisecracked that it finally has the very curious effect of seeming to be rude to its own characters.

The people in "The Goodbye Girl" are very nice indeed, at least when we first meet them. They are a desperately cheerful young woman named Paula (Marsha Mason), a former Broadway hoofer who has a precocious 10-year-old daughter named Lucy (Quinn Cummings) and terrible luck with men, and Elliot Garfield (Richard Dreyfuss), a maniacally egocentric young Chicago actor who's come to New York to star in an Off Off Broadway production of "Richard III."

Paula and Elliot loathe each other at first sight, for good reason. Paula's former lover has just sneaked off to Italy after having sublet to Elliot the apartment in which Paula and Lucy are living. Paula and Lucy refuse to give up the premises and Elliot refuses to acknowledge the right of their occupancy. After thus meeting cute, they compromise, deciding to share the flat while keeping their respective distances.

"The Goodbye Girl," which opened yesterday at Loews Tower East Theater, may be the perfect American comedy for an age in which opportunism is not only an acceptable way of getting ahead in the world, but also a fashionable style of conversation, patterned largely, I suspect, on the manners of television talk-show guests who trample one another for the camera's attention. It's as if Zsa Zsa Gabor had become our Euphues.

The courtship of Paula and Elliot is conducted mostly in terms of outrage, insult and misunderstanding. They don't talk to each other—they compete for the last word. A lot of this, especially early in the film, is quite funny, but eventually it overtakes the characters and the situations so that, to keep the comedy moving, Mr. Simon himself appears to take over, making the characters say and do uncharacteristic things to get the laugh.

Thus Paula, who has done her share of sleeping around, must behave as if she were both jealous and morally outraged when Elliot brings home an actress-friend to rehearse one evening.

THE GOODBYE GIRL, directed by Herbert Ross; screenplay by Neil Simon; produced by Ray Stark; director of photography, David M. Walsh; editor, John F. Burnett; music scored and adapted by Dave Grusin; a Rastar production, distributed by Warner Brothers. Running time: 110 minutes. At Loews Tower East Theater, Third Avenue near 72d Street. This film has been rated PG.

Elliot Garfield	Richard Dreyfuss
Paula McFadden	Marsha Mason
Lucy McFadden	Quinn Cummings
Mark	Paul Benedict
Donna	Barbara Rhoades
Mrs. Crosby	Theresa Merritt
Linda	Marilyn Sokol

We also are asked to believe that Elliot, who is essentially sane though ambitious, would go along with a ridiculously silly production of "Richard III" in which the title character is conceived as a Billy DeWolfe drag-queen.

In certain situations, Mr. Simon's insults and wisecracks work naturally, as in "The Sunshine Boys," about the two old vaudevillians who hate each other while being mutually dependent. It was also very comic in "The Odd Couple," whose two heroes were really early sketches for the Sunshine Boys. His gift for parody was marvelously apparent in "Murder by Death." However, something essential seems to be missing when he attempts to write with feeling about men and women. As he views the war between the sexes, it's a contest of unisex gag writers.

The thing that always confuses my reactions to Mr. Simon's more outrageous inventions—such as the nutty "Richard III" production here—is that many of them are funny by themselves, but they don't fit easily together. Mr. Simon doesn't hesitate to sentimentalize little Lucy, played with eerie self-

Richard Dreyfuss and Marsha Mason in the Neil Simon comedy, *The Goodbye Girl.*

assurance by Miss Cummings, while stuffing her mouth with lines that would do justice to Groucho Marx.

Herbert Ross, this year's "hot" director (what with "The Turning Point" already out and Mr. Simon's new play, "Chapter Two," about to open), who is a man of wit and humane concerns, appears to have put his talent so totally in the service of the Simon script that I have no idea what his contributions to the movie may be. Miss Mason and Mr. Dreyfuss are enthusiastic farceurs who manage to keep their wits about them even when they are doing absurd things. Miss Mason's Paula is especially funny in her early scenes with her daughter when she creates a genuinely comic portrait of a woman who has prepared herself for every possible treachery except the one that turns up.

"The Goodbye Girl," which has been rated PG ("Parental Guidance Suggested"), contains some mildly vulgar language but is otherwise no more or less offensive than a singing commercial that is insidious because it is more clever than most.

WINNER 5 GOLDEN GLOBE NOMINATIONS
(COMEDY OR MUSICAL)
BEST PICTURE-BEST ACTOR-Richard Dreyfuss-BEST ACTRESS-Marsha Mason
BEST SUPPORTING ACTRESS-Quinn Cummings
BEST SCREENPLAY-Neil Simon

Neil Simon's
the GOODBYE GIRL

Richard Dreyfuss
BEST ACTOR OF THE YEAR
Los Angeles
Film Critics Award

A RAY STARK PRODUCTION OF A HERBERT ROSS FILM
NEIL SIMON'S
"THE GOODBYE GIRL"
RICHARD DREYFUSS · MARSHA MASON
and introducing QUINN CUMMINGS as Lucy
Written by NEIL SIMON · Produced by RAY STARK · Directed by HERBERT ROSS
Music Scored and Adapted by DAVE GRUSIN · Song "Goodbye Girl"
Written and Performed by DAVID GATES · a RASTAR Feature · Prints by MGM Labs

Tales Out of School

'The Graduate' Arrives on Local Screens

The Cast

THE GRADUATE, screenplay by Calder Willingham and Buck Henry, based on the novel by Charles Webb; directed by Mike Nichols and produced by Lawrence Turman; presented by Joseph E. Levine and released by Embassy Pictures. At the Coronet Theater, Third Avenue at 59th Street, and the Lincoln Art Theater, 57th Street and Broadway. Running time: 105 minutes.

Mrs. Robinson	Anne Bancroft
Ben Braddock	Dustin Hoffman
Elaine Robinson	Katharine Ross
Mr. Braddock	William Daniels
Mr. Robinson	Murray Hamilton
Mrs. Braddock	Elizabeth Wilson
Carl Smith	Brian Avery
Mr. Maguire	Walter Brooke
Mr. McCleery	Norman Fell
Lady No. 2	Elizabeth Fraser
Mrs. Singleman	Alice Ghostley
Room Clerk	Buck Henry
Miss De Witt	Marion Lorne

By BOSLEY CROWTHER

SUDDENLY, here toward the year's end, when the new films are plunging toward the wire and the prospects of an Oscar-worthy long shot coming through get progressively more dim, there sweeps ahead a film that is not only one of the best of the year, but also one of the best seriocomic social satires we've had from Hollywood since Preston Sturges was making them.

It is Mike Nichols's and Lawrence Turman's devastating and uproarious "The Graduate," which came yesterday to the Lincoln Art and the Coronet.

Mark it right down in your datebook as a picture you'll have to see—and maybe see twice to savor all its sharp satiric wit and cinematic treats. For in telling a pungent story of the sudden confusions and dismays of a bland young man fresh out of college who is plunged headlong into the intellectual vacuum of his affluent parents' circle of friends, it fashions a scarifying picture of the raw vulgarity of the swimming-pool rich, and it does so with a lively and exciting expressiveness through vivid cinema.

•

Further, it offers an image of silver-spoonfed, bewildered youth, standing expectantly but with misgiving where the brook and the swimming-pool meet, that is developed so wistfully and winningly by Dustin Hoffman, an amazing new young star, that it makes you feel a little tearful and choked-up while it is making you laugh yourself raw.

(continued)

EXCLUSIVE LIMITED ENGAGEMENT

ACADEMY AWARD WINNER

BEST DIRECTOR—MIKE NICHOLS

JOSEPH E. LEVINE PRESENTS

A MIKE NICHOLS LAWRENCE TURMAN PRODUCTION

THE GRADUATE

STARRING ANNE BANCROFT AND DUSTIN HOFFMAN · KATHARINE ROSS
SCREENPLAY BY CALDER WILLINGHAM AND BUCK HENRY   SONGS BY PAUL SIMON
PERFORMED BY SIMON AND GARFUNKEL   PRODUCED BY LAWRENCE TURMAN
DIRECTED BY MIKE NICHOLS   TECHNICOLOR® PANAVISION®
AN AVCO EMBASSY FILM

STARTS TOMORROW   *AVCO EMBASSY EAST*
59th St. bet. 3rd & 2nd Aves.—688-1717
12:40, 2:25, 4:15, 6:00, 8:00, 10:00

In outline, it may sound skimpy and perhaps a little crude — possibly even salacious in a manner now common in films. For all it is, in essence, is the story of this bright but reticent young man who returns from an Eastern college to his parent's swanky home in Beverly Hills, gets seduced rather quickly by the restless wife of his father's law partner, then falls in love with the lady's daughter and finds himself helplessly trapped in a rather sticky dilemma until he is able to dislodge himself through a familiar romantic ploy.

That's all. And yet in pursuing this simple story line, which has been adorned with delicious incidents and crackling dialogue in the screenplay by Calder Willingham and Buck Henry, based on a novel by Charles Webb, the still exploring Mr. Nichols has done such sly and surprising things with his actors and with his camera—or, rather—Robert Surtees's camera—that the over-all picture has the quality of a very extensive and revealing social scan.

With Mr. Hoffman's stolid, deadpanned performance, he gets a wonderfully compassionate sense of the ironic and pathetic immaturity of a mere baccalaureate scholar turned loose in an immature society. He is a character very much reminiscent of Holden Caulfield in J. D. Salinger's "Catcher in the Rye."

And with Anne Bancroft's sullenly contemptuous and voracious performance as the older woman who yearns for youth, Mr. Nichols has twined in the netting the casual crudeness and yet the pathos of this type.

Katharine Ross, another comparative newcomer, is beautifully fluid and true as the typical college - senior daughter whose sensitivities are helplessly exposed for brutal abrasion by her parents and by the permissive society in which she lives. Murray Hamilton is piercing as her father—a seemingly self-indulgent type who is sharply revealed as bewildered and wounded in one fine, funny scene. And William Daniels and Elizabeth Wilson fairly set your teeth on edge as the ha-cha, insensitive parents of the lonely young man.

Enhancing the veracity of the picture is first-rate staging in true locations and on well-dressed sets, all looking right in excellent color. And a rich, poignant musical score that features dandy modern folk music, sung (off-screen, of course) by the team of Simon and Garfunkel, has the sound of today's moody youngsters—"The Sound of Silence," as one lyric says.

Funny, outrageous and touching, "The Graduate" is a sophisticated film that puts Mr. Nichols and his associates on a level with any of the best satirists working abroad today.

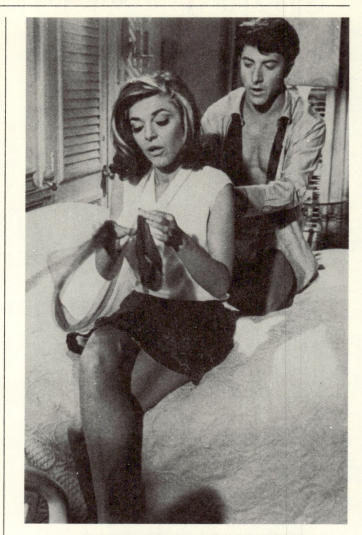

Anne Bancroft, Katherine Ross and Dustin Hoffman in scenes from *The Graduate*.

Grand Hotel

GRAND HOTEL, an adaptation of Vicki Baum's play; directed by Edmund Goulding; produced by Metro-Goldwyn-Mayer. At the Astor Theatre.

Grusinskaya, the Dancer........Greta Garbo
The Baron...............John Barrymore
Flaemmchen, the Stenographer..Joan Crawford
Preysing....................Wallace Beery
Otto Kringelein............Lionel Barrymore
Senf.....................Jean Hersholt
Meierheim.................Robert McWade
Zinnowitz................Purnell B. Pratt
Pimenov...............Ferdinand Gottschalk
Suzette.................Rafaela Ottiano
Chauffeur................Morgan Wallace
Gerstenkorn..............Tully Marshall
Rohna....................Frank Conroy
Schweimann...............Murray Kinnell
Dr. Waltz................Edwin Maxwell

By MORDAUNT HALL.

For the first showing last night of the film of Vicki Baum's stage work, "Grand Hotel," those worshipers of the stars of the Hollywood firmament choked the sidewalk outside the Astor and also the theatre lobby, while policemen afoot and on horse urged the throng to keep moving. And from across Broadway blinding beams of light added to the general excitement.

Inside the theatre it was for a time difficult to move but very slowly, for many of those who had tickets pressed into the aisles and behind the orchestra seats with the evident hope of catching a glimpse of one or another cinema celebrity. But once microphone music came from the stage the spectators hastened to their places and soon the introductory scene of the much talked of motion picture was emblazoned on the screen. It was that of the telephone operators in the Grand Hotel and then the pushing and shouting was a thing of the past.

It is a production thoroughly worthy of all the talk it has created and the several motion-picture luminaries deserve to feel very proud of their performances, particularly Greta Garbo and Lionel Barrymore. So far as the direction is concerned, Edmund Goulding has done an excellent piece of work, but occasionally it seems as though he relies too much on close-ups. Nevertheless he has sustained a steady momentum in darting here and there in the busy hostelry and working up to an effective dramatic pitch at the psychological moment. In all, the picture adheres faithfully to the original and while it undoubtedly lacks the life and depth and color of the play, by means of excellent characterizations it keeps the audience on the qui vive.

It is indubitably a capital subject to bring to the screen, for it benefits by the sweeping scope of the camera and in swaying from room to room and from the lobby to the telephone switchboard, Mr. Goulding gives some markedly fine photographic effects. But it should be stated that in one scene he permits an extremely gruesome idea to creep in. This will probably be eliminated at some of the future exhibitions.

Miss Garbo, of course, impersonates the dancer, Grusinskaya, played on the stage by Eugénie Leontovich. Miss Garbo, possibly appreciating that she was supported by a galaxy of efficient performers, decided that she would do her utmost to make her rôle shine. And she succeeds admirably. She is stunning in her early scenes and charming in the love scene with Baron Geigern, portrayed by John Barrymore with his usual savoir faire. And later, wearing a chinchilla coat, she is gay and lighthearted, for love has beckoned to the temperamental dancer. Grusinskaya leaves the screen hopeful of meeting the Baron at the railroad station, but the audience knows that the good-natured and sympathetic thief has met his doom at the hands of the ignoble Preysing, a part acted by Wallace Beery.

It fell to Lionel Barrymore's lot to play Otto Kringelein, the humble bookkeeper who decides in an introductory scene that, as he has not long to live, he will go out of this world in a blaze of glory. Mr. Barrymore brings out every possible note of this sensitive person, who talks with bated breath to the Baron, entertains with champagne and caviar; loathes his employer, the hard-fisted, sensual Preysing, for whom he has worked for a pittance. He is going to die and therefore what cares he if Preysing discharges him? But, instead of passing away, he entrains for Paris with the attractive stenographer, Flaemmchen, who is seen in the person of Joan Crawford. Through Mr. Barrymore's skillful interpretation one gleans the satisfaction of this obsequious human adding machine has in hobnobbing with people of the world and in living in the corner suite of the Grand Hotel. Mr. Barrymore is superb when he as Kringelein finds himself tipsy, tipsy but elated. If ever an actor got under the skin of a character Mr. Barrymore does here.

And, although Miss Garbo and Lionel Barrymore deliver talented portrayals, it does not mean that any aspersion is to be cast at the work of others in the cast. Miss Crawford, for instance, is splendid as Flaemmchen. She, too, does all that is possible to vie with the others in the cast. Then there is John Barrymore as the Baron. Nobody could hope to see such a type better acted. This Baron is handsome, a little sly, eager for money, but always thoughtful and friendly when it comes to his association with Kringelein. He steals Kringelein's wallet, but, when he hears Kringelein bewailing his loss, he "finds" the wallet, and how glad is Kringelein!

As for Mr. Beery, it may seem that while his performance does not quite compare with that of Siegfried Rumann, the stage Preysing, it is nevertheless a very worthy characterization. Mr. Beery is sufficiently ponderous and forbidding as Preysing, but in having to assume a German accent he is not quite in his element. But those who did not see Mr. Rumann will undoubtedly decide that Mr. Beery's performance is good enough.

No review of this picture would be complete without a mention of the genuinely pleasing work of Ferdinand Gottschalk, who acts the loyal underling of Grusinskaya. Lewis Stone also does well as Dr. Otternschlag and Jean Hersholt is up to his usual high standard as the porter, Senf, whose chief interest during the running of the story is the condition of his wife, who finally gives birth to a child as the story comes to a close. And it is Dr. Otternschlag who is given to saying that "people come and people go, and nothing ever happens in the Grand Hotel."

And the audience has seen manslaughter, gambling, a baron bent on stealing pearls, love affairs, a business deal and various other doings. And "nothing ever happens!"

Greta Garbo and John Barrymore in *Grand Hotel*.

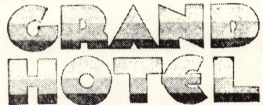

ALL YOU NEED TO KNOW
— (you know the rest!)

GRAND HOTEL

Greta GARBO
John BARRYMORE
Joan CRAWFORD
Wallace BEERY
Lionel BARRYMORE
Louis Stone
Jean Hersholt

A Metro Goldwyn Mayer Picture
Directed by Edmund Goulding from Vicki Baum's Play

TIME OF SHOWING:

Daily — 2:40 — 8:40
Sunday & Holidays — 3 — 6 — 8:40

SCALE OF PRICES:

Daily Matinees — 50c — 75c — $1.00
Sat. Mats. — 50c — 75c — $1.00 — $1.50
Nights — 50c — 75c — $1.00 — $1.50 — $2.00

ASTOR

BROADWAY AT 45th STREET

John Travolta   Olivia Newton-John

GREASE is the word

PARAMOUNT PICTURES PRESENTS

A ROBERT STIGWOOD/ALLAN CARR PRODUCTION

JOHN TRAVOLTA   OLIVIA NEWTON-JOHN in "GREASE"

and STOCKARD CHANNING as Rizzo with special guest appearances by EVE ARDEN, FRANKIE AVALON

JOAN BLONDELL, EDD BYRNES, SID CAESAR, ALICE GHOSTLEY, DODY GOODMAN, SHA·NA·NA

Screenplay by BRONTE WOODARD Adaptation by ALLAN CARR Based on the original musical by JIM JACOBS and WARREN CASEY

Produced on the Broadway Stage by KENNETH WAISSMAN and MAXINE FOX in association with ANTHONY D'AMATO Choreography - PATRICIA BIRCH

Produced by ROBERT STIGWOOD and ALLAN CARR Directed by RANDAL KLEISER

PG PARENTAL GUIDANCE SUGGESTED Soundtrack Album available on RSO Records & Tapes Read the paperback from Pocket Books ©1978 PARAMOUNT PICTURES CORPORATION

★ DOLBY STEREO

98

A Slick Version of 'Grease'

By VINCENT CANBY

"GREASE," the film version of the still-running Broadway musical show, is not really the 1950's teen-age movie musical it thinks it is, but a contemporary fantasy about a 1950's teen-age musical—a larger, funnier, wittier and more imaginative-than-Hollywood movie with a life that is all its own. It uses the Eisenhower era — the characters, costumes, gestures and, particularly, the music—to create a time and place that have less to do with any real 50's than with a kind of show business that is both timeless and old-fashioned, both sentimental and wise. The movie, which opens today at Loews State 2 and other theaters, is also terrific fun.

Because I seem to be one of the few persons who has never seen the Broadway show, I'm not sure how the movie differs from the original, yet it's apparent that the film's score, which is one of the best things about the production, has been liberally supplemented by new material and new-old material, including "Love Is a Many Splendored Thing," which has never before sounded so marvelously, soaringly inane.

Somewhat in the manner of "Close Encounters of the Third Kind," which recalls the science-fiction films of the 50's in a manner more elegant and more benign, than anything that was ever made then, "Grease" is a multimillion-dollar evocation of the B-picture quickies that Sam Katzman used to turn out in the 50's ("Don't Knock the Rock," 1957) and that American International carried to the sea in the 1960's ("Beach Party," 1963).

Fantasy of the 50's

GREASE, directed by Randal Kleiser; screenplay Bronte Woodward, adapted by Allan Carr from the Broadway musical by Jim Jacobs and Warren Casey; produced by Robert Stigwood and Mr. Carr; dances and musical sequences staged and choreographed by Patricia Birch; music supervision Bill Oakes; director of photography, Bill Butler; editor, John F. Burnett; distributed by Paramount Pictures. Running time: 110 minutes. At Loews State 2, Broadway at 45th Street, and other theaters. This film has been rated PG.

Danny	John Travolta
Sandy	Olivia Newton-John
Rizzo	Stockard Channing
Kenickie	Jeff Conway
Frenchy	Didi Conn
Principal McGee	Eve Arden
Teen Angel	Frankie Avalon
Vi	Joan Blondell
Vince Fontaine	Edd Byrnes
Coach Calhoun	Sid Caesar
Mrs. Murdock	Alice Ghostley
Blanche	Dody Goodman
Johnny Casino and the Gamblers	Sha-Na-Na
Jan	Jamie Donnelly
Marty	Dinah Manoff
Doody	Barry Pearl
Sonny	Michael Tucci
Putzie	Kelly Ward
Patty Simcox	Susan Buckner
Eugene	Eddie Deezen
Tom Chisum	Lorenzo Lamas
Leo	Dennis C. Stewart
Cha Cha	Annette Charles
Mr. Rudie	Dick Patterson
Nurse Wilkins	Fannie Flagg
Mr. Lynch	Darrell Zwerling
Waitress	Ellen Travolta

The gang at old Rydell High, which is the universe of "Grease," is unlike any high school class you've ever seen except in the movies. For one thing, they're all rather long in the tooth to be playing kids who'd hang around malt shops. For another, they are loaded with the kind of talent and exuberance you don't often find very far from a musical stage. They not only portray characters but effectively make comments on them.

Olivia Newton-John, the recording star in her American film debut, is simultaneously very funny and utterly charming as the film's ingénue, a demure, virginal Sandra Dee-type. She

The film's producers, Robert Stigwood and Allen Carr, and director, Randel Kleiser (whose first theatrical feature this is), have also supplemented the cast of comparative youngsters with a whole crowd of actors we associate with the 50's, and who seem here to have survived with barely a visible dent.

Eve Arden, a fixture of the 50's as Our Miss Brooks, plays Rydell High's unflappable principal; Sid Caesar is the football coach; Edd Byrnes comes on briefly as the lecherous host of a teen-age TV show that decides to spotlight Rydell in a network program; Joan Blondell is the harassed waitress at the corner soda fountain, and, maybe funniest of all, is Frankie Avalon, who appears in a dream sequence to counsel an unhappy student ("Beauty School Dropout").

Bronte Woodward has adapted the possesses true screen presence as well as a sweet, sure singing voice, while the Sandra Dee I remember had a voice that seemed to have been manufactured in Universal's speech-and-special-effects department.

John Travolta, as Miss Newton-John's costar, a not-so-malevolent gang-leader, is better than he was in "Saturday Night Fever." I'm still not sure if he's a great actor, but he's a fine performer with the kind of energy and humor that are brought to life by the musical numbers.

Stockard Channing, as the high school's tramp who has a dirty mouth and a heart of gold, would (if it were possible) stop the show twice, once with a pasty put-on of poor Olivia ("Look at Me, I'm Sandra Dee") and another when she attempts, in song, to explain why it's more honorable to be loose than uptight ("There Are Worse Things I Could Do").

Olivia Newton-John and John Travolta in the 50's teenage musical, *Grease.*

'The Great Dictator,' by and With Charlie Chaplin, Tragi-Comic Fable of the Unhappy Lot of Decent Folk in a Totalitarian Land, at the Astor and Capitol

THE GREAT DICTATOR, based on an original story written, directed and produced by Charles Chaplin and released through United Artists; musical direction by Meredith Willson. At the Astor and Capitol Theatres.

PEOPLE OF THE PALACE
Adenoid Hynkel, Dictator of Tomania, Charles Chaplin
Benzini Napaloni, Dictator of Bacteria, Jack Oakie
Schultz.................Reginald Gardiner
Garbitsch...................Henry Daniell
Herring......................Billy Gilbert
Mme. Napaloni................Grace Hayle
Bacterian Ambassador.....Carter de Haven

PEOPLE OF THE GHETTO
A Jewish Barber...........Charles Chaplin
Hannah..................Paulette Goddard
Mr. Jaeckel..........Maurice Moscovich
Mrs. Jaeckel................Emma Dunn
Mr. Mann.................Bernard Gorcey
Mr. Agar......................Paul Weigel
Also Chester Conklin, Esther Michelson, Hank Mann, Florence Wright, Eddie Gribbon, Robert O. Davis, Eddie Dunn, Nita Pike and Peter Lynn.

By BOSLEY CROWTHER

Now that the waiting is over and the shivers of suspense at an end, let the trumpets be sounded and the banners flung against the sky. For the little tramp, Charlie Chaplin, finally emerged last night from behind the close-guarded curtains which have concealed his activities these past two years and presented himself in triumphal splendor as "The Great Dictator"—or you know who.

No event in the history of the screen has ever been anticipated with more hopeful excitement than the première of this film, which occurred simultaneously at the Astor and Capitol Theatres; no picture ever made has promised more momentous consequences. The prospect of little "Charlot," the most universally loved character in all the world, directing his superlative talent for ridicule against the most dangerously evil man alive has loomed as a titanic jest, a transcendent paradox. And the happy report this morning is that it comes off magnificently. "The Great Dictator" may not be the finest picture ever made—in fact, it possesses several disappointing shortcomings. But, despite them, it turns out to be a truly superb accomplishment by a truly great artist—and, from one point of view, perhaps the most significant film ever produced.

Let this be understood, however: it is no catch-penny buffoonery, no droll and gentle-humored social satire in the manner of Chaplin's earlier films. "The Great Dictator" is essentially a tragic picture—or tragi-comic in the classic sense—and it has strongly bitter overtones. For it is a lacerating fable of the unhappy lot of decent folk in a totalitarian land, of all the hateful oppression which has crushed the humanity out of men's souls. And, especially, it is a withering revelation, through genuinely inspired mimicry, of the tragic weaknesses, the overblown conceit and even the blank insanity of a dictator. Hitler, of course.

The main story line is quite simple, though knotted with many complications. A little Jewish barber returns to his shop in the ghetto of an imaginary city (obviously Berlin) after a prolonged lapse of perception due to an injury in the World War. He does not know that the State is now under the sign of the double-cross, that storm troopers patrol the streets, that Jews are cruelly persecuted and that the all-powerful ruler of the land is one Hynkel, a megalomaniac, to whom he bears—as a foreword states—a "coincidental re-

Charlie Chaplin returns to the screen with the role of *The Great Dictator.*

semblance." Thus, the little barber suffers a bitter disillusionment when he naively attempts to resist; he is beaten and eventually forced to flee to a neighboring country. But there he is mistaken for Hynkel, who has simultaneously annexed this neighboring land. And pushed upon a platform to make a conqueror's speech, he delivers instead a passionate appeal for human kindness and reason and brotherly love.

Thus the story throws in pointed contrast the good man against the evil one—the genial, self-effacing but courageous little man of the street against the cold pretentious tyrant. Both are played by Chaplin, of course, in a highly comic vein, beneath which runs a note of eternal sadness. The little barber is our beloved Charlie of old—the fellow with the splay feet, baggy pants, trick mustache and battered bowler. And, as always, he is the pathetic butt of heartless circumstances, beaten, driven, but ever prepared to bounce back. In this role Chaplin performs two of the most superb bits of pantomime he has ever done—one during a sequence in which he and four other characters eat puddings containing coins to determine which shall sacrifice his life to kill the dictator, and the other a bit in which he shaves a man to the rhythm of Brahms's Hungarian Rhapsody.

But it is as the dictator that Chaplin displays his true genius. Whatever fate it was that decreed Adolf Hitler should look like Charlie must have ordained this opportunity, for the caricature of the former is devastating. The feeble, affected hand-salute, the inclination for striking ludicrous attitudes, the fabulous fits of rage and violent facial contortions—all the vulnerable spots of Hitler's exterior are pierced by Chaplin's pantomimic shafts. He is at his best in a wild senseless burst of guttural oratory—a compound of German, Yiddish and Katzenjammer double-talk; and he reaches positively exalted heights in a plaintive dance which he does with a large balloon representing the globe, bouncing it into the air, pirouetting beneath it—and then bursting into tears when the balloon finally pops.

Another splendid sequence is that in which Hynkel and Napaloni, a neighboring dictator, meet and bargain. Napaloni, played by Jack Oakie, is a bluff, expansive creature—the anthesis of neurotic Hynkel—and the two actors contrive in this part of the film one of the most hilarious lampoons ever performed on the screen. Others in the cast are excellent—Paulette Goddard as a little laundry girl, Henry Daniell as a Minister of Propaganda, Billy Gilbert as a Minister of War—but Oakie ranges right alongside Chaplin. And that is tops.

On the debit side, the picture is overlong, it is inclined to be repetitious and the speech with which it ended—the appeal for reason and kindness—is completely out of joint with that which has gone before. In it Chaplin steps out of character and addresses his heart to the audience. The effect is bewildering, and what should be the climax becomes flat and seemingly maudlin. But the sincerity with which Chaplin voices his appeal and the expression of tragedy which is clear in his face are strangely overpowering. Suddenly one perceives in bald relief the things which make "The Great Dictator" great—the courage and faith and surpassing love for mankind which are in the heart of Charlie Chaplin.

For laughing purposes!

Today . . . and every day there are

31,640 UNRESERVED SEATS AT THE **CAPITOL**
(7 Continuous Performances . . . 4520 Seats for Each Performance. Doors Open 9 A. M.)

2,024 Reserved Seats at the **ASTOR**
(Twice Daily, 2:45 & 8:45. 1,012 Seats at Each Performance. Buy Seats NOW in Advance for Subsequent Performances.)

Charlie Chaplin
in his new comedy

The Great DICTATOR

Produced, written and directed by CHARLES CHAPLIN
with PAULETTE GODDARD

JACK OAKIE · HENRY DANIELL · REGINALD GARDINER
BILLY GILBERT · MAURICE MOSCOVICH
Released thru United Artists

CAPITOL THEATRE
B'WAY & 51st STREET
Regular continuous performances. Come any time and see a complete show. Doors open at 9 a.m.
PRICES:
Before 5 p.m., Orchestra and Balcony, 75c. (Saturday, Sunday and Holidays Before 3 p.m.) After 5 p.m., Orchestra and Balcony, $1.10. (Saturday, Sunday and Holidays after 3 p.m.) All Prices Include Tax.

ASTOR THEATRE
B'WAY & 45th STREET
Matinees at 2:45. Evenings at 8:45. (Extra Midnight Show Saturday and Extra 6 p.m. show on Sunday.)
PRICES:
Matinees, 75c, 85c, $1.10. (Saturday, Sunday and Holiday Matinees; also Midnight and Extra Shows—75c, 85c, $1.10, $1.65.) Evenings, $1.10, $1.65, $2.20 (including Saturday, Sunday & Holidays). All Prices Include Tax.

Don't forget — Reserved Seats now on sale at the Astor for all subsequent performances. Mail Orders for Astor filled in order of receipt.

'Guess Who's Coming to Dinner' Arrives

Tracy-Hepburn Picture Opens at 2 Theaters

By BOSLEY CROWTHER

"GUESS WHO'S COMING TO DINNER," which came to the Beekman and the Victoria yesterday, is a most delightfully acted and gracefully entertaining film, fashioned much in the manner of a stage drawing-room comedy, that seems to be about something much more serious and challenging than it actually is.

It seems to be about the social bias encountered by a San Francisco miss, daughter of liberal and socially prominent parents, who wants to marry a distinguished Negro scientist and suddenly finds herself opposed by her own father and the father of her fiancé. It seems to pose directly the question contained in that old hypocritical line: "I've got nothing at all against Negroes, but would you want your sister (daughter) to marry one?"

This certainly is the issue that swiftly and startlingly confronts Spencer Tracy and Katharine Hepburn when their daughter, Katharine Houghton, breezes home from a short vacation in Hawaii with beaming Sidney Poitier in tow, and bluntly announces with firm finality that they are going to be wed. And it continues to appear to be the issue as the parents of Mr. Poitier arrive unexpectedly for dinner and the two families sit down face to face to consider this unsettling aberration, a la the families in "Abie's Irish Rose."

●

But actually the bleakness of this issue has already begun to fade long before the dumbfounded Negro parents arrive from Los Angeles. The mother of the girl, a New Deal liberal and a blue-stocking of the sort that Miss Hepburn has played with crisp dexterity and assurance so many times, has plunked positively for the marriage, after her first indication of surprise, and seems almost as joyous about it as if it were her own.

An old monsignor friend of the family, played jovially by Cecil Kellaway, has approved it with as cheerful affirmation as he would give to handing the girl a lollipop. And, of course, the girl her-

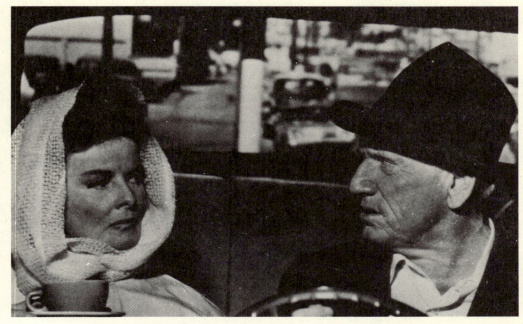

Katherine Hepburn and Spencer Tracy in *Guess Who's Coming to Dinner.*

The Cast

GUESS WHO'S COMING TO DINNER, written by William Rose; produced and directed by Stanley Kramer; released by Columbia Pictures. At the Victoria Theater, Broadway and 46th Street, and the Beekman Theater, 65th Street at Second Avenue. Running time 112 minutes.

Matt Drayton	Spencer Tracy
John Prentice	Sidney Poitier
Christina Drayton	Katharine Hepburn
Joey Drayton	Katharine Houghton
Monsignor Ryan	Cecil Kellaway
Mrs. Prentice	Beach Richards
Mr. Prentice	Roy E. Glenn Sr.
Tillie	Isabell Sanford
Hillary St. George	Virginia Christine
Carr Hop	Alexandra Hay
Delivery Boy	Skip Martin

self is so determined and so blissfully confident that nothing can obstruct her resolution that the issue hangs on one big question mark.

That is the judgment of the father—the father of the intended bride. Will he oppose the marriage? Will he bolt his liberal posture and say "No"? Or is he merely manifesting the misgivings and hesitations of any father of any girl who wants to marry a man much older than she is, whom she has known for only 10 days?

●

This is, indeed, the aggravation that sticks in Mr. Tracy's craw during the hours of his grumpy indecision before the parents of Mr. Poitier arrive—this concern that his daughter is undertaking a delicate marriage in too much haste. And, like so many similar anxieties of Mr. Tracy in previous films, it makes sense.

To be sure, the apparent issue of a difference in race is raised when the father of Mr. Poitier puts it bluntly to Mr. Tracy and to his son. Then it comes as a shock wave of intemperance as Roy E. Glenn Sr. hurls it forth with a fury and indignation that astonishes everyone. But it soon is absorbed in a verbal matting of nice philosophizing about the power of love, before Mr. Tracy accepts the situation and they all go in to a family dinner —with wine.

If one were taking this cheerful disquisition on the problems of mixed marriage seriously, there are several observations and pointed questions that would have to be raised. Is this a normal conjunction of a white girl and a Negro man that Stanley Kramer, the producer-director and his scriptwriter, William Rose, have arranged?

Is the poison of bigotry and bias conceivable in the attitudes of intelligent, liberal parents towards their daughter when she wants to wed a brilliant, charming Negro who is a candidate for a Nobel Prize? Is a sudden, powerful romance likely between an eminent man of this sort and the starry-eyed college senior Miss Houghton rapturously plays?

Let's not pursue those questions, for they will only tend to disturb the euphoria and likely enjoyment of this witty and glistening film. Mr. Rose has written a deliciously swift and pithy script, and Mr. Kramer has made it spin brightly in a stylish ambience of social comedy.

Mr. Tracy and Miss Hepburn are superior—he the crusty, sardonic old boy who speaks from a store of flinty wisdom but whose heart overflows with tender love; and she the seemingly airy patrician whose eyes often well with compassionate tears.

Mr. Poitier is also splendid within the strictures of a rather stuffy type that might also be questioned, if one were dissecting this film, and Beah Richards is deeply touching as his mother, which is the most profound and dignified role. Isabelle Sanford gets off some nifties, in a somewhat Dick Gregoryish vein, as the family's Negro maid who has the strongest bias against mixed marriages.

"Civil rights is one thing but this here is something else," she sniffs in a burst of incisive recognition that might also characterize the blue-chip film.

One might add that it has the further value of strong personal sentiment, in that it offers Mr. Tracy so graciously in the last role he played before his death.

A Robust Drama

'Guns of Navarone' Is at Two Theatres

By BOSLEY CROWTHER

WITH "The Guns of Navarone," Carl Foreman is beginning to blast himself a niche in the hall of fame of adventure-film producers that is surmounted by the bust of Cecil B. DeMille.

This big, robust action drama, which boomed into the Criterion last night and will begin a simultaneous engagement at the Murray Hill today, is one of those muscle-loaded pictures in the thundering tradition of DeMille, which means more emphasis is placed on melodrama than on character or credibility.

Written by Mr. Foreman, from a novel by Alistair MacLean, and produced by him on the island of Rhodes in the Aegean Sea and in a British studio, it tells a straight-away story of a tough team of Allied saboteurs who secretly land on a Nazi-held Greek island in a difficult time of World War II and accomplish a desperate mission of blowing up two critical sea-commanding guns.

•

We tell you the mission is accomplished, even though this is the point of the suspense, because the fact that it will be is foregone by the time the film is halfway through. Missions designed from standard blueprints, as this one plainly is, always succeed. The only question for the knowing moviegoer is how the individual fellows will behave, and this, it is very soon made evident, depends almost wholly on chance.

For the fellows designed by Mr. Foreman, best known for his screen play of "High Noon," are two-dimensional characters cast in assorted heroic moulds. There is the lean-limbed, laconic mountain-climber, played by Gregory Peck, who accepts his assignment with great misgiving and becomes the resolute leader before the end. There's the tough old Greek army officer, played by Anthony Quinn, who has the courage of a lion and the simplicity of a goat.

There's the droll, slightly saucy British sergeant who is an expert with dynamite and is the pessimist of the outfit. Who but David Niven would play him? And there's

the dour bulldog (Stanley Baker), the Greek lad from Brooklyn (James Darren) and the crisp British major, the original leader who is early injured (Anthony Quayle).

There are also a couple of women (Gia Scala and Irene Papas) who turn up and render certain tactical assistance (nothing more) as partisans. But they're all such predictable people you're likely to get thoroughly bored with them before the guns are blown up, the British destroyers sail past and "Rule Britannia" is triumphantly played.

There's a terrible and painful experience of scaling a sea-facing cliff, with the agonies and near-disasters of the climbers recorded by cameras close to them. And there are many ticklish set-tos with the Nazis, captures and escapes, before two of the men reach the gun gallery and start setting their charges against time.

Say this, too. Even though the picture runs more than two hours and a half, it moves swiftly and gets where it is going. J. Lee Thompson has directed it with pace and has seen to it that the actors give the impression of being stout and bold.

The Cast

THE GUNS OF NAVARONE, screen play by Carl Foreman, from the novel by Alistair MacLean; directed by J. Lee Thompson; produced by Mr. Foreman and presented by Columbia Pictures. At the Criterion Theatre, Broadway and Forty-third Street and the Murray Hill Theatre, Third Avenue and Thirty-fourth Street. Running time: 155 minutes.

Mallory	Gregory Peck
Miller	David Niven
Andrea	Anthony Quinn
Brown	Stanley Baker
Franklin	Anthony Quayle
Maria	Irene Papas
Anna	Gia Scala
Pappadimos	James Darren
Jensen	James Robertson Justice
Barnsby	Richard Harris
Cohn	Bryan Forbes
Baker	Allan Cuthbertson
Weaver	Michael Trubshawe
Nicholai	Tutte Lemkow
Commandant	Albert Lieven
Group Captain	Norman Wooland

James Darren, Stanley Baker, David Niven, Gregory Peck, Anthony Quinn and Anthony Quayle in *Guns of Navarone*.

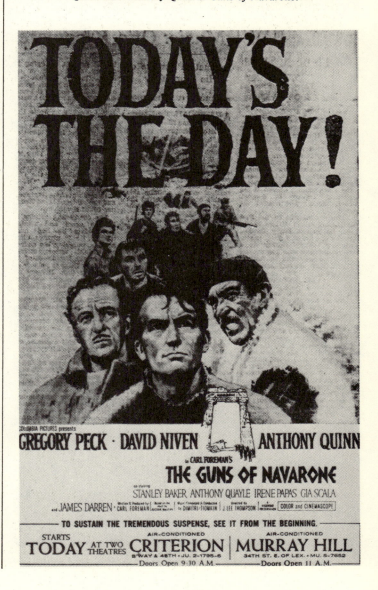

TODAY'S THE DAY!

COLUMBIA PICTURES presents

GREGORY PECK · DAVID NIVEN · ANTHONY QUINN

in CARL FOREMAN'S

THE GUNS OF NAVARONE

also starring STANLEY BAKER · ANTHONY QUAYLE · IRENE PAPAS · GIA SCALA

and JAMES DARREN · Written and Produced by CARL FOREMAN · Music Composed and Conducted by DIMITRI TIOMKIN · Directed by J. LEE THOMPSON · COLOR and CINEMASCOPE

TO SUSTAIN THE TREMENDOUS SUSPENSE, SEE IT FROM THE BEGINNING.

STARTS TODAY AT TWO THEATRES

AIR-CONDITIONED
CRITERION
B'WAY & 45TH · JU. 2-1795-6
Doors Open 9:30 A.M.

AIR-CONDITIONED
MURRAY HILL
34TH ST. E. OF LEX · MU. 5-7652
Doors Open 11 A.M.

Scenes from *A Hard Day's Night* with Director, Richard Lester posing with the Beatles during shooting (bottom).

The Four Beatles in 'A Hard Day's Night'

British Singers Make Debut as Film Stars

By BOSLEY CROWTHER

THIS is going to surprise you—it may knock you right out of your chair—but the new film with those incredible chaps, the Beatles, is a whale of a comedy.

I wouldn't believe it either, if I hadn't seen it with my own astonished eyes, which have long since become accustomed to seeing disasters happen when newly fledged pop-singing sensations are hastily rushed to the screen. But this first fiction film of the Beatles, entitled "A Hard Day's Night," which exploded last night at the Astor, the Trans-Lux East and other theaters hereabouts, has so much good humor going for it that it is awfully hard to resist.

In the first place, it's a wonderfully lively and altogether good-natured spoof of the juvenile madness called "Beatlemania," the current spreading craze of otherwise healthy young people for the four British lads with the shaggy hair.

The opening shots, behind the credits, are of three of the fellows running ahead of a mob of howling admirers chasing after them as they break away from a theater where they have played a singing engagement and race for a waiting train. And all the way through the picture,

The Cast

A HARD DAY'S NIGHT, screenplay by Alun Owen; directed by Richard Lester and produced by Walter Shenson for United Artists. At the Astor, Broadway at 45th Street; the Trans-Lux East, Third Avenue at 58th Street, and other theaters in the metropolitan area. Running time: 87 minutes.

John	John Lennon
Paul	Paul McCartney
George	George Harrison
Ringo	Ringo Starr
Grandfather	Wilfrid Brambell
Norm	Norman Rossington
T V Director	Victor Spinetti
Snake	John Junkin
Millie	Anna Quayle
Simon	Kenneth Haigh
Man on Train	Richard Vernon
Hotel Waiter	Eddie Malin

there are frenzied episodes of the Beatles' encounters with squealing fans and with reporters who ask silly questions, all in a facile, witty vein.

But more than this, it's a fine conglomeration of madcap clowning in the old Marx Brothers' style, and it is done with such a dazzling use of camera that it tickles the intellect and electrifies the nerves.

This is the major distinction of this commercially sure-fire film: It is much more sophisticated in theme and technique than its seemingly frivolous matter promises. With practically nothing substantial in the way of a story to tell — nothing more than a loosely strung fable of how the boys take under their wings the wacky old grandfather of one of them while preparing for a London television show—it discovers a nifty little satire in the paradox of the old man being

more of a problem, more of "a troublemaker and a mixer," than the boys.

"'e's a nice old man isn't 'e?," notes one of the fellows when they first meet Grand-dad on a train. And another replies, with courteous unction, which parodies the standard comment about the Beatles themselves, "'e's very clean."

This line, which runs through the picture, may be too subtle for the happily squealing kids who will no doubt be its major audience, but the oldsters may profitably dig. And, of course, everybody will be able to enjoy the rollicking, madcap fun.

There's no use in trying to chart it. It comes in fast-flowing spurts of sight gags and throw-away dialogue that is flipped about recklessly. Alun Owen, who wrote the screenplay, may have dug it all out of his brain, but Richard Lester has directed at such a brisk clip that it seems to come spontaneously.

And just one musical sequence, for instance, when the

boys tumble wildly out of doors and race eccentrically about a patterned playground to the tune of their song "Can't Buy Me Love," hits a surrealistic tempo that approaches audio-visual poetry.

Sure, the frequent and brazen "yah-yah-yahing" of the fellows when they break into song may be grating. To ears not tuned to it, it has moronic monotony. But it is always relieved by pictorial compositions that suggest travesties—or, at least, intelligent awareness of the absurdity of the Beatle craze.

Unless you know the fellows, it is hard to identify them, except for Ringo Starr, the big-nosed one, who does a saucy comic sequence on his own. But they're all good —surprisingly natural in the cinema-reality style that Mr. Lester expertly maintains. And Wilfrid Brambell as the old man is dandy, a delightfully comic Irishman. Many others are also funny.

It is good to know there are people in this world, up to and including the major parties, who don't take the Beatles seriously.

Wilfrid Brambell and Ringo Starr in scene from new movie

UNITED ARTISTS
UA PREMIERE SHOWCASE PRESENTATION

Regular Performances START TODAY

Starring in their first full-length, hilarious, action-packed film!

THE BEATLES

"A HARD DAY'S NIGHT"

6 brand new songs

A Hard Day's Night
If I Fell
And I Love Her
I Should Have Known Better
I'm Happy Just To Dance With You
Tell Me Why

PLUS YOUR BEATLES FAVORITES!
★ She Loves You ★ All My Loving
★ I Want to Be Your Man ★ Don't Bother Me ★ Can't Buy Me Love

also starring WILFRID BRAMBELL

produced by WALTER SHENSON   screenplay by ALUN OWEN

directed by RICHARD LESTER   released thru UNITED ARTISTS

Hear the Beatles on the one, the only, the original sound track album from United Artists Records!

Gary Cooper won an Oscar for best actor for his role in *High Noon*.

High Noon a Western of Rare Achievement

HIGH NOON, screen play by Carl Foreman: directed by Fred Zinnemann; produced by Stanley Kramer. A Stanley Kramer Production released by United Artists. At the Mayfair.

Will Kane	Gary Cooper
Jonas Henderson	Thomas Mitchell
Harvey Pell	Lloyd Bridges
Helen Ramirez	Katy Jurado
Amy Kane	Grace Kelly
Percy Mettrick	Otto Kruger
Martin Howe	Lon Chaney
William Fuller	Henry Morgan
Frank Miller	Ian MacDonald
Mildred Fuller	Eve McVeagh
Cooper	Harry Shannon
Jack Colby	Lee Van Cleef
James Pierce	Bob Wilke
Ben Miller	Sheb Woolley
Sam	Tom London
Station Master	Ted Stanhope
Gillis	Larry Blake
Barber	William Phillips

By BOSLEY CROWTHER

Every five years or so, somebody—somebody of talent and taste, with a full appreciation of legend and a strong trace of poetry in their soul—scoops up a handful of clichés from the vast lore of Western films and turns them into a thrilling and inspiring work of art in this genre. Such a rare and exciting achievement is Stanley Kramer's production, "High Noon," which was placed on exhibition at the Mayfair yesterday.

Which one of several individuals is most fully responsible for this job is a difficult matter to determine and nothing about which to quarrel. It could be Mr. Kramer, who got the picture made, and it be Scriptwriter Carl Foreman, who prepared the story for the screen. Certainly Director Fred Zinnemann had a great deal to do with it and possibly Gary Cooper, as the star, had a hand in the job. An accurate apportionment of credits is not a matter of critical concern.

What is important is that someone—or all of them together, we would say—has turned out a Western drama that is the best of its kind in several years. Familiar but far from conventional in the fabric of story and theme and marked by a sure illumination of human character, this tale of a brave and stubborn sheriff in a town full of do-nothings and cowards has the rhythm and roll of a ballad spun in pictorial terms. And, over all, it has a stunning comprehension of that thing we call courage in a man and the thorniness of being courageous in a world of bullies and poltroons.

Like most works of art, it is simple — simple in the structure of its plot and comparatively simple in the layout of its fundamental issues and morals. Plot-wise, it is the story of a sheriff in a small Western town, on the day of his scheduled retirement, faced with a terrible ordeal. At 10:30 in the morning, just a few minutes after he has been wed, he learns that a dreaded desperado is arriving in town on the noon train. The bad man has got a pardon from a rap on which the sheriff sent him up, and the sheriff knows that the killer is coming back to town to get him.

Here is the first important question: shall the sheriff slip away, as his new wife and several decent citizens reasonably urge him to do, or shall he face, here and now, the crisis which he knows he can never escape? And once he has answered this question, the second and greater problem is the maintenance of his resolution as noon approaches and he finds himself alone—one man, without a single sidekick, against a killer and three attendant thugs; one man who has the courage to take on a perilous, righteous job.

How Mr. Foreman has surrounded this simple and forceful tale with tremendous dramatic implications is a thing we can't glibly state in words. It is a matter of skill in movie-writing, but, more than that, it is the putting down, in terms of visually simplified images, a pattern of poetic ideas. And how Mr. Zinnemann has transmitted this pattern in pictorial terms is something which we can only urge you to go yourself to see.

One sample worth framing, however, is the brilliant assembly of shots that holds the tale in taut suspension just before the fatal hour of noon. The issues have been established, the townsfolk have fallen away and the sheriff, alone with his destiny, has sat down at his desk to wait. Over his shoulder, Mr. Zinnemann shows us a white sheet of paper on which is scrawled "last will and testament" by a slowly moving pen. Then he gives us a shot (oft repeated) of the pendulum of the clock, and then a shot looking off into the distance of the prairie down the empty railroad tracks. In quick succession, then, he shows us, the tense faces of men waiting in the church and in the local saloon, the still streets outside, the three thugs waiting at the station, the tracks again, the wife of the sheriff waiting and the face of the sheriff himself. Then, suddenly, away in the distance, there is the whistle of the train and, looking down the tracks again, he shows us a whisp of smoke from the approaching train. In a style of consummate realism, Mr. Zinnemann has done a splendid job.

And so has the cast, under his direction. Mr. Cooper is at the top of his form in a type of role that has trickled like water off his back for years. And Lloyd Bridges as a vengeful young deputy, Katy Jurado as a Mexican adventuress, Thomas Mitchell as a prudent townsman, Otto Kruger as a craven judge and Grace Kelly as the new wife of the sheriff are the best of many in key roles.

Meaningful in its implications, as well as loaded with interest and suspense, "High Noon" is a western to challenge "Stagecoach" for the all-time championship.

STANLEY KRAMER PRODUCTIONS presents

GARY COOPER

THERE IS NOTHING UNDER THE SUN LIKE THE HIGH ADVENTURE OF "HIGH NOON"!

"HIGH NOON"

STANLEY KRAMER PRODUCTIONS presents
GARY COOPER in "HIGH NOON"
with THOMAS MITCHELL · LLOYD BRIDGES · KATY JURADO
GRACE KELLY · OTTO KRUGER · Lon Chaney · Henry Morgan
DIRECTED BY FRED ZINNEMANN · Screen Play by Carl Foreman
Music Composed and Directed by Dimitri Tiomkin · Director of Photography Floyd Crosby, A.S.C.
RELEASED THRU UNITED ARTISTS

'High Sierra,' at the Strand, Considers the Tragic and Dramatic Plight of the Last Gangster

HIGH SIERRA; screen play by John Huston and W. R. Burnett; based on the novel by W. R. Burnett; directed by Raoul Walsh for Warner Brothers. At the Strand.

Marie	Ida Lupino
Roy Earle	Humphrey Bogart
"Babe"	Alan Curtis
Red	Arthur Kennedy
Velma	Joan Leslie
"Doc" Banton	Henry Hull
Pa	Henry Travers
Healy	Jerome Cowan
Mrs. Baughnam	Minna Gombell
Jake Kranmer	Barton MacLane
Ma	Elizabeth Risdon
Louis Mendoza	Cornel Wilde
Big Mac	Donald MacBride
Mr. Baughmam	Paul Harvey
Blondie	Isabel Jewell
Algernon	Willie Best

By BOSLEY CROWTHER

We wouldn't know for certain whether the twilight of the American gangster is here. But the Warner Brothers, who should know if anybody does, have apparently taken it for granted and, in a solemn Wagnerian mood, are giving that titanic figure a send-off befitting a first-string god in the film called "High Sierra," which arrived yesterday at the Strand. Yessir, Siegfried himself never rose to more heroic heights than does Mr. Humphrey Bogart, the last of the great gunmen, when, lodged on a high mountain crag with an army of coppers below, he shouts defiance at his tormentors ere his noble soul take flight. It's truly magnificent, that's all.

As a matter of fact—and aside from the virtues of the film itself—it is rather touching to behold the Warners pay such a glowing tribute, for no one has made a better thing out of the legendary gangster than they have. No one has greater reason to grow nostalgic about the bad boys of yesterday who, as one of the characters in "High Sierra" reverently remarks, are "all either dead or doing time now in Alcatraz." So, indeed, we are deeply moved by this honest payment of respects to an aging and graying veteran of the Nineteen Thirty banditti who makes his last stand his best. Somehow, it seems quite fitting.

Of course, that is exactly the way the Warners and every one concerned intended it should seem. For the story which is told is that of a notorious hold-up man who is sprung out of an Illinois prison by an old gangland pal who wants him in California for a big job. But the gunman has got some ideas about freedom and the joy of living. He wants to marry a simple little girl he meets on the road heading West; he wants to do good things because, you see, he really has a good heart.

Well, you know what that means. It's just as old "Doc" Banton tells him ("Doc" being the quack who tends "Big Mac"). He says, "Remember what Johnny Dillinger said about guys like you and him; he said you're just rushing toward death—that's it, you're rushing toward death." And that's the truth. For the big holdup job gets messed up by a couple of "jitterbugs" who are assisting on it, the girl turns out a great disappointment, the gunman is rendered a fugitive with a moll and a dog who love him and finally he is brought to bay on that peak in the High Sierras. And there he dies gallantly. It's a wonder the American flag wasn't wrapped about his broken corpse.

As gangster pictures go, this one has everything—speed, excitement, suspense and that ennobling suggestion of futility which makes for irony and pity. Mr. Bogart plays the leading role with a perfection of hard-boiled vitality, and Ida Lupino, Arthur Kennedy, Alan Curtis and a newcomer named Joan Leslie handle lesser roles effectively. Especially, is Miss Lupino impressive as the adoring moll. As gangster pictures go—if they do—it's a perfect epilogue. Count on the old guard and Warners: they die but never surrender.

The Peak of Excitement!

THIS STORY IS A WORLD BEATER! says MARK HELLINGER

HIGH SIERRA

By the author of "Little Caesar"   WARNER BROS. PICTURE

MARIE, just a two-decker and killer's companion—yet deep down a love-hungry woman yearning for the real thing . . .

IDA LUPINO

'MAD DOG' EARLE, defiant of every law of man . . . until he found man didn't make the law of High Sierra. Played by

HUMPHREY BOGART

Ida Lupino and Humphrey Bogart in *High Sierra*.

Basil Rathbone Plays Sherlock Holmes in the Roxy's 'Hound of the Baskervilles'—New Film at Strand

By FRANK S. NUGENT

In an atmosphere of dense fog perfectly suited to the mental processes of Dr. Watson, Sherlock Holmes is out stalking "The Hound of the Baskervilles" again, this time at the Roxy by request of Twentieth Century-Fox—a circumstance which makes it difficult to resist saying something about Fox chasing the Hound. Holmes is being played by Basil Rathbone, Dr. Watson by Nigel Bruce and the Hound by—but that's the question. For, unless you're up on Conan Doyle, you'll have to discover for yourself whether it's a real mastiff or just a four-legged curse that has been dogging the Baskervilles since Magna Carta.

Putting its straightest face upon the matter and being as weird as all get-out, the film succeeds rather well in reproducing Sir Arthur's macabre detective story along forthright cinema lines. The technicians have whipped up a moor at least twice as desolate as any ghost-story moor has need to be, the mist swirls steadily, the savage howl of the Baskerville hound is heard at all the melodramatically appropriate intervals and Mr. Holmes himself, with hunting cap, calabash and omniscience, whispers from time to time, "It's murder, Watson, murder!"

THE HOUND OF THE BASKERVILLES, screen play by Ernest Pascal based on the story by the late Sir Arthur Conan Doyle; directed by Sidney Lanfield; a Twentieth Century-Fox production. At the Roxy.

Sir Henry Baskerville	Richard Greene
Sherlock Holmes	Basil Rathbone
Beryl Stapleton	Wendy Barrie
Dr. Watson	Nigel Bruce
Dr. James Mortimer	Lionel Atwill
Barryman	John Carradine
Frankland	Barlowe Borland
Mrs. Jenifer Mortimer	Beryl Mercer
John Stapleton	Morton Lowry
Sir Hugo Baskerville	Ralph Forbes
Cabby	E. E. Clive
Mrs. Barryman	Eily Malyon
Convict	Nigel de Bruller
Mrs. Hudson	Mary Gordon

Of course, we had the advantage over Sherlock in having read the book, so we knew all the time how his grim mystery would out. There's just the least reason to believe, too, that most of the others in the audience had their finger on the arch-plotter long before Holmes caught on. But even so, it's fairly good fun and like old times to be seeing Sherlock again and hearing him say, after a nervous twitch of his sensitive nostrils, "Watson, the needle!" Mr. Rathbone really put something into that line.

DOORS OPEN 10 A. M.
Sir Arthur Conan Doyle's
THE HOUND OF THE BASKERVILLES
RICHARD GREENE · BASIL RATHBONE
★ GALA REVUE ON THE STAGE ★
25¢ ROXY 15¢

Appearing in their Sherlock Holmes and Dr. Watson roles are Basil Rathbone and Nigel Bruce in *The Hound of the Baskervilles*.

'House of Wax,' Warners' 3-D Film With Vincent Price, Has Premiere at Paramount

HOUSE OF WAX, screen play by Crane Wilbur, based on a story by Charles Belden; directed by Andre de Toth; produced by Bryan Foy in Natural Vision for Warner Brothers. At the Paramount.

Prof. Henry Jarrod	Vincent Price
Lieut. Tom Brennan	Frank Lovejoy
Sue Allen	Phyllis Kirk
Cathy Gray	Carolyn Jones
Scott Andrews	Paul Picerni
Matthew Burke	Roy Roberts
Mrs. Andrews	Angela Clarke
Sidney Wallace	Paul Cavanagh
Sgt. Jim Shane	Dabbs Greer
Igor	Charles Buchinsky
Barker	Reggie Rymal
Bruce Allison	Philip Tonge

By BOSLEY CROWTHER

A slight paraphrase of the first message sent over telegraph wires might signal the staggering appearance of the first major stereoscopic film. "House of Wax," the historic production unveiled at the Paramount yesterday in as wild a display of noise and nonsense as has rattled a movie screen in years, may well cause a dazed and deafened viewer, amazed and bewildered, to inquire in wonder and genuine trepidation: What hath the Warner Brothers wrought?

For this mixture of antique melodrama, three-dimensional photography, ghoulish sensationalism and so-called directed sound (which means noises coming at you from all parts of the theatre) raises so many serious questions of achievement and responsibility that a friend of the motion picture medium has ample reason to be baffled and concerned.

It isn't only that the story projected in this first major whack with 3-D is a bundle of horrifying claptrap that was cheap and obvious twenty years ago—which is precisely how long ago it was the Warners first made it under the title of "The Mystery of the Wax Museum." Even then it was a raw, distasteful fable fit only to frighten simple souls with the menace of a crazy, fire-scarred sculptor embalming his victims in a waxworks chamber of horrors.

And now, as a story, it is no different. It is still a fantastic conceit, highlighted by a fire in the wax museum and the subsequent depredations of a repulsively disfigured ghoul who establishes a new museum with wax-encased cadavers snatched from the morgue. And its performance by Vincent Price as the monstrous hero, Phyllis Kirk as a potential victim, Frank Lovejoy as a baffled detective and several others in assorted comic-strip roles, under Andre De Toth's direction, is in a consistently stiff and graceless style.

Nor is it that the stereo-photography, while more effective than any other yet seen in New York theatres, is of but moderate advantage to the film. The picture is in Technicolor (as was the previous "The Mystery of the Wax Museum") and the illusion of contour and depth in the images, as viewed through polaroid glasses, is good. On a few occasions, such as a scene in which a barker bounces a rubber ball toward the audience or figures tumble forward in the picture, the shock effect is pronounced. But the so-called added dimension of "deepness" is of slight significance.

The major causes for anxiety presented by this film are in the savagery of its conception and the intolerable artlessness of its sound.

Likewise, the noisy sound of footsteps clattering in the back of the theatre a moment after an actor has appeared to rush forward from the screen is completely illogical and unnerving. It sounds like a riot outside.

But the most frightening thing about this picture is the thought of the imitation it will encourage, if it proves to draw customers to the theatre, which it more than likely will do. Some may accept this dismal prospect with the same casualness they accord the idiocies and eventually comical monstrosities of the film. But not so this reviewer. It's a prospect we view with alarm. Dimly we foresee movie audiences embalmed in three-dimensional wax and sound.

Vincent Price appearing in the first major attempt at a 3-D movie, *House of Wax.*

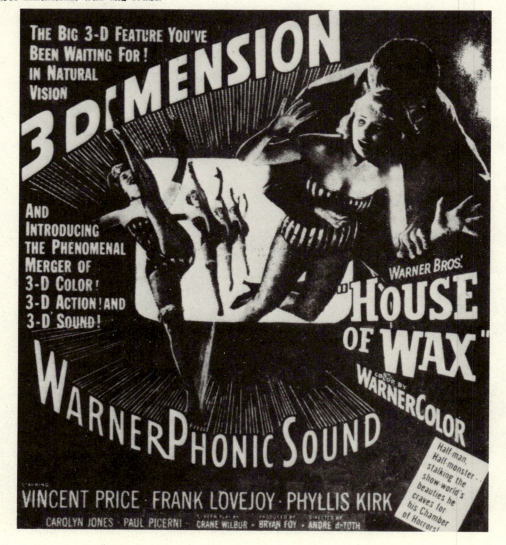

TRIO OF STARS IN CINEMASCOPE

Monroe, Grable, Bacall Illustrate 'How to Marry a Millionaire' at Globe and Loew's State

HOW TO MARRY A MILLIONAIRE, screen play by Nunnally Johnson, based on plays by Zoe Akins, Dale Eunson and Katherine Albert; directed by Jean Negulesco; produced by Mr. Johnson for Twentieth Century-Fox. At the Globe and Loew's State.

Pola	Marilyn Monroe
Loco	Betty Grable
Schatz Page	Lauren Bacall
Freddie Denmark	David Wayne
Eben	Rory Calhoun
Tom Brookman	Cameron Mitchell
J. Stewart Merrill	Alex D'Arcy
Waldo Brewster	Fred Clark
J. D. Hanley	William Powell
Mike, Elevator Man	George Dunn
Benton	Percy Helton
Cab Driver	Robert Adler
Elevator Operator	Harry Carter
Mr. Otis	Tudor Owen
Antoine	Maurice Marsac

By BOSLEY CROWTHER

In the lingo of merchandising there is a neat word—"packaging"—for the business of putting up a product in a container of deceptive size and show. And that, in manner of speaking, is the word for what Twentieth Century-Fox has done in fetching an average portion of very light comedy in its "How to Marry a Millionaire."

Around a frivolous story of the maneuvering of three dumb blondes to hook themselves wealthy husbands, regardless of the usual ardent urge, the Fox boys have tossed the imposing wrapper of their new wide-screen Cinema-Scope and put the whole thing forth as an opportunity in entertainment that you can't afford to miss. Within the mammoth dimensions of their giant-economy-size

screen, they have dribbled a moderate measure of conventional, wise-cracking fun. As premiums, to take up the air space, they have put Betty Grable, Marilyn Monroe and Lauren Bacall. And that constitutes the bargain package. It is obtainable at Loew's State and the Globe.

Why beat around the bush about it? This chucklesome account of how three girls—all of them beautiful New York models—go gunning for rich old bucks looks even more skimpy and trivial on the big panel screen than it is. Plucked from a play by Zoe Akins, "The Greeks Had a Word for It"—which was done as a film with Madge Evans, Ina Claire and Joan Blondell long years ago—it does find some nimble, obvious humor in the hard-working efforts of the dames and in the wriggling evasions of their nominated prey.

Miss Grable, as a breezy huntress who cuts out a skittish gent, Fred Clark, and shamelessly pursues him right up to his snow-bound lodge in Maine, is the funniest of the ladies. And she does work the simple running-gag of thinking she is going to an Elks' convention for as much meager jest as it contains. Her off-screen capitulation to a forest ranger, Rory Calhoun, is by far the most sensible and painless bit of feminine behavior in the film.

Their Rich Quarry Enacted by Fred Clark, Alex D'Arcy and William Powell

As the hard-headed "brain" of the trio, Miss Bacall has a cold and waspish way of regimenting her playmates or plunging for the heart of William Powell, and her last-minute switch to Cameron Mitchell is a grudging and cheerless giving-in.

However, the baby-faced mugging of the famously shaped Miss Monroe does compensate in some measure for the truculence of Miss Bacall. Her natural reluctance to wear eyeglasses when she is spreading the glamour accounts for some funny farce business of missing signals and walking into walls. As the gentlemen of her favor, Alex D'Arcy and David Wayne throw a slight bit of comical flavor into the thinness of the film.

But the substance is still insufficient for the vast spread of screen which CinemaScope throws across the front of the theatre, and the impression it leaves is that of nonsense from a few people in a great big hall.

It is true that producer Nunnally Johnson, who also wrote the script, and Jean Negulesco, who directed, have attempted to fill the mammoth screen with extravagant scenic adornments and some fine panoramic displays. Some shots of the New York skyline as seen from the Upper Bay, of La Guardia and Kansas City airports and of snow-covered timberland (in Maine) are visually exciting. The color, when firm, is very good. But the total effect of these glimpses is one of proud but nonessential showing off.

Coronation Parade Shown

As a matter of fact, these cut-in pictures seem almost as unmatched and remote as some excellent footage included on the program, showing a bit of Britain's Coronation parade. The straight panoramic picturization of masses of marching troops in the drizzle of a famous day in London is more stirring than the feature film.

Betty Grable, Rory Calhoun, Lauren Bacall, Cameron Mitchell, Marilyn Monroe and David Wayne in a scene from *How To Marry A Millionaire.*

ALL THIS and CinemaScope TOO!
YOU SEE IT WITHOUT GLASSES

Marilyn
MONROE

Betty
GRABLE

Lauren
BACALL

of the Big-Time, Grand-Time, Great-Time Show of All Time!

BRANDT'S
GLOBE
B'WAY at 46th
Continuous Performances
DOORS OPEN 8:30 A.M.

Formal Invitational
Premiere Tonight
at 8:30 P.M.

How To Marry A Millionaire
TECHNICOLOR

LOEW'S
STATE
B'WAY at 45th
Continuous Performances
DOORS OPEN 9 A.M.

The First Great Shorts in
CinemaScope

EXTRA! WALT DISNEY'S
Technicolor Cartoon
"TOOT, WHISTLE, PLUNK and BOOM"

20th Century-Fox presents
"THE CORONATION
PARADE" · Technicolor

'The Hucksters,' Starring Gable and Kerr, Opens at Capitol

THE HUCKSTERS, screen play by Luther Davis; adapted by Edward Choderov and George Wells from the novel by Frederic Wakeman; directed by Jack Conway; produced by Arthur Hornblow Jr. for Metro-Goldwyn-Mayer. At the Capitol.

Victor Norman	Clark Gable
Kay Dorrance	Deborah Kerr
Evan Llewellyn Evans	Sydney Greenstreet
Mr. Kimberly	Adolphe Menjou
Jean Ogolvie	Ava Gardner
Buddy Hare	Keenan Wynn
Dave Lash	Edward Arnold
Cooke	Richard Gaines
Max Herman	Frank Albertson
Georgie Gaver	Douglas Fowley
Michael Michaelson	Clinton Sundberg
Mrs. Kimberly	Gloria Holden
Valet	Aubrey Mather
Betty	Connie Gilchrist
Regina Kennedy	Kathryn Card
Miss Hammer	Lillian Bronson
Secretary	Vera Marshe
Allison	Ralph Bunker

By BOSLEY CROWTHER

Not to prolong your anxiety, let's get it said right off that the film version of "The Hucksters," which came to the Capitol yesterday, is a considerable re-write of the original, scrubbed and polished with Beautee soap. Virtually all of the coarseness which was in Frederic Wakeman's dubious book has been neatly eliminated and replaced by a wholesome romance. Much of the sting in the satire of the radio business, which was the novel's singular charm, has been tempered into farce comedy. And the role of Victor Norman has been built up.

That being clearly recorded and the implications absorbed, we can now go ahead and tell you that the film is amusing—but too long. And we can also carefully warn you that, unless you like Clark Cable very much, you are going to find him monotonous in this hour-and-fifty-five-minute film. For Mr. Gable, in the role of Vic Norman, the smartest, slickest thing in radio, is off the screen for all of five minutes—maybe eight. The rest of the time, he's on. And although he makes Vic Norman as round, as firm and as fully packed as he was in the book—which means an incredible character—that's a long time to look at one man.

It's a long time to look at Mr. Gable and his cynical attitudes, especially with several other characters begging favorably for more revealing time. There's Deborah Kerr, for instance, as a beautiful, English-born widow who falls in love with this radio-agency genius. We could do with a little more of her. Not that her rather radiant passion for this well-tailored roughneck makes much sense, but Miss Kerr is a very soothing person and she elevates the tone of the film.

We could also do very nicely with a great deal more of Adolphe Menjou as a harassed radio-agency executive and with Sydney Greenstreet as a freakish soap tycoon. For the fact is that the best parts of the picture—as they were the best parts of the book—are those in which the maddening eccentricities of the soap advertiser are indulged, in which the frank ostentations of this maniac are held up to ridicule and the horrible banalities of the radio are moderately burlesqued. Mr. Menjou and Mr.

Greenstreet are entertaining and fascinating.

But then, as we say, the whole picture seems to have been deliberately designed to give more attention to Mr. Gable than to the kidding of radio. And the consequence is a disproportion in story and personality. The inherent interest in "The Hucksters" is its comment upon a mad business. The emphasis in the picture is upon the growth of an insincere man. Unfortunately, neither Mr. Wakeman nor the fellows who write the script have given us enough of a character to justify his predominance.

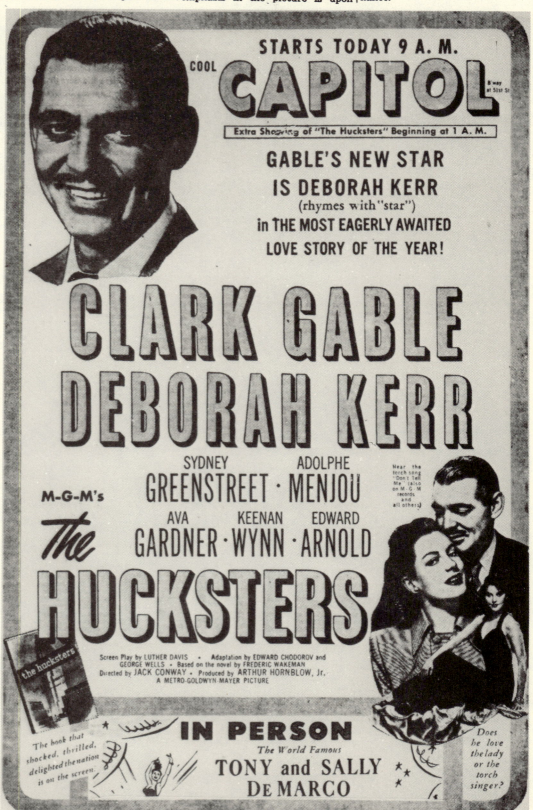

STARTS TODAY 9 A.M.

COOL **CAPITOL** B'way at 51st St

Extra Showing of "The Hucksters" Beginning at 1 A.M.

GABLE'S NEW STAR IS DEBORAH KERR (rhymes with "star") in THE MOST EAGERLY AWAITED LOVE STORY OF THE YEAR!

CLARK GABLE DEBORAH KERR

SYDNEY GREENSTREET · ADOLPHE MENJOU

AVA GARDNER · KEENAN WYNN · EDWARD ARNOLD

M-G-M's **The HUCKSTERS**

Hear the torch song "Don't Tell Me" (also on M-G-M records and all others)

Screen Play by LUTHER DAVIS · Adaptation by EDWARD CHODOROV and GEORGE WELLS · Based on the novel by FREDERIC WAKEMAN Directed by JACK CONWAY · Produced by ARTHUR HORNBLOW, Jr. A METRO-GOLDWYN MAYER PICTURE

The book that shocked, thrilled, delighted the nation is on the screen!

IN PERSON The World Famous TONY and SALLY De MARCO

Does he love the lady or the torch singer?

The Hideous Bell-Ringer

THE HUNCHBACK OF NOTRE DAME, with Lon Chaney, Ernest Torrence, Tully Marshall, Pat., Ruth Miller, Norman Kerry, Nigel de Bruller, Raymond Hatton, John Cossar, Harry Von Meter, Roy Laidlaw, Albert McQuarrie, Jay Hunt, Harry Devere, Eulalie Jensen, Gladys Brockwell, Winifred Bryson, Pearl Tupper, Eva Lewis, Jane Sherman, Helen Brunneau, Gladys Johnston and others. At the Astor Theatre.

As the central figure in the film conception of Victor Hugo's "The Hunchback of Notre Dame," Lon Chaney portrays Quasimodo, the ape-like bellringer of the famed cathedral, as a fearsome, frightful, crooked creature, one eye bulging but blind, knees that interfere, sharp, saw-edged protruding teeth, high, swollen cheek bones and a dented and twisted nose—a "monstrous joke of nature." He gives an unrestrained but remarkable performance in this production, which opened last night at the Astor Theatre, where there gathered familiar faces of the stage and screen, literary lights and men-about-town.

Naturally there is much in this picture which is not pleasant any more than the works of Poe, some of Eugene O'Neill's strokes of genius, the stories of Thomas Burke, Stacey Aumonier and many of the masters of the pen in the olden days. It is, however, a strong production, on which no pains or money have been spared to depict the seamy side of old Paris. The "set" of the cathedral is really marvelous, having the appearance of stolidity and massiveness, and in sequences looking down from it to the streets below give one a dizzy idea of height. If there were nothing else to see in this film it would be worth while to gaze upon the faithful copy of Notre Dame.

The streets of Paris of yesteryear are also well constructed, but if they were not so mudless and dustless they would be more real and less like stage settings.

Chaney throws his whole soul into making Quasimodo as repugnant as anything human could very well be, even to decorating his breast and back with hair. He is remarkably agile and impressive when showing his fearlessness for a great height, and the strength of his awful hands by climbing down the façade of the cathedral, and on one occasion down a rope, looking like a mammoth monkey on a stick. And yet in this distorted body there was gratitude, for Esmeralda is carried to sanctuary from the gibbet by this muscular ogre.

Undoubtedly the most picturesque person in this photodrama is Clopin, the king of beggars and assassins, a character that Ernest Torrence plays and appears to enjoy. He is introduced several times in the so-called court of miracles, where the halt become nimble and the blind see. Torrence is a commanding figure, seated on a block-like throne, handing down his laws to his hordes.

The highest dramatic sequence in this film is where Clopin calls upon his filthy crew to storm the cathedral, and the director, Wallace Worsley, has made this a most telling, inspiring incident. The ragged, half-starved mob comes forth at Clopin's behest from the sewers, the alleys, the underground muckpots and the hovels in which many of them dwell, and, with gathered numbers as they rush along, they charge upon the church with torches, sticks and knives. Quasimodo strains himself lifting heavy granite blocks, which he drops over on the advancing mendi-cants and murderers, finally hurling a heavy teak beam on the frenzied lot. It pinions four under it when it falls, but unfortunately they seem to be too neat in their fall to be realistic. Eventually this beam is used as a battering ram, and one sees, as if from the cathedral towers, the diligent antlike mortals banging the ram on the oaken portals of the cathedral.

Patsy Ruth Miller has the part of Esmeralda, a truly pretty, chubby girl, whose only fault is the over-decorating of her upper lip, which was too perfectly "bowed." However, her acting is unusually good in the many difficult scenes in which she has to appear. Her paramour, Captain Phoebus, is capably portrayed by Norman Kerry.

Louis XI. is played by the careful Tully Marshall, who makes every scene in which he appears count for something.

Throughout this drama there is one humorous sequence—one which is pictured in an interesting manner. It is where Quasimodo appears before the court for kidnapping Esmeralda. The Judge is deaf, but is too proud to admit it. The hunchback doesn't care a rap about his similar affliction and admits it. The prisoner says one thing, and the Judge, not understanding a single word, pretends to have heard, forthwith ordering Quasimodo to be flogged with twenty lashes.

There are a number of changes, obviously necessary, which have been made in this adaptation. The story is subservient to the atmosphere and the acting. It is merely that a girl befriended Quasimodo when he was arrested for a nocturnal attack, inspired by the wicked brother of the Archdeacon. She is arrested finally herself, accused of having stabbed Captain Phoebus, with whom she was in love, and is saved by the hideous bell-ringer. However, the film holds the interest because of the excellent acting and "sets" and the splendid atmosphere throughout the drama. True, the cast has certain weaknesses, but they are not obtrusive. It is a drama which will appeal to all those who are interested in fine screen acting, artistic settings and a remarkable handling of crowds who don't mind a grotesque figure and a grim atmosphere.

AUDIENCE STOOD UP AND CHEERED

The reception accorded

Carl Laemmle's production

"The HUNCHBACK OF NOTRE DAME"

featuring LON CHANEY

One of the greatest ever received by a motion picture.

Seats Now On Sale For First 4 Weeks

MAT. TODAY, 2:30.   TONIGHT, 8:30.

ASTOR THEATRE, B'way, 45 St. TWICE DAILY, 2:30-8:30.

NOTE: Due to the urgent popular demand, the remarkable art lobby in the Astor Theatre will be open to the public daily from 10 A. M.

Patsy Ruth Miller as Esmerelda, tends to the monstrous Quasimodo.

'In the Heat of the Night,' a Racial Drama

Poitier Plays Northern Detective in South

By BOSLEY CROWTHER

THE hot surge of racial hate and prejudice that is so evident and critical now in so many places in this country, not alone in the traditional area of the Deep South, is fictionally isolated in an ugly little Mississippi town in the new film, "In the Heat of the Night," which opened at the Capitol and the 86th Street East yesterday.

Here the corrosiveness of prejudice is manifested by a clutch of town police and a few weaseling nabobs and red-necks toward a Negro detective from the North who happens to be picked up as a suspect in a white man's murder while he is passing through town. But the surge of this evil feeling is also manifested by the Negro himself after he has been cleared of suspicion and ruefully recruited to help solve the crime. And in this juxtaposition of resentments between whites and blacks is vividly and forcefully illustrated one of the awful dilemmas of our times.

•

But here Norman Jewison has taken a hard, outspoken script, prepared by Stirling Silliphant from an undistinguished novel by John Ball, and, with stinging performances contributed by Rod Steiger as the chief of police and Sidney Poitier as the detective, he has turned it into a film that has the look and sound of actuality and the pounding pulse of truth.

The Cast

IN THE HEAT OF THE NIGHT; screenplay by Stirling Silliphant, based on the novel by John Ball; directed by Norman Jewison; produced by Walter Mirisch; presented by the Mirisch Corporation, and released through United Artists. At the Capitol Theater, Broadway and 51st Street, and the 86th Street East Theater, east of Third Avenue. Running time: 109 minutes.

Virgil Tibbs	Sidney Poitier
Bill Gillespie	Rod Steiger
Sam Wood	Warren Oates
Mrs. Leslie Colbert	Lee Grant
Purdy	James Patterson
Delores Purdy	Quentin Dean
Eric Endicott	Larry Gates
Webb Schubert	William Schallart
Mrs. Bellamy (Mama Caleba)	Beah Richards
Harvey Oberst	Scott Wilson
Philip Colbert	Jack Teter
Packy Harrison	Matt Clark
Ralph Henshaw	Anthony James
H. E. Handerson	Kermit Murdock
Jess	Khalil Bezaleel
George Courtney	Peter Whitney

The line of its fascination is not so much its melodramatic plot. It is not in the touch-and-go discovery by the detective of who it was who bumped off that prominent northern industrialist in town to start an integrated mill, or in the gantlet of perils of bodily injury from snarling red-necks that Mr. Poitier constantly runs. Actually, the mystery story is a rather routine and arbitrary one and it is brought to a hasty conclusion in a flurry of coincidences and explanations that leave one confused and unconvinced.

The fascination of it is in the crackling confrontations between the arrogant small town white policeman, with all his layers of ignorance and prejudice, and the sophisticated Negro detective with his steely armor of contempt and mistrust.

It is in the alert and cryptic caution with which these two professional cops face off, the white man arrogant and rueful but respectful of the black man's evident skill and the latter enraged and disgusted by the other's insulting attitudes.

Faces Steiger in Film Delineating Prejudice

And it is in the magnificent manner in which Mr. Steiger and Mr. Poitier act their roles, each giving physical authority and personal depth to the fallible human beings they are.

Fascinating, too, are the natures and details of other characters who swarm and sweat through a crisis in a believable Mississippi town —Warren Oates and Peter Whitney as raw cops, William Schallert and Larry Gates as powerful whites, Scott Wilson as a renegade red-neck and Quentin Dean as a slippery little slut.

The end of it all is not conclusive. It does not imply that the state of prejudice and antagonism in the community is any different from what it was at the start. But it does suggest that a rapport between two totally antagonistic men may be reached in a state of interdependence. And that's something to be showing so forcefully on the screen.

Sidney Poitier and Lee Grant in *In The Heat Of The Night*.

"AN ALTOGETHER EXCELLENT FILM THAT IS QUITE POSSIBLY THE BEST WE HAVE HAD FROM THE U.S. THIS YEAR!" —LIFE MAGAZINE

THE MIRISCH CORPORATION Presents

SIDNEY POITIER   ROD STEIGER

in THE NORMAN JEWISON · WALTER MIRISCH PRODUCTION

"IN THE HEAT OF THE NIGHT".

co-starring
WARREN OATES
LEE GRANT

Screenplay by
STIRLING SILLIPHANT

Produced by
WALTER MIRISCH

Directed by
NORMAN JEWISON

COLOR by DeLuxe   MUSIC–QUINCY JONES · "IN THE HEAT OF THE NIGHT" sung by RAY CHARLES

ORIGINAL MOTION PICTURE SOUNDTRACK AVAILABLE ON UNITED ARTISTS RECORDS

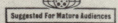
Suggested For Mature Audiences

UNITED ARTISTS

Jailhouse Rock
The Cast

JAILHOUSE ROCK, screenplay by Guy Trosper, based on a Ned Young story; directed by Richard Thorpe; produced by Pandro S. Berman for Metro-Goldwyn-Mayer. At Loew's neighborhood theatres.

Vince Everett	Elvis Presley
Peggy	Judy Tyler
Hunk Houghton	Mickey Shaughnessy
Mr. Shores	Vaughn Taylor
Sherry Wilson	Jennifer Holden

ACTION OF THE TIGER, screenplay by Robert Carson; directed by Terence Young; produced by Kenneth Harper for Metro-Goldwyn-Mayer.

Carson	Van Johnson
Tracy	Martine Carol
Trifon	Herbert Lom
Henri	Gustavo Rocco
Mara	Anna Garber

"JAILHOUSE ROCK," a Metro - Goldwyn - Mayer showcase for Elvis Presley, opening yesterday on the Loew's neighborhood circuit, carries ol' El all the way from the hoosegow to Hollywood, where our boy turns into a sour, spoiled (millionaire) apple. A pal beats some sense back into him though.

This, the third Presley picture, reverentially produced by Pandro S. Berman and directed by Richard Thorpe, also features two talented performers, Mickey Shaughnessy and Judy Tyler. The former plays a kind of Luther Billis of a state pen, who should be forgiven for developing his young cellmate's talent. Although she isn't allotted one single note here, Miss Tyler is the lovely little brunette from Broadway's "Pipe Dream," tragically killed after making her film debut.

For reasons best known to Guy Trosper, who wrote the script, these two delightfully capable people are forced to hang onto the hero's flying mane and ego for the entire picture.

Here's what happens. Defending a frail lady barfly, Elvis conks a bully and draws a brief sentence for manslaughter. Toughened considerably, he later forms a record company with Miss Tyler, as the money and fame roll in. "Uh got wars [wires] 'n' letters from all over the wurl'," he gloats at one point. Presley fans may not like the idea of his being a churlish, egotistical wonder boy of television and the screen for a good half of the picture.

Elvis stays front and center, of course, muttering his lines sheepishly, and wooing Miss Tyler by collapsing like a rag doll and hooking a chin on her shoulder.

The sound technicians must have closed in, for this time most of his singing can actually be understood. And in

two numbers, "Treat Me Nice" and the title song, done as a convict jamboree, Elvis breaks loose with his St. Vitus specialty. Ten to one, next time he'll make it—finally getting those kneecaps turned inside out and cracking them together like coconuts. Never say die, El.

Billed in second place is a slow-moving, far-fetched adventure drama (also from Metro) called "Action of the Tiger," that has Van Johnson leading an escape safari out of Communist Albania. Martine Carol co-stars, Kenneth Harper produced and Terence Young directed. Filmed largely on location, apparently in Greece, the mountainous backgrounds and the color are stunning. And wasted.

H. H. T.

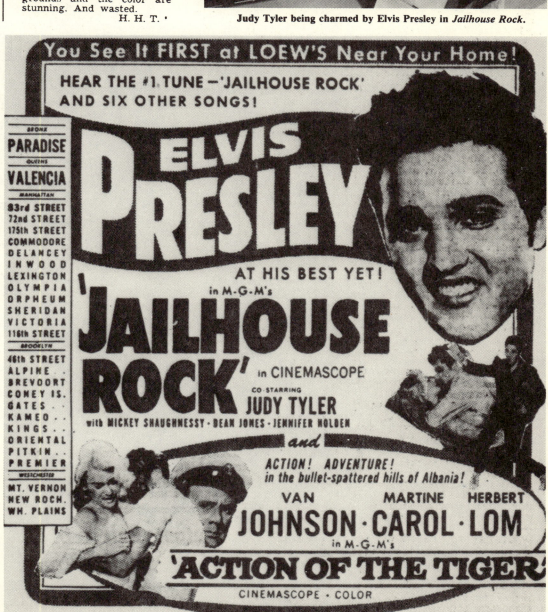

Judy Tyler being charmed by Elvis Presley in *Jailhouse Rock*.

You See It FIRST at LOEW'S Near Your Home!

HEAR THE #1 TUNE — 'JAILHOUSE ROCK' AND SIX OTHER SONGS!

BRONX
PARADISE
QUEENS
VALENCIA
MANHATTAN
83rd STREET
72nd STREET
175th STREET
COMMODORE
DELANCEY
INWOOD
LEXINGTON
OLYMPIA
ORPHEUM
SHERIDAN
VICTORIA
116th STREET
BROOKLYN
46th STREET
ALPINE
BREVOORT
CONEY IS.
GATES
KAMEO
KINGS
ORIENTAL
PITKIN
PREMIER
WESTCHESTER
MT. VERNON
NEW ROCH.
WH. PLAINS

ELVIS PRESLEY

AT HIS BEST YET!
in M-G-M's
'JAILHOUSE ROCK'
in CINEMASCOPE
CO-STARRING
JUDY TYLER
with MICKEY SHAUGHNESSY · DEAN JONES · JENNIFER HOLDEN

and

ACTION! ADVENTURE!
in the bullet-spattered hills of Albania!

VAN   MARTINE   HERBERT
JOHNSON · CAROL · LOM
in M-G-M's
'ACTION OF THE TIGER'
CINEMASCOPE · COLOR

Entrapped by 'Jaws' of Fear

JAWS, directed by Steven Spielberg; screenplay by Peter Benchley and Carl Gottlieb, based on the novel by Mr. Benchley; produced by Richard D. Zanuck and David Brown; director of photography, Bill Butler; editor, Verna Fields; music, John Williams; live shark footage, Ron and Valerie Taylor; underwater photography, Rexford Metz; special effects, Robert A. Mattey; distributed by Universal Pictures. Running time: 124 minutes. At the Rivoli Theater, Broadway at 49th Street; Orpheum Theater, 86th Street near Third Avenue, and 34th Street East Theater, near Second Avenue. This film has been rated PG.

Brody	Roy Scheider
Quint	Robert Shaw
Hooper	Richard Dreyfuss
Ellen Brody	Lorraine Gary
Vaughn	Murray Hamilton
Meadows	Carl Gottlieb
Interviewer	Peter Benchley

By VINCENT CANBY

If you are what you eat, then one of the sharks in "Jaws" is a beer can, half a mackerel and a Louisiana license plate. Another is a pretty young woman, a cylinder of oxygen, a small boy, a scout master and still more. The other characters in the film are nowhere nearly so fully packed.

"Jaws" which opened yesterday at three theaters, is the film version of Peter Benchley's best-selling novel about a man-eating great white shark that terrorizes an East Coast resort community, which now looks very much like Martha's Vineyard, where the film was shot.

It's a noisy, busy movie that has less on its mind than any child on a beach might have. It has been cleverly directed by Steven Spielberg ("Sugarland Express") for maximum shock impact and short-term suspense, and the special effects are so good that even the mechanical sharks are as convincing as the people.

"Jaws" is, at heart, the old standby, a science-fiction film. It opens according to time-honored tradition with a happy-go-lucky innocent being suddenly ravaged by the mad monster, which, in "Jaws," comes from the depths of inner space — the sea as well as man's nightmares. Thereafter "Jaws" follows the formula with fidelity.

Only one person in the community (the chief of police) realizes the true horror of what has happened, while the philistines (the Mayor, the merchants and the tourism people) pooh-pooh his warnings. The monster strikes again. An expert (an oceanographer) is brought in who confirms everyone's wildest fears, at which point the community bands together to hire an eccentric specialist (a shark fisherman) to secure their salvation.

If you think about "Jaws" for more than 45 seconds you will recognize it as nonsense, but it's the sort of nonsense that can be a good deal of fun if you like to have the wits scared out of you at irregular intervals.

It's a measure of how the film operates that not once do we feel particular sympathy for any of the shark's victims, or even the mother of one, a woman who has an embarrassingly tearful scene that at one point threatens to bring the film to a halt. This kind of fiction doesn't inspire humane responses. Just the opposite. We sigh with relief after each attack, smug in our awareness that it happened to them, not us.

In the best films characters are revealed in terms of the action. In movies like "Jaws," characters are simply functions of the action. They're at its service. Characters are like stage hands who move props around and deliver information when it's necessary, which is pretty much what Roy Scheider (the police chief), Robert Shaw (the shark fisherman) and Richard Dreyfuss (the oceanographer) do.

It may not look like much but it puts good actors to the test. They have to work very hard just to appear alive, and Mr. Scheider, Mr. Shaw and Mr. Dreyfuss come across with wit and easy self-assurance.

A UNIVERSAL PICTURE TECHNICOLOR PANAVISION

PG PARENTAL GUIDANCE SUGGESTED
SOME MATERIAL MAY NOT BE SUITABLE FOR PRE-TEENAGERS

...MAY BE TOO INTENSE FOR YOUNGER CHILDREN

(See it from the beginning!)

— NOW PLAYING —
at a Conveniently Located Blue Ribbon Theatre

The machine that frightened millions in *Jaws.*

Al Jolson and the Vitaphone

THE JAZZ SINGER, with Al Jolson, May McAvoy, Warner Orland, Eugenie Besserer, Cantor Josef Rosenblatt, Otto Lederer, Bobbie Gordon, Richard Tucker, Natt Carr, William Demarest, Anders Randolf and Will Walling; based on the play by Samson Raphaelson; directed by Alan Crosland; Vitaphone interpolations of Mr. Jolson's songs and orchestral accompaniment by Vitaphone. At Warners' Theatre.

In a story that is very much like that of his own life, Al Jolson at Warners' Theatre last night made his screen début in the picturization of Samson Raphaelson's play "The Jazz Singer," and through the interpolation of the Vitaphone and the audience had the rare opportunity of hearing Mr. Jolson sing several of his own songs and also render most effectively the Jewish hymn "Kol Nidre."

Mr. Jolson's persuasive vocal efforts were received with rousing applause. In fact, not since the first presentation of Vitaphone features, more than a year ago at the same playhouse, has anything like the ovation been heard in a motion-picture theatre. And when the film came to an end Mr. Jolson himself expressed his sincere appreciation of the Vitaphoned film, declaring that he was so happy that he could not stop the tears.

The Vitaphoned songs and some dialogue have been introduced most adroitly. This in itself is an ambitious move, for in the expression of song the Vitaphone vitalizes the production enormously. The dialogue is not so effective, for it does not always catch the nuances of speech or inflections of the voice so that one is not aware of the mechanical features.

The Warner Brothers astutely realized that a film conception of "The Jazz Singer" was one of the few subjects that would lend itself to the use of the Vitaphone. It was also a happy idea to persuade Mr. Jolson to play the leading rôle, for few men could have approached the task of singing and acting so well as he does in this photoplay. His "voice with a tear" compelled silence, and possibly all that disappointed the people in the packed theatre was the fact that they could not call upon him or his image at least for an encore. They had to content themselves with clapping and whistling after Mr. Jolson's shadow finished a realistic song. It was also the voice of Jolson, with its dramatic sweep, its pathos and soft slurring tones.

One of the most interesting sequences of the picture itself is where Mr. Jolson as Jack Robin (formerly Jakie Rabbinowitz) is perceived talking to Mary Dale (May McAvoy) as he smears his face with black. It is done gradually, and yet the dexterity with which Mr. Jolson outlines his mouth is readily appreciated. You see Jack Robin, the young man who at last has his big opportunity, with a couple of smudges of black on his features, and then his cheeks, his nose, his forehead and the back of his neck are blackened. It is also an engaging scene where Jack's mother comes to the Winter Garden and sees him for the first time as a black-face entertainer.

There is naturally a good deal of sentiment attached to the narrative, which is one wherein Cantor Rabinowitz is eager that his son Jakie shall become a cantor to keep up the traditions of the family. The old man's anger is aroused when one night he hears that Jakie has been singing jazz songs in a saloon. The boy's heart and soul are with the modern music. He runs away from home and tours the country until, through a friend he is engaged by a New York producer to sing in the Winter Garden. His début is to be made on the Day of Atonement, and, incidentally, when his father is dying. Toward the end, however, the old cantor on his deathbed hears his son canting the "Kol Nidre."

Some time afterward Jack Robin is perceived and heard singing "Mammy," while his old mother occupies a seat in the front row. Here Mr. Jolson puts all the force of his personality into the song as he walks out beyond the footlights and some times with clasped hands, he sings as if to his own mother.

The success of this production is due to a large degree to Mr. Jolson's Vitaphoned renditions. There are quite a few moments when the picture drags, because Alan Crosland, the director, has given too much footage to discussion and to the attempts of the theatrical manager (in character) to prevail upon Jack Robin not to permit sentiment to sway him (Jack) when his great opportunity is at hand. There are also times when one would expect the Vitaphoned portion to be either more subdued or stopped as the camera swings to other scenes. The voice is usually just the same whether the image of the singer is close to the camera or quite far away.

Warner Oland does capable work as Cantor Rabinowitz. May McAvoy is attractive, but has little to do as Mary Dale. In most of her scenes Eugenie Besserer acts with sympathetic restraint. Cantor Josef Rosenblatt contributes an excellent Vitaphoned concert number in the course of the narrative.

Al Jolson with May McAvoy in his first film, *The Jazz Singer*.

Jolson "Out-Jolsons" Jolson in "THE JAZZ SINGER"!

Based upon the play by SAMSON RAPHAELSON as produced on the spoken stage by LEWIS & GORDON and SAM H. HARRIS

CANTOR JOSEF ROSENBLATT is seen and heard on the VITAPHONE during the concert scene of "THE JAZZ SINGER"

¶ We apologize to the thousands who were turned away from last night's premiere. ¶ If the WARNER THEATRE were as large as Madison Square Garden, we still would not have been able to accommodate the crowds that clamored for admission. ¶ There will be two performances daily at 2:45 & 8:45, and we respectfully suggest that you purchase tickets well in advance.

WARNER BROS. SUPREME TRIUMPH!

AL JOLSON in "THE JAZZ SINGER" with VITAPHONE

A WARNER BROS. PRODUCTION   Directed by Alan Crosland

WARNER THEA. B'way at 52d St. TWICE DAILY—2:45 & 8:45. SUN. MAT. at 3. MATS. 50c-75c-$1.10 except Sat. & Sun. NIGHTS 75c to $2.20

Yul Brynner won an Oscar for best actor for his role as the King of Siam in *The King and I.*

'The King and I'

The Cast

THE KING AND I, screen play by Ernest Lehman;
music by Richard Rodgers and book and lyrics by
Oscar Hammerstein 2d from the musical play based
on the book "Anna and the King of Siam, by
Margaret Landon; produced by Charles Brackett and
directed by Walter Lang for Twentieth Century-Fox.
At the Roxy.

Anna	Deborah Kerr
The King	Yul Brynner
Tuptim	Rita Moreno
Kralahome	Martin Benson
Lady Thiang	Terry Saunders
Louis Leonowens	Rex Thompson
Lun Tha	Carlos Rivas
Prince Chulalongkorn	Patrick Adiarte
British Ambassador	Alan Mowbray
Ramsay	Geoffrey Toone
Eliza	Yuriko
Simon Legree	Marion Jim
Keeper of the Dogs	Robert Banas
Uncle Thomas	Dusty Worrall
Specialty Dancer	Gemze de Lappe

By BOSLEY CROWTHER

WHATEVER pictorial magnificence "The King and I" may have had upon the stage—and, goodness knows, it had plenty, in addition to other things—it has twice as much in the film version which Twentieth Century-Fox delivered last night to the Roxy. It also has other things.

It has, first of all, the full content of that charmingly droll and poignant "book" that Mr. Hammerstein crystallized so smartly from Margaret Landon's "Anna and the King of Siam." Every bit of the humor and vibrant humanity that flowed through the tender story of the English school-teacher and the quizzical king is richly preserved in the screen play that Ernest Lehman has prepared. And it is got onto the screen with snap and vigor under the direction of Walter Lang.

It has, too, the ardor and abundance of Mr. Rodgers' magnificent musical score, which rings out as lyrically and clearly as those clusters of Siamese bells. Most of the memorable numbers are here and are beautifully done, from "I Whistle a Happy Tune" to the zealous and rollicking "Shall We Dance?" And the few that have been omitted—the slave girl Tuptim's "My Lord and Master" is one, and another is Anna's acrimonious "Shall I Tell You What I Think of You?"—are not missed in the general extravagance of melody and décor.

Also, it has the great advantage of a handsome and talented cast, headed by the unsurpassed Yul Brynner and lovely Deborah Kerr. Mr. Brynner, whose original performance of the volatile King of Siam was so utterly virile and commanding that he took possession of the role, repeats it here in a manner that the close-in camera finds fresh with pride and power. Mr. Brynner has a handsomeness of features and a subtlety of expression that were not so evident on the stage.

His comprehension of the ty-rant whose passionate avidity for "scientific" knowledge and enlightenment often clashes with his traditional arrogance and will is such that there come from his performance all sorts of dazzling little glints of a complex personality battling bravely and mightily for air. The king is the heart of this story, and Mr. Brynner makes him vigorous and big.

But Miss Kerr matches him boldly. Her beauty, her spirit and her English style come as close to approximating those of the late Gertrude Lawrence as could be, and the voice of Marni Nixon adds a thrilling lyricism to her songs. The point of the story, as all know, is that you should never underestimate a woman's power. Miss Kerr makes it trenchant and enjoyable. She and Mr. Brynner are a team.

Rita Moreno as the lovelorn Tuptim and Carlos Rivas as her Burmese beau are relegated to small roles, but they handle them gracefully and manage to put a haunting poignance into "We Kiss in a Shadow," the lovers' song. Terry Saunders is attractive as the "first wife," Patrick Adiarte is trim as the young prince and Martin Benson does very nicely with the abbreviated role of the prime minister.

However, as we said in the beginning, it is the pictorial magnificence of the appropriately regal production that especially distinguishes this film. Done with a taste in decoration and costuming that is forceful and rare, the whole thing has a harmony of the visuals that is splendid in excellent color and CinemaScope. The imagery is beautifully climaxed in the "Little Hut of Uncle Thomas" ballet, which sort of wraps up the quaintness, the humor and the exquisite delicacy of the issues in this fine film.

If you don't go to see it, believe us, you'll be missing a grand and moving thing.

On the Roxy stage, a new stage and ice revue, "Manhattan Moods," features Barbara Hunt and Harold Ronk, vocalists; Nicky Powers and Leslie Sang, dancers; and the Ice Roxyettes and the Skating Blades.

AIR CONDITIONED

NOW! ROXY DOORS OPEN 10:30 A.M.

CI 7-6000   7th Ave. & 50th St.

Darryl F. Zanuck
PRESENTS

RODGERS & HAMMERSTEIN'S

The King and I

from 20th CENTURY-FOX starring

DEBORAH KERR + YUL BRYNNER

COLOR by DE LUXE in

CinemaScope 55

"IT'S SENSATIONAL!"
—HEDDA HOPPER

"The finest thing that has come out of Hollywood!"
—LOUIS SOBOL

PRODUCED BY
CHARLES BRACKETT
DIRECTED BY
WALTER LANG
SCREENPLAY BY
ERNEST LEHMAN
MUSIC BY
RICHARD RODGERS
BOOK AND LYRICS BY
OSCAR HAMMERSTEIN II
CHOREOGRAPHY BY
JEROME ROBBINS

PLUS ON STAGE
"Manhattan Moods"

King Kong

KING KONG, based on a story by the late Edgar Wallace and Merian C. Cooper; directed by Mr. Cooper; presented by RKO Radio Pictures. At the Radio City Music Hall and RKO Roxy.

Ann Redman	Fay Wray
Denham	Robert Armstrong
Driscoll	Bruce Cabot
Englehorn	Frank Reicher
Weston	Sam Hardy
Native Chief	Noble Johnson
Second Mate	James Flavin
Witch King	Steve Clemento
Lumpy	Victor Long

By MORDAUNT HALL.

At both the Radio City Music Hall and the RKO Roxy, which have a combined seating capacity of 10,000, the main attraction now is a fantastic film known as "King Kong." The story of this feature was begun by the late Edgar Wallace and finished by Merian C. Cooper, who with his old associate, Ernest B. Schoedsack, is responsible for the production. It essays to give the spectator a vivid conception of the terrifying experiences of a producer of jungle pictures and his colleagues, who capture a gigantic ape, something like fifty feet tall, and bring it to New York. The narrative is worked out in a decidedly compelling fashion, which is mindful of what was done in the old silent film, "The Lost World."

Through multiple exposures, processed "shots" and a variety of angles of camera wizardry the producers set forth an adequate story and furnish enough thrills for any devotee of such tales.

Although there are vivid battles between prehistoric monsters on the island which Denham, the picture maker, insists on visiting, it is when the enormous ape, called Kong, is brought to this city that the excitement reaches its highest pitch. Imagine a 50-foot beast with a girl in one paw climbing up the outside of the Empire State Building, and after putting the girl on a ledge, clutching at airplanes, the pilots of which are pouring bullets from machine guns into the monster's body.

It often seems as though Ann Redman, who goes through more terror than any of the other characters in the film, would faint, but she always appears to be able to scream. Her body is like a doll in the claw of the gigantic beast, who in the course of his wanderings through Manhattan tears down a section of the elevated railroad and tosses a car filled with passengers to the street. Automobiles are mere missiles for this Kong, who occasionally reveals that he relishes his invincibility by patting his chest.

Denham is an intrepid person, but it is presumed that when the ape is killed he has had quite enough of searching for places with strange monsters. In the opening episode he is about to leave on the freighter for the island supposed to have been discovered by some sailor, when he goes ashore to find a girl whom he wants to act in his picture. In course of time he espies Ann, played by the attractive Fay Wray, and there ensues a happy voyage. Finally through the fog the island is sighted and Denham, the ship's officers and sailors, all armed, go ashore. It soon develops that the savages, who offer up sacrifices in the form of human beings to Kong, their super-king, keep him in an area surrounded by a great wall. Kong has miles in which to roam and fight with brontosauri and dinosauri and other huge creatures.

There is a door to the wall. After Denham and the others from the ship have had quite enough of the island, Kong succeeds in bursting open the door, but he is captured through gas bombs hurled at him by the white men. How they ever get him on the vessel is not explained, for the next thing you know is that Kong is on exhibition in Gotham, presumably in Madison Square Garden.

During certain episodes in this film Kong, with Ann in his paw, goes about his battles, sometimes putting her on a fifty-foot high tree branch while he polishes off an adversary. When he is perceived on exhibition in New York he is a frightening spectacle, but Denham thinks that he has the beast safely shackled. The newspaper photographers irritate even him with their flashlights, and after several efforts he breaks the steel bands and eventually gets away. He looks for Ann on the highways and byways of New York. He climbs up hotel façades and his head fills a whole window, his white teeth and red mouth adding to the terror of the spectacle.

Everywhere he moves he crushes out lives. He finally discovers Ann, and being a perspicacious ape, he decides that the safest place for himself and Ann is the tower of the Empire State structure.

Needless to say that this picture was received by many a giggle to cover up fright. Constant exclamations issued from the Radio City Music Hall yesterday. "What a man!" observed one youth when the ape forced down the great oaken door on the island. Human beings seem so small that one is reminded of Defoe's "Gulliver's Travels." One step and this beast traverses half a block. If buildings hinder his progress he pushes them down, and below him the people look like Lilliputians.

Miss Wray goes through her ordeal with great courage. Robert Armstrong gives a vigorous and compelling impersonation of Denham. Bruce Cabot, Frank Reicher, Sam Hardy, Noble Johnson and James Flavin add to the interest of this weird tale.

Beauty and the beasts. Fay Wray recoils in a treetop as King Kong fights a Tyrannosaurus in *King Kong*.

'King Kong' Bigger, Not Better, In a Return to Screen of Crime

By VINCENT CANBY

When it is played as a straight adventure-fantasy, Dino De Laurentiis's $25-million remake of "King Kong" is inoffensive, uncomplicated fun, as well as a dazzling display of what the special-effects people can do when commissioned to construct a 40-foot-tall ape who can walk, make fondling gestures, is slightly cross-eyed, and smiles a lot.

It's something to make you cringe with embarrassment, though, when it attempts to disarm all criticism by kidding itself (proclaim the ads, "the most exciting original motion picture event of all time") in lines of dialogue that are intended as instant camp ("You goddamned male chauvinist ape!"). I suppose that when you spend as much as Mr. De Laurentiis did on this, you've got to have something for everybody, including the witless.

The nicest thing about the 1933 "King Kong," made by Merian C. Cooper and Ernest B. Schoedsack, was that it was no big deal. One could marvel at the wizardly special effects created by Willis O'Brien and not be overwhelmed by an awareness of the terrific time and expense that went into them. Its heart was genuinely light. Not this time.

Why, I think we have a right to ask, would anyone want to remake it? "King Kong" is a classic, but it's not "Hamlet." There's only one way to do it, and that's been done. Having acknowledged these biases, one might as well relax and let it happen.

John Guillermin, the director, and Lorenzo Semple Jr., the writer, display real affection for old-time movie magic and nonsense that come through in spite of a physical production only slightly less elaborate than that of Elizabeth Taylor's "Cleopatra."

The Cast

KING KONG, directed by John Guillermin; screenplay by Lorenzo Semple Jr., based on a story by Edgar Wallace and Merian C. Cooper; produced by Dino De Laurentiis; executive producers, Federico De Laurentiis and Christian Ferry; director of photography, Richard H. Kline; music, John Barry; editor, Ralph E. Winters; distributed by Paramount Pictures. Running time: 135 minutes. At Loew's State I, Broadway at 45th Street, Loew's Orpheum, 86th Street near Third Avenue, and other theaters. This film has been rated PG.

Jack Prescott	Jeff Bridges
Fred Wilson	Charles Grodin
Dwan	Jessica Lange
Captain Ross	John Randolph
Bagley	Rene Auberjonois
Boan	Julius Harris
Joe Perko	Jack O'Halloran
Sunfish	Dennis Fimple
Carnahan	Ed Lauter
Garcia	Jorge Moreno

Especially effective are the opening sections of the film that lay out —with a respectful gravity that is truly comic—the scientific mumbo jumbo that softens us for the make-believe to come: a team of oil experts from a cartel named Petrox sets out to find a mysterious uncharted South Pacific island that is perpetually enclosed in a cloud of carbon dioxide, indicating that the earth beneath is a virtually bottomless reservoir of petroleum.

There's talk about the worldwide energy crisis, and we are shown satellite photographs meant to allay suspicions that even if such an island could have remained undiscovered throughout all of World War II, our spy-in-the-sky system, which can apparently read the fine print on Kremlin documents, would certainly have chanced upon it long before this.

It may well be that we don't need such explanations. Part of the appeal of "King Kong" today, as it was in 1933, is based on the wish to believe that there may still be places in this world unpenetrated by Petrox, Pepsico, General Motors, Sony and the Clubs Mediterranee.

•

The film builds well to Kong's initial appearance, after we are almost an hour into the story, when he comes clomping out of the jungle to claim his monthly sacrifice, who is not, of course, Fay Wray, but Jessica Lange, a beautiful New York model who plays a would-be actress named Dwan. Though Dwan sets Kong's heart aflame, she's more likely to set everyone else's teeth on edge.

This is no reflection on Miss Lange. It's the script. In their attempt to update a fairy tale, the film makers have turned a conventional heroine into a pseudo-Marilyn Monroe character who seems less dizzy than certifiably daft, aggressively unpleasant and out of place in this sort of movie.

One of my objections to the film is the substitution of the twin towers of the Trade Center for the Empire State Building, used in the original film. The World Trade Center is a very boring piece of architecture. The Empire State Building is not. Though Kong's last fight with Army helicopters is beautifully (and bloodily) done, the setting trivializes it.

The monster from the Dino De Laurentiis remake of the movie, *King Kong*.

The most exciting original motion picture event of all time.

King Kong

Copyright © MCMLXXVI by Dino De Laurentiis Corporation. All Rights Reserved

Dino De Laurentiis presents a John Guillermin Film

"King Kong"

starring Jeff Bridges Charles Grodin Introducing Jessica Lange

Screenplay by Lorenzo Semple Jr. Produced by Dino De Laurentiis Directed by John Guillermin Music Composed and Conducted by John Barry Panavision® in Color A Paramount Release

PG PARENTAL GUIDANCE SUGGESTED THIS MATERIAL MAY NOT BE SUITABLE FOR PRE-TEENAGERS

Read The Creation of Dino De Laurentiis' KING KONG from Pocket Books

Original sound track album and tapes on Reprise Records.

Life in a Shabby Texas Town on the Plains

By VINCENT CANBY

Peter Bogdanovich's fine second film, "The Last Picture Show," adapted from Larry McMurtry's novel by McMurtry and Bogdanovich, has the effect of a lovely, leisurely, horizontal pan-shot across the life of Anarene, Tex., a small, shabby town on a plain so flat that to raise the eye even 10 degrees would be to see only an endless sky.

In an unbroken arc of narrative, beautifully photographed (by Robert Surtees) in the blunt, black-and-white tones I associate with pictures in a high school yearbook, the film tells a series of interlocking stories of love and loss that are on the sentimental edge of "Winesburg, Ohio," but that illuminate a good deal more of one segment of the American experience than any other American film in recent memory.

●

It is 1951, the time of Truman, of Korea, of Jo Stafford, of "I, the Jury" as a best-selling paperback, when tank-town movie houses like the Royal Theater had to close because the citizens of Anarene, like most other Americans, were discovering, in television, a more convenient

dream machine that brought with it further isolation from community — a phenomenon analyzed by Philip Slater, the sociologist, as America's pursuit of loneliness.

"The Last Picture Show" is not sociology, even though it is sociologically true, nor is it another exercise in romantic nostalgia on the order of Robert Mulligan's "Summer of '42." It is filled with carefully researched details of time and place, but although these details are the essential décor of the film, they are not the essence. It is a movie that doesn't look back; rather, it starts off and ends in its own time, as much as does such a completely dissimilar, contemporary story as that of "Sunday, Bloody Sunday."

●

"The Last Picture Show" is about both Anarene and Sonny Crawford, the high school senior and football co-captain (with his best friend, Duane Jackson, of the always defeated Anarene team), through whose sensibilities the film is felt. As Bogdanovich seldom takes his story very far from Anarene, he sees "The Last Picture Show" entirely in terms of the maturation of Sonny, in the course of the emotional crises and confrontations that have become the staples

The Cast

THE LAST PICTURE SHOW, directed by Peter Bogdanovich; screenplay by Larry McMurtry and Mr. Bogdanovich, based on the novel by Mr. McMurtry; director of photography, Robert Surtees; produced by Stephen J. Friedman; for release by Columbia Pictures. At the New York Film Festival, Vivian Beaumont Theater. Running time: 118 minutes. (The Motion Picture Association of America's Production Code and Rating Administration classifies this film: "R—restricted, under 17 requires accompanying parent or adult guardian.")

Sonny Crawford	Timothy Bottoms
Duane Jackson	Jeff Bridges
Jacy Farrow	Cybill Shepherd
Sam the Lion	Ben Johnson
Ruth Popper	Cloris Leachman
Lois Farrow	Ellen Burstyn
Genevieve	Eileen Brennan
Abilene	Clu Gulager
Billy	Sam Bottoms
Charlene Duggs	Sharon Taggart
Lester Marlow	Randy Quaid
Coach Popper	Bill Thurman

of all sorts of American coming-of-age literature, from "Penrod" to "Peyton Place" and "Portnoy's Complaint."

They are familiar staples, but they are treated with such humor, such sympathy and with the expectation of a few overwrought scenes, reticence that "The Last Picture Show" becomes an adventure in rediscovery—of a very decent, straight forward kind of movie, as well as of—and I rather hesitate to use such a square phrase —human values.

●

Timothy Bottoms, who gave most of his performance in "Johnny Got His Gun" as a voice on the soundtrack for the mummy-wrapped, quadruple-amputee hero, is fine as Sonny Crawford, but then I liked just about everyone in the huge cast.

This includes Jeff Bridges (son to Lloyd, younger brother to Beau), as Duane; Cybill Shepherd, as the prettiest, richest girl in town, who is

almost too bad to be true; Cloris Leachman, as the coach's wife, who gives Sonny some idea of what love might be; Ellen Burstyn (who was so good in "Alex in Wonderland"), as a tough, Dorothy Malone type of middle-aged beauty (middle-aged? she's all of 40!) who is one of the few people in Anarene to have recognized what life is and come to terms with it; and Ben Johnson, as the old man who most influences Sonny's life.

●

I do have some small quibbles about the film. Bogdanovich and McMurtry have done everything possible to get the entire novel on screen, yet they have mysteriously omitted certain elements, such as Sonny's family life—if any—and the reasons why the coach's wife is such a pushover for a teen-age lover. The movie is, perhaps, too horizontal, too objective.

I didn't see Bogdanovich's first film, "Targets," but "The Last Picture Show" indicates that Bogdanovich, the movie critic, had already taken Jack Valenti's advice when, last winter, the film industry spokesman described critics as physicians who should heal themselves—by making movies—if they wanted to be taken seriously as critics. Bogdanovich has.

"The Last Picture Show" was screened at the New York Film Festival Saturday and opened yesterday at the new Columbia I Theater. My only fear is that some unfortunates are going to confuse it with Dennis Hopper's "The Last Movie," to which "The Last Picture Show" is kin only by title.

YESTERDAY'S REVIEWS MAKE

THE LAST PICTURE SHOW

THE MOVIE YOU WILL WANT TO SEE TODAY!

COLUMBIA PICTURES Presents
A BBS PRODUCTION
THE LAST PICTURE SHOW
A Film By PETER BOGDANOVICH

starring TIMOTHY BOTTOMS/JEFF BRIDGES/ELLEN BURSTYN/BEN JOHNSON/CLORIS LEACHMAN/ introducing
CYBILL SHEPHERD as Jacy PETER BOGDANOVICH/LARRY McMURTRY and PETER BOGDANOVICH/LARRY McMURTRY
Executive Producer BERT SCHNEIDER/STEPHEN J. FRIEDMAN Original Soundtrack Album on MGM Records

Official Selection New York Film Festival

R

A UNITED ARTISTS THEATRE
Columbia I 2nd Avenue at 64th St. Tel: 832-1670
12:00, 2:00, 4:00, 6:00, 8:00, 10:00 P.M.

Cloris Leachman and Timothy Bottoms in *The Last Picture Show.*

"Little Caesar" Notable for Acting of Edward G. Robinson

NEW GANG FILM AT STRAND.

"Little Caesar" Notable for Acting of Edward G. Robinson.

LITTLE CAESAR, with Edward G. Robinson, Douglas Fairbanks Jr., Glenda Farrell, Sidney Blackmer, Thomas Jackson, Ralph Ince, William Collier Jr., Maurice Black, Stanley Fields and George E. Stone; from the novel by W. R. Burnett, directed by Mervyn LeRoy; newsreel and Vitaphone short features. At the Strand.

"Little Caesar," based on W. R. Burnett's novel of Chicago gangdom, was welcomed to the Strand yesterday by unusual crowds. The story deals with the career of Cesare Bandello, alias Rico, alias Little Caesar, a disagreeable lad who started by robbing gasoline stations and soared to startling heights in his "profession" by reason of his belief in his high destiny.

The production is ordinary and would rank as just one more gangster film but for two things. One is the excellence of Mr. Burnett's credible and compact story. The other is Edward G. Robinson's wonderfully effective performance. Little Caesar becomes at Mr. Robinson's hands a figure out of Greek epic tragedy, a cold, ignorant, merciless killer, driven on and on by an insatiable lust for power, the plaything of a force that is greater than himself.

Douglas Fairbanks Jr. as Rico's pal, who brings about his friend's downfall by trying to live a decent life away from his old haunts, is miscast, and in addition suffers by comparison with the reality of Mr. Robinson's portrayal. At times Mr. Fairbanks talks and acts like the cheap Italian thug he is supposed to represent, but more often he is the pleasant, sincere youth who has been seen to so much better advantage elsewhere.

Little Caesar comes to the big town and joins Sam Vettori's gang, one of the two principal "mobs" in that city. Both gangs are under the supervision of Pete Montana, who in turn owes his allegiance to a mysterious "Big Boy," the king of the underworld. Early in his career Little Caesar plans and executes a raid on a cabaret protected by the rival gang, and in so doing kills a crime commissioner. Thereafter, step by step, he ousts Vettori, Pete Montana and the rival gang leader, and soon only "Big Boy" bars his way to complete mastery of the city's underworld.

His pal, Joe Massara, is threatened with the fatal "spot" because he knows too much, and that young man's sweetheart turns State's evidence. The "mob" is broken and scattered, and Little Caesar is cornered and killed by a crafty detective's appeal to the gangster's vanity. Glenda Farrell is excellently authentic as Massara's "moll," and William Collier Jr. contributes a moving performance in a minor rôle. Thomas Jackson as the detective is also noteworthy.

Edward G. Robinson challenging his best friend, Douglas Fairbanks, Jr. in a scene from *Little Caesar*.

"LISTEN . . . RICO . . . You may be Little Caesar to your gang of cut-throats, but to me you're just a lot of loud talk . . . I'm through . . . Get me? . . . I'm leaving you flat . . . I'm going to get married . . . And I'm going straight from now on . . . If you try to stop me, you'll stop a bullet labelled Little Caesar!"

"LITTLE CAESAR"
EDWARD G. ROBINSON
DOUG. FAIRBANKS, JR.

Better than "Doorway to Hell"

STRAND B'way & 47th St.

Continuous . . . Popular Prices . . . Midnite Shows

Edward G. Robinson as *Little Caesar*.

Shirley Temple, Adolphe Menjou and Dorothy Dell in the New Film at the Paramount.

LITTLE MISS MARKER, based on the story by Damon Runyon; music and lyrics by Ralph Rainger and Leo Robin; directed by Alexander Hall; a Paramount production. At the Paramount.

Sorrowful Jones	Adolphe Menjou
Bangles Carson	Dorothy Dell
Big Steve	Charles Bickford
Miss Marker	Shirley Temple
Regret	Lynn Overman
Doc Chesley	Frank McGlynn Sr.
Sun Rise	Jack Sheehan
Grinder	Gary Owen
Dizzy Memphis	Willie Best
Eddie	Puggy White
Buggs	Tammany Young
Bonnie the Gouge	Sam Hardy
Marky's father	Edward Earle
Sore Toe	John Kelly
Canvas-Back	Warren Hymer
Dr. Ingalls	Frank Conroy
Reardon	James Burke
Sarah	Mildred Gover
Mrs. Walsh	Lucille Ward
Doctor	Craufurd Kent

By MORDAUNT HALL.

How a child of 4 touched the hearts of a band of race-track ruffians is told in "Little Miss Marker," the current film at the Paramount. This picture is a delight in many respects, for it has been produced so pleasingly and with such efficient portrayals that only a dyed-in-the-wool cynic could fail to be affected by its sterling humor and pathos. The story, one written by Damon Runyon, is blessed with originality and it has been adapted to the screen in an understanding fashion.

Considering that some of the adult characters are known by such names as Sorrowful Jones, Bangles Carson, a torch singer; Big Steve, Regret, Sun Rise, Dizzy Memphis, Buggs, Sore Toe and Bonnie the Gouge, it is surprising that the tale possesses so much tenderness and charm. The closing incidents may seem superfluous and somewhat melodramatic, but even so they are set forth with a measure of suspense.

Little Shirley Temple, the lovely tiny lass of "Stand Up and Cheer," is virtually the stellar performer in the present work, and no more engaging child has been beheld on the screen. She appears as Little Miss Marker, so named because she is left with the bookmaker, Sorrowful Jones (Adolphe Menjou), virtually in pawn for her father's $20 bet. Jones is averse to taking the so-called "markers," but Marky, as she eventually becomes known, attracts his attention. The father does not return and it is understood that he ended his unhappy existence with a bullet.

Marky, who at the moment is filled with a child's story of King Arthur, looks upon the rough persons she encounters as Knights of the Round Table. She picks her Sir Launcelot, Sir Galahad, Sir Percival, and Bangles Carson is, of course, Lady Guinevere.

The gloomy Jones, incidentally no fashion plate, finds himself in the somewhat awkward predicament of having to care for the youngster. While he is preparing a bed for her with chairs, she bounces into the big bed and then insists on Jones reading to her until she falls asleep. He reads from a race-track sheet and the names of the horses and some of the turf colloquialisms rather fascinate the youngster.

All these turf touts, from the forbidding specimens to others who can boast of better looks, take an interest in Marky, but several of the child's Knights ridicule Jones, particularly when he, a past master in parsimony, pays out more than $50 for clothes for Marky. The pagan Jones also is asked by Marky about God and soon the bookmaker dictates a little prayer which Marky repeats after him. She makes requests of her own accord, including asking God for new clothes for Sorrowful Jones. And the next day he goes forth and invests in a suit.

As time goes on, environment tarnishes Marky and she forgets her knights in shining armor and her appealing simple patter is lost in a flood of argot. This prompts the race-track crooks and Bangles Carson to have a round-table dinner in a private room of a nightclub, with all the guests arrayed in costumes, Marky being dressed as a Princess. Two cheap pugilists arrive at the party in armor. Apparently this show of King Arthur's knights does not convince the juvenile sophisticate, but when her charger in trappings—actually a race horse which had been doped on several occasions—is brought into the room Marky surrenders.

The penultimate phase of the narrative is somewhat lurid, but it does not detract from the effectiveness of what has gone before. Tiny Shirley Temple is a joy to behold and her spontaneity and cheer in speaking her lines are nothing short of amazing. Mr. Menjou has given much fine acting to pictures, but he has never done anything better than his characterization of Sorrowful Jones. Dorothy Dell as Bangles Carson also contributes real talent. Lynn Overman, Sam Hardy, Warren Hymer and Frank McGlynn Sr. are among those who make the most of their good opportunities.

On the stage is Dave Apollon's "Continental Revue," with Mr. Apollon, Danzi Goodell, Diffin and Draper, Bob Ripa, Nora Williams, Jean, Ruth and Gail, the Eight Débutantes and the Hawaiian Band.

Adolphe Menjou reads a "bedtime story" to Shirley Temple from the daily racing sheet in *Little Miss Marker*.

Today at the Paramount

She was an I.O.U. for 20 Bucks

Hocked to the toughest muggs on Broadway—this million dollar baby carved romance into the hearts of Broadway chiselers . . . .

DAMON RUNYON'S

"Little Miss MARKER"

A Paramount Picture with

SHIRLEY TEMPLE

The child wonder star of "Stand Up and Cheer"

ADOLPHE MENJOU • DOROTHY DELL
CHARLES BICKFORD • LYNNE OVERMAN
a B. P. Schulberg Production

On Stage
DAVE APOLLON
and His Continental Revue
featuring a cast of 50

NEW YORK
Paramount

'Lolita,' Vladimir Nabokov's Adaptation of His Novel

Sue Lyon and Mason in Leading Roles

The Cast

LOLITA, screen play by Vladimir Nabokov, based on his novel of the same name; directed by Stanley Kubrick; produced by James B. Harris; presented by Metro-Goldwyn-Mayer. At Loew's State Theatre, Broadway and Forty-fifth Street, and the Murray Hill Theatre, Thirty-fourth Street east of Lexington Avenue. Running time: 152 minutes.

Humbert Humbert	James Mason
Charlotte Haze	Shelley Winters
Clare Quilty	Peter Sellers
Lolita Haze	Sue Lyon
Vivian Darkbloom	Marianne Stone
Jean Farlow	Diana Decker
John Farlow	Jerry Stovin
Dick	Gary Cockrell
Mona Farlow	Suzanne Gibbs
Lorna	Roberta Shore
Roy	Eric Lane
Nurse Mary Lore	Lois Maxwell
Swine	William Greene
Louise	Isobel Lucas
Hospital Receptionist	Maxine Holden

By BOSLEY CROWTHER

HOW did they ever make a movie of "Lolita?" The answer to that question, posed in the advertisements of the picture, which arrived at the Loew's State and the Murray Hill last night, is as simple as this. They didn't.

They made a movie from a script in which the characters have the same names as the characters in the book, the plot bears a resemblance to the original and some of the incidents are vaguely similar. But the "Lolita" that Vladimir Nabokov wrote as a novel and the "Lolita" he wrote to be a film, directed by Stanley Kubrick, are two conspicuously different things.

•

In the first place, the character of Lolita, the perversely precocious child who had such affect on the libido of the middle-aged hero in the book, is not a child in the movie. She looks to be a good 17 years old, possessed of a striking figure and a devilishly haughty teen-age air. The distinction is fine, we will grant you, but she is definitely not a "nymphet." As played by Sue Lyon, a newcomer, she reminds one of Carroll Baker's "Baby Doll."

Right away, this removes the factor of perverted desire that is in the book and renders the passion of the hero more normal and understandable. It also renders the drama more in line with others we have seen. Older men have often pined for younger females. This is nothing new on the screen.

Further, the structure and the climate of the movie are not the same as those of the book. The movie starts with the melodramatic incident that brings the novel to a close, then flashes back to the beginning and tells its story in a decreasingly humorous vein. Thus the viewer is warned by this weird preface that the ending is going to be grim. The device tends to shade the early satire and pulls the punch from Mr. Nabokov's curious tale.

But once this is said about the movie — and once the reader has been advised not to expect the distractingly sultry climate and sardonic mischievousness of the book — it must be said that Mr. Kubrick has got a lot of fun and frolic in his film. He has also got a bit of pathos and irony toward the end. Unfortunately, there are some strange confusions of style and mood as it moves along.

The best part comes early in the picture when Mr. Nabokov and Mr. Kubrick are making sport of their hero's bug-eyed infatuation with Lolita and his artful circumvention of her mother. Here the satire is somewhat gross but booming, assisted greatly by a wonderfully deft job of comical fumbling by Shelley Winters.

James Mason, Sue Lyons and Shelley Winters in the Nabakov adaption of *Lolita*.

STARTS TODAY **FIRST-RUN** IN YOUR NEIGHBORHOOD AT NO ADVANCE IN PRICES

THE MOST CONTROVERSIAL MOTION PICTURE OF THE DECADE!

"OUTRAGEOUS!" —LOOK "BRILLIANT!" —LIFE "HILARIOUS!" —THE NEW YORKER

LOLITA

FOR PERSONS OVER 18 YEARS OF AGE

METRO-GOLDWYN-MAYER presents in association with SEVEN ARTS PRODUCTIONS · JAMES B. HARRIS and STANLEY KUBRICK'S **LOLITA**

Starring **JAMES MASON** · **SHELLEY WINTERS** · **PETER SELLERS** as "Quilty" and Introducing **SUE LYON** as "Lolita"

Directed by **STANLEY KUBRICK** · Screenplay by **VLADIMIR NABOKOV** based on his novel "Lolita" Produced by **JAMES B. HARRIS** APPROVED BY THE PRODUCTION CODE ADMINISTRATION

and A TOP FEATURETTE IN COLOR! **"PLEASURE HIGHWAY"** A CAPTIVATING TOUR INTO THE HEART OF AFRICA

Perfection and a 'Love Story'

'Erich Segal's Romantic Tale Begins Run

By VINCENT CANBY

What can you say about a movie about a 25-year-old girl who died?

That it is beautiful. And romantic. That it contains a fantasy for just about everyone, perhaps with the exception of Herbert Marcuse. That it looks to be clean and pure and without artifice, even though it is possibly as sophisticated as any commercial American movie ever made. That my admiration for the mechanics of it slops over into a real admiration for the movie itself.

I'm talking, of course, about "Love Story," the movie from which Erich Segal extracted his best-selling nonnovel, mostly, it seems, by appending "she said's" and "I said's" and an occasional "I remonstrated" to the dialogue in his original screenplay.

•

The film, which opened yesterday at the Loew's State I and Tower East Theaters, is about a love affair so perfect that even the death that terminates it becomes a symbol of its perfection.

When, at the end, Jenny (née Cavilleri), the self-styled social zero from Cranston, R. I., the daughter of an Italian baker, is dying of a carefully unidentified blood disease in the arms of her husband, Oliver Barrett 4th, the preppie millionaire from Boston, there is nothing to disfigure love, or faith, or even the complexion. It's as if she were suffering from some kind of vaguely unpleasant Elizabeth Arden treatment. Jenny doesn't die. She just slips away in beauty.

The knowledge that Jenny will—how should I put it—disappear not only gives the movie its shape (it is told in flashback), but it also endows everything — from a snowball fight in the Harvard Yard to a confrontation with snob parents in Ispwich —with an intensity that is no less sweet for being fraudulent.

Curiously, the novel, which I found almost unreadable (I think it might be as readily absorbed if kept under one's pillow), plays very well as a movie, principally, I suspect because Jenny is not really Jenny but Ali MacGraw, a kind of all-American, Radcliffe madonna figure, and Oliver Barrett

4th is really Ryan O'Neal, an intense, sensitive young man whose handsomeness has a sort of crookedness to it that keeps him from being a threat to male members of the audience. They are both lovely.

Francis Lai's background score, mixes Bach and Mozart and Handel with Lai, and resolutely avoids rock. Although Jenny does disappear at the end, everyone in the audience can take heart in identification—the ladies, because they can see how much will be missed, and the gentlemen, who will have the honor of being abandoned by one of fiction's most blessed females. I might add that Oliver, though distraught, is also very rich, and he has promised Jenny to be a merry widower.

I can't remember any movie of such comparable high-style kitsch since Leo McCarey's "Love Affair" (1939) and his 1957 remake, "An Affair to Remember." The only really depressing thing about "Love Story" is the thought of all of the terrible imitations that will inevitably follow it.

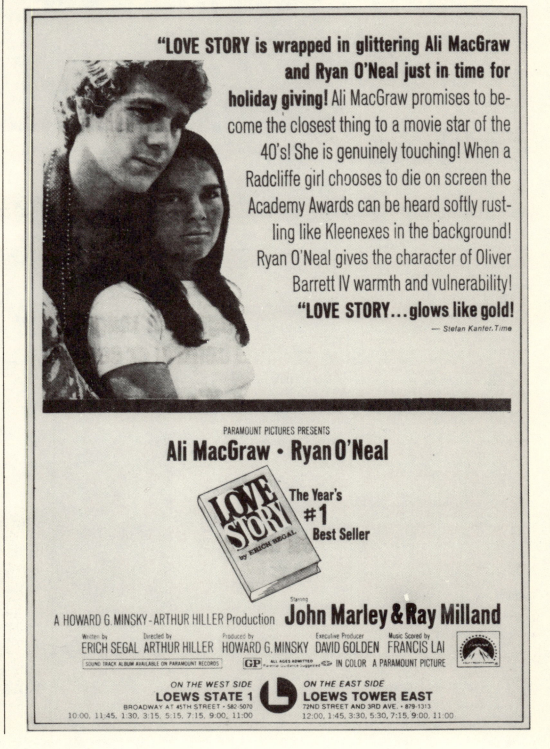

"LOVE STORY is wrapped in glittering Ali MacGraw and Ryan O'Neal just in time for holiday giving! Ali MacGraw promises to become the closest thing to a movie star of the 40's! She is genuinely touching! When a Radcliffe girl chooses to die on screen the Academy Awards can be heard softly rustling like Kleenexes in the background! Ryan O'Neal gives the character of Oliver Barrett IV warmth and vulnerability! "LOVE STORY... glows like gold!"

— Stefan Kanfer, Time

PARAMOUNT PICTURES PRESENTS

Ali MacGraw · Ryan O'Neal

LOVE STORY by ERICH SEGAL

The Year's #1 Best Seller

Starring

John Marley & Ray Milland

A HOWARD G. MINSKY - ARTHUR HILLER Production

Written by ERICH SEGAL Directed by ARTHUR HILLER Produced by HOWARD G. MINSKY Executive Producer DAVID GOLDEN Music Scored by FRANCIS LAI

SOUND TRACK ALBUM AVAILABLE ON PARAMOUNT RECORDS GP ALL AGES ADMITTED Parental Guidance Suggested IN COLOR A PARAMOUNT PICTURE

ON THE WEST SIDE
LOEWS STATE 1
BROADWAY AT 45TH STREET · 582-5070
10:00, 11:45, 1:30, 3:15, 5:15, 7:15, 9:00, 11:00

ON THE EAST SIDE
LOEWS TOWER EAST
72ND STREET AND 3RD AVE. · 879-1313
12:00, 1:45, 3:30, 5:30, 7:15, 9:00, 11:00

Japanese Idea

'Magnificent Seven,' a U. S. Western, Opens

ODDLY enough, more than one review of the Japanese import called "The Magnificent Seven" (here — else, where, "Seven Samurai") contended that this brilliantly blood-curdling action film could easily be rearranged as a Hollywood Western. This is precisely what happened yesterday at neighborhood theatres, four years later.

Even with some highly fetching Mexican scenery in color, this United Artists release, thrusting Yul Brynner well to the fore, is a pallid, pretentious and overlong reflection of the Japanese original.

Don't expect anything like the ice-cold suspense, the superb juxtaposition of revealing human vignettes and especially the pile-driver tempo of the first "Seven." Remember the plot? Seven professional warriors were hired by a quaking, remote medieval village to rid them of bandits.

•

We now have the same story, basically, set in a bleak, terrified little farming outpost below the Rio Grande in, supposedly, the post-Civil War era. And it soon becomes apparent, in John Sturges' stately, overly detailed direction, that the picture is going to take its own sweet time, moving at a thoughtful, snail's pace.

For instance, the long introduction (after a good scene involving a funeral) shows Mr. Brynner as a mysterious man among men, ambling about Texas in black Western togs, suavely accepting a money deal from some Mexican farmers, then leisurely rounding up six gun-toting colleagues. Just why their leader, Mr. Brynner, decides to "chase some flies from a little Mexican village" (his words) we never really know. Not for money, he implies repeatedly. For that matter, why is such a blandly intelligent man simply bumming around? Mr. Brynner just is not a cowboy.

A gifted director like Mr. Sturges (who also produced) can't be held entirely responsible for this endless dawdling prologue, since William Roberts' scenario increasingly flattens the action with phi-

The Casts

THE MAGNIFICENT SEVEN, screen play by William Roberts, based on a Japanese film; directed and produced by John Sturges; a Mirisch-Alpha Picture released through United Artists. Running time: 126 minutes.

Chris	Yul Brynner
Calvera	Eli Wallach
Vin	Steve McQueen
Chico	Horst Buchholz
Harry	Brad Dexter
O'Reilly	Charles Bronson
Lee	Robert Vaughn
Britt	James Coburn
Old Man	Vladimir Sokoloff
Petra	Rosenda Monteros
Hilario	Jorge Martinez de Hoyos

and

THE BOY AND THE PIRATES, screen play by Lillie Hayward and Jerry Sackheim; directed and produced by Bert I. Gordon; released through United Artists. Both at neighborhood theatres. Running time: eighty-two minutes.

Jimmy Warren	Charles Herbert
Katrina Van Keif	Susan Gordon
Blackbeard	Murvyn Vye
Snipe	Paul Guilfoyle
Abu, the Genie	Joseph Turkel

losophical talk on all sides and some easy cliches. (One of the seven, a firm actor named Charles Bronson, loves children. The neurotic young hothead of the group, shrilly played by Horst Buchholz, pairs off with a pretty Mexican girl.)

Once the gun slingers arrive in the village, Mr. Sturges has managed to convey the frightened isolation of the tiny community and the natives' ironic, suspicious acceptance of their hired saviors. And two battle sequences are dusty, slam-bang affairs, although some mighty far-fetched nobility finally saves the day.

Steve McQueen (especially), Brad Dexter, Robert Vaughn and James Coburn are okay as the other four visitors. Jorge Martinez de Hoyos and Vladimir Sokoloff are solid as two Mexicans, and Eli Wallach, as the bandit leader, is excellent. Elmer Bernstein's music supplies the loudest prairie blast we've heard since "Giant" (Dimitri Tiomkin). Japan is still ahead.

The Magnificent Seven starring Yul Brynner, Steve McQueen, Horst Buchholz, Charles Bronson, Robert Vaughn, Brad Dexter and James Coburn.

FIRST ALL-OVER-NEW YORK SHOWING

They were seven...and they fought like seven hundred!

YUL BRYNNER
The Magnificent Seven

Co-starring ELI WALLACH · Steve McQUEEN · CHARLES BRONSON · ROBERT VAUGHN

And introducing HORST BUCHHOLZ

Screenplay by WILLIAM ROBERTS · Produced and Directed by JOHN STURGES
A MIRISCH-ALPHA PICTURE · Filmed in Panavision · Color by DeLuxe
Executive Producer WALTER MIRISCH · Music ELMER BERNSTEIN

'The Maltese Falcon,' a Fast Mystery-Thriller With Quality and Charm, at the Strand

THE MALTESE FALCON; based on the novel by Dashiell Hammett. Screen play by John Huston; directed by Mr. Huston; produced by Hal B. Wallis for Warner Bros. Pictures, Inc. At the Strand.

Samuel Spade	Humphrey Bogart
Brigid O'Shaughnessy	Mary Astor
Iva Archer	Gladys George
Joel Cairo	Peter Lorre
Detective Lieutenant	Barton MacLane
Effie Perine	Lee Patrick
Kasper Gutman	Sidney Greenstreet
Detective Polhaus	Ward Bond
Miles Archer	Jerome Cowan
Wilmer Cook	Elisha Cook Jr.
Luke	James Burke
Frank Richman	Murray Alper
Bryan	John Hamilton

By BOSLEY CROWTHER

The Warners have been strangely bashful about their new mystery film, "The Maltese Falcon," and about the young man, John Huston, whose first directorial job it is. Maybe they thought it best to bring both along under wraps, seeing as how the picture is a remake of an old Dashiell Hammett yarn done ten years ago, and Mr. Huston is a fledgling whose previous efforts have been devoted to writing scripts. And maybe—which is somehow more likely—they wanted to give every one a nice surprise. For "The Maltese Falcon," which swooped down onto the screen of the Strand yesterday, only turns out to be the best mystery thriller of the year, and young Mr. Huston gives promise of becoming one of the smartest directors in the field.

For some reason, Hollywood has neglected the sophisticated crime film of late, and England, for reasons which are obvious, hasn't been sending her quota in recent months. In fact, we had almost forgotten how devilishly delightful such films can be when done with taste and understanding and a feeling for the fine line of suspense. But now, with "The Maltese Falcon," the Warners and Mr. Huston give us again something of the old thrill we got from Alfred Hitchcock's brilliant melodramas or from "The Thin Man" before he died of hunger.

This is not to imply, however, that Mr. Huston has imitated any one. He has worked out his own style, which is brisk and supremely hardboiled. We didn't see the first "Falcon," which had Ricardo Cortez and Bebe Daniels in its cast. But we'll wager it wasn't half as tough nor half as flavored with idioms as is this present version, in which Humphrey Bogart hits his peak. For the trick which Mr. Huston has pulled is a combination of American ruggedness with the suavity of the English crime school—a blend of mind and muscle—plus a slight touch of pathos.

Perhaps you know the story (it was one of Mr. Hammett's best): of a private detective in San Francisco who becomes involved through a beautiful but evasive dame in a complicated plot to gain possession of a fabulous jeweled statuette. As Mr. Huston has adapted it, the mystery is as thick as a wall and the facts are completely obscure as the picture gets under way. But slowly the bits fall together, the complications draw out and a monstrous but logical intrigue of international proportions is revealed.

Much of the quality of the picture lies in its excellent revelation of character. Mr. Bogart is a shrewd, tough detective with a mind that cuts like a blade, a temperament that sometimes betrays him, and a code of morals which is coolly cynical. Mary Astor is well nigh perfect as the beautiful woman whose cupidity is forever to be suspect. Sidney Greenstreet, from the Theatre Guild's roster, is magnificent as a cultivated English crook, and Peter Lorre, Elisha Cook Jr., Lee Patrick, Barton MacLane all contribute stunning characters. (Also, if you look closely, you'll see Walter Huston, John's father, in a bit part.)

Don't miss "The Maltese Falcon" if your taste is for mystery fare. It's the slickest exercise in cerebration that has hit the screen in many months, and it is also one of the most compelling nervous-laughter provokers yet.

Humphrey Bogart, Peter Lorre, Mary Astor and Sydney Greenstreet in *The Maltese Falcon.*

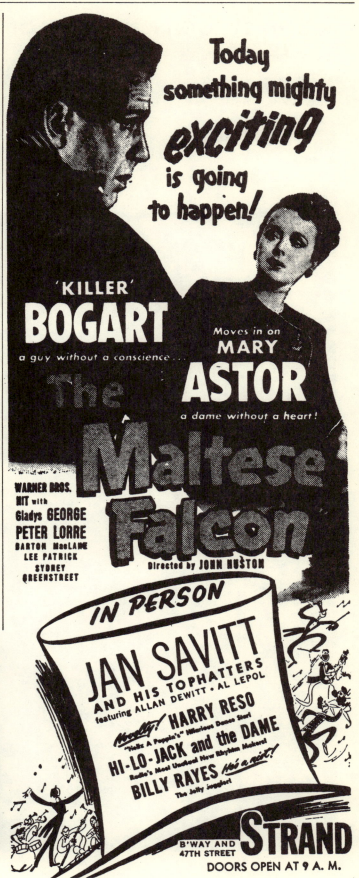

Today something mighty **exciting** is going to happen!

'KILLER' **BOGART**
a guy without a conscience...

Moves in on MARY **ASTOR**
a dame without a heart!

The **Maltese Falcon**

WARNER BROS. HIT with
Gladys GEORGE
PETER LORRE
BARTON MacLANE
LEE PATRICK
SYDNEY GREENSTREET

Directed by JOHN HUSTON

IN PERSON

JAN SAVITT
AND HIS TOPHATTERS
featuring ALLAN DEWITT · AL LEPOL

HARRY RESO

HI-LO-JACK and the DAME

BILLY RAYES
The Jolly Jingler!

STRAND
B'WAY AND 47TH STREET

DOORS OPEN AT 9 A. M.

A Sturdy Conscience, a Steadfast Heart

'A Man for All Seasons' Opens at Fine Arts

By BOSLEY CROWTHER

FRED ZINNEMANN has done a fine job of putting upon the screen the solid substance of "A Man for All Seasons," Robert Bolt's play about Sir Thomas More, and in doing so he presents us with an awesome view of a sturdy conscience and a steadfast heart.

Within such magnificent settings as only England itself could provide to convey the resplendence and color of the play's 16th-century mise en scène, and with Paul Scofield playing Sir Thomas as he did so superbly on the stage, Mr. Zinnemann has crystallized the essence of this drama in such pictorial terms as to render even its abstractions vibrant. The film opened at the Fine Arts last night.

I lay stress upon the screen, because the play is essentially a showing of just one prolonged conflict of wills, one extended exposition of a man's refusal to swerve from his spiritual and intellectual convictions at the insistence of his King. And such ideological disagreements are difficult to state in visual terms, no matter how pyrotechnic the proponents and opponents may be.

It is to Mr. Zinnemann's credit that he has not allowed his excellent cast to resort to pyrotechnics, except

The Cast

A MAN FOR ALL SEASONS, screenplay by Robert Bolt based on his play of the same name; produced and directed by Fred Zinnemann with William N. Graf as executive producer; a Highland Production distributed by Columbia Pictures. At the Fine Arts Theater, 58th Street between Park and Lexington Avenues. Running time: 130 minutes.

Sir Thomas More	Paul Scofield
Alice More	Wendy Hiller
Thomas Cromwell	Leo McKern
King Henry VIII	Robert Shaw
Cardinal Wolsey	Orson Welles
Margaret More	Susannah York
The Duke of Norfolk	Nigel Davenport
Rich	John Hurt
William Roper	Corin Redgrave
Anne Boleyn	Vanessa Redgrave
Matthew	Colin Blakely
Averil Machin	Yootha Joyce

in the singular case of Robert Shaw's tempestuous performance of the unbalanced Henry VIII. Mr. Shaw is permittedly eccentric, like the sweep of a hurricane—now roaring with seeming refreshment, now ominously calm, now wild with wrath—as he shapes a frightening portrait of the headstrong, heretical King who demands that More give acquiescence to his marriage with Anne Boleyn.

But Mr. Scofield is brilliant in his exercise of temperance and restraint, of disciplined wisdom and humor, as he variously confronts his restless King or Cardinal Wolsey, who is played by Orson Welles with subtle, startling glints of poisonous evil that, in this day, are extraordinary for him. Mr. Scofield is equally disciplined and forceful in his several dialectical duels with the King's advocate, Thomas Cromwell, who is played by Leo McKern with truly diabolical malevolence, or in his playful discourses with his son-in-law, William Roper, whom Corin Redgrave makes a bit of a flop.

In fact, it is this delineation of More's sterling strength and character, his intellectual vigor and remarkable emotional control, that endow this film with dynamism in even its most talky scenes. And, heaven knows, it is talky—full of long theological discourses and political implications that you must know your history to understand.

Likewise, it is repetitive in tracing the painful course of More to his final showdown before a rigged high court, where he is betrayed by a young Judas, and thence to the merciful block. And along this route, some of his sessions, especially with Master Rich, the sycophant of John Hurt, who betrays him, are much too involved and difficult.

But throughout, Mr. Scofield manages to use the glowing words of Mr. Bolt and his own histrionic magnificence to give a luminescence and power, integrity and honor, to this man who will not "yes" his King. And he also gets some deep emotion in his ultimate farewell

(continued)

Paul Scofield won an Oscar with his portrayal of Sir Thomas More in *A Man For All Seasons.*

scene with his stalwart wife, played by Wendy Hiller, and his daughter, played (too softly) by Susannah York.

It is notable that Mr. Bolt, in writing his own screenplay, has dropped the Common Man, who was a glib and ubiquitous character of vulgar wit and cynicism on the stage. By this stroke, he has eliminated the built-in point of view of the commonality to these grand monarchial intrigues that was helpful to a balance of the whole.

Moreover, the staging of the drama on the screen in a naturalistic style, with authentic medieval locations and sharply detailed sets designed by John Box, removes it from

Paul Scofield and Susannah York in a scene from *A Man For All Seasons*.

the ambience of philosophical reflection achieved in the abstract set of the stage production and puts it in the aspect of historical literalness. Both of these significant changes put a burden of stark illusion on the film.

I would say that the film misses the humor and pragmatism of the Common Man, and it sacrifices some scope of vision with the loss of the abstract set. But it gains great pictorial conviction with the naturalistic style and the beautiful color photography of Ted Moore.

"A Man for All Seasons" is a picture that inspires admiration, courage and thought.

PREMIERE TONIGHT 8 P.M.!

The award-winning stage-triumph brings new excitement to the screen... with its grandeur and its gripping drama!

COLUMBIA PICTURES presents
FRED ZINNEMANN'S
FILM OF

A MAN FOR ALL SEASONS

From the play by
ROBERT BOLT

co-starring
WENDY HILLER
LEO McKERN
ROBERT SHAW
ORSON WELLES
SUSANNAH YORK

and
PAUL SCOFIELD as Thomas More

with
NIGEL DAVENPORT
JOHN HURT and CORIN REDGRAVE

The Screen: Woody Allen's 'Manhattan'

By VINCENT CANBY

AS California is our idealized future, a place where there is no downtown because the suburbs have moved in instead of out, hip Manhattan represents our idealized present. Existence in Manhattan is so fleeting that one sometimes wishes one could predate oneself, as do the weekly magazines, in this way to avoid life's litter basket, for a few days, anyway.

"Manhattan," Woody Allen's extraordinarily fine and funny new film, is about many things, including a time and place where fashion probably blights more lives, more quickly, than any amounts of booze, drugs, radioactive fallout and saturated animal fats. In this Manhattan, it's no longer a question of keeping up, but of staying ahead. The person on this week's cover is a leading candidate for next year's feature story that asks, "Whatever happened to . . . ?"

•

To survive in alien landscapes, animals develop bizarre defense mechanisms, often at a certain cost. Ostriches can run fast, but they are unable to fly. Sharks have teeth like the slicing blade in a Cuisinart, yet if they take a stationary snooze, their lungs fill with water and they drown. They must always keep moving.

This is pretty much the fate of a number of people who move through and around the Manhattan of Isaac Davis (Mr. Allen), a successful comedy writer who quits his television job to write a novel. As Isaac Davis is Mr. Allen's most fully realized, most achingly besieged male character, so is "Manhattan" his most moving and expansive work to date. It's as serious as "Interiors" — if one must use that often foolish word — but far less constricted and self-conscious. In "Manhattan," Mr. Allen is working in a milieu he knows well and with characters he understands and appreciates, especially when they are drowning.

In addition to being the director and co-author — with Marshall Brickman — of the film, Mr. Allen is its most important presence. He gives "Manhattan" a point of reference just as he did 10 years ago when the character he played was named Virgil Starkwell in "Take the Money and Run." How Virgil and Woody have grown!

"Manhattan" moves on from both "Interiors" and "Annie Hall," being more effectively critical and more compassionate than the first and more witty and clear-eyed than the second. There is a sense of applied romance here, especially in the soundtrack use

(continued)

Diane Keaton with Woody Allen

Slice of the Big Apple

MANHATTAN, directed by Woody Allen; written by Mr. Allen and Marshall Brickman; director of photography, Gordon Willis; film editor, Susan E. Morse; music by George Gershwin; performed by the New York Philharmonic; conducted by Zubin Mehta; produced by Charles H. Joffe. At the Baronet, 993 Third Avenue; Little Carnegie, 57th Street east of Seventh Avenue; 34th Street East, near Second Avenue, and other theaters. Running time: 93 minutes. This film is rated R.

Isaac Davis	Woody Allen
Mary Wilke	Diane Keaton
Yale	Michael Murphy
Tracy	Mariel Hemingway
Jill	Meryl Streep
Emily	Anne Byrne
Connie	Karen Ludwig
Dennis	Michael O'Donoghue
Party Guest	Victor Truro
Party Guest	Tisa Farrow
Party Guest	Helen Hanft
Guest of Honor	Bella Abzug
Television Director	Gary Weis
Television Producer	Kenny Vance
Televison Actor No. 1	Charles Levin
Television Actor No. 2	Karen Allen
Television Actor No. 3	David Rasche
Isaac's son, Willie	Damion Sheller
Jeremiah	Wallace Shawn
Shakespearean Actor	Mark Linn Baker
Shakespearean Actress	Frances Conroy
Porsche Owner No. 1	Frances Conroy
Porsche Owner No. 2	Bill Anthony
Pizzeria Waiter	Ray Serra

of some of the lushest melodies ever written by George Gershwin, as well as in Mr. Allen's decision to have Gordon Willis photograph "Manhattan" in the kind of velvety black-and-white I associate with old M-G-M films like "East Side, West Side" and "The Bad and the Beautiful." The movie looks so good that it looks unreal, which, in this day and age of film and fashion, is to go so far out that you're back in.

"Manhattan" is, of course, about love, or, more accurately, about relationships. Among those who are attempting to relate to Isaac Davis are Mary Wilke (Diane Keaton), a journalist who carries on like an Annie Hall who has been analyzed out of her shyness into the shape of an aggressively neurotic woman doomed to make a mess of things, and Tracy (Mariel Hemingway), a beautiful, 17-year-old nymphet with a turned-down mouth and a trust in her 42-year-old lover, Isaac, that is also doomed. In addition, there is Yale (Michael Murphy), Isaac's best friend, who hands Mary over to Isaac for as long as it suits his (Yale's) purposes.

On the fringe of the film, observing the events with the grim determination of someone who has made a decision that must be stuck by, is Isaac's former wife, Jill (Meryl Streep), who left Isaac and, with their small son, moved in with her feamle lover, in such circumstances to write a best-selling book about her life titled "Marriage, Divorce and Selfhood."

•

"Manhattan," which opens today at the Baronet and other theaters, is mostly about Isaac's efforts to get some purchase on his life after he initiates a breakup with his illegal, teenage mistress — a marvelous scene set at a soda fountain, with Tracy slurping down a large malted while her life goes smash — and his attempt to forge a relationship with the deeply troubled Mary Wilke. Unlike all of his friends

except the still-learning Tracy, Isaac believes in monogamy. "I think people should mate for life," he says, "like pigeons and Catholics."

What happens is not the substance of "Manhattan" as much as how it happens. The movie is full of moments that are uproariously funny and others that are sometimes shattering for the degree in which they evoke civilized desolation.

The screenplay is so vivid you may feel as if you've met characters who are only references in the dialogue. One of these is Mary Wilke's psychiatrist, Donny, who calls her up at 3 A.M. and weeps. The on-screen characters are beautifully played by, among others, Mr. Murphy and Miss Streep. Miss Keaton and Miss Hemingway are superb — the effect of Miss Hemingway's performance being directly responsible for the unexpected impact of Mr. Allen's penultimate moment in the film, which should not be described here.

I suspect there will be much more to say about "Manhattan" in the future. Mr. Allen's progress as one of our major film makers is proceeding so rapidly that we who watch him have to pause occasionally to catch our breath.

Dianne Keaton with Woody Allen in his new romantic comedy, *Manhattan*.

"MANHATTAN' IS A MASTERPIECE. A PERFECT BLENDING OF STYLE, SUBSTANCE, HUMOR AND HUMANITY!"
—Richard Schickel, Time

WOODY ALLEN
DIANE KEATON
MICHAEL MURPHY
MARIEL HEMINGWAY
MERYL STREEP
ANNE BYRNE

MANHATTAN

"MANHATTAN"   Music by   GEORGE GERSHWIN
A JACK ROLLINS-CHARLES H. JOFFE Production
Written by WOODY ALLEN and MARSHALL BRICKMAN
Directed by WOODY ALLEN   Produced by CHARLES H. JOFFE
Executive Producer ROBERT GREENHUT   Director of Photography GORDON WILLIS
United Artists   [R]

WALTER READE 5	MANHATTAN WALTER READE 5	WALTER READE 5
BARONET	LITTLE CARNEGIE	34th ST. EAST
59th St at 3rd Ave EL5-1663	57th St East of 7th Ave 246-5123	Near 2nd Ave MU3-0255
12:00, 1:50, 3:40, 9:30, 7:20, 9:10, 11:00	12:00, 1:50, 3:40, 5:30, 7:20, 9:10, 11:00	12:00, 1:50, 3:40, 7:20, 9:10, 11:00

NASSAU	SUFFOLK
UA MEADOWBROOK #2	WHITMAN
East Meadow (516) 732-7552	Hunting (516) 423-1300
7, 8:40, 10:20	1, 2:40, 6:25, 6:10, 8:00, 9:90

NEW JERSEY	GENERAL CINEMAS
UA CINEMA 46 #1	MENLO PARK CINEMA #2
Totowa (201)256-8484	Menlo Park Rt 1 (201)549-6767
2, 4, 6, 8:10, 10:20	2, 3:40, 9:30, 7:08, 8:40, 10:10

A Bronx Butcher in Love

'Marty,' Adapted From TV, Stars Borgnine

MARTY, screen play and story by Paddy Chayefsky; directed by Delbert Mann; produced by Harold Hecht. A Harold Hecht-Burt Lancaster Presentation released by United Artists. At the Sutton.
Marty .... Ernest Borgnine
Clara .... Betsy Blair
Mrs. Pilletti .... Esther Minciotti
Catherine .... Augusta Ciolli
Angie .... Joe Mantell
Virginia .... Karen Steele
Thomas .... Jerry Paris
Ralph .... Frank Sutton
The Kid .... Walter Kelley
Joe .... Robin Morse

By BOSLEY CROWTHER

NO matter what the movie people may say or think about television, they have it to thank for "Marty," which came to the Sutton yesterday. This neat little character study of a lonely fellow and a lonely girl who find each other in the prowling mob at a Bronx dance hall and get together despite their families and their friends was original-ly done as a TV drama, and its present transposition to the screen has been accomplished by its TV director, Delbert Mann, as his first film achieve-ment.

The transfer is well worth a tribute, for "Marty" makes a warm and winning film, full of the sort of candid comment on plain, drab people that sel-dom reaches the screen. And Ernest Borgnine as the fellow and Betsy Blair as the girl— not to mention three or four others — give performances that burn into the mind. Ex-cept for a rather sudden end-ing that leaves a couple of threads untied and the emo-tional climax not quite played out, it is a trim and reward-ing show.

In essence, this ninety-minute playlet, which Paddy Chayef-sky has prepared from his own TV original, is just a good-natured, wistful kicking around of some of the socially awkward folkways of the great urban middle class. The hero, a stocky, moon-faced butcher, is 34 years old—un-married, uninspired, unimag-inative and lost in boredom and loneliness. He lives with his quaint Italian mother and he spends dull time with his equally helpless friends whose ideal of femininity is a busty pick - up, whose intellectual level is Mickey Spillane.

Into the life of this fellow— at the Stardust Dance Hall on a Saturday night—comes a not young, not glamorous schoolteacher who is as bleak-ly bored and lonely as he. She, too, has known the ignominy and the anguish of being shunned. She, too, has just about exhausted any hope of getting a mate. And even though our hero gallantly as-sures her "You're not really as much of a dog as you think you are," she needs much more than assurance. By the stand-ards of the Bronx set, she's a dog.

There is the simple situa-tion. Lonely boy meets lonely girl. Lonely boy takes lonely girl to meet his mama and then he takes her home. All the next day, he bears the criticism of his suddenly jeal-ous mother and his friends. Then he conquers his torpor and telephones her. That is the end of the film.

But within the dramatic time-lapse of a little more than twenty-four hours, our hero breaks through the inhibitions of his fearful and inferior at-titudes. He poignantly recog-nizes someone just as lost and desperate as he. And he amus-ingly and bravely grabs for her over the pitiful scoffing of his friends.

Mr. Chayefsky's script is loaded with accurate and vivid dialogue, so blunt and insensi-tive in places that it makes the listener's heart bleed while striking a chord of humor with its candor and colorfulness. And Mr. Mann's excellent staging has got the feel and the flavor of the Bronx, where all of the picture's exteriors and many of its interiors were filmed.

As for Mr. Borgnine's per-formance, it is a beautiful blend of the crude and the strangely gentle and sensitive in a monosyllabic man. It is amazing to see such a per-formance from the actor who played the Stockade sadist in "From Here to Eternity." And Miss Blair is wonderfully re-vealing of the unspoken ner-vousness and hope in the girl who will settle for sincerity. The two make an excellent team.

As the disquieted mother of the hero, Esther Minciotti is superb, and Augusta Ciolli is devastating as a grimly de-pendent aunt. Jerry Paris is briefly amusing as the aunt's conscience-smitten son, and Joe Mantell is funny and in-cisive as the hero's pal. With all the others they present a dandy study in this Harold Hecht-Burt Lancaster film.

Betsy Blair and Ernest Borgnine in *Marty*.

AMERICAN PREMIERE TOMORROW 10:30 A. M.

SUTTON
East 57th Street · PLaza 9-1411

this is "MARTY"
a wonderful guy... once you've met him, you'll never forget him!

The New York Times

FRIDAY, SEPTEMBER 25, 1964.

Screen: 'Mary Poppins'

Julie Andrews Stars as Famous Nanny

By BOSLEY CROWTHER

THAT wonderful English nursemaid, Mary Poppins, who has charmed millions of children (and grown-ups) throughout the world since she first entered literary service under the encouragement of Miss P. L. Travers in 1934, has finally been embodied in a movie. And a most wonderful, cheering movie it is, with Julie Andrews, the original Eliza of "My Fair Lady," playing the title role and with its splices and seams fairly splitting with Poppins marvels turned out by the Walt Disney studio.

•

In case you are a Mary Poppins zealot who dotes on her just as she is, don't let the intrusion of Mr. Disney and his myrmidons worry you one bit. Be thankful for it and praise heaven there are such as they still making films. For the visual and aural felicities they have added to this sparkling color film —the enchantments of a beautiful production, some deliciously animated sequences, some exciting and nimble dancing and a spinning musical score—make it the nicest entertainment that has opened at the Music Hall this year.

And, of course, if you know Mary Poppins, you know that no one would dare to try to fool around with her appearance and her stanch individuality. Even the great Mr. Disney would find himself being subdued by a prim nanny flying through his window and warning crisply, "That will be quite enough of that." This is the genuine Mary Poppins that comes sailing in on an east wind, her open umbrella canted over on the starboard tack, to take on the care of the Banks children, Jane and Michael, in their parents' London home, and vastly uplift the spirits of that father-dominated family.

It is she, played superbly by Miss Andrews, with her button-shoed feet splayed out to give her an unshakable footing and a look of complete authority, who calmly proceeds to show her charges that wonders will never cease and that there's nothing like a spoonful of sugar to sweeten the nastiest medicine. And it is she, with her unrelenting discipline and her disarmingly angelic face, who fills this film with a sense of wholesome substance and the serenity of self-confidence.

But don't think that Mary Poppins is simply a nursery martinet. She is a wonderfully agile spirit with a gift for expansion and fun. To her, it is not the least amazing that she can fly with an umbrella, slide upstairs on banisters on which ordinary people slide down, walk through chalk drawings on the pavement into glittering magical worlds and take her young charges along with her, to their surprise and delight.

•

And it is in the performances of these wonders that Mr. Disney and his people assist in their most felicitous fashion. Flying characters are easy for them. There's nothing at all unusual about sliding a nanny upstairs. And when it comes to surrounding live persons with adorable animated cartoons, they are, of course, the past masters. They are close to their best in this film.

By far the most fanciful passage is a winning one in

The Cast

MARY POPPINS, screenplay by Bill Walsh and Don DaGradi, based on the "Mary Poppins" books by P. L. Travers; directed by Robert Stevenson; co-produced by Walt Disney and Bill Walsh; a Buena Vista Distribution Co., Inc., release. At the Radio City Music Hall. Running time: 140 minutes.

Mary Poppins	Julie Andrews
Bert	Dick Van Dyke
Mr. Banks	David Tomlinson
Mrs. Banks	Glynis Johns
Uncle Albert	Ed Wynn
Ellen	Hermione Baddeley
Jane Banks	Karen Dotrice
Michael Banks	Matthew Garber
Katie Nanna	Elsa Lanchester
Constable Jones	Arthur Treacher
Admiral Boom	Reginald Owen
Mrs. Brill	Reta Shaw
Mr. Dawes, Jr.	Arthur Malet
The Bird Woman	Jane Darwell
Mr. Grubbs	Cyril Delevanti
Mr. Tomes	Lester Matthews
Mr. Mousley	Clive L. Halliday
Mr. Binnacle	Don Barclay
Miss Lark	Marjorie Bennett
Mrs. Corry	Alma Lawton
Miss Persimmon	Marjorie Eaton

which Mary Poppins, her two young people and Bert, the sidewalk artist and match-seller, pass into a cartoon wonderland where barnyard animals frolic. And there's a tinkling carousel, on the horses of which the four voyagers go bouncing off on adventuresome jaunts.

To a thoroughly rollicking musical number," Jolly Holiday," they get mixed up in a

cartoon fox-hunt, with a darling Irish fox, and ride on into the Derby horse-race, which, needless to say, Mary Poppins wins.

Maybe it's our imagination, but there's something about the tunes that Richard M. and Robert B. Sherman have written for this film that reminds us of the tunes in "My Fair Lady." And also the Edwardian costumes and the mellow London settings recollect that hit. A brilliant ballet in which Miss Andrews and Dick Van Dyke as Bert scatter and leap with a gang of sooty chimney-sweeps on the London rooftops is reminiscent, too. The comparison is not unflattering to either. "Mary Poppins" is a fair-lady film.

Bouquets don't go only to Miss Andrews. Mr. Van Dyke is joyous as Bert, the gay and irrepressible street merchant who is the companion of Mary Poppins and the kids. The latter, performed by Karen Dotrice and Matthew Garber, are just as they should be, and their parents—appropriately eccentric—are done beautifully by David Tomlinson and Glynis Johns.

Julie Andrews with Dick Van Dyke, Karen Dotrice and Matthew Garber in Walt Disney's,
Mary Poppins.

'M*A*S*H' Film Blends Atheism, Gore, Humor

By ROGER GREENSPUN

To my knowledge Robert Altman's "M*A*S*H" is the first major American movie openly to ridicule belief in God—not phony belief; real belief. It is also one of the few (though by no means the first) American screen comedies openly to admit the cruelty of its humor. And it is at pains to blend that humor with more operating room gore than I have ever seen in any movie from any place.

All of which may promote a certain air of good feeling in the audience, an attitude of self-congratulation that they have the guts to take the gore, the inhumanity to appreciate the humor, and the sanity to admire the impiety — directed against a major who prays for himself, his Army buddies and even "our Commander in Chief."

Actually "M*A*S*H", which opened yesterday at the Baronet, accepts without question several current pieties (for example, concern for a child's life, but not a grown man's soul), but its general bent is toward emotional freedom, cool wit, and shocking good sense.

Based upon a barely passable novel of the same name (the title stands for Mobile Army Surgical Hospital, but "MASH," of course, stands

The Cast

M*A*S*H, directed by Robert Altman; screenplay by Ring Lardner Jr., from the novel by Richard Hooker; director of photography, Harold E. Stine; music by Johnny Mandel; produced by Ingo Preminger; released by 20th-Century-Fox. At the Baronet Theater, 59th Street at Third Avenue. Running time: 116 minutes. (The Motion Picture Association of America's Production Code and Rating Administration classifies this film: "R—restricted—persons under 16 not admitted, unless accompanied by parent or adult guardian.")

Hawkeye	Donald Sutherland
Trapper John	Elliott Gould
Duke	Tom Skerritt
Maj. Hot Lips	Sally Kellerman
Maj. Frank Burns	Robert Duvall
Lieutenant Dish	Jo Ann Pflug
Dago Red	Rene Auberjonois
Col. Henry Blake	Roger Bowen
Radar O'Reilly	Gary Burghoff
Sgt. Maj. Vollmer	Fred Williamson
Spearchucker	David Arkin
Me Lay	Michael Murphy
Ho-Jon	Kim Atwood
Lieutenant Leslie	Indus Arthur
Painless Pole	John Shuck
General Hammond	G. Wood

for a few other things as well.) "M*A*S*H" takes place mostly in Korea during the war. However, aside from the steady processing of bloody meat through the operating room, the film is not so much concerned with the war as with life inside the Army hospital unit and especially with the quality of life created by the three hot-shot young surgeons (Donald Sutherland, Elliott Gould and Tom Skerritt) who make most things happen.

But, unlike "Catch-22," with which it has already been incorrectly compared (I mean the novel, not the legendary unfinished movie) "M*A*S*H" makes no profoundly radical criticism

either of war or of the Army. Although it is impudent, bold, and often very funny, it lacks the sense of order (even in the midst of disorder) that seems the special province of successful comedy. I think that M*A*S*H," for all its local virtues, is not successful. Its humor comes mostly in bits and pieces, and even in its climax, an utterly unsporting football game between the MASH unit and an evacuation hospital, it fails to build toward either significant confrontation or recognition. At the end, the film simply runs out of steam, says good-by to its major characters, and calls final attention to itself as a movie—surely the saddest and most overworked of cop-out devices in the comic film repertory.

Robert Altman's method has been to fill the frame to a great depth with overlapping bits of action and strands of dialogue. The tracking camera serves as an agent of discovery. To a very great degree, "M*A*S*H" substitutes field of view for point of view, and although I think this substitution has a lot to do with the movie's ultimate weakness, the choice is not without its intelligent rewards.

Insane announcements over the hospital's intercom system, Japanese-accented popular American songs from Armed Forces Radio in Tokyo, bungling corpsmen, drivers, nurses—and again and again the brilliantly understood procedures of the operating room—come together to define the spirit of the film.

In one brief night scene, some MASH-men and the

chief nurse meet to divide the winnings of the football game. In the distance, a jeep drives by, carrying a white-shrouded corpse. The nurse glances at it for a second, and then turns back to her happy friends — and we have a momentary view of the ironic complexities of life that "M*A*S*H" means to contain.

The entire cast seems superb, partly, I think, because Altman (whose previous work, largely on television, I do not know) knows exactly where to cut away.

Among the leads, Elliott Gould suggests the right degree of coolly belligerent self-containment, but Donald Sutherland (in a very elaborate performance) supports his kind of detachment with vocal mannerisms that occasionally become annoying. Sally Kellerman plays the chief nurse, Maj. Hot Lips Houlihan—and how she earns her name is the funniest and nastiest sequence of the film. Her character changes—from comic heavy to something like romantic lead — but M*A*S*H really has no way of handling character change, so she mostly fades into the background.

Early in the film she is the butt of some dreadfully humiliating gags, and with her expressive, vulnerable face, she is disturbing to laugh at. It is as if she had returned from some noble-nonsense war movie of the 1940's to suggest an area of human response that the masterly sophistications of "M*A*S*H" are unaware of.

A humorous anti-war statement was made with the irreverent film, M*A*S*H*, starring Donald Sutherland, Elliot Gould and Sally Kellerman.

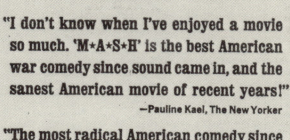

WORLD PREMIERE TODAY 12 NOON

"1970 HAS IT'S FIRST SMASH HIT!" —William Wolf, Cue

M*A*S*H

"I don't know when I've enjoyed a movie so much. 'M*A*S*H' is the best American war comedy since sound came in, and the sanest American movie of recent years!"
—Pauline Kael, The New Yorker

"The most radical American comedy since 'Dr. Strangelove'. 'M*A*S*H' begins where other anti-war films end!" —Time Magazine

"If you believe in God, America, Virginity, Temperance, Not Swearing, Military Discipline and the Sacred Relationship Between Doctor and Patient, pass on to the next review, please. No? Well, you've been warned. 'M*A*S*H' is the deftest, leftest, assiest, grassiest, side-splittingest, throat-slittingest medi-comedy that ever told the Five Deadly Virtues to go stuff it."
—Brad Darrach, Life Movies

"Hilarious...Raises unholy hell!"
—Playboy

"A hip service comedy that goes far beyond the call of duty — to distinguished service, indeed."
—Judith Crist

R RESTRICTED Under 17 requires accompanying Parent or Adult Guardian

20th Century-Fox presents **M*A*S*H** An Ingo Preminger Production

Starring DONALD SUTHERLAND · ELLIOTT GOULD · TOM SKERRITT Co-Starring SALLY KELLERMAN · ROBERT DUVALL · JO ANN PFLUG · RENE AUBERJONOIS
Produced by INGO PREMINGER Directed by ROBERT ALTMAN Screenplay by RING LARDNER, Jr. From a novel by RICHARD HOOKER Music by JOHNNY MANDEL PANAVISION COLOR by DeLuxe

WORLD PREMIERE TODAY

THE **Baronet** A WALTER READE THEATRE
59th St at 3rd Ave · PL 5-1663
12, 2, 4, 6, 8, 10

'Midnight Cowboy'

Dustin Hoffman and Jon Voight Are Starred

JOE BUCK is 6 feet tall and has the kind of innocence that preserves dumb good looks. Joe Buck fancies himself a cowboy, but his spurs were earned while riding a gas range in a Houston hamburger joint. Ratso Rizzo, his buddy and part-time pimp from the Bronx, is short, gimpy and verminous. Although they are a comparatively bizarre couple, they go unnoticed when they arrive at one of those hallucinogenic "Village" parties where the only thing straight is the booze that no one drinks. Everybody is too busy smoking pot, popping pills and being chic. Joe Buck, everhopeful stud, drawls: "I think we better find someone an' tell 'em that we're here."

Trying to tell someone that he's there is the story of Joe Buck's life—28 years of anxiety and dispossession fenced off by Priapian conquests that always, somehow, leave him a little lonelier than he was before. Joe is a funny, dim-witted variation on the lonely, homosexual dream-hero who used to wander disguised through so much drama and literature associated with the nineteen-fifties.

•

"Midnight Cowboy," which opened yesterday at the Coronet Theater, is a slick, brutal (but not brutalizing) movie version of James Leo Herlihy's 1965 novel. It is tough and good in important ways, although its style is oddly romantic and at variance with the laconic material. It may be that movies of this sort (like most war movies) automatically celebrate everything they touch. We know they are movies—isolated, simplified reflections of life—and thus we can enjoy the spectacle of degradation and loss while feeling superior to it and safe.

I had something of this same feeling about "Darling," which was directed by John Schlesinger and in which Julie Christie suffered, more or less upwardly, on her way to fame and fortune in a movie as glossy as the life it satirized. There is nothing obviously glossy in "Midnight Cowboy," but it contains a lot of superior laugh-

ter that has the same softening effect.

Schlesinger is most successful in his use of actors. Dustin Hoffman, as Ratso (his first movie performance since "The Graduate"), is something found under an old door in a vacant lot. With his hair matted back, his ears sticking out and his runty walk, Hoffman looks like a sly, defeated rat and talks with a voice that might have been created by Mel Blanc for a despondent Bugs Bunny. Jon Voight is equally fine as Joe Buck, a tall, handsome young man ,whose open face somehow manages to register the fuzziest of conflicting emotions within a very dim mind.

Waldo Frank's screenplay follows the Herlihy novel in most of the surface events. Joe Buck, a Texas dishwasher without friend or family, comes to New York to make his fortune as a stud to all the rich ladies who have been deprived of their rights by faggot eastern gentlemen. Instead, he winds up a half-hearted 42d Street hustler whose first and only

friend is a lame, largely ineffectual con artist.

•

As long as the focus is on this world of cafeterias and abandoned tenements, of desperate conjunctions in movie balconies and doorways, of catchup and beans and canned heat, "Midnight Cowboy" is so rough and vivid that it's almost unbearable. Less effective are abbreviated, almost subliminal fantasies and flashbacks. Most of these are designed to fill in the story of the young Joe Buck, a little boy whose knowledge of life was learned in front of a TV set while his grandmother, goodtime Sally Buck, ran a Texas beauty parlor and lived with

The Cast

MIDNIGHT COWBOY, screenplay by Waldo Salt, based on the novel by James Leo Herlihy. Directed by John Schlesinger; produced by Jerome Hellman; a Jerome Hellman-John Schlesinger Production, presented by United Artists. At the Coronet Theater, Third Avenue at 59th Street. Running time: 113 minutes.

Ratso	Dustin Hoffman
Joe Buck	Jon Voight
Cass	Sylvia Miles
Mr. O'Daniel	John McGiver
Shirley	Brenda Vaccaro
Towny	Barnard Hughes
Sally Buck	Ruth White
Gretel McAlbertson	Viva

a series of cowboy-father images for Joe.

Schlesinger has given his leads superb support with character actors like Ruth White ((Sally Buck); John McGiver, Brenda Vaccaro, Barnard Hughes and Sylvia Miles. Miss Miles is especially good as the aging hooker Joe picks up under the mistaken impression she is a society lady. The one rather wooden performance, oddly, is that of superstar Viva, who plays a "Village" zombie with none of the flair she exhibits in Andy Warhol's improvisations.

"Midnight Cowboy" often seems to be exploiting its material for sensational or comic effect, but it is ultimately a moving experience that captures the quality of a time and a place. It's not a movie for the ages, but, having seen it, you won't ever again feel detached as you walk down West 42d Street, avoiding the eyes of the drifters, stepping around the little islands of hustlers and closing your nostrils to the smell of rancid griddles.

VINCENT CANBY

Brenda Vaccaro and Jon Voight in a party scene from *Midnight Cowboy*

A JEROME HELLMAN–JOHN SCHLESINGER PRODUCTION

DUSTIN HOFFMAN
JON VOIGHT
"MIDNIGHT COWBOY"

BRENDA VACCARO   JOHN McGIVER   RUTH WHITE   SYLVIA MILES   BARNARD HUGHES

Screenplay by WALDO SALT Based on the novel by JAMES LEO HERLIHY Produced by JEROME HELLMAN Directed by JOHN SCHLESINGER

Music Supervision by JOHN BARRY "EVERYBODY'S TALKIN'" sung by NILSSON   ORIGINAL MOTION PICTURE SCORE AVAILABLE ON UNITED ARTISTS RECORDS

COLOR by DeLuxe

WORLD PREMIERE TONIGHT AT 8:30 P. M.

A limited number of seats will be sold to the public for this performance.

THE Coronet
59th St. at 3rd Ave. EL 5-1663

PERSONS UNDER 17 NOT ADMITTED Ⓧ

'Mildred Pierce,' Warner Drama Starring Joan Crawford, New Bill at the Strand—Western Thriller Moves Into Gotham

MILDRED PIERCE, screen play by Ranald MacDougall and Catherine Turney, based on the James M. Cain novel; directed by Michael Curtiz and produced by Jerry Wald for Warner Brothers. At the Strand.

Mildred Pierce	Joan Crawford
Wally	Jack Carson
Monty Beragon	Zachary Scott
Ida	Eve Arden
Bert Pierce	Bruce Bennett
Veda Pierce	Ann Blyth
Kay Pierce	Jo Ann Marlowe
Dr. Gale	Manart Kippen
Mrs. Biederhof	Leo Patrick
Inspector Peterson	Moroni Olson
Mr. Chris	George Tobias
Mrs. Forrester	Barbara Brown
Mr. Williams	Charles Trowbridge
Ted Forrester	John Compton
Lottie	Butterfly McQueen
Mr. Jones	Chester Clute

Joan Crawford is playing a most troubled lady, and giving a sincere and generally effective characterization of same, in the new drama of James M. Cain origin, "Mildred Pierce," which the Warners presented yesterday at the Strand. But somehow all Miss Crawford's gallant suffering, even with the fillip of murder-mystery that was added to the novel by its screen adaptors, left this spectator strangely unmoved. For it does not seem reasonable that a level-headed person like Mildred Pierce, who builds a fabulously successful chain of restaurants on practically nothing, could be so completely dominated by a selfish and grasping daughter, who spells trouble in capital letters.

This Veda Pierce, for whom poor Mildred works the polish off her nails and makes a loveless second marriage with a socially prominent parasite just to give the girl "background," is as mean and tricky as they come. Yet we couldn't help feeling that if Mildred had put Veda over her knee twice a day at the age of fourteen she might have grown up rather differently. But no, Mildred showers the brat with kindness, suffers the humiliation of seeing Veda make love to the worthless stepfather and then, in a final burst of nobility— and/or mother love— tries to cover up her daughter's shame.

If you can accept this rather demanding premise— and there were not a few ladies in the Strand who were frequently blotting tears with evident enjoyment— then "Mildred Pierce" is just the tortured drama you've been waiting for. Michael Curtiz has directed the story with cunning dramatic artifice for most of its 111 minutes, but has let the character of Veda get out of hand. Ann Blyth interprets Veda with such devastating emphasis that she is quite incredible on the whole. She is an even less convincing protagonist on the screen than she was in Mr. Cain's original chronicle of the tribulations of Mildred Pierce.

It is a tribute to Miss Crawford's art that Mildred, who is deserted by her first husband and suffers the death of her younger daughter in the home of her wayward spouse's inamorata, comes through the ordeal as well as she does. Jack Carson is noisy as a brassy friend whose constant pawing of Mildred is not in the best of taste, Bruce Bennett and Zachary Scott are the first and second husbands, respectively, the one being mostly sulky, the other offensively roughish. Eve Arden is her customary hardboiled self, and that's quite alright with us.

"Mildred Pierce" lacks the driving force of stimulating drama, and its denouement hardly comes as a surprise, but it is cut from a pattern that has been hugely successful in the past and it probably will be this time too.   T. M. P.

THE KIND OF WOMAN MOST MEN WANT
—but shouldn't have!

It's that sizzling best-seller on the screen! WARNERS'

Mildred Pierce

STARRING
JOAN CRAWFORD · JACK CARSON · ZACHARY SCOTT

EVE ARDEN · ANN BLYTH · BRUCE BENNETT · Directed by MICHAEL CURTIZ · Produced by JERRY WALD

IN PERSON
RUSS MORGAN
AND HIS ORCHESTRA featuring MARJORIE LEE
TOMMY DIX
THREE STOOGES
Also! THE GRAYSONS

STRAND

TODAY! Doors open 9 A.M. • B'way & 47th St.

Joan Crawford as the mother determined to give her daughter, Ann Blyth, a good life in *Mildred Pierce*.

Joan Crawford and Zachary Scott in *Mildred Pierce*.

John Huston's 'The Misfits'

Gable and Monroe Star in Script by Miller

By BOSLEY CROWTHER

THERE is this to be said for the people that Clark Gable, Marilyn Monroe, et al, play in John Huston's new film, "The Misfits," which came to the Capitol yesterday: they are not what you might call status seekers or

The Cast

THE MISFITS, screen play by Arthur Miller; directed by John Huston; produced by Frank E. Taylor; released by United Artists. At the Capitol Theatre, Broadway and Fifty-first Street. Running time: 124 minutes.
Gay Langland ....Clark Gable
Roslyn Taber ....Marilyn Monroe
Perce Howland ....Montgomery Clift
Isabelle Steers ....Thelma Ritter
Guido ....Eli Wallach
Old Man ....James Barton
Church Lady ....Estelle Winwood
Raymond Taber ....Kevin McCarthy
Young Boy ....Dennis Shaw

organization men. They are simply lowdown variations

of the old - fashioned genus tramp.

They are nice tramps, it's true—chummy fellows and equally chummy girls, cowboys, garage mechanics and assorted divorcées, who happen to gravitate together in Reno, Nev., that toddling town, and soak up a little whisky before taking off to catch some mustangs in the hills. They are scatterbrained, whimsical, lonely and, in the case of the character of Miss Monroe, inclined to adore all living creatures and have a quivering revulsion to pain.

They are amusing people to be with, for a little while, anyhow. But they are shallow and inconsequential, and that is the dang-busted trouble with this film.

Right at the start, Arthur Miller, who wrote the original script, drops a hint on what is coming and the line that the film is going to take. "Cowboys," he has a jolly woman, played by Thelma Ritter, say, "are the last real men in the world, but they're as reliable as jackrabbits." And that's it.

Everyone in this film is unreliable, wild, slightly kookie. As William Saroyan once put it, "There's no foundation all the way down the line."

Mr. Gable is a leathery old cowboy with a realistic slant on most plain things, but even he has to go a little nutty and sentimental at the end. Eli Wallach as a rolling-stone mechanic is a bundle of impulses and appetites, sometimes very funny, sometimes repulsive and sad. Montgo-

mery Clift as a vagrant rodeo rider is as slug-nutty as they come, equally cavalier toward injuries and toward his gnawing loneliness for his Mom. And Miss Monroe——well, she is completely blank and unfathomable as a new divorcée who shed her husband because "you could touch him but he wasn't there."

Unfortunately for the film's structure, everything turns upon her—the congregation of the fellows, like a pack of dogs, the buildup of cross-purposed courtships and the sentimental backflip at the end. But there is really not much about her that is very exciting or interesting. Mr. Miller makes a pass at explanation. He has someone tell her: "When you smile, it's like the sun coming up."

Toward the end, something happens. The three fellows go into the hills to catch wild horses to sell for dog meat, and the divorcée goes along. The wrangling is vivid and thrilling and everyone is having a good time, until the woman discovers what the horses are being captured for. Then she kicks up such a ruckus—and Mr. Huston lets his cameras show so much of the pitiful plight of the creatures—that the screen is full of shock and the audience is left in breathless horror until she persuades Mr. Gable to let the horses go.

It has something to do with her sense of freedom. What, we wouldn't know.

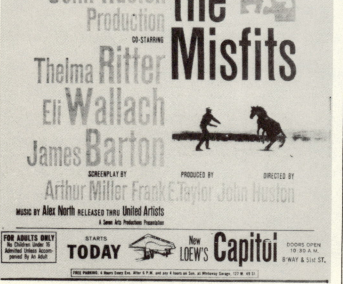

Marilyn Monroe and Clark Gable in their last film, *The Misfits*.

Frank Capra's 'Mr. Smith Goes to Washington' at the Music Hall Sets a Seasonal High in Comedy

MR. SMITH GOES TO WASHINGTON, screen play by Sidney Buchman based on a story by Lewis R. Foster; directed and produced by Frank Capra for Columbia Pictures. At the Radio City Music Hall.

Saunders	Jean Arthur
Jefferson Smith	James Stewart
Senator Joseph Paine	Claude Rains
Jim Taylor	Edward Arnold
Governor Hopper	Guy Kibbee
Diz Moore	Thomas Mitchell
Chick McGann	Eugene Pallette
Ma Smith	Beulah Bondi
Senate Majority Leader	H. B. Warner
President of the Senate	Harry Carey
Susan Paine	Astrid Allwyn
Mrs. Hopper	Ruth Donnelly
Senator MacPherson	Grant Mitchell
Senator Monroe	Porter Hall
Senate Minority Leader	Pierre Watkin
Nosey	Charles Lane
Bill Griffith	William Demarest
Carl Cook	Dick Elliott

By FRANK S. NUGENT

Scorning such cinemacerated branches of the government as the FBI, the Army, Coast Guard and Department of State which, by usage, have become Warner exclusives any way, Columbia's Frank Capra has gone after the greatest game of all, the Senate, in "Mr. Smith Goes to Washington," his new comedy at the Music Hall. In doing so, he is operating, of course, under the protection of that unwritten clause in the Bill of Rights entitling every voting citizen to at least one free swing at the Senate. Mr. Capra's swing is from the floor and in the best of humor; if it fails to rock that august body to its heels—from laughter as much as injured dignity—it won't be his fault but the Senate's and we should really begin to worry about the upper house.

For Mr. Capra is a believer in democracy as well as a stout-hearted humorist. Although he is subjecting the Capitol's bill-collectors to a deal of quizzing and to a scrutiny which is not always tender, he still regards them with affection and hope as the implements, however imperfect they may be, of our kind of government. Most directors would not have attempted to express that faith otherwise than in terms of drama or melodrama. Capra, like the juggler who performed at the Virgin's shrine, has had to employ the only medium he knows. And his comedy has become, in consequence, not merely a brilliant jest, but a stirring and even inspiring testament to liberty and freedom, to simplicity and honesty and to the innate dignity of just the average man.

That may seem altogether too profound a way of looking at Mr. Capra's Mr. Smith, who is blood brother of our old friend, Mr. Deeds. Jefferson Smith came to Washington as a short-term Senator. He came with his eyes and mouth open, with the blessing of the Boy Rangers and a party boss's prayer that he won't tumble to the graft clause in the bill the senior Senator was sneaking into law. But Senator Smith tumbled; dazedly, because he couldn't quite believe the senior Senator was less than godlike; helplessly, because the aroused political machine framed him four ways from Sunday and had him up for expulsion before he could say Jack Garner. But the right somehow triumphs, especially when there's a canny young secretary on Senator Smith's side to in-

struct him in the ungentle art of the filibuster and preserve his faith, and ours, in democracy.

If that synopsis is balder than the Capitol's dome, it is because there is not space here for all the story detail, the character touches, the lightning flashes of humor and poignance that have gone into Mr. Capra's two-hour show. He has paced it beautifully and held it in perfect balance, weaving his romance lightly through the political phases of his comedy, flicking a sardonic eye over the Washington scene, racing out to the hinterland to watch public opinion being made and returning miraculously in time to tie all the story threads together into a serious and meaningful dramatic pattern. Sidney Buchman, who wrote the script, has his claim on this credit, too, for his is a cogent and workmanlike script, with lines worthy of its cast.

And there, finally, Mr. Capra has been really fortunate. As Jefferson Smith, James Stewart is a joy for this season, if not forever. He has too many good scenes, but we like to remember the way his voice cracked when he got up to read his bill, and the way he dropped his hat when he met the senior Senator's daughter, and the way he whistled at the Senators when they turned their backs on him in the filibuster. (He just wanted them to turn around so he could be sure they still had faces.) Jean Arthur, as the secretary—lucky girl being secretary to both Deeds and Smith—tosses a line and bats an eye with delightful drollery. Claude Rains, as the senior Senator, Edward Arnold, as the party steam-roller, Thomas Mitchell, as a roguish correspondent, are splendid all.

Have we forgotten to mention it? "Mr. Smith" is one of the best shows of the year. More fun, even, than the Senate itself.

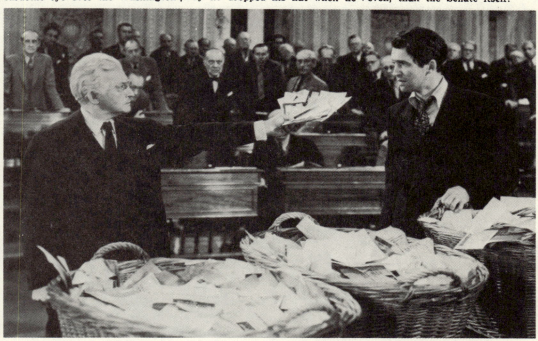

Claude Raines, the dishonest senior senator, and Jimmy Stewart, the naive colleague, in *Mr. Smith Goes to Washington*.

Jean Arthur, Jimmy Stewart and Thomas Mitchell in *Mr. Smith Goes to Washington*.

RADIO CITY
MUSIC HALL

Showplace of the Nation • **Rockefeller Center**

WORLD PREMIERE · **STARTS TODAY** Doors Open 11:00 A. M.

Out of the hearts of its people... out of the very soil of America... a great director creates his most stirring human spectacle of the laughter...the love...the pain... and the joy of the everyday business of living! Stirring...in the seeing! Precious...in the remembering! Enacted by one of the most perfect casts ever assembled in one picture!

•

*Creator of "You Can't Take It With You", "Lost Horizon", "Mr. Deeds Goes To Town", "It Happened One Night", and other Music Hall successes!

FRANK CAPRA'S*
Mr. Smith Goes To Washington

co-starring

Jean **ARTHUR** ★ James **STEWART**

with

CLAUDE **RAINS** • EDWARD **ARNOLD** • GUY **KIBBEE** • THOMAS **MITCHELL** • BEULAH **BONDI**

Directed by **FRANK CAPRA** • A COLUMBIA PICTURE

ON THE GREAT STAGE

"JEROME KERN CAVALCADE"—a gay, pictorial pageant—saluting a great American screenplay with the melodies of a great American composer . . . produced by Leonidoff, settings by Bruno Maine . . . featuring Jan Peerce, Melissa Mason, Walter Cassel, George Holmes, with the Music Hall Rockettes, Corps de Ballet and Choral Ensemble. Symphony Orchestra, under the direction of Erno Rapee.

Picture at: 11:20, 2:09, 4:55, 7:40, 10:28 • Stage Show at: 1:30, 4:19, 7:05, 9:50

FIRST MEZZANINE SEATS MAY BE RESERVED IN ADVANCE • Phone CIrcle 6-4600

Ample Parking Space in Rockefeller Center Garage, 48th to 49th Streets between 5th and 6th Avenues

Lots of Chocolates for Miss Eliza Doolittle

'My Fair Lady' Bows at the Criterion

By BOSLEY CROWTHER

AS Henry Higgins might have whooped, "By George, they've got it!" They've made a superlative film from the musical stage show "My Fair Lady"—a film that enchantingly conveys the rich endowments of the famous stage production in a fresh and flowing cinematic form. The happiest single thing about it is that Audrey Hepburn superbly justifies the decision of the producer, Jack L. Warner, to get her to play the title role that Julie Andrews so charmingly and popularly originated on the stage.

All things considered, it is the brilliance of Miss Hepburn as the Cockney waif who is transformed by Prof. Henry Higgins into an elegant female facade that gives an extra touch of subtle magic and individuality to the film, which had a bejeweled and bangled premiere at the Criterion last night.

•

Other elements and values that are captured so exquisitely in this film are but artful elaborations and intensifications of the stage material as achieved by the special virtuosities and unique flexibilities of the screen.

There are the basic libretto and music of Alan Jay Lerner and Frederick Loewe, which were inspired by the wit and wisdom in the dramatic comedy, "Pygmalion," of George Bernard Shaw. With Mr. Lerner serving as the screen playwright, the structure and, indeed, the very words of the musical play as it was performed on Broadway for six and a half years are preserved. And every piece of music of the original score is used.

There is punctilious duplication of the motifs and patterns of the décor and the Edwardian costumes and scenery, which Cecil Beaton designed for the stage. The only difference is that they're expanded. For instance, the Covent Garden set becomes a stunningly populated market, full of characters and movement in the film; and the embassy ball, to which the heroine is transported Cinderellalike, becomes a dazzling array of regal splendor, as far as the eye can reach, when laid out for ritualistic emphasis on the Super-Panavision color screen. Since Mr. Beaton's décor was fresh and flawless, it is super-fresh and flawless in the film.

•

In the role of Professor Higgins, Rex Harrison still displays the egregious egotism and ferocity that he so vividly displayed on the stage, and Stanley Holloway still comes through like thunder as Eliza's antisocial dustman dad.

Yes, it's all here, the essence of the stage show—the pungent humor and satiric wit of the conception of a linguistic expert making a lady of a guttersnipe by teaching her manners and how to speak, the pomp and mellow grace of a romantic and goneforever age, the delightful intoxication of music that sings in one's ears.

The added something is what Miss Hepburn brings—and what George Cukor as the director has been able to distill from the script.

For want of the scales of a jeweler, let's just say that what Miss Hepburn brings is a fine sensitivity of feeling and a phenomenal histrionic skill. Her Covent Garden flower girl is not just a doxy of the streets. She's a terrifying example of the elemental self-assertion of the female sex. When they try to plunge her into a bathtub, as they do in an added scene, which is a wonderfully comical creation of montage and pantomime, she fights with the fury of a tigress. She is not one to submit to the still obscure customs and refinements of a society that is alien to her.

But when she reaches the point where she can parrot the correct words to describe the rain in Spain, she acknowledges the thrill of achieving this bleak refinement with an electrical gleam in her eyes. And when she celebrates the male approval she receives for accomplishing this goal, she gives a delightful demonstration of ecstasy and energy by racing about the Higgins mansion to the music of "I Could Have Danced All Night."

•

It is true that Marni Nixon provides the lyric voice that seems to emerge from Miss Hepburn, but it is an excellent voice, expertly synchronized. And everything Miss Hepburn mimes to it is in sensitive tune with the melodies and words.

Miss Hepburn is most expressive in the beautiful scenes where she achieves the manners and speech of a lady, yet fails to achieve that one thing she needs for a sense of belonging—that is, the recognition of the man she loves.

Mr. Cukor has maneuvered Miss Hepburn and Mr. Harrison so deftly in these scenes that she has one perpetually alternating between chuckling laughter and dabbing the moisture from one's eyes.

The Cast

MY FAIR LADY, screenplay by Alan Jay Lerner, based on the stage musical by Mr. Lerner and Frederick Loewe, from "Pygmalion," by George Bernard Shaw; directed by George Cukor and produced by Jack L. Warner. Presented by Warner Bros. Pictures. At the Criterion Theater, Broadway and 45th Street. Running time: 170 minutes.

Eliza	Audrey Hepburn
Henry Higgins	Rex Harrison
Alfred Doolittle	Stanley Holloway
Colonel Pickering	Wilfrid Hyde White
Mrs. Higgins	Gladys Cooper
Freddie	Jeremy Brett
Zoltan Karpathy	Theodore Bikel
Mrs. Pearce	Mona Washbourne
Mrs. Eynsford-Hill	Isobel Elsom
Butler	John Holland

Rex Harrison and Audrey Hepburn in an early scene from *My Fair Lady.*

148

The New York Times

SATURDAY, MARCH 16, 1940.

W. C. Fields and Mae West Are Seen in 'My Little Chickadee' at the Roxy—Joe Penner in New Film

MY LITTLE CHICKADEE, from a screen play by Mae West and W. C. Fields; directed by Edward Cline; produced by Lester Cowan for Universal. At the Roxy.

Flower Belle Lee	Mae West
Cuthbert J. Twillie	W. C. Fields
Jeff Badger	Joseph Calleia
Wayne Carter	Dick Foran
Amos Budge	Donald Meek
Ermingarde Foster	Anne Nagel
Mrs. Gideon	Margaret Hamilton
Aunt Lou	Ruth Donnelly
Cousin Zeb	Fuzzy Knight
Hotel Clerk	Harlan Briggs
Milton	George Moran
Uncle John	Willard Robertson

By FRANK S. NUGENT

Noel Coward once had a line about two empty paper bags belaboring each other, but we never thought we should one day be scoundrel enough to remember it in connection with a picture harboring W. C. Fields and Mae West. "My Little Chickadee," at the Roxy, in which the two comic soloists are trying to sing a duet, is an effort greatly strained. With the best will in the world, it just isn't funny—not even when the great William Claude ogles Miss West and roguishly invites her to come up and see him some time; not even when La West, commenting on her escape from the "Masked Bandit," explains "It was a tight spot, but I managed to wiggle out of it." And those are the film's high-water marks.

The low water mark is more clearly defined, for the film is at low tide most of the time in the quality of its humor, in the broad treatment its players and directors have given it, in the caliber of the audience it seems intended to please and in the generally bad odor it

exudes. Miss West's humor, like Miss West herself, appears to be growing broader with the years and begins to turn upon the lady: it's one thing to burlesque sex and quite another to be burlesqued by it. Mr. Fields, largely the innocent victim of some one else's bad taste, inevitably is tempted to juggle a few mud pies himself. It puts a heavy strain on an old admiration to endure the old boy's keyhole-peeping and door-champing at Flower Belle's boudoir, to see him become just another member of the adulant entourage Miss West thoughtfully creates for all her pictures.

The story this time is of Flower Belle Lee (guess who) and of Cuthbert J. Twillie, who are united in the bonds of matrimony-in-name-only because Flower Belle needs a consort for legal reasons and because Cuthbert has . . . well, never mind what Cuthbert finds interesting in Flower Belle. The point is that they are married by a gambler and cut a swath—at least Miss West does—in Greasewood City, where all the men develop asthma when Flower Belle enters a barroom and where Mr. Twillie becomes Sheriff, tends bar, plays a game of poker or two and tells a couple of whoppers about Injun fights and the time he swatted a female barfly. If they had let him alone things might have been better; but, as it runs, Fields ends where the West begins.

W.C. Fields in *My Little Chickadee*.

W.C. Fields and his leading ladies, Margaret Hamilton and Mae West, in *My Little Chickadee*.

Chayefsky's 'Network' Bites Hard As a Film Satire of TV Industry

By VINCENT CANBY

After a long and rewarding career with the UBS Television network as one of America's most respected news commentators, Howard Beale (Peter Finch) is being given the sack. Because his ratings have begun to slip and his show's share of the national audience is nil, this heir to the ideals of Edward R. Murrow has been found wanting. He's obsolete. The night after receiving the bad news, Howard signs off the air by urging his viewers to tune in to his final show next week. He will, he says cheerily, commit suicide on camera.

The next night, against the better judgment of his employers, Howard is allowed to go back on the air to apologize. Instead, he launches into a tirade full of obscenities about the dreary quality of American life in general and corporate television's inhumanity in particular. More apoplexy in the UBS board room, but Howard Beale has just catapulted himself into a new career as television's biggest new star. He's also flipped, being certifiably insane.

"Network," written by Paddy Chayefsky and directed by Sidney Lumet, is about the fall, rise and fall of Howard Beale and about television's running horrendously and hilariously amok. It's about dangerous maneuvers in the executive suites and about old-fashioned newsmen like Max Schumacher (William Holden), who have scruples and are therefore impotent. It's also about Arab oil, conglomerates and new-fashioned hucksters like Diana Christensen (Faye Dunaway), a television executive whose sensitive reading of the viewing audience ("the American people are turning sullen") prompts her to put a seeress on the 11 o'clock news (to predict what will happen tomorrow) and to promote the lunatic coming-apart of Howard Beale as America's most popular personality since Will Rogers.

"Network," which opened yesterday at the Sutton Theater, is, as its ads proclaim, outrageous. It's also brilliantly, cruelly funny, a topical American comedy that confirms Paddy Chayefsky's position as a major new American satirist. Paddy Chayefsky? Major? New? A satirist? Exactly.

Mr. Chayefsky, who made his name initially as television's poet of the small and everyday, has evolved through work like "The Latent Heterosexual" and "The Hospital" into one of our very very few, card-carrying satirists with access to the mass market. His humor is not gentle or generous. It's about as stern and apocalyptic as it's possible to be without alienating the very audience for which it is intended.

Which leads me to wonder what it will mean when "Network" becomes—as I'm sure it will—a huge commercial hit with, one assumes, the same audiences whose tastes supposedly dictate the lunacies that Mr. Chayefsky describes in "Network." Could it be that Mr. Chayefsky has not carried his outrage far enough or that American audiences are so jaded that they will try anything once, say, "Network" or Russian roulette? I'm not sure.

I expect that a lot of people will sniff at the film on the ground that a number of the absurdities Mr. Chayefsky and Mr. Lumet chronicle so carefully couldn't happen, which is to miss the point of what they're up to. These wickedly distorted views of the way television looks, sounds and, indeed, is, are the satirist's cardiogram of the hidden heart, not just of television.

Robert Duvall, the superb Dr. Watson in "The Seven-Per-Cent Solution," is fine as the network hatchet man, subservient only to the head of the conglomerate that owns the network. This fellow, a folksy messiah beautifully played but also of the society that supports it and is, in turn, supported.

"Network" has soft moments. A scene in which the aging, philandering Mr. Holden finally walks out on Miss Dunaway, predicting emotional disaster for such a heartless creature, is of a dopey sentimentality that belongs to another movie, even though both characters are completely credible. Miss Dunaway, in particular, is successful in making touching and funny a woman of psychopathic ambition and lack of feeling.

by Ned Beatty, is the mouthpiece for some of Mr. Chayefsky's bluntest thoughts about the current state of the wealth of nations.

"Network" can be faulted both for going too far and not far enough, but it's also something that very few commercial films are these days. It's alive. This, I suspect, is the Lumet drive. It's also the wit of performers like Mr. Finch, Mr. Holden and Miss Dunaway. As the crazy prophet within the film says of himself. "Network" is vivid and flashing. It's connected into life.

The Cast

NETWORK, directed by Sidney Lumet; screenplay by Paddy Chayefsky; produced by Howard Gottfried; director of photography, Owen Roizman; editor, Alan Heim; music, Elliott Lawrence; a Metro-Goldwyn-Mayer presentation, distributed by United Artists. Running time: 120 minutes. At the Sutton Theater, 57th Street east of Third Avenue. This film has been rated R.

Diane Christensen	Faye Dunaway
Max Schumacher	William Holden
Howard Beale	Peter Finch
Frank Hackett	Robert Duvall
Nelson Chaney	Wesley Addy
Arthur Jensen	Ned Beatty
Great Ahmend Kahn	Arthur Burghardt
Bill Herron	Darryl Hickman
Edward George Ruddy	William Prince
Helen Miggs	Sasha von Scherler
Louise Schumacher	Beatrice Straight
Laureen Hoobs	Marlene Warfield

Faye Dunaway, full of corporate ambitions, and Peter Finch, just plain fed up in *Network*.

Prepare yourself for a perfectly outrageous motion picture.

NETWORK

Television will never be the same

METRO-GOLDWYN-MAYER presents

FAYE DUNAWAY **WILLIAM HOLDEN** **PETER FINCH** **ROBERT DUVALL** in

NETWORK

BY **PADDY CHAYEFSKY**

Directed by **SIDNEY LUMET**   Produced by **HOWARD GOTTFRIED**

MGM   United Artists

World Premiere Sunday   **SUTTON**

'A Night At The Opera'- Three of the Four Marx Brothers at the Capitol

A NIGHT AT THE OPERA, based on a story by James Kevin McGuinness; screen play by George S. Kaufman and Morrie Ryskind; music score by Herbert Stothart; music and lyrics by Nacio Herb Brown and Arthur Freed, and Kaper, Jurmann and Ned Washington; directed by Sam Wood; a Metro-Goldwyn-Mayer production. At the Capitol.

Otis B. Driftwood	Groucho Marx
Fiorello	Chico Marx
Tomasso	Harpo Marx
Rosa	Kitty Carlisle
Ricardo	Allan Jones
Lassparri	Walter King
Gottlieb	Siegfried Rumann
Mrs. Claypool	Margaret Dumont
Captain	Edward Keane
Henderson	Robert Emmet O'Connor

By ANDRE SENNWALD.

The merry Marx boys, whittled down from a quartet to a trio, have arrived in town with the loudest and funniest screen comedy of the Winter season. If "A Night at the Opera" is a trifle below their best, it is also considerably above the standard of laughter that has been our portion since they quit the screen. George S. Kaufman and Morrie Ryskind have given them a resounding slapstick to play with and they wield it with maniacal delight.

Even when their gags sound as if they were carved out of Wheeler and Woolsey with an axe, the boys continue to be rapturously mad. You may have wondered what the trouble has been with the operatic films. You will discover the answer at the Capitol: the Marx Brothers weren't in them.

The Marxist assault on grand opera makes a shambles of that comparatively sacred institution. Groucho, you see, is a phony musical impresario who has attached himself to a dignified lady in the hope of separating her from a portion of her $8,000,000. Chico is managing an ambitious Italian tenor against the tenor's will and better judgment. Harpo, the mischievous pixie, is up to his old habit of getting in everybody's way. Their adventures as impostors, stowaways and hunted madmen progress to a delirious climax at a performance of "Il Trovatore" in what is evi-dently intended to be the Metropolitan. Here the comedy bursts its shackles and spatters into magnificent fragments as the brothers, with the police and the opera management hard on their heels, pop in and out of the performance and transform Verdi into low buffoonery.

Among other things "A Night at the Opera" finally does justice to Harpo, whose pantomimic genius sometimes has a habit of getting lost behind Groucho's machine-gun patter. The whimsical little fellow, half pagan and half innocent child, manages to be in the approximate centre of all the film's best moments. There is his superbly demoniac pantomime at the breakfast table, where he puts the food and crockery to curious uses and winds up by making a sandwich with Groucho's cigar. At one point the sly authors arrange a situation around him that threatens to bludgeon him into breaking his golden silence. That occurs when the brothers are being fêted at City Hall in the guise of three eminent Italian aviators whose beards and uniforms they have borrowed. But Harpo wriggles out of the obligation to make a speech by a device that you will have to see to believe.

It would be pleasant to report that the omission of Zeppo, the romantic juvenile of the gang, also means the elimination of the conventional musical comedy romance. That isn't quite so, although the boys do keep the amorous business from becoming too tiresome. "A Night at the Opera" is especially fortunate in its straight people. Margaret Dumont, that fine and gracious stooge in all the Marx Brothers pictures, is proficient once again as the dignified art patroness who falls under Groucho's baleful eye. Siegfried Rumann is an excellent exponent of outraged respectability as the opera impresario. Robert Emmet O'Connor also is an asset as a cynical Irish detective who finds the boys a little too formidable for him.

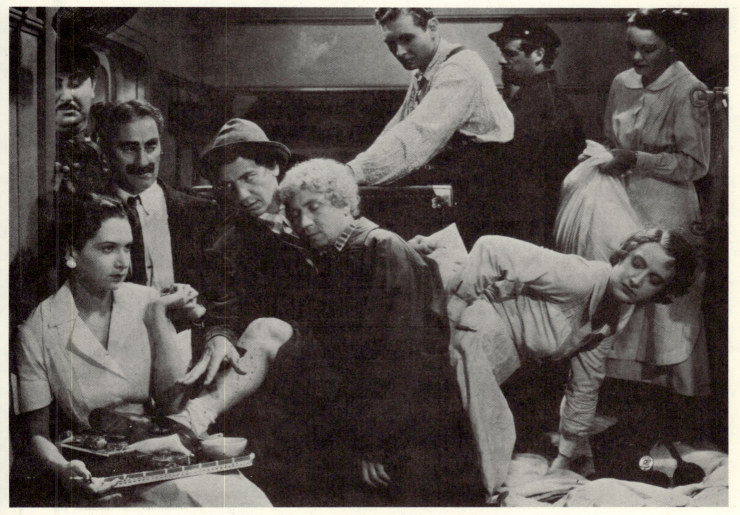

The Marx Brothers in their hilarious spoof on grand opera, *A Night At The Opera.*

The COMEDY that COST A MILLION!

Nothing like it in all the history of screen hilarity! At a cost of $1,000,000, M-G-M has plotted the BIG COMEDY SHOW that you'll vote the funniest ever made! A year to make! And when you see this mammoth fun festival, jammed with 1,000 laughs, crammed with a song and spectacle, beauty and hilarity, you'll agree it's the COMEDY SENSATION OF ALL TIME!

A Night at the Opera
starring
GROUCHO · CHICO · HARPO ·
MARX BROTHERS
with KITTY CARLISLE and ALLAN JONES

WALLACE BEERY: "Three times as funny as anything I've ever seen...but after all there's three times as many comedians in the picture."

WALTER WINCHELL (N. Y. Mirror) "Reports on the new Marx Bros. picture are so sugary...the wags all concerned will be called Groucho, Chico, Harpo and Bravo."

JEANETTE MacDONALD: "'A Night at the Opera' is one of the greatest as well as the funniest I have ever seen."

Extra on Screen
CHARLES "CHIC" SALE as LINCOLN in 'The PERFECT TRIBUTE'
Metro Color Cartoon "Alias St. Nick"

The Fun Starts TODAY
CAPITOL
BROADWAY AT 51st STREET
MAJOR EDWARD BOWES, Managing Director

DOORS OPEN
10:15 A.M.
25c TILL 1 P.M.

Hal Roach Presents a Splendid Film Version of John Steinbeck's 'Of Mice and Men' at the Roxy

OF MICE AND MEN, screen play by Eugene Solow adapted from the John Steinbeck play; directed and produced by Lewis Milestone; a Hal Roach presentation; released by United Artists. At the Roxy.

George	Burgess Meredith
Mae	Betty Field
Lennie	Lon Chaney Jr.
Slim	Charles Bickford
Candy	Roman Bohnen
Curley	Bob Steele
Whit	Noah Beery Jr.
Jackson	Oscar O'Shea
Carlson	Granville Bates
Crooks	Leigh Whipper

By FRANK S. NUGENT

His biographers report that John Steinbeck's pet aversions are Hollywood and New York. Happily the feeling is not reciprocated. Hollywood, which brought his "Grapes of Wrath" so magnificently to the screen, has been no less reverent toward the strangely dramatic and compassionate tale that Steinbeck called "Of Mice and Men." And New York, unless we have miscalculated again, will endorse its film version, at the Roxy, as heartily as it has endorsed the film of the Joads. The pictures have little in common as narrative, but they have much in common as art: the same deft handling of their material, the same understanding of people, the same ability to focus interest sharply and reward it with honest craftsmanship and skill.

"Of Mice and Men" is news no longer. It has the familiarity of a widely sold novelette, of a successful play that won the New York Drama Critics Circle award as the best American contribution to the 1937-38 season. It would be idle, we think, to say that it has found new meaning, new depth, new significance as a film. Nor should such added value be required. Lewis Milestone, who directed it; Eugene Solow, who adapted it, and Burgess Meredith, Lon Chaney Jr., Betty Field and the others who have performed it, have done more than well in simply realizing the drama's established values. "Of Mice and Men" need not have been better as a play than it was as a novelette; it need not be better as a picture, so long as it is just as good.

Book and play have been followed as literally as the screen demands and the Hays office permits. There is a short prologue; the camera enlarges the play's vista to include the fields where the barley-buckers worked, the messroom, the town cafe where the hands might spend their wages; but nothing has been added that does not belong, nothing has been removed that was important to the proper telling of the story. If we must be reduced to comparisons we should say the film has been better cast in almost every role: Young Mr. Chaney does not quite erase the memory of Broderick Crawford's Lennie, but Mr. Meredith's George is an improvement on the flat, recitative interpretation by the play's Wallace Ford, and Miss Field is superb (an abused but useful word) as Mae.

Mr. Steinbeck wrote, as you probably are aware, the pathetic, fate-ridden drama of two bundle stiffs who dreamed, and kindled other men's dreams, of owning their own little ranch and living off "the fatta the lan'." George used to talk about it to Lennie, and Lennie, whose mind wasn't clear "on accounta he'd been kicked in the head by a horse," used to crow with delight at the notion of having to tend the rabbits and be permitted to stroke their soft fur. Lennie liked the feel of smooth things, but he was so strong his touch killed them—a bird, a mouse, a white-and-brown puppy, and finally Mae, the foreman's wife, who had silky hair. So the posse went out to hunt him down, and George knew he had to find Lennie first to tell him again about the time they'd have their own little place—and to hold a gun to the back of his happily nodding head.

In summary this has a cruel, bizarre, ridiculous sound. But it doesn't seem that way on the screen. Tragedy dignifies people, even such little people as Lennie, George, Candy and Mae. Mr. Steinbeck and his adapters have seen the end all too clearly, the end of George's dream and Lennie's life. With sound dramatic instinct they have not sought to hasten the inevitable, or stave it off. Doom takes its course and bides its moment; there is hysteria in waiting for the crisis to come. And during the waiting there is the rewarding opportunity to meet some of Steinbeck's interesting people, to listen to them talk, to be amused or moved by the things they say and do. For here again, as in "Grapes of Wrath," we have the feeling of seeing another third, or thirtieth, of the nation, not merely a troupe of play-actors living in a world of make-believe.

No small share of that credit belongs to the men and the one young woman Hal Roach has recruited for his production. Miss Field has added stature to the role of the foreman's wife by relieving her of the play's box-office-conscious order that she behave like a hoyden. Mae, in the film, is entitled to some respect—and never more so than in the splendid scene she has with Lennie when they share a cross-purposed soliloquy. Bob Steele's Curly, Leigh Whipper's Crooks (the only carry-over from the play), Roman Bohnen's Candy, Charles Bickford's Slim and the others, have been scarcely less valuable in their several ways. We noted but one flaw in Mr. Milestone's direction: his refusal to hush the off-screen musicians when Candy's old dog was being taken outside to be shot. A metronome, anything, would have been better than modified "Hearts and Flowers." And that's the only fault we can find with Mr. Steinbeck's second Hollywood-to-New York contribution.

Lennie and the farmer's wife, Betty Field, in *Of Mice and Men*.

Ranch hands Bob Steele and Charles Bickford tease poor, dumb Lennie, played by Lon Chaney, Jr., in *Of Mice and Men*.

A Truly Great Motion Picture!

John Steinbeck's best-selling novel and prize-winning play has been wrought into a magnificent screen drama of compelling power... sincerely human... impressively realistic ...emotionally stirring!

Hal Roach presents

"OF MICE and MEN"

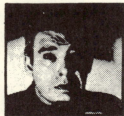

Burgess Meredith as "George"..."I could have lived off the fat o' the land!"

Betty Field as "Mae" ..."I got nobody to talk to—nobody to be with!"

Lon Chaney, Jr. as "Lennie"...I didn't mean to do no bad thing!"

by the author of "The GRAPES of WRATH"

JOHN STEINBECK

with

Burgess **MEREDITH** • Betty **FIELD** • Lon **CHANEY, Jr.**

Produced and Directed by

LEWIS MILESTONE

Released Thru United Artists

★ ON THE ROXY STAGE ★

A Joyous New Variety Presentation with

THE PETERS SISTERS • THREE SWIFTS
PEG-LEG BATES • The GAE FOSTER GIRLS
PAUL ASH and ROXY ORCHESTRA

Starts **TODAY** Doors Open 11 A. M.

THOUSANDS PAID $3.30 TO SEE THE STAGE PLAY! Broadway hailed it a "sensation" in its long run at the famed Music Box Theatre!

Any Day Any Seat to 1 P.M. 25¢ **ROXY** Children Under 12 Always 15¢

SHOW VALUE OF THE NATION • 7th AVE. & 50th ST.

'On the Beach'

The Cast

ON THE BEACH, screen play by John Paxton, based on the book by Nevil Shute; directed and produced by Stanley Kramer; released by United Artists. At the Astor Theatre, Broadway and Forty-fifth Street. Running time: 134 minutes.

Dwight Towers	Gregory Peck
Moira Davidson	Ava Gardner
Julian Osborn	Fred Astaire
Peter Holmes	Anthony Perkins
Mary Holmes	Donna Anderson
Admiral Bridie	John Tate
Lieutenant Hosgood	Lola Brooks
Ferrel	Guy Doleman
Swain	John Meillon
Sundstrom	Harp McGuire
Benson	Ken Wayne
Davis	Richard Meikle
Ackerman	Joe McCormick
Davidson	Lou Vernon

By BOSLEY CROWTHER

THERE is an initial impulse to say of Stanley Kramer's "On the Beach," the new film that he and John Paxton have refined from the novel of Nevil Shute, that it is concerned with the imagined annihilation of all mankind on this earth, the slow poisoning of the last pocket of surviving humans by radioactive fall-out from a nuclear war.

And that would be absolutely accurate, so far as the situation and plot are concerned. For the crisis in this deeply moving picture, which opened at the Astor last night—and in theatres in seventeen other places all around the world—is that which confronts a group of people in Australia in 1964 as they helplessly await the inexorable onset of a lethal cloud of atomic dust.

Death and complete annihilation of the human race are certainly the menaces that hang over all the characters in this film. They are specified at the beginning in the most candid and awesome terms.

A nuclear war someone started (it is never clarified who) has caused fall-out that has completely decimated the entire northern hemisphere. Now the fall-out is slowly drifting southward; the last people in Australia have five months to enjoy what is left of living and prepare themselves for the end.

So, as they grasp the situation, as an American submarine and its crew go north as far as Alaska in hopes of finding a clearing atmosphere and as the final days come upon them (when they learn there is no hope), the ever-present realization of themselves—and the audience—is death.

Yet the basic theme of this drama and its major concern is life, the wondrous thing that man's own vast knowledge and ultimate folly seem about to destroy. And everything done by the characters, every thought they utter and move they make, indicates their fervor, tenacity and courage in the face of doom.

The American submarine captain will not accept that his wife and children are dead, a young Australian naval lieutenant and his wife look forward to having a second child, a worldly and blasé woman who has wasted life tries to find true love, a seasoned and cynical atomic scientist tunes his cherished possession, a racing car.

In putting this fanciful but arresting story of Mr. Shute on the screen, Mr. Kramer and his assistants have most forcibly emphasized this point: life is a beautiful treasure and man should do all he can to save it from annihilation, while there is still time.

The great merit of this picture, aside from its entertaining qualities, is the fact that it carries a passionate conviction that man is worth saving, after all.

The submarine crew: Fred Astaire, Anthony Perkins, and Gregory Peck.

IF YOU NEVER SEE ANOTHER MOTION PICTURE IN YOUR LIFE YOU MUST SEE ON THE BEACH

GREGORY PECK · AVA GARDNER · FRED ASTAIRE · ANTHONY PERKINS

STANLEY KRAMER'S PRODUCTION OF ON THE BEACH

THE BIGGEST STORY OF OUR TIME!

introducing DONNA ANDERSON

Screenplay by JOHN PAXTON
From the novel by NEVIL SHUTE
Produced and Directed by STANLEY KRAMER
Released thru UNITED UA ARTISTS

The NEW Astor THEATRE
BROADWAY & 45th STREET

Tonight at 8:30 p.m.
...The new Astor, an entirely new concept in motion picture theatres, will open its doors. Conceived as a complete composition of abstract art, it embodies the ultimate in perfect entertainment enjoyment, luxuriousness and comfort. The Astor has been completely rebuilt from sidewalk to screen and represents a dramatic new concept in entertainment presentation.

Tomorrow at 9:30 a.m.
...Will mark the start of Continuous Performances. For maximum enjoyment, there is a completely new, electronically-controlled projection and stereophonic acoustical system, and a crystal-clear variable giant screen. For the maximum in comfort, there are roomy, luxurious lounge seats in white naugahyde with ample leg room. Be among the first to see—and be seen—at the Astor!

Premiere Tonight! 8:30 P.M. Benefit American Academy of Dramatic Arts · Tickets Now On Sale At Boxoffice · Continuous Performances Start Tomorrow · Doors Open 8:30 A.M.

The New York Times

THURSDAY, JULY 29, 1954.

Astor Offers 'On the Waterfront'

Brando Stars in Film Directed by Kazan

ON THE WATERFRONT; screen play by Budd Schulberg; based on an original story by Mr. Schulberg and suggested by the series of Pulitzer Prize-winning articles by Malcolm Johnson; directed by Elia Kazan; produced by Sam Spiegel; a Horizon picture presented by Columbia; at the Astor.

Terry Malloy	Marlon Brando
Edie Doyle	Eva Marie Saint
Father Barry	Karl Malden
Johnny Friendly	Lee J. Cobb
Charley Malloy	Rod Steiger
"Pop" Doyle	John Hamilton
"Kayo" Dugan	Pat Henning
Glover	Leif Erickson
Big Mac	James Westerfield
Truck	Tony Galento
Tillie	Tami Mauriello
Barney	Abe Simon
Mott	John Heldabrand
Moose	Rudy Bond
Luke	Don Blackman
Jimmy	Arthur Keegan
J. P.	Barry Macollum
Specs	Mike O'Dowd
Gillette	Marty Balsam
Slim	Fred Gwynne
Tommy	Thomas Handley
Mrs. Collins	Anne Hegira

A SMALL but obviously dedicated group of realists has forged artistry, anger and some horrible truths into "On the Waterfront," as violent and indelible a film record of man's inhumanity to man as has come to light this year. And, while this explosive indictment of the vultures and the meek prey of the docksides, which was unveiled at the Astor yesterday, occasionally is only surface dramatization and an oversimplification of the personalities and evils of our waterfront, it is, nevertheless, an uncommonly powerful, exciting and imaginative use of the screen by gifted professionals.

Although journalism and television already have made the brutal feudalism of the wharves a part of current history, "On the Waterfront" adds a graphic dimension to these sordid pages. Credit for this achievement cannot be relegated to a specific few. Scenarist Budd Schulberg, who, since 1949, has lived with the story stemming from Malcolm Johnson's crusading newspaper articles; director Elia Kazan; the principals headed by Marlon Brando; producer Sam Spiegel; Columbia, which is presenting this independently made production; Leonard Bernstein, who herein is making his debut as a movie composer, and Boris Kaufman, the cinematographer, convincingly have illustrated the murder and mayhem of the waterfront's sleazy jungles.

They also have limned a bestial and venal boss longshoreman; the "shape-up" by which only his obedient, mulct, vassals can earn a day's pay; the hard and strange code that demands that these sullen men die rather than talk about these injustices and a crime commission that helps bring some light into their dark lives. Perhaps these annals of crime are too labyrinthine to be fully

Eva Marie Saint and Marlon Brando in *On the Waterfront*.

and incisively captured by cameras. Suffice it to say, however, that while Mr. Kazan and Mr. Schulberg have not dug as deeply as they might, they have chosen a proper and highly effective cast and setting for their grim adventure. Moving cameras and crews to the crowded rookeries of Hoboken's quayside, where the film was shot in its entirety, they have told with amazing speed and force the story of Terry Malloy, ex-prize fighter and inarticulate tool of tough, ruthless and crooked labor leader, Johnny Friendly. The labor leader is an absolute un-

regenerated monarch of the docks who will blithely shake down his own men as well as ship owners; he will take cuts of pay envelopes and lend his impecunious union members money at usurious rates and he will have his pistol-toting goons dispatch anyone foolish enough to squeal to the crime commission attempting to investigate these practices.

It is the story also of one of these courageous few about to "sing" to the commission — a luckless longshoreman unwit-

tingly set up for the kill by Terry Malloy, who is in his soft spot only because his older brother is the boss' slick, right-hand man. It is the tale of Terry's meeting with the dead man's agonized sister and a fearless, neighborhood priest, who, by love and reason, bring the vicious picture into focus for him. And, it is the account of the murder of Terry's brother; the rampaging younger man's defiant testimony before the commission and the climactic bloody battle that wrests the union from the boss' tenacious grasp.

Journalism may have made these ingredients familiar and certainly more inclusive and multi-dimension, but Mr. Kazan's direction, his outstanding cast and Mr. Schulberg's pithy and punchy dialogue give them distinction and terrific impact. Under the director's expert guidance, Marlon Brando's Terry Malloy is a shatteringly poignant portrait of an amoral, confused, illiterate citizen of the lower depths who is goaded into decency by love, hate and murder. His groping for words, use of the vernacular, care of his beloved pigeons, pugilist's walk and gestures and his discoveries of love and the immensity of the crimes surrounding him are highlights of a beautiful and moving portrayal.

In casting Eva Marie Saint --a newcomer to movies from TV and Broadway—Mr. Kazan has come up with a pretty and blond artisan who does not have to depend on these attributes. Her parochial school training is no bar to love with the proper stranger. Amid scenes of carnage, she gives tenderness and sensitivity to genuine romance. Karl Malden, whose importance in the scheme of this drama seems overemphasized, is, however, a tower of strength as the militant man of the cloth. Rod Steiger, another newcomer to films, is excellent as Brando's fearful brother. The pair have a final scene that is a harsh and touching revelation of their frailties.

Lee J. Cobb is muscularly effective as the labor boss. John Hamilton and Pat Henning are typical "longshoremen," gents who look at home in a hold, and Tony Galento, Tami Mauriello and Abe Simon —erstwhile heavyweight boxing contenders, who portray Cobb's chief goons—are citizens no one would want to meet in a dark alley. Despite its happy ending; its preachments and a somewhat slick approach to some of the facets of dockside strife and tribulations, "On the Waterfront" is moviemaking of a rare and high order.   A. W.

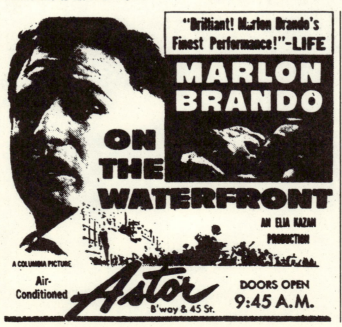

"Brilliant! Marlon Brando's Finest Performance!"—LIFE

MARLON BRANDO

ON THE WATERFRONT

AN ELIA KAZAN PRODUCTION

A COLUMBIA PICTURE

Air-Conditioned

Astor
B'way & 45 St.

DOORS OPEN 9:45 A.M.

D. W. Griffith has been approached by representatives of two South American nations who want him to make historical films dealing with their respective countries, it is reported, but note this:

"One of the conditions provided," adds the announcement, "is that Mr. Griffith shall make two versions, one suitable for the South American eye, and the other tamed to the standard of the North American censor."

It is said that the South Americans were impressed with Mr. Griffith's treatment of a historical subject in the current "Orphans of the Storm," at the Apollo Theatre, and perhaps they were aware of how little incentive Mr. Griffith needs to indulge his love of the spectacular in history. It is interesting to note here, therefore, just how slight was the trace of the French Revolution in the original stage version of "The Two Orphans," from which Mr. Griffith started. The action of the play occurred about two years before the storming of the Bastile, and its only direct reference to the Revolution, according to a witness who has examined the old melodrama, came when de Vaudry remarked that he had seen a play containing expressions of revolutionary sentiments forbidden by the police, which, however, had not been suppressed, the King finding himself forced to yield to the people, who insisted that the play be let alone. Then the following dialogue took place:

De Presles—The King compelled to yield? If that is true, royalty has lowered its dignity.

Vaudrey—No, Marquis. It is the people who are asserting theirs.

De Presles—Why, if this goes on, they will not be satisfied until they suppress one's titles and privileges.

Vaudrey—That would not at all surprise me.

Picard—Excuse me, sir, but that is as ridiculous as though you were to say that one of these days the Parisiens would arise and demolish the Bastille!

Vaudrey—Who knows?

And from that came the idea of all the revolutionary scenes and Danton's ride in "Orphans of the Storm."

Incidentally, "Orphans of the Storm" affords an interesting illustration of how a photoplay, commonly supposed to be much less fluid than a stage production, may be revised after its formal presentation. It is well known, of course, that film may be cut and pasted almost indefinitely, so that scenes shown originally may be eliminated, and others at first held out inserted wherever an exhibitor chooses, but Mr. Griffith has gone further than this. Since the opening of "Orphans of the Storm" at the Apollo he has himself observed, and has engaged others to observe, the reactions of spectators, and as a result he has not only deleted certain scenes, but has made others at his studio in Mamaroneck and put them into the photoplay. Frank Puglia as Pierre, for instance, has been brought to life and kept alive for the happy ending; Creighton Hale has been given additional space as the amusing Picard; the Carmagnole dancers now have more to do, and the scene at the guillotine has been made less horrifically detailed, according to reports from the front of the house.

Three men kissed her

The First on the Cheek

In that beautiful garden of de Praille, with its great trees, gorgeous women, wine, dancing, mad revelry—

And within ten minutes he had lost the world, because of it.

The Second Kissed Her on the Mouth

He was rich and young and handsome, indeed the most handsome man of all the millions in the country.

And he was sent away, far out of the country, because of that kiss.

The Third Kissed Her on the Forehead

He was Danton, the nation's hero . . . and the nation turned against him. Ruler by a nod . . . unseated by a kiss, for later . . .

It Is the Story of the Three Kisses

of Henriette Girard, the little love girl, who brought her blind orphan sister to Paris.

Of intrigue, romance, adventure, love . . . love that is happy, fierce, consuming, glorifying. It is the story of the two orphans in D. W. Griffith's arresting and enchanting masterpiece, "Orphans of the Storm" as shown in the Apollo Theatre.

Lillian and Dorothy Gish in *Orphans of the Storm.*

A Fantastic Melodrama

THE PHANTOM OF THE OPERA, with Lon Chaney, Mary Philbin, Norman Kerry, Arthur Edmund Carewe, Snitz Edwards, Gibson Gowland, Bernard Siegel, John Sainpolis, Virginia Pearson, Olive Ann Alcorn, Edward Cecil, John Miljaun, Grace Marvin, Alexander Bevani, Anton Vaverka, William Tyroler, George B. Williams, Bruce Covington, Edith Yorke and Cesare Gravina. Adapted from Gaston LeRoux's novel. Directed by Rupert Julian with supplementary direction by Edward Sedgwick. Special ballet prologue. At the Astor.

By MORDAUNT HALL.

Up to the present the motion picture producer cannot be accused of hiding his light under a bushel at the opening exhibition of one of his pet pictures.

"The Phantom of the Opera" is an ultra fantastic melodrama, an ambitious production in which there is much to marvel at in the scenic effects. It has been produced with a sort of mechanical precision, and the story reminds one somewhat of a writer who always seeks for alliterative combinations. The narrative could have been fashioned in a more subtle manner and would then have been more interesting to the few. As it stands it will strike popular fancy, and the stage settings will appeal to everybody.

In this presentation one perceives an effect of the interior of the Paris Opera, with people peering from the boxes and flocks of faces in the orchestra seats. There is the giant curtain which swings to with a graceful sweep, and a decorative and glistening central chandelier. All this is pictured in color, some of it a trifle weak, but most of the scenes quite effective.

Another prismatic sequence is that dealing with a mask ball in the Paris Opera, where one beholds the uniforms of all colors, with touches of bright blues and glowing reds. There is the famous staircase, down which passes the Phantom, who, in a cheery moment for the gala event, has decided to appear in flowing crimson and a mask of a death's head. There are the affrighted figurantes who whisper and blanche at the thought that this stalking figure may be the awful Phantom who dwells in the subterranean cellars under the Temple of Music.

You see the bed once owned by Gaby de Lys, which resembles a boat swung from three pillars; then there is a coffin bed in which the Phantom is supposed to rest his weary limbs, and dozens of other interesting features which are flashed here and there on the screen.

Lon Chaney impersonates the Phantom. It is a rôle suited to his liking, and one which he handles with a certain skill, a little exaggerated at times, but none the less compelling. One has to remember that this is a fantastic tale and therefore strange things can happen; and they do.

The idea is an excellent one, but the changes in the picture, and the re-cutting, it, have made some of the scenes abrupt. There is the Chief of the Secret Police, whose rôle has been throttled, as he obviously ought to play a far more important part in the story than he does. And there is throughout this film a decided uncertainty concerning France and her people. Norman Kerry figures as the hero, Raoul de Chagny, and never for an instant does he impress one other than having stepped into a uniform that did not belong to him. His facial expressions are often annoying, especially in one supposedly dramatic sequence where he smiles at the heroine, ignoring the awful presence of the Phantom. In more than one stretch he is introduced leaning against a door or standing erect near a pillar.

Mary Philbin fills the rôle of Christine Daae, with whom, for some mysterious reason, the Phantom has fallen in love. This strange person who is so much feared, is thought to be frightful of face, so forbidding that the few who have seen him have fled in terror. He wears a mask. Christine knew less about him than any of the other girls in the opera, and when a "voice like an angel" taught her from the other side of a wall how to sing, she never suspected that her benefactor and the Phantom were one.

Carlotta, the prima donna of the Opéra, is warned that she must not sing Marguerite in "Faust" on a certain night or there will be dire disaster. The new management of the Opéra decide to permit Christine to sing the part, seeing that the Phantom wished it, but in a later sequence Carlotta returns to her favorite rôle and the management takes possession of the box wherein the Phantom is supposed to sit. All goes well up to a certain point, when suddenly the singer's note is presumed to clash with the gigantic chandelier and it crashes from the ceiling upon the audience far below. This is quite an effective bit, although, as an accident, it seems to be forgotten much sooner than one would expect.

The Phantom, or Erik, as he pleases to call himself at times, has an inclined plane to his underground domicile and when he beguiles the dazed Christine to come below with him he puts her on a horse and she is taken down, down and down, where we are told there is the seepage of the Seine which river incidentally is more than a mile away from the Opéra. The Phantom is just as much at home on the roof of the Opéra as he is below and in this picture people are permitted to wander at will through the building, and yet the police can't lay their hands on the hideous looking Phantom.

The most dramatic touch is where Christine in the cellar abode is listening to the masked Phantom—he wears a weird, childish-looking mask with plump cheeks—as he plays the organ. Then she steals up behind him, as he is apparently entranced with his own playing, and, after hesitating suddenly snatches the mask from the Phantom's face and at once faints at the horrible ugliness of the man. In the theatre last night a woman behind us stifled a scream when this happened, as this is the first glimpse one has of the Phantom's physiognomy. He is hollow-eyed, with a turned-up nose which has long nostrils. His teeth are long and separated and his forehead is high. There is no doubt that he is a repellant sight.

Miss Philbin is only satisfactory in some of her scenes, and she ought to have been able to make many of them far more telling. Actually the outstanding performances in this production are delivered by Lon Chaney and Arthur Edmund Carewe, who is cast as the Persian, or the head of the secret police.

This is a well-dressed thriller, with a capable acting by the villain, a stiff and stilted hero and an insipid heroine. So far as the story is concerned, it looks as if too many cooks had rather spoiled the broth, which was served up in novel form by Gaston LeRoux.

Lon Chaney and Mary Philbin in *The Phantom of the Opera*.

New York "Got the Spirit" Last Night
— and —
The PHANTOM "Got" them!!

THOUSANDS
Thrilled—Gasped—Laughed
Applauded—Cheered—Acclaimed
THE EXTRAORDINARY, FANTASTIC, ROMANTIC THRILLER

The PHANTOM of the OPERA
with
LON CHANEY
MARY PHILBIN
NORMAN KERRY

A Universal Picture—Presented by Carl Laemmle

Directed by RUPERT JULIAN

Supplementary Direction by Edward Sedgwick

COMPLETE GALA PERFORMANCE including PHANTOM STAGE EFFECTS by THURSTON, THE GREAT MAGICIAN, and the gorgeous BALLET under direction of ALBERTINA RASCH is given in its entirety in the evening and at all

☞ NOTICE

MATINEES
50c to $1.00
EVES. 50c to $1.50

ASTOR THEATRE
Broadway at 45th Street

TWICE DAILY, 2:30—8:30
SEATS SELLING FOUR WEEKS IN ADVANCE

"Get the Spirit — See the Phantom"

Monkey Business
By RENATA ADLER

PLANET OF THE APES, written by Rod Serling and Michael Wilson, based on the novel by Pierre Boulle; directed by Franklin J. Schaffner and produced by Arthur P. Jacobs; an APJAC production released by 20th Century-Fox. At the Capitol Theater, Broadway and 51st Street, and the 72d Street Playhouse, east of Second Avenue. Running time: 119 minutes.

Taylor	Charlton Heston
Zaius	Maurice Evans
Zira	Kim Hunter
Cornelius	Roddy McDowall
President of Assembly	James Whitmore
Honorius	James Daly
Landon	Robert Gunner
Dodge	Jeff Burton
Nova	Linda Harrison

"PLANET OF THE APES," which opened yesterday at the Capitol and the 72d Street Playhouse, is an anti-war film and a science-fiction liberal tract, based on a novel by Pierre Boulle (who also wrote "The Bridge on the River Kwai"). It is no good at all, but fun, at moments, to watch.

A most unconvincing space-ship containing three men and one woman, who dies at once, arrives on a desolate-looking planet. One of the movie's misfortunes lies in trying to maintain suspense about what planet it is. The men debark. One of them is a relatively new movie type, a Negro based on some recent, good Sidney Poitier roles — intelligent, scholarly, no good at sports at all. Another is an all-American boy. They are not around for long. The third is Charlton Heston.

He falls in with the planet's only human inhabitants, some Neanderthal flower children who have lost the power of speech. They are raided and enslaved by the apes of the title—who seem to represent militarism, fascism and police brutality. The apes live in towns with Gaudi-like architecture. They have a religion and funerals with speeches like "I never met an ape I didn't like," and "He was a model for all of us, a gorilla to remember." Some of them have grounds to believe, heretically, that apes evolved from men. They put Heston on trial, as men did the half-apes in Vercors's novel "You Shall Know Them." All this leads to some dialogue that is funny, and some that tries to be. Also some that tries to be serious.

Maurice Evans, Kim Hunter, Roddy McDowall and many others are cast as apes, with wonderful anthropoid masks covering their faces. They wiggle their noses and one hardly notices any loss in normal human facial expression. Linda Harrison is cast as Heston's Neanderthal flower girl. She wiggles her hips when she wants to say something.　　　　R.A.

"THE YEAR IS 3987 AND YOU ARE THERE!"
—Daily News

"'PLANET OF THE APES' is an enthralling thriller ...a science fiction mind-bender, hyped by the tingling realism of the camera work and the action sequences. Extraordinary photography giving a chill of suspense...a new frightening perspective!"—Kathleen Carroll, New York Daily News

"SCIENCE FICTION WITH A REAL STINGER IN ITS TAIL. A startling reversal of things as we know them on earth. Evolution has turned out differently. The great apes are in charge; mankind is regarded as speechless, brainless primitives who overbreed, must be periodically hunted in order to reduce their numbers, and supply a kind of sport. There is a shocking commentary on the destiny of this earth, making this a picture that could focus more self examination than most science fiction. Fascinating, imaginative, and painstakingly produced."—Archer Winsten, New York Post

20TH CENTURY-FOX PRESENTS
CHARLTON HESTON
in an ARTHUR P. JACOBS production
pLANET OF THE APES

AN UNUSUAL AND IMPORTANT MOTION PICTURE FROM THE PEN OF PIERRE BOULLE, AUTHOR OF "THE BRIDGE ON THE RIVER KWAI"

CO-STARRING RODDY McDOWALL · MAURICE EVANS · KIM HUNTER · JAMES WHITMORE · JAMES DALY · INTRODUCING LINDA HARRISON AS NOVA

PRODUCED BY APJAC PRODUCTIONS · ASSOCIATE PRODUCER MORT ABRAHAMS · DIRECTED BY FRANKLIN J. SCHAFFNER · SCREENPLAY BY MICHAEL WILSON AND ROD SERLING · MUSIC BY JERRY GOLDSMITH · BASED ON A NOVEL BY PIERRE BOULLE · PANAVISION® · COLOR BY DELUXE

CONTINUOUS PERFORMANCES
Loew's CAPITOL / A.I.T.'s 72ST. PLAYHOUSE

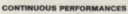

Charlton Heston encounters an uncomfortable twist to evolution in *Planet of the Apes*. The two apes in the foreground are Kim Hunter and Roddy McDowell.

Sudden Shocks

Hitchcock's 'Psycho' Bows at 2 Houses

By BOSLEY CROWTHER

YOU had better have a pretty strong stomach and be prepared for a couple of grisly shocks when you go to see Alfred Hitchcock's "Psycho," which a great many people are sure to do. For Mr. Hitchcock, an old hand at frightening people, comes at you with a club in this frankly intended blood-curdler, which opened at the DeMille and Baronet yesterday.

There is not an abundance of subtlety or the lately familiar Hitchcock bent toward significant and colorful scenery in this obviously low-budget job. With a minimum of complication, it gets off to a black-and-white start with the arrival of a fugitive girl with a stolen bankroll right at an eerie motel.

●

Well, perhaps it doesn't get her there too swiftly. That's another little thing about this film. It does seem slowly paced for Mr. Hitchcock and given over to a lot of small detail. But when it does get her to the motel and apparently settled for the night, it turns out this isolated haven is, indeed, a haunted house.

The young man who diffidently tends it — he is Anthony Perkins and the girl is Janet Leigh—is a queer duck, given to smirks and giggles and swift dashes up to a stark Victorian mansion on a hill. There, it appears, he has a mother—a cantankerous old woman—concealed. And that mother, as it soon develops, is deft at creeping up with a knife and sticking holes into people, drawing considerable blood.

That's the way it is with Mr. Hitchcock's picture—slow buildups to sudden shocks that are old-fashioned melodramatics, however effective and sure, until a couple of people have been gruesomely punctured and the mystery of the haunted house has been revealed. Then it may be a matter of question whether Mr. Hitchcock's points of psychology, the sort highly favored by Krafft-Ebing, are as reliable as his melodramatic stunts.

Frankly, we feel his explanations are a bit of leg-pulling by a man who has been known to resort to such tactics in his former films.

The Cast

PSYCHO, screen play by Joseph Stefano, from a novel by Robert Bloch; directed and produced by Alfred Hitchcock for Paramount Pictures. At the Baronet Theatre, Third Avenue and Fifty-ninth Street, and DeMille Theatre, Broadway and Forty-seventh Street. Running time: 109 minutes.
Norman Bates ....Anthony Perkins
Lila Crane ....Vera Miles
Sam Loomis ....John Gavin
Marion Crane ....Janet Leigh
Milton Arbogast ....Martin Balsam
Sheriff Chambers ......John McIntire
Dr. Richmond ....Simon Oakland
Mr. Cassidy ....Frank Albertson
Caroline ....Pat Hitchcock
Mr. Lowery ....Vaughn Taylor
Mrs. Chambers ....Lurene Tuttle

The consequence is his denouement falls quite flat for us. But the acting is fair. Mr. Perkins and Miss Leigh perform with verve, and Vera Miles, John Gavin and Martin Balsam do well enough in other roles.

The one thing we would note with disappointment is that, among the stuffed birds that adorn the motel office of Mr. Perkins, there are no significant bats.

Anthony Perkins and Janet Leigh in Hitchcock's, *Psycho*.

No one... BUT NO ONE... will be admitted to the theatre after the start of each performance of PSYCHO.

A new kind of drama and excitement from the screen's master of suspense... as his cameras move into the icy blackness of the unexplored!

ALFRED HITCHCOCK'S

PSYCHO

* This is to help you enjoy PSYCHO more. By the way, after you see the picture, please don't give away the ending. It's the only one we have.

starring
ANTHONY PERKINS
VERA MILES
JOHN GAVIN
MARTIN BALSAM
JOHN McINTIRE
and JANET LEIGH as MARION CRANE

Directed by ALFRED HITCHCOCK
Screenplay by JOSEPH STEFANO
Based on the Novel by Robert Bloch
A PARAMOUNT

STARTS TOMORROW AT 2 THEATRES

The DeMILLE
47th St. and 7th Ave · CO 5-8438

BARONET
59th St. and 3rd Ave · EL 5-1663

AIR CONDITIONED   WALTER READE THEATRES

Splendid Film of du Maurier's 'Rebecca' Is Shown at the Music Hall

REBECCA, adapted by Philip MacDonald and Michael Hogan from the novel by Daphne du Maurier; screen play by Robert E. Sherwood and Joan Harrison; directed by Alfred Hitchcock for Selznick-International; released by United Artists. At the Radio City Music Hall.

Maxim de Winter	Laurence Olivier
Mrs. de Winter	Joan Fontaine
Jack Flavell	George Sanders
Mrs. Danvers	Judith Anderson
Giles	Nigel Bruce
Frank Crawley	Reginald Denny
Colonel Julyan	C. Aubrey Smith
Beatrice	Gladys Cooper
Mrs. Van Hopper	Florence Bates
The Coroner	Melville Cooper
Dr. Baker	Leo G. Carroll
Ben	Leonard Carey
Tabb	Lumsden Hare
Frith	Edward Fielding
Robert	Philip Winter
Chalcroft	Forrester Harvey

By FRANK S. NUGENT

Before getting into a review of "Rebecca," we must say a word about the old empire spirit. Hitch has it—Alfred Hitchcock that is, the English master of movie melodramas, rounder than John Bull, twice as fond of beef, just now (with "Rebecca") accounting for his first six months on movie-colonial work in Hollywood. The question being batted around by the cineastes (hybrid for cinema-esthetes) was whether his peculiarly British, yet peculiarly personal, style could survive Hollywood, the David O. Selznick of "Gone with the Wind," the tropic palms, the minimum requirements of the Screen Writers Guild and the fact that a good steak is hard to come by in Hollywood.

But depend on the native Britisher's empire spirit, the policy of doing in Rome not what the Romans do, but what the Romans jolly well ought to be civilised into doing. Hitch in Hollywood, on the basis of the Selznick "Rebecca" at the Music Hall, is pretty much the Hitch of London's "Lady Vanishes" and "The Thirty-nine Steps," except that his famous and widely-publicized "touch" seems to have developed into a firm, enveloping grasp of Daphne du Maurier's popular novel. His directorial style is less individualized, but it is as facile and penetrating as ever; he hews more to the original story line than to the lines of a Hitch original; he is a bit more respectful of his cast, though not to the degree of close-up worship exacted by Charles Laughton in "Jamaica Inn." What seems to have happened, in brief, is that

Mr. Hitchcock, the famous soloist, suddenly has recognized that, in this engagement, he is working with an all-star troupe. He makes no concession to it and, fortunately, vice versa.

So "Rebecca"—to come to it finally—is an altogether brilliant film, haunting, suspenseful, handsome and handsomely played. Miss du Maurier's tale of the second mistress of Manderley, a simple and modest and self-effacing girl who seemed to have no chance against every one's—even her husband's—memories of the first, tragically deceased Mrs. de Winter, was one that demanded a film treatment evocative of a menacing mood, fraught with all manner of hidden meaning, gaited to the pace of an executioner approaching the fatal block. That, as you need not be told, is Hitchcock's meat and brandy. In "Rebecca" his cameras murmur "Beware!" when a black spaniel raises his head and lowers it between his paws again; a smashed china cupid takes on all the dark significance of a blood-stained dagger; a closed door taunts, mocks and terrifies; a monogrammed address book becomes as accusative as a district attorney.

Miss du Maurier's novel was an "I" book, its story told by the second, hapless Mrs. de Winter. Through Mr. Hitchcock's method, the film is first-personal too, so that its frail young heroine's diffident blunders, her fears, her tears are silly only at first, and then are silly no longer, but torture us too. Rebecca's ghost and the Bluebeard room in Manderley become very real horrors as Mr. Hitchcock and his players unfold their macabre tale, and the English countryside is demon-ridden for all the brightness of the sun through its trees and the Gothic serenity of its manor house.

But here we have been giving Mr. Hitchcock and Miss du Maurier all the credit when so much of it belongs to Robert Sherwood, Philip MacDonald, Michael Hogan and Joan Harrison who adapted the novel so skillfully, and to the players who have re-created it so beautifully. Laurence Olivier's brooding Maxim de Winter is a performance that almost needs not to be commented upon, for Mr. Olivier last year played Heathcliffe, who also was a study in dark melancholy, broken fitfully by gleams of sunny laughter. Maxim is the Heathcliffe kind of man and Mr. Olivier seems that too. The real surprise, and the greatest delight of them all, is Joan Fontaine's second Mrs. de Winter, who deserves her own paragraph, so here it is:

"Rebecca" stands or falls on the ability of the book's "I" to escape caricature. She was humiliatingly, embarrassingly, mortifyingly shy, a bit on the dowdy side, socially unaccomplished, a little dull; sweet, of course, and very much in love with—and in awe of—the lord of the manor who took her for his second lady. Miss du Maurier never really convinced me any one could behave quite as the second Mrs. de Winter behaved and still be sweet, modest, attractive and alive. But Miss Fontaine does it—and does it not simply with her eyes, her mouth, her hands and her words, but with her spine. Possibly it's unethical to criticize performance anatomically. Still we insist Miss Fontaine has the most expressive spine—and shoulders!—we've bothered to notice this season.

The others, without reference to their spines—except that of Judith Anderson's housekeeper, Mrs. Danvers, which is most menacingly rigid—are splendidly in character: George Sanders as the blackguard, Nigel Bruce and Gladys Cooper as the blunt relatives, Reginald Denny as the dutiful estate manager, Edward Fielding as the butler and—of course—Florence Bates as a magnificent specimen of the ill-bred, moneyed, resort-infesting, servant-abusing dowager. Hitch was fortunate to find himself in such good company but we feel they were doubly so in finding themselves in his.

RADIO CITY MUSIC HALL
Showplace of the Nation • Rockefeller Center

The strangely fascinating drama of the mistress of Manderley and her haunting spell . . . shadows of the printed page quickened to vivid life . . . the master of suspense and mood, Alfred Hitchcock, holds the heart breathless by his superb artistry, provoking an excitement never before achieved. "Rebecca"—perfectly cast, impeccably produced — establishes David O. Selznick, Hollywood's greatest producer, as the foremost interpreter of literature of our times.

STARTS TODAY
Doors Open 9:00 A. M.

Rebecca
starring
LAURENCE OLIVIER · JOAN FONTAINE
with George Sanders • Judith Anderson • C. Aubrey Smith
PRODUCED BY DAVID O. SELZNICK
From the novel by Daphne du Maurier
Directed by Alfred Hitchcock
Released thru United Artists

Music Hall Patrons Will Remember These Great Selznick Pictures
•
Little Lord Fauntleroy • Garden of Allah • A Star is Born • Prisoner of Zenda • Nothing Sacred • Adventures of Tom Sawyer • The Young in Heart • Made for Each Other • Intermezzo

ON THE GREAT STAGE

"Tropical Nights"—enchantment, color and gay revelry beneath the southern skies, in four spectacular, swiftly paced scenes . . . produced by Leonidoff, settings by Bruno Maine . . . featuring Betty Bruce, Mlle. Nirska, Carlos Ramirez, Hilda Eckler, Nicholas Daks, with Music Hall Rockettes, Corps de Ballet, Choral Ensemble. Symphony Orchestra, under direction of Erno Rapee.

Picture at: 9:05, 11:50, 2:30, 5:10, 7:50, 10:33 • Stage Show at 11:15, 2:00, 4:40, 7:20, 10:00
FIRST MEZZANINE SEATS MAY BE RESERVED IN ADVANCE • Telephone Circle 6-4600
Parking Space Rockefeller Center Garage, 48th to 49th Streets between 5th and 6th Avenues

Joan Fontaine, Laurence Olivier, George Sanders, Judith Anderson and C. Aubrey Smith in the Hitchcock spine-tingler, *Rebecca*.

Delinquency

'Rebel Without Cause' Has Debut at Astor

REBEL WITHOUT A CAUSE, screen play by Stewart Stern, from an adaptation by Irving Shulman and a story by Nicholas Ray; directed by Mr. Ray; produced by David Weisbart for Warner Brothers presentation. At the Astor.

Jim	James Dean
Judy	Natalie Wood
Jim's Father	Jim Backus
Jim's Mother	Ann Doran
Judy's Mother	Rochelle Hudson
Judy's Father	William Hopper
Plato	Sal Mineo
Buzz	Corey Allen
Goon	Dennis Hopper
Ray	Edward Platt
Mil	Steffi Sidney
Maid	Marietta Canty
Lecturer	Ian Wolfe
Crunch	Frank Mazzola

By BOSLEY CROWTHER

IT is a violent, brutal and disturbing picture of modern teen-agers that Warner Brothers presents in its new melodrama at the Astor, "Rebel Without a Cause." Young people neglected by their parents or given no understanding and moral support by fathers and mothers who are themselves unable to achieve balance and security in their homes are the bristling heroes and heroines of this excessively graphic exercise. Like "Blackboard Jungle" before it, it is a picture to make the hair stand on end.

The foremost of these youthful characters, played by the late James Dean, Natalie Wood and Sal Mineo, are several social cuts above the vocational high school hoodlums in that previous film. They are children of well-to-do parents, living in comfortable homes and attending a well-appointed high school in the vicinity of Los Angeles. But they are none the less mordant in their manners and handy with switch-blade knives. They are, in the final demonstration, lonely creatures in their own strange, cultist world.

Screenwriter Stewart Stern's proposal that these youngsters would be the way they are for the skimpy reasons he shows us may be a little hard to believe. Mr. Dean, he says, is a mixed-up rebel because his father lacks decisiveness and strength. "If he only had the guts to knock Mom cold once!" Mr. Dean mumbles longingly. And Miss Wood is wild and sadistic, prone to run with surly juveniles because her worrisome father stopped kissing her when she was 16.

As for Mr. Mineo, he is a thoroughly lost and hero-searching lad because his parents have left him completely in the care of a maid.

But convincing or not in motivations, this tale of tempestuous kids and their weird ways of conducting their social relations is tense with explosive incidents. There is a horrifying duel with switch-blade cutlery between the re-

luctant Mr. Dean and another lad (Corey Allen) on a terrace outside a planetarium, where the youngsters have just received a lecture on the tininess of man. There is a shocking presentation of a "chicky run" in stolen automobiles (the first boy to jump from two autos racing toward the brink of a cliff is a "chicken" or coward). And there's a brutal scene in which three hoodlums, villainous school-boys in black-leather jackets and cowboy boots, beat up the terrified Mr. Mineo in an empty swimming pool.

To set against such hideous details is a wistful and truly poignant stretch where in Mr. Dean and Miss Wood as lonely exiles from their own homes try to pretend they are happy grown-ups in an old mansion. There are some excruciating flashes of accuracy and truth in this film.

However, we do wish the young actors, including Mr. Dean, had not been so intent on imitating Marlon Brando in varying degrees. The tendency, possibly typical of the behavior of certain youths, may therefore be a subtle commentary but it grows mo-

Sal Mineo, James Dean and Natalie Wood.

notonous. And we'd be more convinced by Jim Backus and Ann Doran as parents of Mr. Dean if they weren't so obviously silly and ineffectual in treating with the boy.

There is, too, a pictorial slickness about the whole thing in color and Cinema-Scope that battles at times with the realism in the direction of Nicholas Ray.

Natalie Wood and James Dean play misdirected teenagers in *Rebel Without a Cause.*

Jim Stark—a kid in the year 1955—
what makes him tick...like a bomb?

WARNER BROS. PUT ALL THE FORCE OF THE SCREEN INTO A CHALLENGING DRAMA
OF TODAY'S TEENAGERS!

JAMES DEAN

The overnight sensation of 'East of Eden.'

...and they both come from 'good' families!

"REBEL WITHOUT A CAUSE"

CINEMASCOPE AND WARNERCOLOR

ALSO STARRING NATALIE WOOD WITH SAL MINEO · JIM BACKUS · ANN DORAN · COREY ALLEN · WILLIAM HOPPER

SCREEN PLAY BY STEWART STERN · PRODUCED BY DAVID WEISBART · DIRECTED BY NICHOLAS RAY · Music by Leonard Rosenman

TODAY 9:30 A.M. · ASTOR

B'WAY AT 45TH ST.
LATE FILM 12:07 A.M.

164

'Road to Morocco,' With Bing Crosby, Bob Hope, Dorothy Lamour at Paramount

ROAD TO MOROCCO; original screen play by Frank Butler and Don Hartman; directed by David Butler for Paramount; music and lyrics by Johnny Burke and James Van Heusen. At the Paramount.

Jeff Peters	Bing Crosby
Turkey Jackson	Bob Hope
Princess Shalmar	Dorothy Lamour
Mullay Kasim	Anthony Quinn
Mihirmah	Dona Drake
Hyder Khan	Vladimir Sokoloff
Ahmed Fey	Mikhail Rasumny
Neb Jolla	George Givot
Oso Bucco	Andrew Tombes
Yusef	Leon Belasco

By BOSLEY CROWTHER

Let us be thankful that Paramount is still blessed with Bing Crosby and Bob Hope, and that it has set its cameras to tailing these two irrepressible wags on another fantastic excursion, "Road to Morocco," which came to the Paramount yesterday. For the screen, under present circumstances, can hold no more diverting lure than the prospect of Hope and Crosby ambling, as they have done before, through an utterly slap-happy picture, picking up Dorothy Lamour along the way and tossing acid wisecracks at each other without a thought for reason or sense. That is what they are doing in this current reprise on trips to Singapore and Zanzibar and, as a consequence, "Road to Morocco" is Route 1 to delightful "escape."

Of course, that may sound a bit ambiguous, considering Morocco's current significance in the news. But you mustn't forget that geography means nothing in a Crosby-Hope film. The only purpose it serves in this instance is to justify a fairy-tale background of oriental splendors, turbaned villains, Miss Lamour and Dona Drake in scant attire, and a line in a song whereby the heroes indicate that they are Morocco-bound.

Otherwise this lot of slap-stick nonsense, wherein Paramount's priceless pair of pantaloons whale each other with insults instead of custard pies, might take place in any locality, including Hollywood, in which the Messrs. Hope and Crosby could be cast up on a strange and fearful shore, amid the most forbidding surroundings—until Miss Lamour comes along It might be set down in any country where Miss Lamour could be a gauze-gowned princess and Bing and Bob could wrangle hotly about which one should win her fair hand, then later go through mad and fast adventures when they have to shove a native shiek aside.

For, really, this "Road to Morocco" runs through that beautiful land of whacky make-believe, so seldom well explored in the movies—a land of magic rings and mirages, a land in which Bing and Bob can suddenly make an inexplicable escape from rigid bonds and then observe that, if they told how they did it, no one would believe them—so they just won't tell. It is, in short, a lampoon of all pictures having to do with exotic romance, played by a couple of wise guys who can make a gag uo everything but lay eggs.

As usual, Mr. Crosby is the sly one, Mr. Hope is the reckless, pop-eyed dope. Mr. Crosby woos the lady with soft talking and a song, "Moonlight Becomes You So." But Mr. Hope does it in a manner which would normally make her laugh herself to death. Together they form a combination which strings the fastest and crispest comedy line in films. Miss Lamour is, as usual in such spots, helpful; she never gets in the way and she sings a ditty called "Constantly" with just the proper shadow of a doubt. And Dons Drake, Anthony Quinn and Mikhail Rasumny furnish picturesque and rib-tickling assists.

The short of it is that "Road to Morocco" is a daffy, laugh-drafting film. And you'll certainly agree with the camel which, at one point, offers the gratuitous remark, "This is the screwiest picture I was ever in."

Dorothy Lamour, Bing Crosby, Bob Hope and Donna Drake in *The Road to Morocco.*

'THE ROBE' SHOWN IN CINEMASCOPE

Movie Based on Douglas' Novel Stars Richard Burton, Jean Simmons, Victor Mature

THE ROBE, screen play by Philip Dunne; adapted by Gina Kaus from the novel by Lloyd C. Douglas; directed by Henry Koster in the CinemaScope process and produced by Frank Ross for Twentieth Century-Fox. At the Roxy.

Marcellus Gallio	Richard Burton
Diana	Jean Simmons
Demetrius	Victor Mature
Peter	Michael Rennie
Caligula	Jay Robinson
Justus	Dean Jagger
Senator Gallio	Torin Thatcher
Pilate	Richard Boone
Miriam	Betta St. John
Paulus	Jeff Morrow
Emperor Tiberius	Ernest Thesiger
Junia	Dawn Addams
Abidor	Leon Askin
Rebecca	Helen Beverley
Quintus	Frank Pulaski

By BOSLEY CROWTHER

Twentieth Century-Fox removed the wrappings last night from its much-heralded CinemaScope production of "The Robe" and revealed a historical drama less compelling than the process by which it is shown. This huge motion picture re-creation in color of the late Lloyd C. Douglas' rich tale of early Christian converts was put on view on the Roxy's new giant screen and proved in itself to be essentially a smashing display of spectacle.

The panoply and splendor of Emperor Tiberius' Rome, the turbulence of Jerusalem and the dustiness of the Holy Land have never been shown with more magnificence or sweep on a movie screen than they are on the great arching panel installed for the showing of "The Robe." And the mightiness of masses and the forms of heroes have never loomed so large as they do in this studied demonstration, projected by CinemaScope. But an unwavering force of personal drama is missed in the size and the length of the show, and a full sense of spiritual experience is lost in the physicalness of the display.

Physical Action Stressed

This is not hard to fathom. The adaptation that Gina Kaus has made from Mr. Douglas' best-selling novel and the screen play that Philip Dunne has penned have emphasized physical action more than the drama of feelings and words. The power of Christ's presence and spirit upon a Roman tribune's slave and then, in time, upon the tribune is not developed in clear dramatic terms; it is simply presented as an assumption upon which the subsequent action turns. The consequence is that the inspiration of the spirit, which is the key to the story that is told, is a matter of sheer deduction from the surge of music and the expressions in eyes.

And when these eyes appear in faces that often loom upon the screen in close-ups of mammoth proportions, and when the music surges and swells from magnified multiple speakers that make up the system's stereophonic sound, the violent assault upon the senses dissipates spiritual intimacy.

Likewise, the slowness of the pacing through many of the major sequences and the intricacies of the plotting, which run the picture for more than two hours, tend to affect the burdened senses with a feeling of frank monotony.

However, the vastness of the images upon the sixty-eight by twenty-four-foot screen, the eye-filling vigor of the action and the beauty of some of the shots compensate with fascinations and excitements that keep the customer upright in his chair. And the performances by the actors are—all things considered—remarkably good.

Richard Burton, the young English actor who distinguished himself previously in Twentieth Century Fox "My Cousin Rachel," is stalwart, spirited and stern as the arrogant Roman tribune who has command of the crucifixion of Christ and who eventually becomes a passionate convert through an obsession about the Savior's robe. Jean Simmons is lovely and impassioned as the Roman maid who loves this headstrong man, Victor Mature is muscular and moody as the early converted Greek slave.

Michael Rennie is solemn and transcendent as Simon Called Peter, whom they call "the big fisherman"; Dean Jagger is full of piety as a humble convert and Jay Robinson is warped and shrill as Caligula. Several other actors comport themselves in minor roles according to the moods of the occasions that Director Henry Koster has decreed.

It is notable that Christ is seen only as a wide-robed figure on a distant hill and a tormented, indistinguishable victim burdened beneath the heavy Cross. In this respect the picture has dignity and restraint.

As for the esthetic nature and cinematic potential of CinemaScope, it is evident that the system has the advantage of great pictorial range. The expanse of the screen across the theatre gives opportunity for panoramic scenes of overwhelming beauty. And in medium shots, such as one here in which four horses charge toward the camera, there may be developed great power. The shape of the screen—wide and narrow—makes for occasional oppressiveness. A sense of the image being pressed down and drawn out inevitably occurs. Close-ups, too, become oppressive. However, the system seems fully flexible, and some exciting employments of it may be anticipated confidently.

Richard Burton in the first movie done in Cinemascope, *The Robe*.

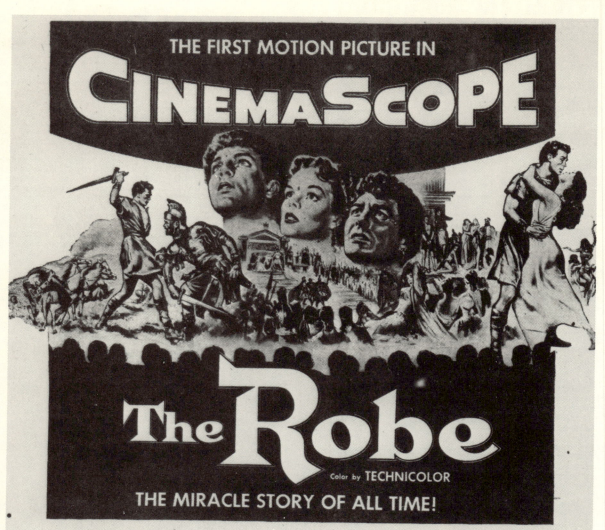

THE FIRST MOTION PICTURE IN

CinemaScope

The Robe

Color by TECHNICOLOR

THE MIRACLE STORY OF ALL TIME!

20th Century-Fox presents the New Dimensional Photographic Marvel!

The Modern Miracle You See Without Glasses!

The Roxy Theatre has been selected to introduce THE ROBE in CinemaScope to the theatre-goers of America. You have read about it...you have heard about it...soon you will see it for the first time.

In every corner of the globe where special demonstrations of CinemaScope were held, this new wonder that achieves life-like reality and infinite depth, was acclaimed the greatest step forward in entertainment history.

Through the Anamorphic Lens Process on the newly created, curved Miracle Mirror Screen...through CinemaScope's new Stereophonic Sound...through

scenes never before matched for life-like quality and breathtaking power, you will become a part of the first CinemaScope production...based on one of the most inspiring novels ever written.

Soon you will be engulfed in THE ROBE...the supreme story of love, faith and overwhelming spectacle, as the imperial might of Rome crashes against the Word of God! Ten years in preparation...two years in production...with a cast of thousands!

Nothing you have ever seen in any theatre will match the scope...the spectacle...the power of 'THE ROBE' in CINEMASCOPE!

20th Century-Fox presents
A CinemaScope PRODUCTION
The Robe
RICHARD BURTON · JEAN SIMMONS · VICTOR MATURE · MICHAEL RENNIE
with Jay Robinson · Dean Jagger
Richard Boone
Produced by FRANK ROSS
Directed by HENRY KOSTER
Screen Play by PHILIP DUNNE
From the Novel by LLOYD C. DOUGLAS

STARTS TOMORROW
Continuous Performances · Doors Open 9 A.M.

ROXY
7th AVENUE & 50th STREET
Formal Invitational Showing Tonight, 8:30 P.M.

168

Pure 30's Make-Believe

By VINCENT CANBY

NOT SINCE "The Great Gatsby" two years ago has any film come into town more absurdly oversold than "Rocky," the sentimental little slum movie that opened yesterday at the Cinema II. As a former head of Paramount Pictures said to me with some irritation at the time "Gatsby" came out, movies shouldn't be penalized for being effectively promoted. That's true. Yet the sort of highpowered publicity (most of it free, it seems) that's been attending the birth of "Rocky" must, in turn, subject the movie to impossible expectations that can boomerang. Be warned.

Sylvester Stallone, who had a role in "The Lords of Flatbush," another "sleeper" that never quite measured up as a hit, both wrote the original screenplay and plays the title role. Rocky is a young man who, by day, is a small-time Mafia collector, the sort of fellow who shows his heart of gold by hesitating to break a client's thumbs, and at night pursues a third-rate boxing career in fleabag sporting arenas.

•

Under the none too decisive direction of John G. Avildsen ("Joe," "Save the Tiger"), Mr. Stallone is all over "Rocky" to such an extent it begins to look like a vanity production. His brother composed one of the film's songs and appears briefly, as does his father, while his dog, a cheerful mastiff named Butkus, plays Rocky's dog. It's as if Mr. Stallone had studied the careers of Martin Scorcese and Francis Ford Coppola and then set out to copy the wrong things.

The screenplay of "Rocky" is purest Hollywood make-believe of the 1930's, but there would be nothing wrong with that, had the film been executed with any verve.

•

It's the story of Rocky and his girlfriend Adrian (Talia Shire), when Rocky, due to circumstances too foolish to go into, is granted the opportunity of his lifetime. He is given a chance to fight the heavyweight champion of the world, a black fighter named Apollo Creed (Carl Weathers), modeled on Muhammad Ali so superficially as to be an almost criminal waste of character. It's not good enough to be libelous, though by making the Alilike fighter such a dope,

His whole life was a million-to-one shot.

ROCKY

A ROBERT CHARTOFF-IRWIN WINKLER PRODUCTION · JOHN G. AVILDSEN FILM · STARRING SYLVESTER STALLONE IN "ROCKY"

ALSO STARRING TALIA SHIRE · BURT YOUNG · CARL WEATHERS AND BURGESS MEREDITH AS MICKEY · WRITTEN BY SYLVESTER STALLONE

PRODUCED BY IRWIN WINKLER AND ROBERT CHARTOFF · DIRECTED BY JOHN G. AVILDSEN · EXECUTIVE PRODUCER GENE KIRKWOOD · MUSIC BY BILL CONTI

PG PARENTAL GUIDANCE SUGGESTED

ORIGINAL MOTION PICTURE SOUNDTRACK ALBUM AND TAPE AVAILABLE ON UNITED ARTISTS RECORDS

United Artists
A Transamerica Company

the film explores areas of latent racism that just may not be all that latent.

That Mr. Weathers is no actor doesn't help things, though there are some very good actors in other supporting roles, and they don't help in any significant way. Burt Young is effective as Rocky's best friend, a beer-guzzling mug, as is Burgess Meredith as Rocky's ancient trainer.

The person who comes off best is Miss Shire, Mr. Coppola's sister who made brief, effective appearances in the two "Godfather" films. She's a real actress, genuinely touching and funny as an incipient spinster who comes late to sexual life. She's so good, in fact, that she almost gives weight to Mr. Stallone's performance, which is the large hole in the center of the film.

For years, Talia Shire's main claim to fame in movie circles was that she was Francis Ford Coppola's sister. Even the Academy Award nomination she got in 1975 for playing the part of Connie Corleone, Al Pacino's head-strong, sluttish sister in Mr. Coppola's "The Godfather, Part II," didn't help erase from some minds the notion that she was just a big director's little sister.

Miss Shire bristled a bit when it was suggested that she got the part in "Rocky" because of her brother. "I got it because I was called to audition, and I went in and gave the best reading I had ever given in my life," she said. "Normally, I'm really bad at readings."

Mr. Stallone's Rocky is less a performance than an impersonation. It's all superficial mannerisms and movements, reminding me of Rodney Dangerfield doing a nightclub monologue. The speech patterns sound right, and what he says is occasionally lifelike, but it's a studied routine, not a character.

It's the sort of performance that could have been put together by watching other actors on television. Most of the film was photographed on location in seedy, Philadelphia neighborhoods, and it's one of the film's ironies that a production that has put such emphasis on realism should seem so fraudulent.

The problem, I think, comes back to Mr. Stallone. Throughout the movie we are asked to believe that his Rocky is compassionate, interesting, even heroic, though the character we see is simply an unconvincing actor imitating a lug

●

"Rocky," which has been rated PG ("parental guidance suggested"), contains some barroom language and a climactic boxing match that is effectively brutal.

Ringside Story

ROCKY, directed by John G. Avildsen; screenplay by Sylvester Stallone; produced by Irwin Winkler and Robert Chartoff; executive producer, Gene Kirkwood; director of photography, James Crabe; editor, Richard Halsey; music, Bill Conti; distributed by United Artists. Running time: 121 minutes. At the Cinema II Theater, Third Avenue near 60th Street. This film has been rated PG.

Rocky	Sylvester Stallone
Adrian	Talia Shire
Paulie	Burt Young
Apollo	Carl Weathers
Mickey	Burgess Meredith
Jergens	Thayer David
Gazzo	Joe Spinell
Mike	Jimmy Gambina

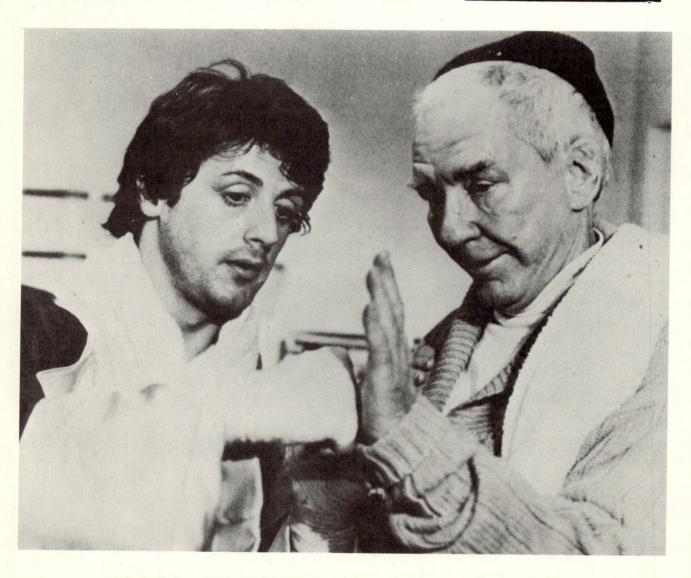

Sylvestor Stallone, author and star of *Rocky*, with Burgess Meredith as Rocky's ancient trainer.

'Room at Top'

The Cast

ROOM AT THE TOP; screen play by Neil Paterson; from the novel by John Braine; directed by Jack Clayton; produced by John and James Woolf; a Romulus Production released by Continental Distributing, Inc. At the Fine Arts, Fifty-eighth Street, west of Lexington Avenue. Running time: 115 minutes.

Joe Lampton	Laurence Harvey
Alice Aisgill	Simone Signoret
Susan Brown	Heather Sears
Mr. Brown	Sir Donald Wolfit
Mrs. Brown	Ambrosine Philpotts
Charles Soames	Donald Houston
Mr. Hoylake	Raymond Huntley
Jack Wales	John Westbrook
George Aisgill	Allan Cuthbertson
June Samson	Mary Peach
Elspeth	Hermione Baddeley
Miss Gilchrist	Avril Elgar
Aunt	Beatrice Varley
Darnley	Stephen Jack
Mayor	John Welsh
Mayoress	Everley Gregg
Mavis	April Olrich

By A. H. WEILER

THE cynical, disenchanted and footloose post-war youths of England, who justifiably have been termed "angry," never have been put into sharper focus than in "Room at the Top." The British-made import, which was unveiled at the Fine Arts Theatre yesterday, glaringly spotlights them in a disk of illumination that reveals genuine drama and passion, truth as well as corruption. Although it takes place 3,000 miles away, it is as close to home as a shattered dream, a broken love affair or a man seeking to make life more rewarding in an uneasy world.

Unlike John Osborne, who, in "Look Back in Anger," merely shouted the sensitive younger Britishers' fiery protests against class distinctions and other contemporary English inequities, John Braine, out of whose brilliant first novel this careful dissection was made, is more adult and scientifically observant about a grievous malaise. Mr. Braine, Neil Paterson, the scenarist, and Jack Clayton, who did a superb job in directing an excitingly effective cast, are angry, too. But they see the picture whole. They are basically moral people who know that, come what may, a price must be paid for revolt sometimes.

As has been noted, Mr. Braine is concerned with a type of schemer, whose accent may be exotic but one who is becoming more and more symbolic of the restless young men of the world. In this case, he is Joe Lampton, born to poverty in a North Country manufacturing town but determined to catapult himself out of a world he never made or wanted. As a civil servant in another city, he meets the nubile and naïve daughter of the richest tycoon who represents the prize and escape he has been waiting for. But this is a consummation not easily achieved. And, when thrown into the orbit of a married woman, ill-used, worldly wise, anxiously groping for real affection, it is fairly obvious that he will succumb first to lust and then to genuine love.

•

That this dual affair is doomed to tragedy is inevitable. But the artisans who fashioned this shaky triangle are neither crude nor insensitive. Joe is a calculating, shrewd and realistic campaigner, yearning for wealth and the opportunity to rid himself of low-caste stigma through marriage with the heiress to a great fortune. He is, however, also pictured as a man in whom all conscience has not been killed. He is a hero without medals and one mourning defeat when he should be enjoying victory.

The director and scenarist also have shown us a multidimensional figure in the married woman he is forced to reject, a deed that indelibly underlines the sadness, desperation and tragedy that surrounds these truly ill-fated lovers. And they have done equally well by the rich, sheltered young girl he marries at long last, an untutored youngster wholly engulfed by the sweetness, wonder and uneasiness of first love and sex.

A prudish observer perhaps might be shocked by some of the drama's explicit dialogue and situations, but these, too, are adult and in context. One also might be thrown by the thick, Yorkshire-like accents of the cast, which strike foreign and harsh on American ears. A viewer might take exception to the slowness of pace as this somber play is first exposed.

But these are minor faults that are heavily outweighed by the superb performances of Simone Signoret, as the married woman clutching at her last chance at happiness, and Laurence Harvey, the seemingly selfish schemer, who discovers that he cannot destroy all of his decency. Heather Sears is gentle, fresh and properly naïve as the heiress he is forced to marry; and Sir Donald Wolfit, as her outspoken, self-made millionaire father; Donald Houston, as Mr. Harvey's room-mate and confidant, and Hermione Baddeley, as Miss Signoret's trusted friend, are among those supporting players who add distinctive bits to an engrossing picture.

Jack Clayton's vigorous and discerning direction has involved them in more than just a routine romantic drama. "Room at the Top" may be basically cheerless and somber, but it has a strikingly effective view.

Simone Signoret and Laurence Harvey in *Room At the Top*.

"Please be gentle with me, Joe...I've never had a lover!"

"ROOM AT THE TOP"

Starring LAURENCE HARVEY · HEATHER SEARS · SIMONE SIGNORET
Directed by Jack Clayton · Produced by John and James Woolf
Screenplay by Neil Paterson from the novel by John Braine
A Romulus Film Ltd Production · A Continental Distributing, Inc. Release

A Motion Picture So Frank... So Boldly Revealing We Recommend It. For Adult Audiences Only!

British Film Academy Winner 1959
"BEST PICTURE OF THE YEAR"
SIMONE SIGNORET—Best Foreign Actress

AMERICAN PREMIERE
STARTS TODAY
Doors Open 12 Noon
FINE ARTS
58th Street bet. Park & Lex. · PLaza 5-603
FEATURE AT: 12, 2, 4, 6, 8, 10

The Prince of Bay Ridge

By JANET MASLIN

TONY IS A HANDSOME, big-hearted guy with a lot more style than he knows what to do with. His job in a paint store doesn't call for much élan, but Tony supplies that anyway, charming the customers and strutting gamely down the street as he makes his deliveries. His room at home is dreary and his family even more so, but Tony has done what he can with Farrah and Rocky and Pacino posters to give the place a little class. Even so, things can get him down—but just when they do, another week is over and it's time to hit the local disco. On the weekend, and on the dance floor, Tony is king.

Tony's whole life, as somebody else in "Saturday Night Fever" manages to point out, is "a cliché." But John Travolta is so earnestly in tune with the character that Tony becomes even more touching than he is familiar and a source of fierce, desperate excitement. The movie, which spends mercifully little time trying to explain Tony, has a violent energy very like his own.

Cliche That Touches

SATURDAY NIGHT FEVER, directed by John Badham; screenplay by Norman Wexler, based on a story by Nik Cohn; director of photography, Ralf D. Bode; editor, David Rawlins; musical numbers staged and choreographed by Lester Wilson; additional music and adaptation by David Shire; original music by Barry Robin and Maurice Gibb; produced by Robert Stigwood; released by Paramount Pictures. At Loews State 1, Broadway and 45th Street; Loews Cine, Third Avenue at 86th Street and 34th Street East, east of Third Avenue. Running time: 119 minutes. This film is classified R.

Tony Manero	John Travolta
Stephanie	Karen Lynn Gorney
Bobby C	Barry Miller
Joey	Joseph Cali
Double J	Paul Pape
Annette	Donna Pescow

"Saturday Night Fever," which opens today at several theaters, begins to flag when, after an initial hour filled with high spirits and jubilant music, it settles down to tell its story; the effect is so deflating that it's almost as though another Monday has rolled around and it's time to get back to work.

It seems that Tony's friends, who are a lively but uninteresting lot are so dead-ended that they're beginning to make him worry about his own future. And Stephanie (Karen Lynn Gorney), who has a job in Manhattan, is such a braggart that she has begun to give him notions of upward mobility.

Ten minutes into the movie, you can be sure that its ending will be at least partly upbeat and that whatever happens will be blunt. But that is still no preparation for all the gruesome tricks Norman Wexler's screenplay uses to get Tony out of Brooklyn.

CATCH THE FEVER

IF YOU'RE NOT SURE YOU HAVE THE FEVER NOW, AFTER TOMORROW, YOU'LL SAY YOU ALWAYS DID.

SATURDAY NIGHT FEVER™

...Catch it

PARAMOUNT PICTURES PRESENTS JOHN TRAVOLTA   KAREN LYNN GORNEY
"SATURDAY NIGHT FEVER" A ROBERT STIGWOOD PRODUCTION
Screenplay by NORMAN WEXLER   Directed by JOHN BADHAM
Executive Producer KEVIN McCORMICK   Produced by ROBERT STIGWOOD
Original music written and performed by the Bee Gees
Soundtrack album available on RSO Records

R RESTRICTED   DOLBY SYSTEM   Read the Bantam paperback. A Paramount...

STARTS TOMORROW

'The Searchers' Find Action

Entertaining Western Opens at Criterion

THE SEARCHERS, screen play by Frank S. Nugent; based upon the novel by Alan LeMay; directed by John Ford and produced by Merian C. Cooper for C. V. Whitney Pictures; a Warner Brothers presentation. At the Criterion.

Ethan Edwards	John Wayne
Martin Pawley	Jeffrey Hunter
Laurie Jorgensen	Vera Miles
Capt. Rev. S. Clayton	Ward Bond
Debbie Edwards	Natalie Wood
Lars Jorgensen	John Qualen
Mrs. Jorgensen	Olive Carey
Chief Scar	Henry Brandon
Charlie McCorry	Ken Curtis
Brad Jorgensen	Harry Carey Jr.
Emilio Figueroa	Antonio Moreno
Mose Harper	Hank Worden
Debbie (as a child)	Lana Wood
Lieutenant Greenhill	Pat Wayne
Look	Beulah Archuletta

By BOSLEY CROWTHER

APPROPRIATELY, C. V. Whitney, the distinguished turfman, is making his debut as a producer of motion pictures with a horse opera, directed by John Ford. This, in the realm of motion pictures, is like having a favorite three-year-old going in the Kentucky Derby with Eddie Arcaro or Dave Erb up.

Thus, it is highly gratifying to be able to report that Mr. Whitney's first film, "The Searchers," came thundering in a winner at the Criterion yesterday. And it is equally gratifying to notice that Mr. Ford hasn't lost his touch.

"The Searchers," for all the suspicions aroused by excessive language in its ads, is really a rip-snorting Western, as brashly entertaining as they come. It starts with the tardy homecoming of a lean Texan from the Civil War and leaps right into a massacre by Commanches and the abduction of two white girls. And then it proceeds for almost two hours to detail the five-year search for the girls that is relentlessly conducted by the Texan, with the ultimate help of just one lad.

That is the story pattern on which Mr. Ford and his gang have plastered a wealth of Western action that has the toughness of leather and the sting of a whip. It bristles and howls with Indian fighting, goes into tense, nerve-rasping brawls between the Texan and his hunting companion, explodes with fiery comedy and lays into some frontier heroics that make the welkin ring.

And when we distribute credit not only to Mr. Ford but to his gang, we do so with frank appreciation. For it is his familiar corps of actors, writer, etc., that helps to give the gusto to this film. From Frank S. Nugent, whose screen play from the novel of Alan LeMay is a pungent thing, right on through the cast and technicians, it is the honest achievement of a well-knit team.

John Wayne is uncommonly commanding as the Texan whose passion for revenge is magnificently uncontaminated by caution or sentiment. Jeffrey Hunter is wonderfully callow and courageous as the lad who goes with him, and Ward Bond makes a dandy fighting parson in an old plug hat and a long linen coat.

John Qualen as a stolid Texas rancher, Olive Carey as his wife, Vera Miles as their militantly romantic daughter, Natalie Wood as one of the abducted girls and a dozen or so other actors are great in supporting roles.

There are only two faults of minor moment that we can find in this slambang Western film. The first is that Mr. Ford, once started, doesn't seem to know when to stop. Episode is piled upon episode, climax upon climax and corpse upon corpse until the whole thing appears to be taking a couple of turns around the course. The justification for it is that it certainly conveys the lengthiness of the hunt, but it leaves one a mite exhausted, especially with the speed at which it goes.

The other fault is that the director has permitted too many outdoor scenes to be set in the obviously synthetic surroundings of the studio stage. Mr. Ford's scenic stuff, shot in color and VistaVision, in the expanse of Monument Valley that he loves, has his customary beauty and grandeur, but some of those campfire scenes could have been shot in a sporting-goods store window. That isn't like Mr. Ford. And it isn't like most of this picture, which is as scratchy as genuine cockleburrs.

John Wayne as the Texan with a passion for revenge in *The Searchers*.

'Sergeant York,' a Sincere Biography of the World War Hero, Makes Its Appearance at the Astor

SERGEANT YORK, an original screen play by Abem Finkel, Harry Chandlee, Howard Koch and John Huston, based on the diary of Sergeant Alvin C. York; directed by Howard Hawks as "a Howard Hawks Production"; produced by Jesse L. Lasky and Hal B. Wallis for Warner Brothers. At the Astor.

Alvin C. York	Gary Cooper
Pastor Rosier Pile	Walter Brennan
Gracie Williams	Joan Leslie
Major Buxton	Stanley Ridges
"Pusher" Ross	George Tobias
Ike Botkin	Ward Bond
Mother York	Margaret Wycherly
Rosie York	June Lockhart
Buck Lipscomb	Noah Beery Jr.
Zeke	Clem Bevans
George York	Dickie Moore
Cordell Hull	Charles Trowbridge
Lem	Howard da Silva
Bert Thomas	David Bruce
Captain Danforth	Harvey Stephens
Sergeant Early	Joseph Sawyer
German Major	Charles Esmond
Zeb Andrews	Robert Porterfield
Sergeant Harry Parsons	Pat Flaherty
Nate Tomkins	Erville Alderson

By BOSLEY CROWTHER

At this time, when a great many people are thinking deep and sober thoughts about the possible involvement of our country in another deadly world war, Warner Brothers and a bewildering multiplicity of collaborative producers and writers have reflected propitiously upon the motives and influence which inspired America's No. 1 hero in the last war. And, in "Sergeant York," which opened last night at the Astor, they have brought forth a simple and dignified screen biography of that famous Tennessee mountaineer who put aside his religious scruples against killing for what he felt was the better good of his country and the lasting benefit of mankind.

It is, in the light of what has happened, a strangely affecting account, this brave and sincerely wrought biography of the lanky Alvin C. York, who left his barren home 'way back in the Cumberland hills to travel across troubled waters and fight for what he hoped would be the best. It is an honest saga of a plain American who believed in fundamentals and acted with clean simplicity. And because the unmentioned sequel to the larger story has been so grim, the personal and well-earned triumph of Sergeant York acquires tragic overtones.

In outline, the film is no more than a straightaway narrative about a "fightin' an' hell-raisin'" mountain farmer named Alvin York who scrabbles a poor living from a piece of rocky high-ground in the Cumberlands and yearns for a "piece of bottom." Then he "gets religion" just about the time this country enters the World War and undergoes a terrific mental ordeal to decide whether he should fight. An American history book wins him over, and he goes on to Europe and to fame because of his single-handed capture of an incredible number of German soldiers. In the end, however, he returns to Tennessee and to a life of simple toil.

Gary Cooper and Joan Leslie in *Sergeant York*.

That is all there is to the story, but in the telling of it—of the first part, anyhow—the picture has all the flavor of true Americana, the blunt and homely humor of backwoodsmen and the raw integrity peculiar to simple folk. This phase of the picture is rich. The manner in which York is persuaded to join the fighting forces and the scenes of actual combat betray an unfortunate artificiality, however—in the battle scenes, especially; and the overly glamorized ending, in which York returns to a spotless little farm, jars sharply with the naturalness which has gone before. The suggestion of deliberate propaganda is readily detected here. However, the performance of Gary Cooper in the title role holds the picture together magnificently, and even the most unfavorable touches are made palatable because of him. He is the gaunt, clumsy yokel, the American hayseed to the life—the proud, industrious, honest, simple citizen who marches in the forefront of this nation's ranks. Walter Brennan as a country parson and storekeeper is a perfect specimen of homo americanus, too, while Robert Porterfield, Clem Bevans, Howard da Silva and George Tobias make excellent "types." Margaret Wycherly as a pinched and inflexible hill-woman bears up too consciously under her manifold woes, and Joan Leslie plays a mountain beauty with little more than a bright smile, a phoney accent and a tight dress.

"Sergeant York" is good native drama, inspiring in parts and full of life. It is a little naive, perhaps, but so are the folks of which it tells. And, basically, it is as full of humility and pride as is the simple prayer which Mother York prays over a meager meal: "The Lord bless these victuals we got and help us to beholden to no one. Amen."

Tennesseeans Hail York

While the real-life hero himself sat among the audience, "Sergeant York," the Warner Brothers film on the life of the Tennessee mountaineer who became America's greatest hero of the last war, held its première last night at the Astor, attended by delegations from Sergeant Alvin C. York's home State, notables of the screen world and government and Army officials.

Preceded by a band from the Corporal George Benkert Jr. Corps, Post 516, Veterans of Foreign Wars at Farmingdale, L. I., Sergeant York arrived at the theatre at 8:45, accompanied by Jesse L. Lasky, who produced the film in collaboration with Hal B. Wallis. Gary Cooper, who portrays the sergeant in the film, arrived soon after. Sergeant York was greeted in the lobby of the theatre by a Tennessee State delegation headed by Colonel George Buxton, his wartime commander of the Eighty-second Division.

Accepting the applause of the audience on behalf of his comrades in the Meuse-Argonne exploit resulting in the capture of 132 Germans, Sergeant York later expressed the wish that the film would contribute to "national unity in this hour of danger," adding that "millions of Americans, like myself, must be facing the same questions, the same uncertainties which we faced and I believe resolved for the right some twenty-four years ago."

An orderly crowd of several hundred persons on the sidewalk watched the arrival of the celebrities.

The picture that can't be topped!

GARY COOPER as the soldier who couldn't be stopped

Sergeant York

A WARNER BROS. PICTURE
with **WALTER BRENNAN**
JOAN LESLIE GEORGE TOBIAS STANLEY RIDGES
A HOWARD HAWKS PROD'N
Produced by JESSE L. LASKY and HAL B. WALLIS

You'll see lovely Joan Leslie as Alvin York's Tennessee sweetheart. It makes her a star!

AIR-CONDITIONED
Astor

TICKETS NOW AVAILABLE FOR ALL PERFORMANCES!
All Seats Reserved • Two Performances Daily 2:45–8:45 p. m. • Midnite
Show Sats. • 6 p. m. Mat. Sundays • Week-day Mats: 75c, 85c, $1.10
Sat., Sun., Holiday Mat: 75c, 85c, $1.10, $1.65 • Evenings: $1.10, $1.65, $2.20
Tel. and Mail Reservations Accepted. Circle 6-4642 • B'way & 45th Street
SPECIAL 6 P. M. MATINEE TOMORROW!

176

Summer Bachelor's Itch

Marilyn Monroe, Tom Ewell Star at State

THE SEVEN YEAR ITCH, screen play by Billy Wilder and George Axelrod, from the play by Mr. Axelrod; directed by Mr. Wilder; produced by Charles K. Feldman and Mr. Wilder. A Charles K. Feldman Group Production, released by Twentieth Century-Fox. At the Loew's State.

The Girl	Marilyn Monroe
Richard Sherman	Tom Ewell
Helen Sherman	Evelyn Keyes
Tom McKenzie	Sonny Tufts
Kruhulik	Robert Strauss
Dr. Brubaker	Oscar Homolka
Miss Morris	Marguerite Chapman
Plumber	Victor Moore
Elaine	Roxanne
Mr. Brady	Donald MacBride
Miss Finch	Carolyn Jones
Ricky	Butch Bernard
Waitress	Doro Merando
Girl	Dorothy Ford

By BOSLEY CROWTHER

THE primal urge in the male animal — particularly one who has been married for seven years when he finds himself left alone for the whole summer in the hot city, with a voluptuous young lady in the apartment upstairs—is one of the principal topics of "The Seven Year Itch" at Loew's State. The other, equally assertive and much more tangible, is Marilyn Monroe.

As the aforesaid voluptuous young lady who comes into close proximity with the highly susceptible male animal, adroitly played by Tom Ewell, Miss Monroe brings a special personality and a certain physical something or other to the film that may not be exactly what the playwright ordered but which definitely convey an idea.

From the moment she steps into the picture, in a garment that drapes her shapely form as though she had been skillfully poured into it, the famous screen star with the silver-blonde tresses and the ingenuously wide-eyed stare emanates one suggestion. And that suggestion rather dominates the film. It is—well, why define it? Miss Monroe clearly plays the title role.

•

In a way, this is out of kilter. For George Axelrod, who wrote the stage play from which the picture is taken and collaborated with Director Billy Wilder on the script, obviously meant that the dominating interest should be the comical anxieties of the character played by Mr. Ewell. The torments of this poor fellow, torn between the thought of his wife and the more immediate and pressing impulses of his libido and his highly fertile brain, are the principal substance of the stage play. They gave it lilt and character.

Marilyn Monroe

And they still have significance in the picture. As a publisher of paper-bound books whose mind is drenched with lurid notions of sin and fatality, Mr. Ewell wrestles tensely with his urges and with his self-induced fantasies when the sexy number from upstairs becomes a real thing in his air-conditioned living room.

But the simple fact is that Mr. Wilder has permitted Miss Monroe, in her skin-fitting dresses and her frank gyrations, to overpower Mr. Ewell. She, without any real dimensions, is the focus of attention in the film.

This may be fortunate, however, as a factor of popularity, for there is a certain emptiness and eventual tedium to the anxieties of Mr. Ewell. Although some of his crises are explosive, in a far-fetched, farcical way, there is a sameness and repetition to the fixes he continuously finds himself in. And, it must be stated quite frankly, color and the CinemaScope screen do not lend an intriguing appearance to his plain and clownish phiz.

Also here is a further factor: In the play, as we recall, the wishful thoughts of the fellow toward the lady were finally realized. In the picture there is no such fulfillment. The rules of the Production Code have compelled a careful evasion that makes his ardor just a little absurd.

Thus it is that the undisguised performance of Miss Monroe, while it may lack depth, gives the show a caloric content that will not lose her any faithful fans. We merely commend her diligence when we say it leaves much—very much—to be desired.

In roles of minor importance Evelyn Keyes as Mr. Ewell's wife, Sonny Tufts as her darkly suspected suitor, Robert Strauss as a nosey janitor and Oscar Homolka as an unsympathetic psychoanalyst do nicely in the rush of episodes. If they, too, seem to lack definition, that is the nature of the film.

CHARLES K. FELDMAN Group Productions present

the seven year itch

COOL LOEW'S STATE
B'WAY & 45th ST.
DOORS OPEN 8:45 A.M.

starring MARILYN MONROE and TOM EWELL
Directed by BILLY WILDER
CINEMASCOPE
COLOR BY DE LUXE
Released by 20th Century-Fox

Marilyn Monroe and Tom Ewell in *The Seven Year Itch.*

Soul Gumshoe

Gordon Parks's 'Shaft' Begins at 2 Theaters

By ROGER GREENSPUN

Shaft is a New York private eye with a shabby office in midtown, a duplex in the Village, a wad of bills (and no small change) to tip with, a working love-hate relation with the cops and friends all over the city. He is also black. When Bumpy Jonas, chief hood in Harlem, tells him that his teen-aged daughter has been kidnapped and he suspects that militants have done it, Shaft takes the case more for $50 an hour than for any love of Bumpy. The case turns out to be a bit complex, a major gang war with racial overtones, though, really, no racial undertones. But Shaft delivers Bumpy his girl. And to his pal, Police Lieut. Vic Androzzi, he delivers the still warm bodies of what seems to be virtually all the white half of East-coast organized crime.

•

Of course, everybody knows you can't make a private-eye movie any more. But if you *could* make a private-eye movie, making it black might be a good idea. Not just for kicks, though there is nothing wrong with kicks, but for truth—or at least as much truth as you need to put into the genre. For who better than a black man to be both underdog and overlord, to understand everybody's motives including his own, to have that freedom of the city that is the point of the detective film and that, at least where many of us live, is no longer a right freely granted to anyone named Marlowe or Harper or even Madigan.

Gordon Parks's "Shaft," which opened yesterday at the DeMille and the 72d Street Playhouse, has surely the best title of any of the one-name movies to have opened in recent years. And though it doesn't have too much else of the best, it has a kind of self-generated good will that makes you want to like it even when for scenes on end you know it is doing everything wrong.

Parks is a well-known and very classy still photographer, a composer, writer and general Renaissance man whose first feature, "The Learning Tree," offered some moments of lovely, rather formal beauty amid vast stretches of conventional

The Cast

SHAFT, directed by Gordon Parks; screenplay by Ernest Tidyman and John D.F. Black, based on the novel by Mr. Tidyman; director of photography, Urs Furrer; music by Isaac Hayes; produced by Joel Freeman; released by Metro-Goldwyn-Mayer. At the DeMille Theater, Broadway and 47th, and the 72d Street Playhouse, east of Second Avenue. Running time: 100 minutes. (The Motion Picture Association of America's Production Code and Rating Administration classifies this film: "R-restricted, under 17 requires accompanying parent or adult guardian.")

John Shaft	Richard Roundtree
Bumpy Jonas	Moses Gunn
Vic Androzzi	Charles Gioffi
Ben Buford	Christopher St. John
Ellie Moore	Gwenn Mitchell
Linda	Margaret Warncke

forms. "Shaft" demonstrates a similar respect for forms, and for formal good looks (though Parks is not this time his own cinematographer), so that much of the time it has the visual style of a Life magazine photographic essay — though its dramatic logic is all Flash Gordon.

Shaft really is wish-fulfillment: the pad, the girls (whom he treats none too well), the fancy leather clothes, the ability to put down absolutely everybody and be paid back in admiration, the instinct for danger, the physical prowess, the fantastic recuperative ability that has him up and around and feeling no pain an hour after taking three machine-gun slugs in the chest.

•

He is also New York's champion jaywalker and a kidder on all levels and master of enough character quirks to keep a whole series of detective movies going—and although Parks is not yet enough at ease in the medium to make these things work, he has ideas and a feeling for the form's more vulgar excitements that may

Shaft! 24 hours a day!
The DeMille Theatre will be open around the clock Today

The mob wanted Harlem back. They got Shaft... up to here.

SHAFT

SHAFT's his name. SHAFT's his game.

M-G-M Presents "SHAFT" A STIRLING SILLIPHANT-ROGER LEWIS PRODUCTION Starring RICHARD ROUNDTREE Co-Starring MOSES GUNN Screenplay by ERNEST TIDYMAN and JOHN D.F. BLACK Based upon the novel by ERNEST TIDYMAN Music by ISAAC HAYES Produced by JOEL FREEMAN Directed by GORDON PARKS METROCOLOR MGM

R

DeMILLE 47th St. & 7th Ave. CO 5-8430
10:30 AM; 12:15 PM; 2:05, 3:40, 5:30, 7:20, 9:05, 10:55, 12:40 AM, 2:10, 3:30, 5:00, 6:30, 7:20, 9:00

72 ST. PLAYHOUSE Between 1st & 2nd Aves.—BU 8-9304
1:30, 3:25, 5:20, 7:10, 9:05, 11:00

in time allow him to overcome his own good taste.

He is at his worst in directing actors, or perhaps in cutting between actors, so that the strong cast (Richard Roundtree, Moses Gunn, Charles Gioffi) seems weak and without much sense of verbal rhythm. But, tin-eared and occasionally glass-eyed, he shows a grace in putting the horror of the city to the purposes of entertainment that seems especially welcome considering the options.

Richard Roundtree and Moses Gunn in *Shaft*.

Shane

SHANE, screen play by A. B. Guthrie Jr., based on the novel by Jack Schaefer with additional dialogue by Jack Sher; directed and produced by George Stevens for Paramount Pictures. At the Radio City Music Hall.

Shane	Alan Ladd
Mrs. Starrett	Jean Arthur
Mr. Starrett	Van Heflin
Joey Starrett	Brandon De Wilde
Wilson	Jack Palance
Chris	Ben Johnson
Lewis	Edgar Buchanan
Ryker	Emile Meyer
Torrey	Elisha Cook Jr.
Mr. Shipstead	Douglas Spencer
Morgan	John Dierkes
Mrs. Torrey	Ellen Corby
Grafton	Paul McVey
Atkey	John Miller
Mrs. Shipstead	Edith Evanson
Wright	Leonard Strong
Johnson	Ray Spiker
Susan Lewis	Janice Carroll
Howells	Martin Mason
Mrs. Lewis	Helen Brown
Mrs. Howells	Nancy Kulp

By BOSLEY CROWTHER

With "High Noon" so lately among us, it scarcely seems possible that the screen should so soon again come up with another great Western film. Yet that is substantially what has happened in the case of George Stevens' "Shane," which made a magnificent appearance at the Music Hall yesterday. Beautifully filmed in Technicolor in the great Wyoming outdoors, under the towering peaks of the Grand Tetons, and shown on a larger screen that enhances the scenic panorama, it may truly be said to be a rich and dramatic mobile painting of the American frontier scene.

For "Shane" contains something more than beauty and the grandeur of the mountains and plains, drenched by the brilliant Western sunshine and the violent, torrential, black-browed rains. It contains a tremendous comprehension of the bitterness and passion of the fueds that existed between the new homesteaders and the cattlemen on the open range. It contains a disturbing revelation of the savagery that prevailed in the hearts of the old gun-fighters, who were simply legal killers under the frontier code. And it also contains a very wonderful understanding of the spirit of a little boy amid all the tensions and excitements and adventures of a frontier home.

As a matter of fact, it is the concept and the presence of this little boy as an innocent and fascinated observer of the brutal struggle his elders wage that permits a refreshing viewpoint on material that's not exactly new. For it's this youngster's frank enthusiasms and naive reactions that are made the solvent of all the crashing drama in A. B. Guthrie Jr.'s script. And it's his youthful face and form, contributed by the precocious young Brandon De Wilde, that Mr. Stevens as director has most creatively worked with through the film.

There is tempestuous violence in a fist-fight that a stranger and the youngster's father wage against a gang of cattlemen hoodlums in a plain-board frontier saloon, but the fight has a freshness about it because it is watched by the youngster from under a door. And there's novelty and charm in this stranger because he is hero-worshipped by the boy. Most particularly, there's eloquence and greatness in a scene of a frontier burial on a hill, but

it gets its keenest punctuation when the boy wanders off to pet a colt.

The story Mr. Stevens is telling is simply that of the bold and stubborn urge of a group of modest homesteaders to hold onto their land and their homes against the threats and harassments of a cattle baron who implements his purpose with paid thugs. And it is brought to its ultimate climax when the stranger, who seeks peace on one of the farms, tackles an ugly gunfighter imported from Cheyenne to do a job on the leader of the homesteaders, the father of the boy.

This ultimate gun-fight, incidentally, makes a beautiful, almost classic scene as Mr. Stevens has staged it in the dismal and dimly lit saloon, with characters slinking in the background as the antagonists, Alan Ladd and Jack Palance, face off in frigid silence before the fatal words fly and the guns blaze. It is a scene which, added to the many that Mr. Stevens has composed in this film, gives the whole thing the quality of a fine album of paintings of the frontier.

And in many respects the characters that Mr. Stevens' actors have drawn might be considered portraits of familiar frontier types. Van Heflin as the leading homesteader is outstanding among those played by Douglas Spencer, Elisha Cook Jr., Edgar Buchanan and Leonard Strong. Mr. Ladd, though slightly swashbuckling as a gunfighter wishing to retire, does well enough by the character, and Jean

Arthur is good as the homesteader's wife. Mr. Palance as the mean, imported gunman; Emile Meyer as the cattleman boss and Paul McVey as the frontier storekeeper give fine portrayals, too. But it is Master De Wilde with his bright face, his clear voice and his resolute boyish ways who steals the affections of the audience and clinches "Shane" as a most unusual film.

Brandon de Wilde as Joey, with Alan Ladd in *Shane*.

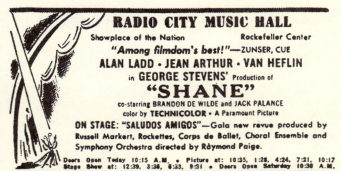

RADIO CITY MUSIC HALL
Showplace of the Nation   Rockefeller Center

"Among filmdom's best!"—ZUNSER, CUE

ALAN LADD • JEAN ARTHUR • VAN HEFLIN
in GEORGE STEVENS' Production of

"SHANE"

co-starring BRANDON DE WILDE and JACK PALANCE
color by TECHNICOLOR • A Paramount Picture

ON STAGE: "SALUDOS AMIGOS"—Gala new revue produced by Russell Markert, Rockettes, Corps de Ballet, Choral Ensemble and Symphony Orchestra directed by Raymond Paige.

Doors Open Today 10:15 A.M. • Picture at: 10:35, 1:28, 4:24, 7:21, 10:17
Stage Show at: 12:39, 3:36, 6:33, 9:31 • Doors Open Saturday 10:30 A.M.

The Sheik As A Photoplay

Edith M. Hull's novel, "The Sheik," which seems to have provided some kind of entertainment for numerous readers and no little amusement for the book reviewers, has followed the path of all popular fiction and may be seen on the screens of the Rivoli and Realto Theatres this week, that is, a photoplay calling itself "The Sheik" and acknowledging Mrs. Hull's story as its parent is being offered. Again the writer must confess that he has not read the novel from which a photoplay under review has been derived. He knew he would have to see the picture sooner or later. Isn't that enough?

Anyhow, the photoplay tells the story of an unusually spiritless English girl who is abducted by an exceedingly gentle desert sheik, but will not admit that she loves him until she is captured by a really rough Arab and realizes how perfectly safe she is with her tamer admirer. Somehow, this doesn't seem to be exactly the idea of Mrs. Hull's novel as reported in the book reviews, but never mind; here's the picture tale of a nice sheik and his agreeable English girl. And you won't be offended by having a white girl marry an Arab either, for the sheik isn't really a native of the desert at all. Oh, no; he's the son of a Spanish father and an English mother who were killed when he was a baby so the old sheik could raise him as his son. These romantic Arabian movies, you know, never have the courage of their romantics.

Agnes Ayres is the girl and Rudolph Valentino is the sheik. Both of them can make the characters they impersonate seem real in a picture, which gives any character a chance to seem real.

George Melford directed the production and although he has given it no cinematographic quality, he has made many elaborate scenes, using the desert effectively a number of times. The only trouble in this connection is that he has used the desert too much, and especially too much in the sun. If realism was his object he has certainly accomplished it. By the time half a dozen of these glaring white desert scenes have followed each other on the screen your eyes are ready to give up. Those who go to see the picture would do well to take their amber glasses with them.

The Rivoli and Rialto programs are enlivened by one of those ingenious and amusing doll comedies periodically issued as "Funny Face" productions without credit to the person or persons who make them. The magazines at these two theatres also emphasize Armistice Week and the Washington conference with pictures of the men prominent during the war and since.

Rudolph Valentino as *The Sheik*.

Theatres Under Direction of Hugo Riesenfeld

Paramount Pictures

THRILLED 20,000 ON
THE OPENING DAY (YESTERDAY)

JESSE L. LASKY presents

GEORGE MELFORD'S PRODUCTION

"The SHEIK"

A PARAMOUNT PICTURE

Agnes Ayres
AND
Rudolph Valentino

By EDITH M. HULL

— AT THE —

RIVOLI
BROADWAY AT 49TH ST.

RIALTO
TIMES SQUARE

THE SILENT DRAMA

The Sheik and his unwilling captive, Agnes Ayres.

The Music Hall Presents Walt Disney's Delightful Fantasy, 'Snow White and the Seven Dwarfs'

SNOW WHITE AND THE SEVEN DWARFS, a feature-length cartoon based on Grimms' fairy tale; adapted by Ted Sears, Otto Englander, Earl Hurd, Dorothy Ann Blank, Richard Creedon, Dick Rickard, Merrill De Maris and Webb Smith; music by Frank Churchill, Leigh Harline and Paul Smith; supervising director, David Hand; produced in Technicolor by Walt Disney for release by RKO-Radio. At the Radio City Music Hall.

By FRANK S. NUGENT

Sheer fantasy, delightful, gay and altogether captivating, touched the screen yesterday when Walt Disney's long-awaited feature-length cartoon of the Grimm fairy tale, "Snow White and the Seven Dwarfs," had its local première at the Radio City Music Hall. Let your fears be quieted at once: Mr. Disney and his amazing technical crew have outdone themselves. The picture more than matches expectations. It is a classic, as important cinematically as "The Birth of a Nation" or the birth of Mickey Mouse. Nothing quite like it has been done before; and already we have grown impolite enough to clamor for an encore. Another helping, please!

You can visualize it best if you imagine a child, with a wondrous, Puckish imagination, nodding over his favorite fairy tale and dreaming a dream in which his story would come true. He would see Snow White, victim of the wicked Queen's jealousy, dressed in rags, singing at her work quite unmindful of the Magic Mirror's warning to the Queen that the Princess, not she, was now the "fairest in the land." Then he would see Snow White's banishment from the castle, her fearful flight from the hobgoblins of the forest, her adoption by all the friendly little creatures of the wood and her refuge at the home of the seven dwarfs.

And then, if this child had a truly marvelous imagination—the kind of impish imagination that Mr. Disney and his men possess—, he might have seen the seven dwarfs as the picture sees them. There are Doc, who sputters and twists his words, and Happy, who is a rollicking little elf, and Grumpy, who is terribly grumpy—at first—, and Sleepy, who drowses, and Sneezy, who acts like a volcano with hay fever, and Bashful, who blushes to the roots of his long white beard, and Dopey. Dopey really deserves a sentence all by himself. No, we'll make it a paragraph, because Dopey is here to stay.

Dopey is the youngest of the seven dwarfs. He is beardless, with a buttony nose, a wide mouth, Gable ears, cross-purpose eyes and the most disarming, winning, helpless, puppy-dog expression that creature ever had. If we had to dissect him, we'd say he was one part little Benny of the comic strips, one part Worry-Wart of the same and one part Pluto, of the Mickey Mouse Plutos. There may, too, be just a dash of Harpo Marx. But he's all Dopey, forever out of step in the dwarfs' processions, doomed to carry the red tail-light when

they go to their jewel mines, and speechless. As Doc explains, "he never tried to talk."

So there they are, all seven of them, to protect the little Princess from her evil stepmother, the Queen, to dance and frolic and cavort—with the woodland creatures—in comic Disneyesque patterns at Snow White's glass-and-gold coffin until Prince Charming imprints "love's first kiss" upon her lips and so releases her from the sleeping death that claimed her after she ate the witch's poisoned apple. For this, you know, is partly the story of Sleeping Beauty.

But no child, of course, could dream a dream like this. For Mr. Disney's humor has the simplicity of extreme sophistication. The little bluebird who overreaches itself and hits a flat note to the horror of its parents; the way the animals help Snow White clean house, with the squirrels using their tails as dusters, the swallows scalloping pies with their feet, the fawns licking the plates clean, the chipmunks twirling cobwebs about their tails and pulling free; or the ticklish tortoise when the rabbits use his ribbed underside as a scrubbing board—all these are beyond a youngster's imagination, but not beyond his delight.

And technically it is superb. In some of the early sequences there may be an uncertainty of line, a jerkiness in the movements of the Princess; but it is corrected later and hand and lip movements assume an uncanny reality. The dwarfs and animals are flawless from the start.

A scene from Snow White and the Seven Dwarfs, Walt Disney's first feature-length cartoon.

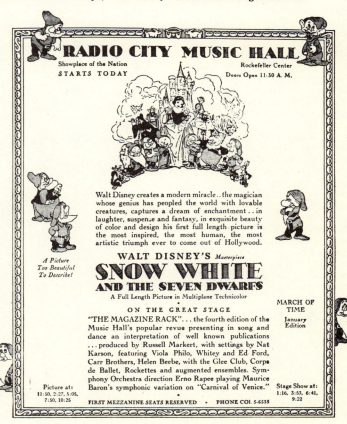

RADIO CITY MUSIC HALL
Showplace of the Nation   Rockefeller Center
STARTS TODAY   Doors Open 11:30 A. M.

Walt Disney creates a modern miracle..the magician whose genius has peopled the world with lovable creatures, captures a dream of enchantment..in laughter, suspense and fantasy, in exquisite beauty of color and design his first full length picture is the most inspired, the most human, the most artistic triumph ever to come out of Hollywood.

WALT DISNEY'S *Masterpiece*
SNOW WHITE
AND THE SEVEN DWARFS
A Full Length Picture in Multiplane Technicolor

ON THE GREAT STAGE
"THE MAGAZINE RACK"...the fourth edition of the Music Hall's popular revue presenting in song and dance an interpretation of well known publications...produced by Russell Markert, with settings by Nat Karson, featuring Viola Philo, Whitey and Ed Ford, Carr Brothers, Helen Beebe, with the Glee Club, Corps de Ballet, Rockettes and augmented ensembles. Symphony Orchestra direction Erno Rapee playing Maurice Baron's symphonic variation on "Carnival of Venice."

A Picture Too Beautiful To Describe

MARCH OF TIME
January Edition

Picture at: 11:50, 2:27, 5:05, 7:50, 10:25
FIRST MEZZANINE SEATS RESERVED • PHONE COL. 5-6555
Stage Show at: 1:16, 3:53, 6:41, 9:22

2-Hour Comedy

By A. H. WEILER

THERE should be no doubt this morning that the members of the happily irreverent film troupe that made "Some Like It Hot" have done something constructive about the old wheeze that begins, "Who was that lady I saw you with?" For, in fashioning this overlong, occasionally labored but often outrageously funny series of variations on an ancient gag, they have come up with a rare, rib-tickling lampoon that should keep them, the customers and the management of the newly refurbished Loew's State, which reopened yesterday, chortling with glee.

Let's face it. Two hours is too long a time to harp on one joke. But Billy Wilder, who produced, directed and collaborated with I. A. L. Diamond on this breeziest of scripts, proves once again that he is as professional as anyone in Hollywood. Mr. Wilder, abetted by such equally proficient operatives as Marilyn Monroe, Jack Lemmon and Tony Curtis, surprisingly has developed a completely unbelievable plot into a broad farce in which authentically comic action vies with snappy and sophisticated dialogue.

It is quite possible also that this uninhibited team was inspired by Mack Sennett and "Charley's Aunt." The slim story, to put it bluntly, simply deals with what happens to a pair of Prohibition Era musicians who witness a gangland murder in Chicago (strongly reminiscent of the St. Valentine's Day massacre) and who seek sanctuary masquerading as dames in an all-girl band in Florida.

But Mr. Wilder and company obviously are not bothered by this flimsy framework. "Some Like It Hot" is as constantly busy as picnickers fighting off angry wasps. Jack Lemmon has a torrid time guzzling gin at an impromptu party in a Pullman upper berth attended by Miss Monroe and the rest of the giddy band. Tony Curtis, switching disguises from bogus girl saxophonist to phony millionaire, amorously pursues Miss Monroe, and vice versa, aboard a "borrowed" yacht. The slightly addled playboy-owner of that ship, played in properly harebrained style by Joe E. Brown, chases Mr. Lemmon with nothing but honorable intentions. And, Chicago's hoods, led by George Raft and Nehemiah Persoff, tear after Lemmon and Curtis, the witnesses to their foul deed, with equal determination.

Who gets whom is not particularly important. A viewer might question the taste of a few of the lines, situations and the prolonged masquerade, but Mr. Wilder and his associates generally make their points with explosive effect. Besides the wild and wooly train sequence, one is reminded of such scenes as Miss Monroe's ardent and naive wooing of Mr. Curtis, Mr. Lemmon's gay fandango with Mr. Brown, a dopey pas-de-deux that ends in their becoming "engaged" and Mr. Persoff's and Mr. Raft's caricatures of hoodlum big shots.

The Cast

SOME LIKE IT HOT; screen play by Billy Wilder and I. A. L. Diamond; suggested by a story by R. Thoeren and M. Logan; produced and directed by Mr. Wilder; a Mirisch Company presentation of an Ashton Production released through United Artists. At Loew's State, Broadway and Forty-fifth Street. Running time: 120 minutes.

Sugar Kane (Kovalchick)	Marilyn Monroe
Joe (Josephine)	Tony Curtis
Jerry (Daphne)	Jack Lemmon
Spats Colombo	George Raft
Mulligan	Pat O'Brien
Osgood Fielding 3d	Joe E. Brown
Little Bonaparte	Nehemiah Persoff
Sue	Joan Shawlee
Toothpick Charlie	George E. Stone
Beinstock	Dave Barry
Spats Colombo's Henchmen	{ Mike Mazurki { Harry Wilson
Poliakoff	Billy Gray
Dolores	Beverly Wills
Nellie	Barbara Drew
Paradise	Edward G. Robinson Jr.

As the band's somewhat simple singer-ukulele player, Miss Monroe, whose figure simply cannot be overlooked, contributes more assets than the obvious ones to this madcap romp. As a pushover for gin and the tonic effect of saxophone players, she sings a couple of whispery old numbers ("Running Wild" and "I Wanna Be Loved by You") and also proves to be the epitome of a dumb blonde and a talented comedienne.

As has been noted, the sight of the Messrs. Curtis and Lemmon teetering around on high heels wears thin awfully quickly, as does Mr. Curtis' vocal imitation of a noted male movie star. But both take to slapstick, double-takes and mugging as though they were charter members of the Keystone Kops. They give vigorous, top-flight performances that add greatly to wacky goings-on.

"Some Like It Hot" does cool off considerably now and again, but Mr. Wilder and his carefree clowns keep it crackling and funny most of the time.

Members of the all-girl band, Tony Curtis, Jack Lemmon and Marilyn Monroe, in *Some Like It Hot*.

'Sounder' Opens

Story of a Negro Boy in Louisiana of 1930's

By ROGER GREENSPUN

It would be so comfortable to praise "Sounder." The story of a boy, David, and his dog, Sounder, and his family, black sharecroppers in Louisiana in the 1930's, it is a film that virtually announces nobility. And the pre-opening reviews quoted in the ads have responded as if on cue, treating "Sounder" not as a movie at all but rather as something unusually worthy, like the United Fund or a UNICEF Christmas card

It is about growing up, a subject with special appeal to the makers of distinguished motion pictures, and it is about growing up poor, black and dignified, and at a time just enough in the past to carry an aura of modern, but not quite contemporary, history. Even the plot — a kindly father caught stealing food for his hungry family, sentenced to a year at hard labor, a year in which his son comes to terms with himself and learns not to accept his lot—has the feeling of historical demonstration.

And if "Sounder," an inteligent enough movie, avoids all the major pitfalls of its type, it also lacks the excitement that may have come from plumbing greater depths and discovering a few tougher, less accessible insights.

"Sounder" was produced by Robert Radnitz, who specializes in children's films, and directed by Martin Ritt ("Hud," "The Molly Maguires," etc.) who poses something of a problem. An earnest, conscientious director, he seems to strive for classical plainness, but to succeed only in being ordinary. When David visits his father's labor camp, a long trip on foot and the centerpiece of the film, Ritt follows him through a series of shots dissolving into one another that are clearly meant to express the journey, but really promote a kind of decorative and oddly inexpressive picture-making.

And the emotional life of the family is figured too often in scenes of fond greeting or of sad farewell—a requirement of the story partly but also, I think, a rather dull willingness to rely on conventional public views of what are essentially private relationships.

The Cast

SOUNDER, directed by Martin Ritt; screenplay by Lonne Elder 3d, from the novel by William H. Armstrong; cinematographer, John Alonzo; music by Taj Mahal; film editor, Sid Levin; produced by Robert B. Radnitz. At the Plaza Theater, 58th Street, east of Madison Avenue and the New Embassy Theater, 46th Street and Broadway. Running time: 105 minutes. This film is classified G.

Rebecca Morgan .... Cicely Tyson
Nathan Lee Morgan ......Paul Winfield
David Lee Morgan .... Kevin Hooks
Mrs. Boatwright ......Carmen Matthews
Ike ....Taj Mahal
Sheriff Young ....James Best
Camille ....Janet MacLachlan

Lonne Elder's screenplay, from the novel by William Armstrong, attempts a universality in its dialogue (e.g., "Where is it you went last night, Nathan?" "I did what I had to do, Rebecca.") that makes everyone sound as if he were reciting from a book. This can be very good where there is a style to match the solemnity, as in, say, the late films of Carl Dreyer, but it is merely unreal here.

Among the performances, all rather expert, only the women are complicated enough to be interesting. These include Janet MacLachlan as the young black teacher who proves equal to David's sense of his own worth, and Cicely Tyson, as the mother who helped give him that sense in the first place.

Miss Tyson seems to understand that part of screen acting is keeping secrets from the camera, and she does suggest a range of personality beneath and beyond the ambitions of this film.

"Sounder" opened yesterday at the Plaza and New Embassy theaters.

"IT IS A MISSING CHAPTER FROM THE GRAPES OF WRATH' AND OF EQUAL STATURE."
—Judith Crist, New York Magazine

Radnitz / MATTEL Productions, Inc. Presents

"SOUNDER"

A Robert B. Radnitz/Martin Ritt Film

starring CICELY TYSON · PAUL WINFIELD
KEVIN HOOKS · co-starring TAJ MAHAL
JANET MACLACHLAN · produced by ROBERT B. RADNITZ
directed by MARTIN RITT · screenplay by LONNE ELDER, III
based on the Newbery Award winning Novel by WILLIAM H. ARMSTRONG

Kevin Hooks and Paul Winfield in the homecoming scene from *Sounder.*

A Ford-Powered 'Stagecoach' Opens at Music Hall

STAGECOACH, based on the story "Stage to Lordsburg," by Ernest Haycox; screen play by Dudley Nichols; directed by John Ford; a Walter Wanger production; released by United Artists. At the Radio City Music Hall.

Dallas	Claire Trevor
Ringo Kid	John Wayne
Buck	Andy Devine
Hatfield	John Carradine
Doc Boone	Thomas Mitchell
Lucy Mallory	Louise Platt
Curly Wilcox	George Bancroft
Lieutenant Blanchard	Tim Holt
Gatewood	Berton Churchill
Peacock	Donald Meek
Chris	Chris Martin
Captain Whitney	Cornelius Keefe
Chris's wife	Elvira Rios
Billy Pickett	Francis Ford
Mrs. Whitney	Florence Lake

By FRANK S. NUGENT

In one superbly expansive gesture, which we (and the Music Hall) can call "Stagecoach," John Ford has swept aside ten years of artifice and talkie compromise and has made a motion picture that sings a song of camera. It moves, and how beautifully it moves, across the plains of Arizona, skirting the sky-reaching mesas of Monument Valley, beneath the piled-up cloud banks which every photographer dreams about, and through all the old-fashioned, but never really outdated, periods of prairie travel in the scalp-raising Seventies, when Geronimo's Apaches were on the warpath. Here, in a sentence, is a movie of the grand old school, a genuine rib-thumper and a beautiful sight to see.

Mr. Ford is not one of your subtle directors, suspending sequences on the wink of an eye or the precisely calculated gleam of a candle in a mirror. He prefers the broadest canvas, the brightest colors, the widest brush and the boldest possible strokes. He hews to the straight narrative line with the well-reasoned confidence of a man who has seen that narrative succeed before. He takes no shadings from his characters: either they play it straight or they don't play at all. He likes his language simple and he doesn't want too much of it. When his Redskins bite the dust, he expects to hear the thud and see the dirt spurt up. Above all, he likes to have things happen out in the open, where his camera can keep them in view.

He has had his way in "Stagecoach" with Walter Wanger's benison, the writing assistance of Dudley Nichols and the complete co-operation of a cast which had the sense to appreciate the protection of being stereotyped. You should know, almost without being told, the station in life (and in frontier melodrama) of the eight passengers on the Overland stage from Tonto to Lordsburg.

To save time, though, here they are: "Doc" Boone, a tipsy man of medicine; Major Hatfield, professional gambler, once a Southern gentleman and a gentleman still; Dallas, a lady of such transparently dubious virtue that she was leaving Tonto by popular request; Mrs. Mallory, who, considering her condition, had every reason to be hastening to her army husband's side; Mr. Gatewood, an absconding banker and windbag; Mr. Peacock, a small and timid whisky salesman destined by Bacchus to be Doc Boone's traveling companion; Sheriff Wilcox and his prisoner, the Ringo Kid. The driver, according to the rules, had to be Slim Summerville or Andy Devine; Mr. Devine got the call.

So onward rolls the stage, nobly sped by its six stout-hearted bays, and out there, somewhere behind the buttes and crags, Geronimo is lurking with his savage band, the United States Cavalry is biding its time to charge to the rescue and the Ringo Kid is impatiently awaiting his cue to stalk down the frontier-town street and blast it out with the three Plummer boys. But foreknowledge doesn't cheat Mr. Ford of his thrills. His attitude, if it spoke its mind, would be: "All right, you know what's coming, but have you ever seen it done like this?" And once you've swallowed your heart again, you'll have to say: "No, sir! Not like this!"

His players have taken easily to their chores, all the way down the list from Claire Trevor's Dallas to Tom Tyler's Hank Plummer. But the cutest coach-rider in the wagon, to our mind, was little Donald Meek as Mr. Peacock, the whisky-drummer. That, of course, is not meant as a slight to Thomas Mitchell as the toping Dr. Boone, to Louise Platt as the wan Mrs. Mallory, George Bancroft as the sheriff or John Wayne as the Ringo Kid. They've all done nobly by a noble horse opera, but none so nobly as its director. This is one stagecoach that's powered by a Ford.

George Bancroft, John Wayne and Claire Trevor in *Stagecoach*, directed by John Ford.

RADIO CITY **MUSIC HALL**
Showplace of the Nation — Rockefeller Center

STARTS TODAY
Doors Open 11:30 A. M.

THOMAS MITCHELL
the doctor

CLAIRE TREVOR
the outcast

JOHN WAYNE
the outlaw

ANDY DEVINE
stagecoach driver

JOHN CARRADINE
the mysterious gambler

BERTON CHURCHILL
the banker

DONALD MEEK
the drummer

LOUISE PLATT
the lady of quality

GEORGE BANCROFT
the U. S. Marshal

Nine strangely-assorted passengers on a stagecoach bound for the most gripping, dramatic journey ever filmed ... across a vast panorama of scenic splendor ... emotions crack and hidden strength and failure come startlingly to the surface ... nine memorable characterizations in an epic, romantic story of the American frontier ... the greatest directorial achievement of John Ford, repeated Academy Award winner.

A Walter Wanger Picture

STAGECOACH

Directed by John Ford

with CLAIRE TREVOR · JOHN WAYNE · ANDY DEVINE · JOHN CARRADINE · THOMAS MITCHELL · LOUISE PLATT · GEORGE BANCROFT · DONALD MEEK · BERTON CHURCHILL
Released thru United Artists

A Star Is Born

A STAR IS BORN, from a story by. William A. Wellman and Robert Carson; screen play by Dorothy Parker, Alan Campbell and Mr. Carson; musical score by Max Steiner; directed by Mr. Wellman; produced by David O. Selznick for Selznick International; released by United Artists. At the Radio City Music Hall.

Esther Blodgett—Vicki Lester	Janet Gaynor
Norman Maine	Fredric March
Oliver Niles	Adolphe Menjou
Lettie	May Robson
Danny McGuire	Andy Devine
Libby	Lionel Stander
Anita Regis	Elizabeth Jenns
Pop Randall	Edgar Kennedy
Casey Burke	Owen Moore
Theodore Smythe	J. C. Nugent
Aunt Mattie	Clara Blandick
Esther's brother	A. W. Sweatt
Miss Phillips (clerk)	Peggy Wood
Harris	Adrian Rosely
Ward	Arthur Hoyt
Posture Coach..Guinn (Big Boy) Williams
Otto Friedl	Vince Barnett
Academy Awards Speaker	Paul Stanton
Billy Moon	Franklin Pangborn

By FRANK S. NUGENT

It is not as dull a Spring as we had thought. Selznick International came to April's defense yesterday with one of the year's best shows, "A Star Is Born," which probably will find the Music Hall's treasurer turning cartwheels in the streets this morning. For here, at least, is good entertainment by any standards. including the artistic, and convincing proof that Hollywood need not travel to Ruritania for its plots: there is drama a-plenty in its own backyard.

"A Star Is Born" is a Hollywood story of, by and for its people. It has the usual preface, attesting to the fictional quality of the characters and incidents depicted, but it is nonetheless the most accurate mirror ever held before the glittering. tinseled. trivial, generous, cruel and ecstatic world that is Hollywood. That, in itself, guarantees its dramatic interest, for there is no place on this twentieth-century earth more fascinating—not even that enchanting make-believe republic which James Hilton called Shangri-La.

Looking at it objectively,' one might argue that William Wellman, Robert Carson. Dorothy Parker and Alan Campbell (who coined the plot) have been passing Confederate money. Their thesis is the old one about the rising star and the falling star in the theatrical firmament whose paths cross. create a pyrotechnic glow where they meet, then flame out tragically as one soars onward in her flight as the other dips sadly and dies. If this were all, then "A Star Is Born" would be no more than commonplace, a jaded repetition of a basic theatrical formula.

But there are vibrance and understanding in their writing, a feeling for telling detail and a sympathy for the people they are touching. It is not a maudlin picture—not nearly so heroic, let us say, as its dramatic corollary, "Stage Door." Janet Gaynor's movie-struck Esther Blodgett is not a caricature; Fredric March's waning Norman Maine is not an outrageous "ham". Adolphe Menjou's Oliver Niles (of Oliver Niles Productions) is no more—and no less—human than many producers are. They are honest. normal, well-intentioned folk; different. of course. for Hollywood would make them so: but we can believe in them and understand them and be moved by their tragedy. Conviction can bring any formula to life.

So then. we have the story of little Esther Blodgett who came to Hollywood and stood beatifically in the concrete footprints of Norman Maine outside Grauman's Chinese Theatre; who somehow—by one of those 100.000-to-1 chances—became the sensational Vicki Lester and Mrs. Norman Maine; who could not arrest her husband's swift descent, nor protect him from being called Mr. Vicki Lester. nor stay him when he stepped gallantly from the scene. Little Esther Blodgett had her success in Hollywood, but she paid for it. "Stage Door" never took that into account.

It is, as we said before, a good picture. It has been capitally played all down the line. Its script is bright, inventive and forceful. Mr. Wellman's direction is expert. Its color—we almost forgot to mention it, so casually was it used—proves Technicolor's value in a modern story, demonstrates that it need not, should not, be restricted to the gaudy costume dramas. Not even its three climaxes, one right after the other, are enough to alter our verdict. The Music Hall, after a long famine, is spreading a feast again.

Janet Gaynor, Frederic March and Adolphe Menjou in a scene from *A Star Is Born.*

RADIO CITY MUSIC HALL

presents with pride

a great human document, another brilliant picture by David Selznick, who produced "Tale of Two Cities", "David Copperfield", "Little Lord Fauntleroy", etc., etc...

★ ★ ★ ★ ★

"A STAR IS BORN"...a sincere and powerful portrayal of real life...romance ...pathos...humor...the bitter and sweet of a career story of today's generation... in Hollywood...a story of unusual interest to every motion picture patron...in beautiful Technicolor...Fredric March and Janet Gaynor in the outstanding performances of their careers ...with Adolphe Menjou and a strong supporting cast.

Starts TODAY
Doors open 11.30 A. M.

JANET GAYNOR
FREDRIC MARCH
in
A Star is Born
IN TECHNICOLOR

with ADOLPHE MENJOU · MAY ROBSON
ANDY DEVINE · LIONEL STANDER

Produced by DAVID O. SELZNICK

Directed by William A. Wellman · Released thru United Artists

'A Star Is Born' Bows

Judy Garland, James Mason in Top Roles

A STAR IS BORN, screen play by Moss Hart, based on the Dorothy Parker, Alan Campbell, Robert Carson screen play; from a story by William A. Wellman and Robert Carson; music and lyrics by Harold Arlen, Ira Gershwin and Leonard Gershe; directed by George Cukor; produced by Sidney Luft for Warner Brothers. At the Paramount and Victoria.

Esther Blodgett	Judy Garland
Norman Maine	James Mason
Libby	Jack Carson
Oliver Niles	Charles Bickford
Danny McGuire	Tom Noonan
A Starlet	Lucy Marlow
Susan	Amanda Blake
Graves	Irving Bacon
Libby's secretary	Hazel Shermet
Glenn Williams	James Brown
Miss Markham	Lotus Robb

By BOSLEY CROWTHER

THOSE who have blissful recollections of David O. Selznick's "A Star Is Born" as probably the most affecting movie ever made about Hollywood may get themselves set for a new experience that should put the former one in the shade when they see Warner Brothers' and George Cukor's remake of the seventeen-year-old film. And those who were no more than toddlers when that classic was starting floods of tears may warm themselves up for one of the grandest heartbreak dramas that has drenched the screen in years.

For the Warners and Mr. Cukor have really and truly gone to town in giving this hackneyed Hollywood story an abundance of fullness and form. They have laid it out in splendid color on the smartly used CinemaScope screen, and they have crowded it with stunning details of the makers and making of films. They have got Judy Garland and James Mason to play the important roles that were filled with such memorable consequence by Janet Gaynor and Fredric March in the original. And they have fattened it up with musical numbers that are among the finest things in the show.

And a show it is, first and foremost. Its virtually legendary account of the romance of an actress headed for stardom and an actor headed downhill would have very little force or freshness in this worldly wise day and age if it weren't played within the lush surroundings of significant performance and fancy show. So it is a build-up of this that gives grandeur and background to the poignance of this film, which was put on with fanfare last evening at the Paramount and Victoria Theatres.

The whole thing runs for three hours, and during this extraordinary time a remarkable range of entertainment is developed upon the screen. There is the sweet and touching love story that Moss Hart has smoothly modernized from the neat synthesis of Hollywood legends, which went into the original.

It is the story of a vocalist with a dance band who catches the bleary, wistful eye of a topnotch male star, now skidding on the downgrade, and gets his help toward motion-picture fame. It is the story of their marriage and their struggle to hold fast to the fragile thing of love as fame and failure divide them—and of the husband's sacrifice at the end. This is the core of the drama, and it is brilliantly visualized.

No one surpasses Mr. Cukor at handling this sort of thing, and he gets performances from Miss Garland and Mr. Mason that make the heart flutter and bleed. Such episodes as their meeting on the night of a benefit show, their talking about marrying on a soundstage under an eavesdropping microphone, their bitter-sweet reaching for each other in a million-dollar beach bungalow, their tormenting ordeal in a night court—these are wonderfully and genuinely played. What matters that logic does not always underlie everything they do? What matters that we never really fathom Mr. Mason's flamboyant Norman Maine? Theirs is a credible enactment of a tragic little try at love in an environment that packages the product. It is the strong tie that binds the whole show.

But there is more that is complementary to it. There is the muchness of music that runs from a fine, haunting torch-song at the outset, "The Man That Got Away," to a mammoth, extensive production number recounting the career of a singer. It is called "Born in a Trunk." Miss Gar-

(continued)

$6,000,000 AND 2½ YEARS TO MAKE IT!

"It is impossible to review 'A Star is Born' as other films are reviewed. It is more than 'super-colossal' and all other stupendous adjectives!"
—LOUELLA PARSONS

JUDY GARLAND · JAMES MASON
'A Star is Born'

ORIGINAL MUSIC BY HAROLD ARLEN AND LYRICS BY IRA GERSHWIN

PRESENTED BY WARNER BROS. IN CinemaScope · TECHNICOLOR · STEREOPHONIC SOUND

ALSO STARRING JACK CARSON · CHARLES BICKFORD
Screen Play by MOSS HART · Directed by GEORGE CUKOR · Musical Direction by RAY HEINDORF
Produced by SIDNEY LUFT A TRANSCONA ENTERPRISES PRODUCTION WARNER BROS.

THE MAN THAT GOT AWAY
"IT'S A NEW WORLD"
"GOTTA HAVE ME GO WITH YOU"
"HERE'S WHAT I'M HERE FOR"
"SOMEONE AT LAST"
"LOSE THAT LONG FACE"

TOMORROW 8:30 A.M. CONTINUOUS PERFORMANCES AT BOTH THEATRES PARAMOUNT AND VICTORIA

FORMAL PREMIERES TONIGHT 8:30 P.M. AT BOTH THEATRES!

Guest of Honor JUDY GARLAND ...AND JUST ABOUT EVERY CELEBRITY IN TOWN WILL BE THERE!

TELECASTS FROM BOTH THEATRES OVER WABC TV (7) 8:00 TO 8:30 P.M.

land is excellent in all things—but most winningly, perhaps, in the song, "Here's What I'm Here For," wherein she dances, sings and pantomimes the universal endeavors of the lady to capture the man. Harold Arlen, Ira Gershwin and Leonard Gershe are the authors of the songs.

●

And there is, through it all, a gentle tracing of clever satire of Hollywood, not as sharp as it was in the original, but sharp enough to be stimulating fun. Charles Bickford's calm and generous producer is a bit on the idealized side and Jack Carson's disagreeable press agent is not as vicious as he's supposed to be. But the sense of an artificial milieu wraps the whole thing, as in cellophane—all in colors that fill the eye with excitement.

It is something to see, this "Star Is Born."

Crowds of enthusiastic on-lookers swirled around the Paramount and Victoria Theatres last night to attend and watch the gala activities surrounding the première of "A Star Is Born." Miss Garland made an appearance at the Victoria and and later arrived at the Paramount for the showing of the film.

The glare of flood lights and popping of flash-bulbs provided customary background for the event which was "covered" by television cameras, radio broadcasters, Armed Forces Overseas radio, press and newsreel photographers. The sidewalks in front of the two theatres were carpeted in the traditional red velvet and searchlights sent shafts of light high in the sky over Broadway.

The audiences at both theatres were made up, to a large extent, by notables from many fields. As they arrived, Martin Block, the master of ceremonies, and George Jessel greeted them.

Judy Garland and Jack Carson.

Judy Garland in the 1954 version of *A Star Is Born*.

'Star Wars'—Trip to a Far Galaxy

By VINCENT CANBY

"STAR WARS," George Lucas's first film since his terrifically successful "American Graffiti," is the movie that the teen-agers in "American Grafiti" would have broken their necks to see. It's also the movie that's going to entertain a lot of contemporary folk who have a soft spot for the virtually ritualized manners of comic-book adventure.

"Star Wars," which opened yesterday at the Astor Plaza, Orpheum and other theaters, is the most beautiful movie serial ever made. It's both an apotheosis of "Flash Gordon" serials and a witty critique that makes associations with a variety of literature that is nothing if not electic: "Quo Vadis?", "Buck Rogers," "Ivanhoe," "Superman," "The Wizard of Oz," "The Gospel According to St. Mathew," the legend of King Arthur and the knights of the Round Table.

All of these works, of course, had earlier left their marks on the kind of science-fiction comic strips that Mr. Lucas, the writer as well as director of "Star Wars," here remembers with affection of such cheerfulness that he avoids facetiousness. The way definitely not to approach "Star Wars," though, is to expect a film of cosmic implications or to footnote it with so many references that one anticipates it as if it were a literary duty. It's fun and funny.

The time, according to the opening credit card, is "a long time ago" and the setting "a galaxy far far away," which gives Mr. Lucas and his associates total freedom to come up with their own landscapes, housing, vehicles, weapons, religion, politics —all of which are variations on the familiar.

•

When the film opens, dark times have fallen upon the galactal empire once ruled, we are given to believe, from a kind of space-age Camelot. Against these evil tyrants there is, in progress, a rebellion led by a certain Princess Leia Organa, a pretty roundfaced young woman of old-fashioned pluck who, before you can catch your breath, has been captured by the guardians of the empire. Their object is to retrive some secret plans that can be the empire's undoing.

That's about all the plot that anyone of voting age should be required to keep track of. The story of "Star Wars" could be written on the head of a pin and still leave room for the Bible. It is, rather, a breathless succession of escapes, pursuits, dangerous missions, unexpected encounters, with each one ending in some kind of defeat until the final one.

These adventures involve, among others, an ever-optimistic young man named Luke Skywalker (Mark Hamill), who is innocent without being naive; Han Solo (Harrison Ford), a free-booting freelance, space-ship caption who goes where he can make the most money, and an old mystic

Comic-Book Sci-Fi

STAR WARS, directed and written by George Lucas; produced by Gary Kurtz; production designer, John Barry; director of photography, Gilbert Taylor; music, John Williams; editors, Paul Hirsch, Marcia Lucas and Richard Chew; a Lucasfilm Ltd. production, distributed by 20th Century Fox. Running time: 123 minutes. At the Astor Plaza, 44th Street west of Broadway, Orpheum Theater, 86th Street near Third Avenue, and other theaters. This film has been rated PG.

Luke Skywalker	Mark Hamill
Han Solo	Harrison Ford
Princess Leia Organa	Carrie Fisher
Grand Moff Tarkin	Peter Cushing
Ben (Obi-Wan) Kenobi	Alec Guinness
See Threepio	Anthony Daniels
Artoo-Deetoo	Kenny Baker
Chewbacca	Peter Mayhew
Lord Darth Vader	David Prowse
Uncle Owen Lars	Phil Brown
Aunt Beru Lars	Shelagh Fraser
Chief Jawa	Jack Purvis
General Dodonna	Alex McCrindie
General Willard	Eddie Byrne
General Taggi	Don Henderson
General Motti	Richard Le Parmentier

named Ben Kenobi (Alec Guinness), one of the last of the Old Guard, a fellow in possession of what's called "the force," a mixture of what appears to be ESP and early Christian faith.

•

The true stars of "Star Wars" are John Barry, who was responsible for the production design, and the people who were responsible for the incredible special effects—space ships, explosions of stars, space battles, hand-to-hand combat with what appear to be lethal neon swords. I have a particular fondness for the look of the interior of a gigantic satellite called the Death Star, **a place full of the kind of waste space one finds today only in old Fifth Avenue mansions and public libraries.**

There's also a very funny sequence in a low-life bar on a remote planet, a frontierlike establishment where they serve customers who look like turtles, apes, pythons and various amalgams of same, but draw the line at robots. Says the bartender piously: "We don't serve *their* kind here."

NOMINATED FOR
10
ACADEMY
AWARDS
— including —
BEST PICTURE
BEST DIRECTOR-George Lucas
BEST ORIGINAL SCREENPLAY-George Lucas
BEST SUPPORTING ACTOR-Alec Guinness
BEST ORIGINAL SCORE

MARK HAMILL · HARRISON FORD · CARRIE FISHER
PETER CUSHING and ALEC GUINNESS
STAR WARS
GEORGE LUCAS · GARY KURTZ · JOHN WILLIAMS
PANAVISION® PRINTS BY DE LUXE® TECHNICOLOR

R$_2$ D$_2$, one of the robots on the team of the "good guys" in *Star Wars*.

GALA Holiday Entertainment *from* **UNIVERSAL** AN MCA COMPANY

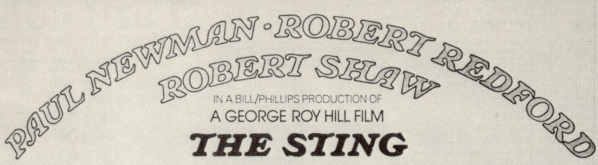
PAUL NEWMAN · ROBERT REDFORD
ROBERT SHAW
IN A BILL/PHILLIPS PRODUCTION OF
A GEORGE ROY HILL FILM

THE STING

A RICHARD D. ZANUCK/DAVID BROWN PRESENTATION

...all it takes is a little Confidence.

Written by
DAVID S. WARD · Directed by **GEORGE ROY HILL** · Produced by **TONY BILL, MICHAEL** and **JULIA PHILLIPS**
Music Adapted by MARVIN HAMLISCH · TECHNICOLOR® A UNIVERSAL PICTURE

ORIGINAL SOUNDTRACK AVAILABLE EXCLUSIVELY ON MCA RECORDS AND TAPES | **PG** PARENTAL GUIDANCE SUGGESTED

(For your fullest enjoyment—you must see this film from the beginning.)

Starts Christmas Day

| ON BROADWAY | ON THE EAST SIDE | IN NEW JERSEY | ON LONG ISLAND |
| **LOEWS STATE 2** · **LOEWS CINE / MURRAY HILL** · **UA BELLEVUE** · **UA SYOSSET** |
| Broadway at 45th St. | 86th St. & 3rd Ave. | 3rd Ave. at 34th St. | Upper Montclair | Jericho Tpke., Syosset |

The New York Times

WEDNESDAY, DECEMBER 26, 1973

30's Confidence Men Are Heroes of 'Sting'

THE STING, directed by George Roy Hill; screenplay by David S. Ward; produced by Tony Bill and Michael and Julia Phillips; director of photography, Robert Surtees; editor, William Reynolds; music, Marvin Hamlisch; a Richard D. Zanuck-David Brown presentation, distributed by Universal Pictures. Running time: 129 minutes. At Loew's State 2 Theater, Broadway at 45 Street, Loew's Cine Theater, Third Avenue near 86th Street, Murray Hill Theater, 34th Street at Third Avenue, and other theaters. This film has been classified PG.

Henry Gondoroff	Paul Newman
Johnny Hooker	Robert Redford
Doyle Lonnegan	Robert Shaw
Lieut. William Snyder	Charles Durning
J. J. Singleton	Ray Walston
Billie	Eileen Brennan
Kid Twist	Harold Gould
eddie Niles	John Heffernan
F.B.I. Agent Polk	Dana Elcar

By VINCENT CANBY

"The Sting," which opened yesterday at Loew's State 2 and other theaters, re-teams the director (George Roy Hill) and stars (Paul Newman and Robert Redford) of "Butch Cassidy and the Sundance Kid" in a comedy about a couple of exuberant confidence men operating in and around Chicago in 1936.

"The Sting" looks and sounds like a musical comedy from which the songs have been removed, leaving only a background score of old-fashioned, toe-tapping piano rags that as easily evoke the pre-World War I teens as the nineteen-thirties.

A lot of the other period details aren't too firmly anchored in time, but the film is so good-natured, so obviously aware of everything it's up to, even its own picturesque frauds, that I opt to go along with it. One forgives its unrelenting efforts to charm, if only because "The Sting" itself is a kind of con game, devoid of the poetic aspirations that weighed down "Butch Cassidy and the Sundance Kid."

Mr. Newman and Mr. Redford, dressed in best, fit-to-kill, snap-brim hat, thirties spendor, looking like a couple of guys in old Arrow shirt ads, are more or less reprising their roles in "Butch Cassidy."

Mr. Newman is Henry Gondoroff, the older con artist in charge of the instruction of Johnny Hooker (Mr. Redford), the bright, eager, younger man who yearns to make what the movie calls the Big Con (swindle), the way tap dancers in the movies about the twenties wanted to play the Palace.

Their quarry is a ruthless, vain, fastidious New York racketeer named Doyle Lonnegan, played by Robert Shaw in the broad manner in which the film was conceived by David S. Ward, who wrote the screenplay, and realized by Mr. Hill.

The director supplements the period sets and costumes with elaborate technical devices to move from one scene into another: wipes, iris-outs, images that turn like pages. Separating sequences are title cards that recall Norman Rockwell's Saturday Evening Post covers. It's all a little too much, but excess is an essential part of the film's style.

"The Sting" has a conventional narrative, with a conventional beginning, middle and end, but what one remembers are the set pieces of the sort that can make a slapped-together Broadway show so entertaining. These include a hilarious, thoroughly crooked poker game on the Twentieth Century Limited in which Henry blows his nose on his tie to the horror of Lonnegan, as well as a chase that lasts approximately two minutes, and the final swindle, the mechanics of which are still none too clear to me.

The only woman with a substantial role in the film is Eileen Brennan, who plays a madam with a heart of gold and enough time off to be able to assist the stars in the final con. "The Sting" is not the kind of film that takes its women very seriously, and the continuing popularity of these male-male co-starring teams should, I suppose, probably prompt some solemn analysis.

It is not, I suspect, a terrible perversion of the romantic movie-team concept idealized by William Powell and Myrna Loy, Clark Gable and Lana Turner but, rather, a variation on the old Dr. Gillespie-Dr. Kildare relationship, with a bit of Laurel and Hardy thrown in. It is also apparently very good box office.

Paul Newman as the ultimate con man in *The Sting*.

'The Sun Also Rises' on View at Roxy

Hemingway Classic

THE SUN ALSO RISES, screen play by Peter Viertel, based on the Ernest Hemingway novel; directed by Henry King; produced by Darryl F. Zanuck for Twentieth Century-Fox. At the Roxy.

Jake Barnes	Tyrone Power
Lady Brett Ashley	Ava Gardner
Robert Cohn	Mel Ferrer
Mike Campbell	Errol Flynn
Bill Gorton	Eddie Albert
Romero	Robert J. Evans
Montoya	Carlos Muzquiz
Georgete	Juliette Greco
Count Mippipopolous	Gregory Ratoff
Doctor	Henry Daniell

IN all probability, many bristling book-readers are going to march into the Roxy for the screen version of Ernest Hemingway's "The Sun Also Rises" with a unanimous, grim conviction: it had better be good. It is.

Bravely tackling one of the most hallowed of all American novels, as his second independent project under the Twentieth Century-Fox banner, Darryl F. Zanuck has assembled a glitteringly spacious and beautiful background canvas, on location in France, Spain and Mexico.

This visual magnificence, in CinemaScope and color, frames a picturesque cast, headed by Tyrone Power, Ava Gardner and Mel Ferrer, that looks hand-picked down to the last bit "extra." Director Henry King has staged a personalized, handsome, big "show," from Peter Viertel's admirably faithful script, which slices a few corners and minor characters from the source.

While the result is emotionally intriguing, rather than powerful, it remains, nevertheless, Hemingway all the way.

Outwardly, the author's revered "lost" American expatriates of the post-war mid-Twenties have changed little in some thirty years. Jake—good old Jake Barnes, played by Mr. Power—is the same cynical Paris Herald writer, the platonic soul-mate of the disillusioned Brett Ashley, portrayed by Miss Gardner, who is trailed, in turn, by their hanger-on crony, Robert Cohn, played by Mr. Ferrer.

Their aimless Parisian prowlings in a superbly atmospheric assortment of vintage bars, hotels and thoroughfares immediately convey Mr. Hemingway's unyielding tone of futility. These rather stilted early scenes, unfortunately, are full of endless, if incomparable, talk.

What amounts to an adult, lifelike charade suddenly bursts forth with a clanging, hypnotically stunning close-up of a Spanish bullfighting town in full traditional fiesta blast. Here, in Pamplona (adroitly juxtaposed with additional Mexican footage), the crossed tensions of the trio begin to attain real urgency.

The derelicts, by now linked up with Bill Gorton (Eddie Albert) and Mike Campbell, Brett's "fiancé," (Errol Flynn), are so smoothly piloted through the fascinating little town by Mr. King that their child-like abandon, their snapping nerves and Brett's climactic dalliance with a young toreador all come across with keen-edged credibility.

•

We doubt, indeed, if Mr. Hemingway's pen, or anybody's, could improve some occasional camera magic: the huge arena itself; Jake's poster-lined stalk through the streets; Brett's first, fleeting glimpse of her young quarry, Romero (perfectly personified by Robert J. Evans—let's forget his Irving Thalberg in "Man of a Thousand Faces).

The picture needs, and lacks, just one great performance, although Mr. Power is certainly a professionally convincing hero. Mr. Ferrer is fine, considering the slight sketchiness of his motivations. A grinning, portly Mr. Flynn and the jovial Mr. Albert fit their roles like gloves.

As for Brett, that tarnished beauty loved for years by so many male readers (including this one), Miss Gardner, with an occasional look of real, fleeting anguish, excellently pegs her predatory aspects. She simply doesn't, or can't, convey the lady's innate, poignant air of breeding, for all Brett's promiscuity. Sorry, Miss Gardner.

Again, thirty years is a long time between mediums. In an age of galvanized tourism, short on introspection, this picture deals with some none-too-youthful barflys who might be called merely idle, rather than (as they insist) "lost." But if Mr. Hemingway's book seems somewhat of a curio on the screen, blame it on the respect, intelligence and technical splendor that roving Hollywood has accorded a classic.

NOW! air conditioned

ROXY
50th ST. & 7th AVE
CI 7-6000

TYRONE POWER
AVA GARDNER
MEL FERRER
ERROL FLYNN
EDDIE ALBERT

in

DARRYL F. ZANUCK'S
most provocative production!
ERNEST HEMINGWAY'S
most tantalizing novel!

20. THE SUN ALSO RISES

Directed by
HENRY KING

Produced by
DARRYL F. ZANUCK

Screenplay by
PETER VIERTEL

CinemaScope   COLOR by DE LUXE   Stereophonic Sound

ON THE STAGE

"SHOWPLANE
at the Roxy"

Juliette Greco from the film version of Hemingway's classic, *The Sun Also Rises.*

Gloria Swanson Returns to the Movies in 'Sunset Boulevard,' Feature at Music Hall

SUNSET BOULEVARD, screen play by Charles Brackett, Billy Wilder and D. M. Marshman Jr.; directed by Mr. Wilder and produced by Mr. Brackett for Paramount Pictures. At the Music Hall.

Joe Gillis	William Holden
Norma Desmond	Gloria Swanson
Max Von Mayerling	Erich von Stroheim
Betty Schaefer	Nancy Olson
Sheldrake	Fred Clark
Morino	Lloyd Gough
Artie Green	Jack Webb
Undertaker	Franklyn Barnum
First Finance Man	Larry Blake
Second Finance Man	Charles Dayton
Themselves	Cecil B. DeMille
	Hedda Hopper
	Buster Keaton
	Anna Q. Nilsson
	H. B. Warner
	Ray Evans
	Jay Livingston

A segment of life in Hollywood is being spread across the screen of the Music Hall in "Sunset Boulevard." Using as the basis of their frank, caustic drama a scandalous situation involving a faded, aging silent screen star and a penniless, cynical young script writer, Charles Brackett and Billy Wilder (with an assist from D. M. Marshman Jr.) have written a powerful story of the ambitions and frustrations that combine to make life in the cardboard city so fascinating to the outside world.

"Sunset Boulevard" is by no means a rounded story of Hollywood, past or present. But it is such a clever compound of truth and legend—and is so richly redolent of the past, yet so contemporaneous—that it seemingly speaks with great authority. "Sunset Boulevard" is that rare blend of pungent writing, expert acting, masterly direction and unobtrusively artistic photography which quickly casts a spell over an audience and holds it enthralled to a shattering climax.

Gloria Swanson was coaxed out of long retirement to portray the pathetic, forgotten film queen, Norma Desmond, and now it can be said that it is inconceivable that anyone else might have been considered for the role. As the wealthy, egotistical relic desperately yearning to hear again the plaudits of the crowd, Miss Swanson dominates the picture. Even in those few scenes when she is not on screen her presence is felt like the heavy scent of tuberoses which hangs over the gloomy, musty splendor of her mementocluttered mansion in Beverly Hills.

Playing the part of Joe Gillis, the script writer, William Holden is doing the finest acting of his career. His range and control of emotions never falters and he engenders a full measure of compassion for a character who is somewhat less than admirable. Hounded by collectors from the auto-finance company, the struggling, disillusioned writer grabs an opportunity to make some money by helping Norma Desmond to fashion a screen play about Salome with which the hopeless egomaniac believes she will make a "return to the millions of people who have never forgiven me for deserting the screen."

Joe Gillis is indignant when Norma insists that he live in her house, but gradually his self respect is corroded by easy comforts and he does nothing strenuous to thwart her unsubtle romanic blandishments. Before an attachment to a girl of his own age jolts him out of this dark abyss and rekindles his writing spark, Joe has become hopelessly entangled in the life of the psychopatic star who holds him down with lavish gifts and an attempted suicide.

With uncommon skill, Brackett and Wilder, who also produced and directed this splendid drama for Paramount Pictures, have kept an essentially tawdry romance from becoming distasteful and embarrassing. Aside from the natural, knowing tone of the dialogue, the realism of the picture is heightened by scenes set inside the actual iron-grilled gates of the Paramount Studio, where Norma Desmond goes for an on-the-set visit with her old comrade, Cecil B. DeMille himself. And the fantastic, Babylonian atmosphere of an incredible past is reflected sharply in the gaudy elegance of the decaying mansion in which Norma Desmond lives.

The hope that propels young people to try their luck in Hollywood is exemplified by Betty Schaefer, a studio reader with writing ambitions who is beautifully portrayed by Nancy Olson.

RADIO CITY MUSIC HALL

Showplace of the Nation   Rockefeller Center

WORLD PREMIERE TODAY
Doors Open 10:30 A. M.

THE HOLLYWOOD STORY

WILLIAM HOLDEN · GLORIA SWANSON · ERICH von STROHEIM

with NANCY OLSON · FRED CLARK · LLOYD GOUGH · JACK WEBB

and Cecil B. DeMille · Hedda Hopper · Buster Keaton · Anna Q. Nilsson

H. B. Warner · Franklyn Farnum

Produced by Charles Brackett · Directed by BILLY WILDER · A Paramount Picture

Gloria Swanson plays the fading silent screen star and William Holden plays a penniless script writer in
Sunset Boulevard.

It's a Bird, It's a Plane, It's a Movie

IN a season in which our motion-picture comic strips have been either heavily mythic ("The Lord of the Rings") or simply pretentious ("Watership Down"), "Superman" is good, clean, simple-minded fun, though it's a movie whose limited appeal is built in. There isn't a thought in this film's head that would be out of place on the side of a box of Wheaties. But to describe as good, clean, simple-minded fun a film on which so much effort, time and talent have been expended is to sound a muted warning.

To enjoy this movie as much as one has a right to expect, one has either to be a Superman nut, the sort of trivia expert who has absorbed all there is to know about the planet Krypton, or to check one's wits at the door, which may be more than a lot of people are prepared to do for longer than two hours.

The Superman comic strip has been carefully, elaborately, sometimes wittily blown up for the big-theater screen, which, though busy, often seems sort of empty. In Christopher Reeve, a young New York stage and television actor who plays Superman and Clark Kent, the mild-mannered newspaper reporter who is Superman's cover, the producers and Richard Donner, the director, have a performer who manages to be both funny and comic-strip heroic without making a fool of himself. Mr. Reeve even looks like something drawn on an easel, being composed entirely of firm lines without a bit of shading. Margot Kidder is also most charming, revealing (is this for the first time?) that Lois Lane is the sort of newspaper reporter who puts two p's in rapist.

The supporting cast is of a caliber one might otherwise expect to see only at fund-raising events for American Indians, the American Film Institute or the March of Dimes. Marlon Brando turns up early in the saga as Superman's dad, Jor-El, who looks rather like George Washington with chrome finish on his hair. Glenn Ford has two scenes as Superman's adopted earth-father.

Gene Hackman, Ned Beatty and Valerie Perrine play the members of the evil trio whose attempts to destroy California (by activating the San Andreas fault) form what might be called the plot. Jackie Cooper plays the harried editor of The Daily Planet, and a number of other major actors, including Terence Stamp, Susannah York, Harry Andrews, Trevor Howard and Maria Schell, play roles so small the actors should wear numbers for immediate identification.

This kind of casting is prodigal but it is an essential element in a film in which extravagance is the dominant style.

The screenplay appears to have been composed by a unisex basketball team — Mario Puzo, who is credited with the original story; David Newman, Leslie Newman (who is the wife of David) and Robert Benton, who in 1966 wrote a Broadway musical about Superman

Super Cast

SUPERMAN, directed by Richard Donner; screenplay by Mario Puzo, David Newman, Leslie Newman and Robert Benton; story by Mario Puzo; creative consultant, Tom Mankiewicz; executive producer, Ilya Salkind, producer, Pierre Spengler; music by John Williams; released by Warner Bros. At Loews Astor Plaza, Loews Orpheum, Murray Hill, and neighborhood theaters. Running time: 142 minutes. This film is rated PG.

Jor-el	Marlon Brando
Lex Luthor	Gene Hackman
Superman/Clark Kent	Christopher Reeve
Otis	Ned Beatty
Perry White	Jackie Cooper
Pa Kent	Glenn Ford
First Elder	Trevor Howard
Lois Lane	Margot Kidder
Non	Jack O'Halloran
Eve Teschmacher	Valerie Perrine
Vond-ah	Maria Schell
General Zod	Terence Stamp
Ma Kent	Phyllis Thaxter
Lara	Susannah York
Young Clark Kent	Jeff East
Jimmy Olsen	Marc McClure
Ursa	Sarah Douglas
Second Elder	Harry Andrews

with Mr. Newman. Tom Mankiewicz receives credit as creative consultant, but, because he is a writer, I assume he might also have written a line or two.

There have been a number of published statements by people connected with the film to the effect that the Superman legend has been treated with-

out condescension, not as camp, which is more or less true, though the movie's brightest moments are those very broad ones supplied by Mr. Hackman, Mr. Beatty and Miss Perrine, whose bosom submits to her bodice only with a fight. Their comic moments recall the best of the old Batman television series.

For all intents and purposes Mr. Brando plays it straight, applying to Krypton's most brilliant scientist a neo-English accent and a mock gravity that are funny because he's the actor he is.

The movie does nothing lightly or quickly. After opening credits that are so portentous they could be announcing the discovery of a new mouthwash, the film spends what seems to be an interminable amount of time (approximately an hour) on Krypton explaining the planet's domestic problems (worse than but not as complicated as Iran's) and Superman's heritage, a sequence climaxed by the destruction of Krypton. The rest of the movie proceeds at the panel-by-panel pace of a comic strip, with Superman/Clark Kent's courting of Lois Lane and fighting for "truth, justice and the American way."

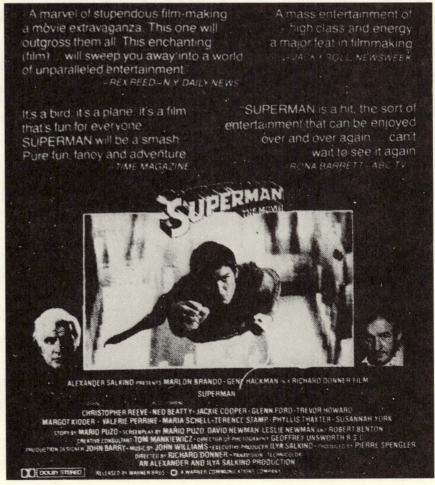

"A marvel of stupendous film-making a movie extravaganza. This one will outgross them all. This enchanting (film) will sweep you away into a world of unparalleled entertainment."
— REX REED – N.Y. DAILY NEWS

"A mass entertainment of high class and energy a major feat in filmmaking."
— JACK KROLL, NEWSWEEK

"It's a bird, it's a plane, it's a film that's fun for everyone. SUPERMAN will be a smash. Pure fun, fancy and adventure."
— TIME MAGAZINE

"SUPERMAN is a hit, the sort of entertainment that can be enjoyed over and over again... can't wait to see it again."
— RONA BARRETT – ABC TV

SUPERMAN THE MOVIE

ALEXANDER SALKIND PRESENTS MARLON BRANDO · GENE HACKMAN in A RICHARD DONNER FILM
SUPERMAN
CHRISTOPHER REEVE · NED BEATTY · JACKIE COOPER · GLENN FORD · TREVOR HOWARD
MARGOT KIDDER · VALERIE PERRINE · MARIA SCHELL · TERENCE STAMP · PHYLLIS THAXTER · SUSANNAH YORK
STORY BY MARIO PUZO SCREENPLAY BY MARIO PUZO, DAVID NEWMAN, LESLIE NEWMAN AND ROBERT BENTON
CREATIVE CONSULTANT: TOM MANKIEWICZ · DIRECTOR OF PHOTOGRAPHY GEOFFREY UNSWORTH B.S.C.
PRODUCTION DESIGNER JOHN BARRY · MUSIC BY JOHN WILLIAMS · EXECUTIVE PRODUCER ILYA SALKIND · PRODUCED BY PIERRE SPENGLER
DIRECTED BY RICHARD DONNER · PANAVISION · TECHNICOLOR
AN ALEXANDER AND ILYA SALKIND PRODUCTION
DOLBY STEREO RELEASED BY WARNER BROS. A WARNER COMMUNICATIONS COMPANY

Christopher Reeve as *Superman*.

Screen: 'Sweet Bird of Youth' Opens

Adaptation of Williams Play at 2 Theatres

By BOSLEY CROWTHER

A new set of gaudy plumage bedecks Tennessee Williams' "Sweet Bird of Youth" in the motion picture version of it that came to the Capitol and Sutton yesterday.

CinemaScope and color, a monster political rally and parade in the seamy Gulf Coast community where the action of the drama takes place, smashing close-ups of tarnished faces and a wildly contrived "happy end" are used to adorn the scraggly body of Mr. Williams' poisonous play.

But underneath all the glitter and added motion provided on the screen (some of which, we must say, is quite exciting and effective in a purely graphic way), we are still up against the same dank characters that slithered and squirmed and grunted and howled across the stage, with the three main ones still being acted by Paul Newman, Rip Torn and Geraldine Page.

Even though they are still horrendous characters, each in his (or her) separate way, oozing meanness like blackstrap molasses and trailing misery like a prisoner's clanking chains—all of which has the surface fascination of the churning of a basketful of snakes — they are still strangely dissociated. They are monsters roaming in Mr.

Williams' space, only occasionally bumping into one another in credible clashes. And this becomes the more obvious on the screen.

Mr. Newman's sneaky Hollywood gigolo who returns to his old home town in the hope of making one more fruitful contact with the papa-hobbled girl he left behind is a vicious, conniving creature—so much so that it's hard to believe he would have the quality to sustain a pure devotion to a pallid, unprofitable girl.

What's he doing back here in this community, stubbornly sticking out his neck and virtually asking for it to be chopped off, when he's almost got it made with a Hollywood doll?

And Miss Page's drunken Hollywood has-been—she's a

FROM:

Tennessee Williams, the author of "Cat on a Hot Tin Roof"
Richard Brooks, the writer-director of "Elmer Gantry"
Pandro S. Berman, the producer of "Butterfield 8"

Metro Goldwyn Mayer presents

PAUL NEWMAN
GERALDINE PAGE

Based on the Play by TENNESSEE WILLIAMS

SWEET BIRD OF YOUTH

He used love like most men use money!

ACADEMY AWARD NOMINEES!
PAUL NEWMAN "BEST ACTOR!" in "The Hustler"
GERALDINE PAGE "BEST ACTRESS!" in "Summer and Smoke"

CINEMASCOPE and METROCOLOR

Provocative Adult Entertainment

CO-STARRING SHIRLEY KNIGHT · ED BEGLEY · RIP TORN

WRITTEN FOR THE SCREEN AND DIRECTED BY RICHARD BROOKS
PRODUCED BY PANDRO S. BERMAN MGM

STARTS TODAY

EXTRA! IN PERSON! TONIGHT AT CAPITOL!
GERALDINE PAGE · SHIRLEY KNIGHT · RIP TORN · MILDRED DUNNOCK · MADELEINE SHERWOOD and distinguished members of The Actors' Studio will attend the Opening Night Showing.

DOORS OPEN 10:30 A.M.
NEW LOEW'S **CAPITOL** B'way & 51st St. FREE PARKING AFTER 6:00 P.M.

DOORS OPEN 11:45 A.M.
SUTTON 57th St. at 3rd Ave.

The Cast

SWEET BIRD OF YOUTH, screen play by Richard Brooks, based on the stage play by Tennessee Williams; directed by Mr. Brooks; produced by Pandro S. Berman for Metro-Goldwyn-Mayer. At the Capitol Theatre, Broadway and Fifty-first Street, and Sutton Theatre, Fifty-seventh Street and Third Avenue. Running time: 120 minutes.

Chance Wayne	Paul Newman
Alexandra Del Lago	Geraldine Page
Heavenly Finley	Shirley Knight
Boss Finley	Ed Begley
Thomas J. Finley Jr.	Rip Torn
Aunt Nonnie	Mildred Dunnock
Miss Lucy	Madeleine Sherwood
Dr. George Scudder	Philip Abbott
Scotty	Corey Allen
Bud	Barry Cahill
Dan Hatcher	Dub Taylor
Leroy	James Douglas
Ben Jackson	Barry Atwater
Mayor Hendricks	Charles Arnt
Mrs. Maribelle Norris	Dorothy Konrad
Prof. Burtus Smith	James Chandler
Deputy	Mike Steen
Sheriff Clark	Kelly Thordsen

shatteringly frightful grotesque, clawing the walls and the bare shoulders of her male companion with equal wild distress. Miss Page makes her a brilliant lot of fiendish femininity (although at times her scenes are played at too great length, so that her artfulness grows a little boring). But what's she doing in this provincial mess? Mr. Williams has dragged her into it and Richard Brooks, writer and director of the film, has naturally kept her involved. But she's really just a marginal monster, contributing her marginal lot of horror.

And Boss Finley, the local political tyrant, father of the girl and also father of the sadistic satrap played coldly by Mr. Torn—he's a horrible, howling Southern roughneck, a strong reminder of Huey Long, splendidly played by Ed Begley, who makes you cringe every time he grins. But he, too, is an unconnected monster. Why does he waste any time with this undistinguished home-comer? And why did he drive him away in the first place, anyhow?

No, this cynical, coruscating drama has a strong look of being contrived, and Mr. Brooks' happy ending for it is implausible and absurd. If there is any point to the whole thing, it is that life is a tangle of defeats and Mr. Williams' language that screams it has a strange, mad poetic quality. The most honest thing about the stage play was that the fetid hero got it in the end. Not only is he spared that desolation in this picture; he gets his old loyal girl instead.

Shirley Knight as the latter and Mildred Dunnock as her squeaky, brow-beaten aunt are a couple of those gauzy Williams females who seem like caricatures on the screen.

"Sweet Bird of Youth," for all its graphics and the vigorous performance of its top roles, has the taint of an engineered soap opera, wherein the soap is simply made of lye, that's all.

Flamboyant 'Taxi Driver' by Scorsese

TAXI DRIVER, directed by Martin Scorsese; screenplay by Paul Schrader; produced by Michael Phillips and Julia Phillips; music, Bernard Herrmann; director of photography, Michael Chapman; editors, Tom Rolf and Melvin Shapiro; distributed by Columbia Pictures. Running time: 112 minutes. At the Coronet Theater, Third Avenue near 59th Street. This film has been rated R.

Travis Bickle	Robert De Niro
Betsy	Cybill Shepherd
Iris	Jodie Foster
Sport	Harvey Keitel
Wizard	Peter Boyle
Charles Palantine	Leonard Harris
Tom	Albert Brooks
Melio	Vic Argo
Gun Salesman	Steven Prince
Passenger	Martin Scorsese
Personnel Officer	Joe Spinell

By VINCENT CANBY

The steam billowing up around the manhole cover in the street is a dead giveaway. Manhattan is a thin cement lid over the entrance to hell, and the lid is full of cracks. Hookers, hustlers, pimps, pushers, frauds and freaks— they're all at large. They form a busy, faceless, unrepentant society that knows a secret litany. On a hot summer night the cement lid becomes a nonstop harangue written in neon: walk, stop, go, come, drink, eat, try, enjoy. Enjoy? That's the biggest laugh. Only the faceless ones — the human garbage — could enjoy it.

This is the sort of thing that Travis Bickle (Robert De Niro) might make note of in his diary. Travis, a loner who comes from somewhere else, drives a Manhattan cab at night. In the day he sleeps in short naps, pops pills to calm down, swigs peach brandy, which he sometimes pours on his breakfast cereal, and goes to porn films to relax. At one point he is aware that his headaches are worse and he suspects that he may have stomach cancer.

Travis Bickle is the hero of Martin Scorsese's flamboyant new film, "Taxi Driver," which opened yesterday at the Coronet. He's as nutty as they come, a psychotic, but as played by Mr. De Niro he's a riveting character inhabiting a landscape that's as much his creation as he is the creation of it.

"Taxi Driver" is in many ways a much more polished film than Mr. Scorsese's other major Manhattan movie, "Mean Streets," but its polish is what ultimately makes it seem less than the sum of its parts. The original screenplay by Paul Schrader, one of Hollywood's new young hopes (writers' division) imposes an intellectual scheme upon Travis's story that finally makes it seem too simple. It robs the film of mystery. At the end you may feel a bit cheated, as you do when the solution of a whodunit fails to match the grandeur of the crime.

But until those final moments "Taxi Driver" is a vivid, galvanizing portrait of a character so particular that you may be astonished that he makes consistent dramatic sense. Psychotics are usually too different, too unreliable, to be dramatically useful except as exotic décor.

Travis Bickle—the collaboration of writer, director and actor —, remains fascinating throughout, probably because he is more than a character who is certifiably insane. He is a projection of all our nightmares of urban alienation, refined in a performance that is effective as much for what Mr. De Niro does as for how he does it. Acting of this sort is rare in films. It is a display of talent, which one gets in the theater, as well as a demonstration of behavior, which is what movies usually offer.

Were Mr. De Niro less an actor, the character would be a sideshow freak. The screenplay, of course, gives him plenty to work with. Until the final sequences, "Taxi Driver" has a kind of manic aimlessness that is a direct reflection of Travis's mind, capable of spurts of common sense and discipline that are isolated in his general confusion. Travis writes in his diary, "I don't believe that one should devote his life to morbid self-attention," and then sets about to make a name for himself by planning a political assassination.

The point of the film (which I can't talk about without giving away the plot), is, I feel, questionable, but the rest of it works. The supporting performances are fine, including those of Jodie Foster (whom I last saw as Becky Thatcher in "Tom Sawyer") as a teen-age hustler, Harvey Keitel as her pimp and Peter Boyle as a muddle-headed Manhattan cab driver.

You may want to argue with "Taxi Driver" at the end, and with good reason, but it won't be a waste of time.

COLUMBIA PICTURES presents

ROBERT DE NIRO

TAXI DRIVER

A BILL/PHILLIPS Production of a MARTIN SCORSESE Film

JODIE FOSTER   ALBERT BROOKS as Tom   HARVEY KEITEL
LEONARD HARRIS   PETER BOYLE as Wizard   and

CYBILL SHEPHERD as Betsy

Written by PAUL SCHRADER   Music BERNARD HERRMANN   Produced by MICHAEL PHILLIPS and JULIA PHILLIPS
Directed by MARTIN SCORSESE   Production Services by Devon/Persky Bright   R RESTRICTED   Columbia Pictures

Remarkable Spectacle

THE TEN COMMANDMENTS, with Theodore Roberts, Charles de Roche, Estelle Taylor, Julia Faye, Terrence Moore, James Neill, Lawson Butt, Clarence Burton, Nobie Johnson, in the great spectacle; in the modern story are Edyth Chapman, Richard Dix, Rod La Roque, Leatrice Joy, Nita Naldi, Robert Edeson, Charles Ogle and Agnes Ayres.

It is probable that no more wonderful spectacle has ever been put before the public in shadow-form than the greatly heralded prelude to Cecil B. DeMille's costly film, which opened last night to a brilliant and eager gathering in the George M. Cohan Theatre. It is called, and it hardly seems necessary to mention the title "The Ten Commandments." It is built in two sections, the spectacle and the melodrama. Two men might have directed this feature, as it goes from the sublime to the out-and-out movie. Not that the latter part is bad, but that almost any melodramatic picture would have fitted into the second section of this photodrama.

But the sight of the Israelites in bondage in Egypt, their slaving before the chariots, their treatment by the despots of the day, the swiftly drawn chariots and their steeds, and the great bas-reliefs of figures whose shin-bones would have made two big men. All this was obviously directed by a genius who held in his hand the cost. There are many impressive colorful scenes of the Israelites in the desert, some of them appearing better and more natural than other such effects we have witnessed on the screen.

Charles de Roche, whom we first met in a minor part of "The Spanish Jade," who recently was seen as a Hindu with Pola Negri in "The Cheat," impersonated the terrible Rameses. He was impressive, and like all the other players in this section of this picture, wore his raiment of cloth and metal as if it were comfortable.

There was the death of all the first borns of the Egyptians, and the great and so-called magnificent Rameses praying to his god throughout the night to put life into his boy's body, and no life came. His god had no power like the God of the Israelites.

Coupled with the orchestration there has been nothing on the film so utterly impressive as the thundering and belching forth of one commandment after another, and the tilting and photography of this particular effect was remarkable. It was the quivering, crashing, resounding blare from the string and wind instruments that did much to assist in the desired effect. The sky clouds, and then seems to burst, and from the ball of smoke appears golden lettering with one or another of the commandments, stress being laid upon those that are considered the most important, if one may say such a thing.

The costumes in this million dollars' worth of prelude are splendidly created, and not in a single instance is there a jarring note in this regard. Theodore Roberts, who recently was seen in the character of a business man with a cigar in his mouth, gave an excellent portrayal of Moses, the Lawgiver. His make-up was faultless, and the sincerity with which he acted this part made the whole affair doubly effective. Undoubtedly it was a series of sequences that made one think, that carried a message, that was done with meticulous precision, and boomed forth so well that it would have needed an unusually perfect modern drama to stand up in comparison with it. In this section, with a good photographic and scenic effect, the crossing through a water flanked path of the Red Sea was shown, and it drew applause from the packed theatre. Prior to that there was the Pillar of Fire which confused and halted the Egyptians hastening after the slaves they had released through fear of the God of the Israelites.

But—and unfortunately we have to say but—the strain on Mr. De Mille told, and as soon as he swept on to his modern drama he was back to the ordinary and certainly uninspired movie, one in which the direction at times had "business" apparently intended to appeal to the very young. Too many "inserts" were shown. In one case there was a letter which was put on the screen three different times, and from what we now remember once would have been sufficient. The cracking walls of a cathedral being constructed by the hapless man in this portion of the film are brought out so many times that it is extremely tedious, and we would also like to say that if an old mother reads her Bible it is no reason why a motion picture director should have her carrying around a volume that weighs about a hundredweight. Also, why have her pictured after death with the same huge Bible? This is a story of two sons, one bad and the other good, a woman from a leper island, and the breaking of all the Commandments by the conscienceless love making, unfaithful and plotting weakling.

At the same time it must be admitted that in this melodrama there are also some excellent and well-thought out ideas, and some eye-smiting shots. There is considerable suspense where the wife of the wicked brother ascends to the top of the scaffolding of the tickety structure, constructed with rotten cement. It is the catching of her heel on a corner that uncovers the cheap and rotten concrete, as she nearly falls. And Mr. De Mille has not forgotten to give his spectators an impression of height in the full sequence.

Whatever has been done in the second instalment of this picture—which in all is said to have cost a million and one-half dollars and classed by Mr. De Mille as "the cheapest picture ever made," because of the reward in sheckels it will reap—one must say that great heights of costuming and direction have been attained in the prelude.

Estelle Taylor in *The Ten Commandments.*

GEO. M. COHAN THEATRE, B'way. and 42nd Street

FIRST MATINEE TODAY AT 2:30

"THE TEN COMMANDMENTS"

Produced by

CECIL B. DeMILLE

Story by Jeanie Macpherson

A Paramount Production

Presentation by Riesenfeld

Twice Daily 2:30 and 8:30. Sunday Mats. at 3

PRICES   Daily Mats. 50c to $1. Nights, Saturday and Hol. Mats. 50c to $2.00. ALL SEATS RESERVED

'That's Entertainment!' Certainly Is

THAT'S ENTERTAINMENT!, scenes from movie musicals by M-G-M from 1929 to 1958; written, produced and directed by Jack Haley Jr.; executive producer, Daniel Melnick; additional music adapted by Henry Mancini; released by United Artists Corporation. At the Ziegfeld Theater, Avenue of the Americas and 54th Street. Running time: 120 minutes. (This film is classified G).

By NORA SAYRE

When Graham Greene was a movie critic in the nineteen-thirties, he detested close-ups of the open mouths of singers; his reviews complained steadily of teeth and tonsils. He would be miserable at "That's Entertainment!," a tour of M-G-M musicals from 1929 to 1958—but those who don't share his phobia will hugely enjoy this movie. Written, produced and directed by Jack Haley Jr., it opened yesterday at the Ziegfeld.

The pleasures are abundant: Gene Kelly squelching sublimely through puddles in "Singin' in the Rain"; Judy Garland singing "Get Happy" over a series of clips of her faces at all ages—the result is a joyful obituary; Donald O'Connor dancing on his knees; Fred Astaire and Eleanor Powell in a breath-stopping duet from "Broadway Melody of 1940." Glimpses of Mr. Kelly, springing about on the scaffolding of a half-constructed building, and Mr. Astaire, dancing with a hat rack, distill the contrasting styles of both great hoofers.

Mr. Kelly's acrobatic talents make you aware of the exertion as much as the dexterity: what he does is triumphantly difficult, and we know that almost no one else could leap so smartly from one spot to another. But, as many have noted, Mr. Astaire makes every step look easy: as he soars and swoops and glides, infinite spectators feel that they could do exactly the same.

Some of the musicals of the early thirties were creaky because dramatic actors were suddenly pushed into a medium that didn't suit them. In "Idiot's Delight," Clark Gable dances and sings abominably, and Joan Crawford—one rigid finger laid against her cheek — prances like a lumberjack. The movie's funniest moment may be the apotheosis of Esther Williams in the early fifties: climactic scenes of that brawny Venus sinking into or rising from the water appear to mock the imagery of the Aquarian age. Incidentally, the big ballet from "American in Paris" seems soupier than ever.

Ars Gratia Artis indeed . . . Today, there's a pang in watching that lion roar above M-G-M's motto, to see the ravaged sets of the studio whose existence was imperiled for a while (although movie production has resumed). Elizabeth Taylor, James Stewart, Mickey Rooney and the other stars who narrate this picture are sentimental about the past—but why shouldn't they be? Meanwhile, most of the numbers—from Jimmy Durante coaching the young Frank Sinatra in "It Happened in Brooklyn" to Leslie Caron drifting in and out of Mr. Kelly's grasp — run long enough so that you can re-experience the original. Hence this isn't nostalgia, it's history.

An American in Paris.

'3 Faces of Eve'

Personalities Study Opens at Victoria

The Cast

THE THREE FACES OF EVE, written, produced and directed by Nunnally Johnson; based on the book by Drs. Corbett H. Thigpen and Hervey M. Cleckley; presented by Twentieth Century-Fox. At the Victoria.

Eve	Joanne Woodward
Ralph White	David Wayne
Dr. Luther	Lee J. Cobb
Dr. Day	Edwin Jerome
Secretary	Alena Murray
Mrs. Black	Nancy Kulp
Mr. Black	Douglas Spencer
Bonnie	Terry Ann Ross
Earl	Ken Scott
Eve—Age 8	Mimi Gibson

By BOSLEY CROWTHER

A YOUNG Georgia woman with a personality that is prone to a severe three-way stretch is the subject of Nunnally Johnson's new drama—or melodrama—"The Three Faces of Eve," which came with a faint jangle of sweet bells into the Victoria yesterday.

When we first come upon this heroine she is a wan and emotionally troubled dame, nervously accompanied by her husband, seeking the aid of a psychiatrist. It seems that she has terrible headaches and strange lapses of memory. The psychiatrist offers some pat suggestions and sends her home to her husband and child.

However, she comes back some time later. Now a second personality has begun to emerge. This one is a loose, lurid creature with a brash go-to-hell attitude. She doesn't care beans for her husband, denies that she's the mother of her child and generally raises mischief when she takes over and goes out on the town.

Naturally, the woman is bewildered when she slips back into her pallid state. The doctor is fascinated. And the dumb husband thinks it's all a fake. He watches a couple of these cycles of changing personality, then washes his hands of the whole business and gets himself a divorce.

Left alone with her psychiatrist, the woman degenerates until she is switching back and forth from one to the other personality almost as fast as she can close and open her eyes. The doctor seems to find it so intriguing that he prompts her to change, like a magician doing a trick. "Let's have Eve Black," he will tell her. "Now, let's go back to Mrs. White." She does.

And then something curious happens. Mrs. White tries to commit suicide, but Eve Black takes possession of the situation and saves herself—or both of herselves—just in time. Whereupon, as she tells the doctor of it, a third personality begins to emerge. This one is sweet, serene, intelligent and conspicuously self-possessed.

Well, this occurrence flips the doctor. Now he has THREE changes that he can ring, and he spins the poor woman around the circuit as though her three personalities were playing tag. Finally, he hits upon something. Seems that when she was a little girl, her mother made her kiss her dead grandmother and that did something awful to her nerves. What it was is not explained to the audience, but once the doctor and the woman have it tagged, they are able to "kill" the other personalities and let the sweet, serene one live.

The last we see of the woman and her recovered daugh they are going off with a fine young fellow name of Earl.

•

This story, which Alistair Cooke sincerely tells us at the beginning is absolutely true—and is, indeed, based upon a clinical study written up by two Georgia psychiatrists, is written, produced and directed by Mr. Johnson with a clean documentary clarity, and played with superlative flexibility and emotional power by Joanne Woodward in the main role.

Miss Woodward, a comparative newcomer, stretches three ways convincingly. David Wayne is pretty good as her crude husband and Lee J. Cobb plays the psychiatrist well.

But when you come right down to it, this is simply a melodramatic exercise—an exhibition of psychiatric hocus-pocus, without any indication of how or why. It makes for a fairly fetching mystery, although it is too verbose and too long. But like the similar film, "Lizzie," before it, it leaves one feeling gypped and gulled at the end.

Joanne Woodward in *The Three Faces of Eve.*

A moment ago she was the nicest girl in town! A moment from now she will be anybody's pick-up! YOU NEVER KNEW SUCH WOMEN EXISTED!

CAN YOU FACE "THE THREE FACES OF EVE"

The most fantastic true personal story ever filmed

EVERY ADULT MUST SEE IT!

IT'S ALL TRUE! SHE MAY BE YOUR NEXT DOOR NEIGHBOR

SEE IT WITH SOMEONE YOU'D LIKE TO MARRY

NO ONE SEATED DURING THE SENSATIONAL ENDING! No one under 14 will be permitted to see it alone!

starring
JOANNE WOODWARD · DAVID WAYNE · LEE J. COBB

From 20th Century-Fox in CinemaScope

Produced and Directed from his screenplay by NUNNALLY JOHNSON

in the wonder of STEREOPHONIC SOUND

NOW! VICTORIA B'way & 46th Street Doors Open 9:30 A.M. Late Film 12:25 A.M.

'To Have and Have Not,' With Humphrey Bogart, at the Hollywood—Arrival of Other New Films at Theatres Here

TO HAVE AND HAVE NOT, screen play by
Jules Furthman and William Faulkner; from
the novel by Ernest Hemingway; produced
and directed by Howard Hawks for Warner
Brothers. At the Hollywood.
Morgan	Humphrey Bogart
Eddie (The Rummy)	Walter Brennan
Marie	Lauren Bacall
Helene De Bursac	Dolores Moran
Crickett	Hoagy Carmichael
Paul De Bursac	Walter Molnar
Lieut. Coyo	Sheldon Leonard
Gerard	Marcel Dalio
Johnson	Walter Sande
Capt. Renard	Dan Seymour
Renard's Bodyguard	Aldo Nadi
Beauclerc	Paul Marion
Mrs. Beauclerc	Patricia Shay
Bartender	Pat West
Emil	Emmet Smith
Horatio	Sir Lancelot

By BOSLEY CROWTHER

Having once cornered Humphrey Bogart in a Casablanca café and beheld his tremendous potential in that sultry and colorful spot, it was logical that the Warners should have wanted to get him there again—or in some place of similar nature, where the currents would flow much the same. A fellow like Mr. Bogart needs a well-coupled circuit, you know. Well, the desire has been accomplished with surprisingly comparable effect in Howard Hawks' production for that studio, "To Have and Have Not," which came to the Hollywood yesterday.

Maybe they say that the story is based on Ernest Hemingway's tale of the same name, and maybe the locale is visually French Martinique four years ago. But there's no use dodging around it: "To Have and Have Not" is "Casablanca" moved west into the somewhat less hectic Caribbean but along the same basic parallel. And, although there are surface alterations in some of the characters, you will meet here substantially the same people as in that other geo-political romance.

For what Mr. Hawks and his script-writers have done to Mr. Hemingway's tale is to shape it out of all recognition into a pattern of worldly intrigue. Now the professional sports fisherman, who was a brute in the original, is a much more tractable fellow where human destinies are involved, and especially is he open to persuasion when a fascinating female waves in. And thus, while pursuing his profession in the region of Martinique, he is coerced to fish in the deep waters of pro and anti-Vichy lawlessness by the push of his own moral suasion and the lure of a very fetching girl.

There is much more character than story in the telling of this tough and tight-lipped tale, and much more atmosphere than action of the usual muscular sort. And that—as was true with "Casablanca"—is generally just as well. For Mr. Bogart is best when his nature is permitted to smoulder in the gloom and his impulse to movement is restricted by a caution bred of cynical doubt. And those are his dispositions which Mr. Hawks has chiefly worked on in this film. As the hard-boiled professional fisherman who gives his ample ingenuity to a cause, Mr.

Bogart is almost as impressive as he was as Rick, the Casablanca host.

And as the wistful bird of passage who moves dauntlessly into his life, Lauren Bacall, a blondish newcomer, is plainly a girl with whom to cope. Slumberous of eye and softly reedy along the lines of Veronica Lake, she acts in the quiet way of catnip and sings a song from deep down in her throat. Accompanied by Hoagy Carmichael, who plays a sweetly sleazy pianist in this film, she mumbles a song of his composing, "How Little We Know," in perfect low-down barroom style. Mr. Carmichael himself also does grandly by a sort of calypso song, which is strictly in keeping with the rambling and melancholy atmosphere.

Hoagy Carmichael with Humphrey Bogart and Lauren Bacall in their first film together, *To Have and Have Not.*

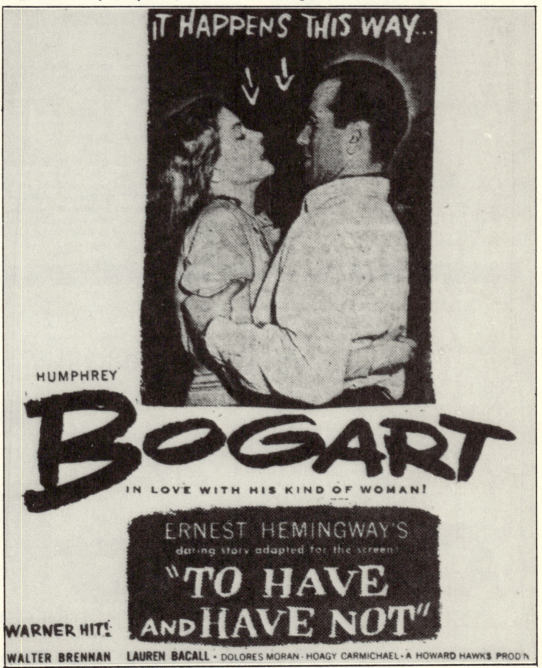

IT HAPPENS THIS WAY...

HUMPHREY
BOGART
IN LOVE WITH HIS KIND OF WOMAN!

ERNEST HEMINGWAY'S
daring story adapted for the screen!
"TO HAVE AND HAVE NOT"

WARNER HIT!
WALTER BRENNAN · LAUREN BACALL · DOLORES MORAN · HOAGY CARMICHAEL · A HOWARD HAWKS PROD'N

'Tom Jones,' a Lusty Comedy

Albert Finney Is Seen in the Title Role

By BOSLEY CROWTHER

PREPARE yourself for what is surely one of the wildest, bawdiest and funniest comedies that a refreshingly agile filmmaker has ever brought to the screen. It is Tony Richardson's production of Henry Fielding's classic novel, "Tom Jones," and it arrived yesterday for what I reckon should be at least a six-month run at Cinema I.

But is it "Tom Jones"? Well, that voluminous and wonderfully entertaining tale of the social and amorous adventures of a young buck in England in the 18th century is the narrative source of the picture. And most of its major episodes recounting life in the beautiful west country and in fashionable London are packed into the film.

But in finding a means of cinema expression in which to convey most suitably to our age the deceptively fastidious rhetoric and ribald wit of the Fielding work, Mr. Richardson and his scenarist,

John Osborne of "Angry Young Man" fame, have worked out a structure and a rhythm that constitute a major creative achievement in themselves.

Their attack on the lusty old novel is completely away from the line of a standard-movie treatment, with its usual endeavor to put a naturalistic reproduction of the original into pictorial terms. And they have whipped up a roaring entertainment that develops its own energy as much from its cinematic gusto as from the racy material it presents.

At the very beginning, for instance, before the main title comes on, they serve astonishing notice that this is to be a lark in movie terms. Home comes the righteous Squire Allworthy to find a bawling infant in his bed and the hint of an amatory scandal lurking somewhere below his stairs.

But do you think this conventional prologue is done in conventional style? Not at all! It is done in mock depictment of an old melodramatic silent film, with the action fast and the cutting frequent, printed titles instead of dialogue and a wild din of spinnet music setting an antique tone. And then, as

the camera hits a close-up of the baby and as the title is superimposed, the voice of a primly sly narrator comes in to say, "Tom Jones, of whom the opinion of all was that he was born to be hanged."

Now it takes off, some years later, with Tom a lusty young man, played with a wonderfully open, guileless and raffish attitude by the brilliant new star, Albert Finney (who is now playing Martin Luther on Broadway), bounding through earthy adventures as Squire Allworthy's ward. And the breakneck pace set in the prologue is miraculously maintained to the measures of a highly contributive musical accompaniment composed by John Addison.

Mr. Addison's score, so full of mischief, instrumental and melodic, swings along with the breathtaking tempo of the action and with Mr. Richardson's camera techniques, which are really most apt revitalizations of flavorsome tricks and stunts.

For instance, he loves to cut an action with a fast across-the-frame or clock-hand wipe or to stop the action at a climactic moment for a split-second freeze before jumping on to the next scene. He will frame a character's face in

an iris. He will even have his actors address the audience in "asides" as when Tom, suspicious of a woman innkeeper, turns to the audience and asks, "Did you see her take 50 pounds from me pocket?" At another point, when Tom is about to embrace the utterly abandoned Mrs. Waters, he considerately places his cap over the eye of the camera.

By such prankish devices, Mr. Richardson gives his film the speed and, indeed, somewhat the character of a Keystone comedy. He conveys, in these cinematic comments, an even fuller enjoyment of the absurd. His is a 20th-century

(continued)

The Cast

TOM JONES, screenplay by John Osborne from the novel by Henry Fielding; produced and directed by Tony Richardson; a Woodfall Production, distributed by Lopert Pictures Corporation. At Cinema I, Third Avenue and 60th Street. Running time: 135 minutes.

Tom Jones	Albert Finney
Sophie Western	Susannah York
Squire Western	Hugh Griffith
Miss Western	Dame Edith Evans
Lady Bellaston	Joan Greenwood
Molly	Diane Cilento
Mrs. Waters	Joyce Redman
Squire Allworthy	George Devine
Lord Fellamar	David Tomlinson
Blifil	David Warner
Partridge	Jack McGowran
Fitzpatrick	George A. Cooper
Thwackum	Peter Bull
Square	John Moffat
Mrs. Fitzpatrick	Rosalind Knight
Parson Supple	James Cairncross
Black George	Wilfrid Lawson
Mrs. Miller	Rosalind Atkinson
Mrs. Wilkins	Angela Baddeley
Mrs. Seagrim	Freda Jackson
Northerton	Julian Glover
Honour	Patsy Rowlands
Bridget Allworthy	Rachel Kempson

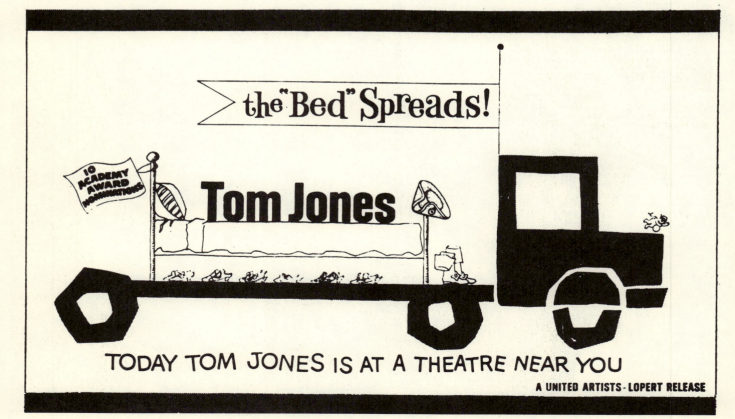

the "Bed" Spreads!

10 ACADEMY AWARD NOMINATIONS

Tom Jones

TODAY TOM JONES IS AT A THEATRE NEAR YOU

A UNITED ARTISTS - LOPERT RELEASE

means of characterizing 18th-century manners and morals.

And what manners and morals he shows us, what characters and episodes! There's the big, brawling fight in the churchyard over Molly, the incorrigible slut (a word often used with rich expression). There's Squire Western's roaring deer hunt, with the camera hand-held and pitching wildly in the midst of the huntsmen and hounds or flying over the scene (in a helicopter), surveying the madness below. There's the pell-mell explosion of characters, righteous and unrighteous, through the halls of the Upton inn after an irate husband has discovered a bit of scandalous going-on.

And what acting! We have mentioned Mr. Finney. He is tops in the title role, but Hugh Griffith is his match as Squire Western, the sporting, cursing, barnyard-mannered goat. Mr. Griffith is everything that Fielding intended him to be—fire-eater, hypocrite, lecher—with a madcap style of his own.

Susannah York as his daughter — the lovely Sophie

whom Tom hopes to wed— is a warm little package of passions; Diane Cilento is all teeth and claws as the insatiable Molly; Joyce Redman is brazen and bold as the naughty Mrs. Waters and in one incomparable scene Mr. Richardson has her and Mr. Finney make eating a meal an act so lewd, yet so utterly clever and unassailable, that it is one of the highlights in the film.

Oh, there are a dozen others that should be mentioned—Joan Greenwood as Lady Bellaston, George Devine as Squire Allworthy, Dame Edith Evans as the sister of Squire Western, David Warner as the insidous Blifil and many more. There's the excellent color photography and the amusing costuming that should be praised. There's even the new "cliff-hanger" ending that Fielding himself might have generously enjoyed.

Perhaps there will be those who will be embarrassed by so much bawdiness on the screen. But I find it too funny to be tasteless, too true to be artistically false. And, what's more, it should set a lot of people to reading that incomparable novel, "Tom Jones."

Albert Finney and Diane Cilento in a scene from the bawdy comedy, *Tom Jones.*

Hugh Griffith and Dame Edith Evans.

'The Towering Inferno' First-Rate Visual Spectacle

THE TOWERING INFERNO, directed by John Guillermin; screenplay by Sterling Silliphant; based on the novels "The Tower" by Richard Martin Stern and "The Glass Inferno" by Thomas N. Scortia and Frank M. Robinson; produced by Irwin Allen; action sequences directed by Mr. Allen; director of photography, Fred Koenekamp; director of action-sequence photography, Joseph Biroc; editors, Harold F. Kress and Carl Kress; music, John Williams; distributed by 20th Century-Fox (domestic) and Warner Bros. (foreign). Running time: 160 minutes. At the National Theater, Broadway at 44th Street, and Trans-Lux East Theatre, Third Avenue at 58th Street. This film has been rated PG.

Michael O'Hallorhan	Steve McQueen
Doug Roberts	Paul Newman
James Duncan	William Holden
Susan Franklin	Faye Dunaway
Harlee Claiborne	Fred Astaire
Patty Simmons	Susan Blakely
Roger Simmons	Richard Chamberlain
Lisolette Mueller	Jennifer Jones
Jernigan	O. J. Simpson
Senator Gary Parker	Robert Vaughn
Dan Bigelow	Robert Wagner
Lorrie	Susan Flannery

By VINCENT CANBY

"The Towering Inferno" is a nearly three-hour suspense film for arsonists, firemen, movie-technology buffs, building inspectors, worry warts.

The film, which opened yesterday at the National and Trans-Lux East Theaters, is a gigantic cautionary tale for people who want the worst to happen. It's this year's best end-of-the-world movie—the world in this case being represented by a 138-story, glass-and-steel San Francisco skyscraper that, on the night of its dedication, becomes history's biggest Roman candle. It doesn't burn down, just up.

It's not a movie that bothers too much about the specifics how it happened (something about cheap wiring). It's mainly concerned with what happens during the holocaust, that is with an almost interminable succession of rescue episodes involving lovers, frauds, villains, a little girl, a small cat, a mayor and his wife and other assorted characters whose life spans conform roughly to their billing: actors at the head of the cast live longest.

•

Granting that end-of-the-world movies are not designed to test the intellect but, rather, to provide second-hand thrills of a visceral sort, "The Towering Inferno" must be everything its producer (Irwin Allen) and its two distribution companies (20th Century-Fox and Warner Bros., paired in a one-shot marriage-of-convenience to finance the film) could have possibly desired.

The special effects are smashing, better than those in "Earthquake" even without the brain-bending Sensurround effect of "Earthquake."

ONE TINY SPARK BECOMES A NIGHT OF BLAZING SUSPENSE

The world's tallest building is on fire. You are there on the 135th floor... no way down... no way out.

The Fire Chief

The Architect

STEVE McQUEEN   PAUL NEWMAN   WILLIAM HOLDEN

IRWIN ALLEN'S

THE TOWERING INFERNO

FAYE DUNAWAY

FRED ASTAIRE · SUSAN BLAKELY · RICHARD CHAMBERLAIN · JENNIFER JONES · O.J. SIMPSON · ROBERT VAUGHN · ROBERT WAGNER

Produced by IRWIN ALLEN · Directed by JOHN GUILLERMIN · Screenplay by STIRLING SILLIPHANT · Music by JOHN WILLIAMS

Based on the novels "The Tower" by RICHARD MARTIN STERN and "The Glass Inferno" by THOMAS N. SCORTIA and FRANK M. ROBINSON

PG PARENTAL GUIDANCE SUGGESTED

The Builder · The Girl Friend · The Con Man · The Wife · The Son-in-Law · The Widow · The Security Man · The Senator · The Publicity Man

GALA INVITATIONAL PREMIERE WEDNESDAY 8 PM AT THE NATIONAL THEATRE
STARS! LIGHTS! CELEBRITIES! DON'T MISS IT!
Benefit—New York Diabetes Association
For ticket information call (212) 697-7760

REGULAR PERFORMANCES START THURSDAY
(70mm and 6 Track Stereophonic Sound)

ON BROADWAY
Mann's
NATIONAL THEATRE
Broadway at 44th St. 869-0950

ON THE EAST SIDE
TRANS-LUX EAST
58th St. & 3rd Ave.
759-2262

ON LONG ISLAND
UA SYOSSET
Jericho Turnpike. 516-921-5810
GALA PREMIERE THURSDAY AT 8:30 PM
Sponsored by the Syosset Fire Department

IN WESTCHESTER
CENTRAL PLAZA 2
Yonkers
914-793-3232

IN NEW JERSEY
BLUE STAR 1
Blue Star Shopping Center
Watchung. 201-322-7007

TOTOWA CINEMA 1
Route 46. Totowa
201-256-8484

No passes accepted during this engagement. Academy members will be admitted with card.

The New York Times

AUGUST 18, 1934.

Wallace Beery and Jackie Cooper in a Film Version of Stevenson's "Treasure Island."

TREASURE ISLAND, adapted from the novel by Robert Louis Stevenson; directed by Victor Fleming; a Metro-Goldwyn-Mayer production. At the Capitol and Loew's Metropolitan.

Long John Silver...........Wallace Beery
Jim Hawkins................Jackie Cooper
Billy Bones..............Lionel Barrymore
Dr. Livesey..................Otto Kruger
Captain Smollett.............Lewis Stone
Squire Trelawney............Nigel Bruce
Ben Gunn...............Charles (Chic) Sale
Pew...................William V. Mong
Black Dog...........Charles McNaughton
Mrs. Hawkins.............Dorothy Peterson

By MORDAUNT HALL.

As fine a lot of cutthroats as ever have infested a film turn up as pirates in the latest cinematic conception of Robert Louis Stevenson's "Treasure Island," which is now on exhibition at the Capitol. Long John Silver appears in the person of Wallace Beery, who does extraordinarily well at hobbling about the sets on one leg and a crutch, with a parrot perched on his shoulder.

Although there are occasional studio interpolations, the present screen offering is a moderately satisfactory production. It has not the force or depth of the parent work and, kind as one might wish to be to the adaptation, it always seems synthetic. However, hitherto on the stage and in two silent films of the same subject, the rôle of Jim Hawkins has been acted by a girl. One is spared this weakness in this picture, for that able juvenile, Jackie Cooper, plays Jim, and, although he may not impress one as being the Jim of the book, he does fairly well.

In the film there are several effective settings, such as those of the Ben Bow Inn, the schooner Hispaniola and the stockade on Skeleton Island. When the time comes to reveal the treasure, Victor Fleming, the director, shows a heap of golden pieces and boxes of jewels, thus making it worth all the trouble taken by Dr. Livesey, Squire Trelawney and the ship's gallant skipper, Captain Smollett.

Charles (Chic) Sale is cast as Ben Gunn who, having been deserted by pirates and left for three years on the island, has one thing uppermost in his mind, and that is a good piece of cheese. In one of the closing incidents Gunn is discovered on the ship's deck with a cheese about the size of the average water melon, and he consumes it very much in the same way a Negro eats the popular fruit.

If this picture does not come up to expectations, it is at least a good deal better than the films of most classics. One feels that its chief shortcomings are an overzealousness to make it exciting and an eagerness to thrust forth comedy relief. If Mr. Beery is not precisely the character drawn by Stevenson, he deserves praise for giving as good a performance as was possible in the circumstances. Lionel Barrymore lends his talent to the part of Billy Bones. Otto Kruger, although too immaculately clad and made-up as Dr. Livesey, acts pleasingly. Nigel Bruce does a good piece of acting as the garrulous Trelawney and Lewis Stone as Captain Smollett is a decided asset. Mr. Sale is not amiss as the crack-brained Ben Gunn.

The principals in the Capitol stage show are George Givot, Peggy Taylor and her Kitchen Pirates, the Four Trojans, Pete, Peaches and Duke, the Chester Hale dancers and Joe Morrison.

Wallace Beery and Jackie Cooper in *Treasure Island*.

Wallace Beery (Long John Silver) introduces Jim Hawkins (Jackie Cooper) to his shipmates in a scene from *Treasure Island*.

Today at the Capitol!

THEY'LL STEAL THEIR WAY TO YOUR HEART

WALLACE **BEERY** JACKIE **COOPER**

LIONEL BARRYMORE
In Robert Louis Stevenson's
Immortal Drama

Treasure Island

The Champ and the Kid return to the screen together, in the greatest of all adventure stories... Anchors aweigh! Follow them to the end of the rainbow of romance! Come...the open seas call ...We're away to "Treasure Island" as literature's greatest classic springs to life on the screen.

with
CHARLES "Chic" SALE · OTTO KRUGER
NIGEL BRUCE · LEWIS STONE
A Metro-Goldwyn-Mayer Picture
Directed by VICTOR FLEMING — *Produced by* HUNT STROMBERG

WALLACE BEERY . . . . . . *as Long John Silver*
JACKIE COOPER . . . . . . *as Little Jim Hawkins*
LIONEL BARRYMORE . . . . . . *as Billy Bones*
OTTO KRUGER . . . . . . *as Dr. Livesey*
LEWIS STONE . . . . . . *as Captain Smollett*
"Chic" Sale *as Ben Gunn*   William V. Mong *as Old Pew*

ON STAGE
GEO. GIVOT
Radio's Greek Ambassador
PEGGY TAYLOR
And Kitchen Pirates
FOUR TROJANS
PETE, PEACHES *and* DUKE
CHESTER HALE GIRLS
and Added Attraction
JOE MORRISON
of "Last Roundup" *Fame*

COOL
Capitol

BROADWAY
AT 50th ST.

MAJOR EDWARD BOWES,
Managing Director

'Treasure of Sierra Madre,' Film of Gold Mining in Mexico, New Feature at Strand

TREASURE OF SIERRA MADRE: Screen play by John Huston; based on the novel by B. Traven; directed by John Huston; produced by Henry Blanke for Warner Brothers Pictures, Inc. At the Strand.

Dobbs	Humphrey Bogart
Howard	Walter Huston
Curtin	Tim Holt
Cody	Bruce Bennett
McCormick	Barton MacLane
Gold Hat	Alfonso Bedoya
Presidente	A. Soto Rangel
El Jefe	Manuel Donde
Pablo	Jose Torvay
Pancho	Margarito Luna
Flashy Girl	Jacqueline Dalay
Mexican Boy	Bobby Blake

By BOSLEY CROWTHER

Greed, a despicable passion out of which other base ferments may spawn, is seldom treated in the movies with the frank and ironic contempt that is vividly manifested toward it in "Treasure of Sierra Madre." And certainly the big stars of the movies are rarely exposed in such cruel light as that which is thrown on Humphrey Bogart in this new picture at the Strand. But the fact that this steel-springed outdoor drama transgresses convention in both respects is a token of the originality and maturity that you can expect of it.

Also, the fact that John Huston, who wrote and directed it from a novel by B. Traven, has resolutely applied the same sort of ruthless realism that was evident in his documentaries of war is further assurance of the trenchant and fascinating nature of the job.

Taking a story of three vagrants on "the beach" in Mexico who pool their scratchy resources and go hunting for gold in the desolate hills, Mr. Huston has shaped a searching drama of the collision of civilization's vicious greeds with the instinct for self-preservation in an environment where all the barriers are down. And, by charting the moods of his prospectors after they have hit a vein of gold, he has done a superb illumination of basic characteristics in men. One might almost reckon that he has filmed an intentional comment here upon the irony of avarice in individuals and in nations today.

But don't let this note of intelligence distract your attention from the fact that Mr. Huston is putting it over in a most vivid and exciting action display. Even the least perceptive patron should find this a swell adventure film. For the details are fast and electric from the moment the three prospectors start into the Mexican mountains, infested with bandits and beasts, until two of them come down empty-handed and the third one, the mean one, comes down dead. There are vicious disputes among them, a suspenseful interlude when a fourth man tries to horn in and some running fights with the banditi that will make your hair stand on end. And since the outdoor action was filmed in Mexico with all the style of a documentary camera, it has integrity in appearance, too.

Most shocking to one-tracked moviegoers, however, will likely be the job that Mr. Bogart does as the prospector who succumbs to the knawing of greed. Physically, morally and mentally, this character goes to pot before our eyes, dissolving from a fairly decent hobo under the corroding chemistry of gold into a hideous wreck of humanity possessed with only one passion—to save his "stuff." And the final appearance of him, before a couple of roving bandits knock him off in a manner of supreme cynicism, is one to which few actors would lend themselves. Mr. Bogart's compensation should be the knowledge that his performance in this film is perhaps the best and most substantial that he has ever done.

Equally, if not more, important to the cohesion of the whole is the job done by Walter Huston, father of John, as a wise old sourdough. For he is the symbol of substance, of philosophy and fatalism, in the film, as well as an unrelenting image of personality and strength. And Mr. Huston plays this ancient with such humor and cosmic gusto that he richly suffuses the picture with human vitality and warmth. In the limited, somewhat negative role of the third prospector, Tim Holt is quietly appealing, while Bruce Bennett is intense as a prospecting lone wolf and Alfonso Bedoya is both colorful and revealing as an animalistic bandit chief.

Humphrey Bogart and Walter Huston in a scene from *Treasure of Sierra Madre,* written and directed by John Huston.

TREASURE...TEMPTATION...TREACHERY!

Men turned tyrant and women sold their souls to possess the gold in a mighty mountain of malice!

HUMPHREY **BOGART**

Hits A New High in High Adventure!

WARNER BROS. PRESENT

TREASURE OF SIERRA MADRE

WITH WALTER HUSTON · TIM HOLT · BRUCE BENNETT

DIRECTED BY JOHN HUSTON

PRODUCED BY HENRY BLANKE

WB

'Turning Point' Limns Ballet Life

THE TURNING POINT, directed by Herbert Ross; screenplay by Arthur Laurents; produced by Mr. Ross and Mr. Laurents; executive producer, Nora Kaye; music adapted and conducted by John Lanchbery; director of photography, Robert Surtees; editor, William Reynolds; distributed by 20th Century-Fox. Running time: 118 minutes. At the Coronet Theater, Third Avenue and 59th Street. This film has been rated PG.

Emma	Anne Bancroft
Deedee	Shirley MacLaine
Yuri	Mikhail Baryshnikov
Emilia	Leslie Towne
Wayne	Tom Skerritt
Acelaide	Martha Scott
Sevilla	Antoinette Sibley
Dahkarova	Alexandra Danilova
Carolyn	Starr Danias
Carter	Marshall Thompson
Michael	James Mitchell
Freddie	Scott Douglas
Arnold	Daniel Levans
Peter	Jurgen Schneider
Rosie	Anthony Zerbe
Ethan	Phillip Saunders
Janina	Lisa Lucas
Florence	Scan Bradbury
Sandra	Hilda Morales
Barney	Donald Petrie
Billy Joe	James Crittenden

Also guest appearances by Lucette Aldous, Fernando Bujones, Richard Crasun, Suzanne Farrell, Marcia Haydee, Peter Martins, Clark Tippet, Marianna Tcherkassky, Martine Van Hamel and Charles Ward.

By VINCENT CANBY

The story to date: 20 years ago Deedee abandoned her ambitions to become a star of the American Ballet Theater and, instead, moved to Oklahoma City with her husband, Wayne, with whom she opened a fabulously successful ballet school, raised three fabulously sweet children, moved into a split-level house and acquired a fabulously long station wagon. Deedee chose love—unlike her best friend, Emma, who chose success and became Ballet Theater's prima ballerina.

As our movie, which is called "The Turning Point," opens, Deedee and Emma are reunited when Ballet Theater comes to Oklahoma City. Old hopes are rekindled for, as all of us know, an old hope never dies in fiction of this sort, no matter how many tears are pumped on it. Emma, who gets 19 curtain calls and has "everything" envies Deedee, while Deedee, the one who got pregnant, still dreams of stardom. Will lthey ever find peace and fulfillment—these two women who now recall their—how shall I put it?—turning points?

To ask that question is to know the worst about this entertaining ne.. movie, an old-fashioned backstage musical transplanted to the world of ballet by three people who not only know it but also love it, sentimental clichés and all.

"The Turning Point," which opened last night at special performances at the Coronet and Baronet Theaters, begins its regular commercial engagement at the Coronet today. It's the work of Herbert Ross, the director; Arthur Laurents, the screenwriter, and Nora Kaye (Mrs. Ross), the former ballerina who is its executive producer. Their curious, collective achievement is in having found so much vitality in the sort of movie that demands that its audiences weep with sympathy for characters who have all they ever wanted but simply don't realize it yet.

Among the film's principal assets are Shirley MacLaine, looking very pretty and almost matronly, but not quite, as the sharp-tongued, intelligent, deep-down furious homemaker, Deedee; and Anne Bancroft as the driven ballerina, Emma, a woman of ravaged beauty and whose frail frame could possibly lift a freight car if she willed it.

The intensity of their lifelong friendship, and rivalry, is carefully and sometimes hilariously detailed as "The Turning Point" follows Deedee's daughter, Emilia, charmingly played by Leslie Browne, her mother and her little brother to New York, where Emilia joins Ballet Theater's school. It's not giving away too much to report that the girl's almost instantaneous success means that one day in the not too distant future she will be replacing her beloved godmother, Emma, as the A.B.T.'s major attraction.

These are more or less the bones of the film, which are hardly bare, what with Emma's having to face the reality of time's passage, and Deedee's having to come to terms with her missed opportunities. Could she have danced the lead in "Anna Karenina" 20 years ago? Probably not, though from what we see of Emma in the role, it's mostly walking through steam.

There are also the emotional crises faced in New York by Emilia, who has an unhappy affair with a young Soviet dancer named Yuri, a role played with cheerful ease by Mikhail Baryshnikov, the young Soviet dancer who chose success in the West several years ago.

As Emilia learns that the love of a young Soviet ballet dancer is not forever—which is just as well when one has her eye on the top of the bill—and as Emma and Deedee are wrestling, once physically in a very funny and moving scene, with their doubts, "The Turning Point" gives us excerpts from more than a dozen ballets that feature, in addition to Mr. Baryshnikov and Miss Browne, the stars and the corps de ballet of Ballet Theater.

All of the men in the film exist as little more than dance partners or as props for the drama. This is partly the result of the focus of the movie in which Miss MacLaine and Miss Bancroft give such powerhouse performances and only Mr. Baryshnikov is allowed to be a man of any substance.

The others, including Tom Skerritt, who plays Miss MacLaine's blandly decent husband, are background figures. Such a comment, I realize, could also be made about any number of Bette Davis, Joan Crawford or Greer Garson movies of long ago.

"The Turning Point" is entertaining, not for discovering new material, but for treating old material with style and romantic feeling that, in this day and age, seem remarkably unafraid.

A moving story. A romantic story.
A story of envy, hatred, friendship, triumph, and love.

ANNE BANCROFT   SHIRLEY MacLAINE

The Turning Point

TWENTIETH CENTURY-FOX Presents A HERBERT ROSS Film
ANNE BANCROFT SHIRLEY MacLaine "THE TURNING POINT" TOM SKERRITT
featuring MIKHAIL BARYSHNIKOV and LESLIE BROWNE
Co-starring MARTHA SCOTT · MARSHALL THOMPSON and ANTHONY ZERBE · AMERICAN BALLET THEATRE
Executive Producer NORA KAYE Written by ARTHUR LAURENTS Produced by HERBERT ROSS and ARTHUR LAURENTS
Directed by HERBERT ROSS   PRINTS BY DE LUXE® NOW IN PAPERBACK FROM SIGNET
MUSIC FROM THE MOTION PICTURE ON 20TH CENTURY RECORDS AND TAPES

EXCLUSIVE ENGAGEMENT
THE Coronet
59th St. at 3rd Ave · EL 5 1663
12:00, 2:10, 4:20, 6:30, 8:40, 10:50

Anne Bancroft and Shirley MacLaine in the backstage film about ballet, The Turning Point.

'2001' Is Up, Up and Away

Kubrick's Odyssey in Space Begins Run

By RENATA ADLER

EVEN the M-G-M lion is stylized and abstracted in Stanley Kubrick's "2001: A Space Odyssey," a film in which infinite care, intelligence, patience, imagination and Cinerama have been devoted to what looks like the apotheosis of the fantasy of a precocious, early nineteen-fifties city boy. The movie, on which Kubrick collaborated with the British science-fiction author Arthur C. Clarke, is nominally about the finding, in the year 2001, of a camera-shy sentient slab on the moon and an expedition to the planet Jupiter to find whatever sentient being the slab is beaming its communications at.

There is evidence in the film of Clarke's belief that men's minds will ultimately develop to the point where they dissolve in a kind of world mind. There is a subplot in the old science-fiction nightmare of man at terminal odds with his computer. There is one ultimate science-fiction voyage of a man (Keir Dullea) through outer and inner space, through the phases of his own life in time thrown out of phase by some higher intelligence, to his death and rebirth in what looked like an intergalactic embryo.

●

But all this is the weakest side of a very complicated, languid movie—in which almost a half-hour passes before the first man appears and the first word is spoken, and an entire hour goes by before the plot even begins to declare itself. Its real energy seem to derive from that bespectacled prodigy reading comic books around the block. The whole sensibility is intellectual fifties child: chess games, body-building exercises, beds on the spacecraft that look like camp bunks, other beds that look like Egyptian mummies, Richard Strauss music, time games, Strauss waltzes, Howard Johnson's, birthday phone calls. In their space uniforms, the voyagers look like Jiminy Crickets. When they want to be let out of the craft they say, "Pod bay doors open," as one might say "Bomb bay doors open" in every movie out of World War II.

When the voyagers go off to plot against HAL, the computer, it might be HAL, the camper, they are ganging up on. When HAL is expiring, he sings "Daisy." Even the problem posed when identical twin computers, previously infallible, disagree is the kind of sentence-that-says-of-itself-I-lie paradox, which—along with the song and the nightmare of ganging up—belong to another age. When the final slab, a combination Prime Mover slab and coffin lid, closes in, it begins to resemble a fifties candy bar.

●

The movie is so completely absorbed in its own problems, its use of color and space, its fanatical devotion to science-fiction detail, that it is somewhere between hypnotic and immensely boring.

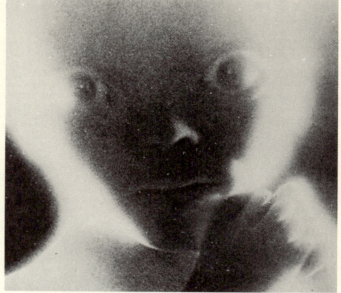

A creature from the future in the Stanley Kubrick-Arthur C. Clarke collaboration, *2001: A Space Odyssey.*

(With intermission, it is three hours long.) Kubrick seems as occupied with the best use of the outer edge of the screen as any painter, and he is particularly fond of simultaneous rotations, revolving, and straight forward motions—the visual equivalent of rubbing the stomach and patting the head. All kinds of minor touches are perfectly done: there are carnivorous apes that look real; when they throw their first bone weapon into the air, Kubrick cuts to a spacecraft; the amiable HAL begins most of his sentences with "Well," and his answer to "How's everything?" is, naturally, "Everything's under control."

There is also a kind of fanaticism about other kinds of authenticity: space travelers look as sickly and exhausted as travelers usually do; they are exposed in space stations to depressing canned music; the viewer is often made to feel that the screen is the window of a spacecraft, and as Kubrick introduces one piece of unfamiliar apparatus after another—a craft that looks, from one angle, like a plumber's helper with a fist on the end of it, a pod that resembles a limbed washing machine—the viewer is always made aware of exactly how it is used and where he is in it.

The special effects in the movie—particularly a voyage, either through Dullea's eye or through the slab and over the surface of Jupiter-Earth and into a period bedroom—are the best I have ever seen; and the number of ways in which the movie conveys visual information (there is very little dialogue) drives it to an outer limit of the visual.

The movie opened yesterday at the Capitol.

The Cast

2001 A SPACE ODYSSEY, screenplay by Stanley Kubrick and Arthur C. Clarke; directed and produced by Mr. Kubrick; presented by Metro-Goldwyn-Mayer. At the Capitol Theater, Broadway and 51st Street. Running time: 160 minutes.
Bowman ....Keir Dullea
Poole ....Gary Lockwood
Dr. Heywood Floyd ...William Sylvester
Moonwatcher ....Dan Richter
HAL 9000 ....Douglas Rain
Smyslov ....Leonard Rossiter
Elena ....Margaret Tyzack
Halvorsen ....Robert Beatty
Michaels ....Sean Sullivan
Mission Controller ....Frank Miller

MGM PRESENTS A STANLEY KUBRICK PRODUCTION

2001: a space odyssey

CINERAMA

STARRING KEIR DULLEA · GARY LOCKWOOD · SCREENPLAY BY STANLEY KUBRICK AND ARTHUR C. CLARKE · PRODUCED AND DIRECTED BY STANLEY KUBRICK
SUPER PANAVISION AND METROCOLOR

Loew's CAPITOL
Broadway & 51 St. · JU 2-5060

The New York Times

SUNDAY, MARCH 5, 1978

'An Unmarried Woman,' Film With Jill Clayburgh

By VINCENT CANBY

What would you do if, after 15 years of what has seemed to be a happy marriage, you're walking down the street with your husband, making plans to rent a house on Fire Island for the summer, when he stops, looks suddenly bereft, and breaks into the sobs of childhood as he says he wants out? He confesses that he has another woman, another life he wants to go to, and he feels so miserable about everything he's shocked when you don't sympathize.

In Paul Mazursky's new comedy. "An Unmarried Woman," about America's dangerously mobile, just-this-side-of-rootless middle class, Erica (Jill Clayburgh) gets bloody mad. She stalks off alone down the street, throws up in a trash basket and, when she at last lets the news sink in, starts to cry in fury, surprise, hurt and fear.

●

As Miss Clayburgh plays this scene, one has a vision of all the immutable things that can be destroyed in less than a minute, from landscapes and ships and reputations to perfect marriages. The scene is beautifully written by Mr. Mazursky. It is high comedy of a sharp, bitter kind, and Michael Murphy is fine as the weasel husband named Martin, but Miss Clayburgh is nothing less than extraordinary in what is the performance of the year to date. In her we see intelligence battling feeling—reason backed against the wall by pushy needs.

In the succeeding weeks, Erica begins to cope. Daily routine helps. She has her job in a SoHo art gallery. She has her teen-age daughter and her women friends, some of whom are in worse shape that she is. One night she gets out of bed and systematically throws out Martin's shaving gear, golf clubs and Adidas sneakers. For a while Erica also has a woman therapist who makes her feel better by appearing serenely understanding (and a tiny bit smug) as she repeats to Erica truisms that can be very comforting to the deeply distressed.

●

"An Unmarried Woman," which opens today at the Beekman, Paramount and Murray Hill Theaters, is Mr. Mazursky's most ambitious movie so far, and the first film to put Miss Clayburgh's talents to full use. She was charming in "Semi-Tough," but otherwise she's had to wade around in things such as "The Silver Streak" and "Gable and Lombard," pretending that mud puddles are swimming pools.

Mr. Mazursky has written a marvelous role for the actress, so I suppose it's not unfair of him to depend on her to carry the movie, which is ultimately not as tough and funny and critical as it is in individual moments. Because Mr. Mazursky has such a sharp eye for the essential props of a certain kind of American life, and because he

The Cast

AN UNMARRIED WOMAN, directed and written by Paul Mazursky; produced by Mr. Mazursky and Tony Ray; director of photography, Arthur Ornitz; editor, Stuart H. Pappe; music, Bill Conti; distributed by 20th Century Fox. Running time: 124 minutes. At the Beekman Theater, 65th Street and Second Avenue; Paramount Theater, Broadway at 61st Street, and Murray Hill Theater, 34th Street near Third Avenue.

Erica	Jill Clayburgh
Saul	Alan Bates
Martin	Michael Murphy
Charlie	Cliff Gorman
Sue	Pat Quinn
Elaine	Kelly Bishop
Patti	Lisa Lucas
Jeanette	Linda Miller
Bob	Andrew Duncan
Dr. Jacobs	Daniel Seltzer
Phil	Matthew Arkin
Tanya	Penelope Russianoff
Jean	Novella Nelson
Edward	Raymond J. Barry
Herb Rowan	Ivan Karp
Claire	Jill Eikenberry
Fred	Michael Tucker
Cabby	Chico Martinez
Hal	Paul Mazursky
Sophie	Donna Perich
Man at party	Vincent Schiavelli

has an ear for the way people talk, one expects him to be a more merciless social satirist than he has any intention of being.

This is especially apparent in the new film after he has introduced us to Erica and her "problem," and after we witness her first desperate, comic attempts to liberate herself sexually

Finding a little companionship proves difficult for Jill Clayburgh in *An Unmarried Woman.*

(with an egocentric Village painter, nicely played by Cliff Gorman). Erica doesn't flounder for long. She meets Mr. Right in the form of an English artist (Alan Bates), who's so manly, wise, affectionate and dependable that he seems to be out of "The Sleeping Beauty."

●

The final quarter of the movie gives the impression not of having been written, directed and acted, but of a tone poem that's been scored with slushy music and paced with swoony camera shots, thus to suggest an alternate title, "An Unmarried Man and A Woman."

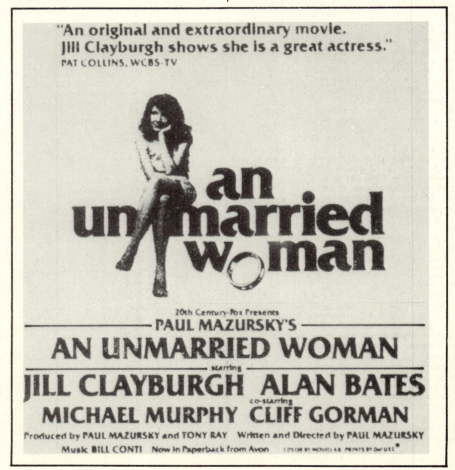

"An original and extraordinary movie. Jill Clayburgh shows she is a great actress."
PAT COLLINS, WCBS-TV

an unmarried woman

20th Century-Fox Presents

PAUL MAZURSKY'S

AN UNMARRIED WOMAN

starring

JILL CLAYBURGH   ALAN BATES

co-starring

MICHAEL MURPHY   CLIFF GORMAN

Produced by PAUL MAZURSKY and TONY RAY   Written and Directed by PAUL MAZURSKY

Music BILL CONTI   Now in Paperback from Avon   COLOR BY MOVIELAB PRINTS BY DeLUXE

The New York Times

THURSDAY, OCTOBER 19, 1961.

'West Side Story' Arrives

Film at the Rivoli Is Called Masterpiece

By BOSLEY CROWTHER

WHAT they have done with "West Side Story" in knocking it down and moving it from stage to screen is to reconstruct its fine material into nothing short of a cinema masterpiece.

In every respect, the re-creation of the Arthur Laurents-Leonard Bernstein musical in the dynamic forms of motion pictures is superbly and appropriately achieved. The drama of New York juvenile gang war, which cried to be released in the freer and less restricted medium of the mobile photograph, is now given range and natural aspect on the large Panavision color screen, and the music and dances that expand it are magnified as true sense-experiences.

The strong blend of drama, dance and music folds into a rich artistic whole. It may be seen at the Rivoli Theatre, where it had its world premiere last night.

Perhaps the most striking aspect of it is the sweep and vitality of the dazzling Jerome Robbins dances that the kids of the seamy West Side do. Here is conveyed the wild emotion that burns in these youngsters' tough, lithe frames. Here are the muscle and the rhythm that bespeak a collective energy.

From the moment the camera swings grandly down out of the sky at the start of the film and discovers the Jets, a gang of tough kids, twitching restlessly in a playground park, bodies move gracefully and fiercely in frequent spontaneous bursts of dance, and even the movements of the characters in the drama have the grace of actors in a ballet.

This pulsing persistence of rhythm all the way through the film—in the obviously organized dances, such as the arrogant show-offs of the Jets, that swirl through playgrounds, alleys, school gymnasiums and parking lots, and in the less conspicuous stagings, such as that of the "rumble" (battle) of the two kids—gives an overbeat of eloquence to the graphic realism of this film and sweeps it along, with Mr. Bernstein's potent music, to the level of an operatic form.

Against, or within, this flow of rhythm is played the tender drama of two nice kids, a Puerto Rican girl and a Polish boy, who meet and fall rapturously in love, despite

The Cast

WEST SIDE STORY, screen play by Ernest Lehman; directed by Robert Wise and Jerome Robbins; produced by Mr. Wise for Mirisch Pictures in association with Seven Arts Productions; released by United Artists. At the Rivoli Theatre, Seventh Avenue and Forty-ninth Street. Running time: 155 minutes.

Maria	Natalie Wood
Tony	Richard Beymer
Riff	Russ Tamblyn
Anita	Rita Moreno
Bernardo	George Chakiris
Ice	Tucker Smith
Action	Tony Mordente
A-rab	David Winters
Baby John	Eliot Feld
Snowboy	Bert Michaels
Anybodys	Sue Oakes
Graziella	Gina Trikonis
Velma	Carole D'Andrea
Chino	Jose De Vega
Pepe	Jay Norman
Indio	Gus Trikonis
Juano	Eddie Verso
Loco	Jaime Rogers
Rocco	Larry Roquemore
Consuelo	Yvonne Othon
Rosalia	Suzie Kaye
Francisca	Joanne Miya
Lieutenant Schrank	Simon Oakland
Officer Krupke	William Bramley
Doc	Ned Glass
Glad Hand	John Astin

the hatred and rivalry of their respective ethnic groups, and are plunged to an end that is tragic, just like Romeo and Juliet.

Every moment of the drama has validity and integrity, got from skillful, tasteful handling of a universal theme. Ernest Lehman's crackling screen play, taken from Arthur Laurent's book, and Robert Wise's incisive direction are faithful and cinema-wise, and the performances are terrific except in one major role.

Richard Beymer's characterization of the boy who meets and loves the girl is a little thin and pretty-pretty, but Natalie Wood is full of luster and charm as the nubile Puerto Rican who is poignantly drawn to him. Rita Moreno is a spitfire as Miss Wood's faithful friend, and George Chakiris is proud

Tonight! Tonight! It all begins tonight!

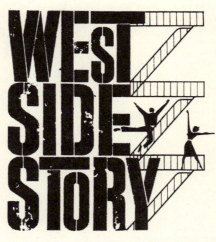

MIRISCH PICTURES PRESENTS

"WEST SIDE STORY"

A ROBERT WISE PRODUCTION

STARRING

NATALIE WOOD

RICHARD BEYMER
RUSS TAMBLYN
RITA MORENO
GEORGE CHAKIRIS

DIRECTED BY
ROBERT WISE AND JEROME ROBBINS
SCREENPLAY BY
ERNEST LEHMAN
ASSOCIATE PRODUCER
SAUL CHAPLIN
CHOREOGRAPHY BY
JEROME ROBBINS
MUSIC BY
LEONARD BERNSTEIN
LYRICS BY
STEPHEN SONDHEIM
BASED UPON THE STAGE PLAY PRODUCED BY
ROBERT E. GRIFFITH AND HAROLD S. PRINCE
BOOK BY
ARTHUR LAURENTS
PLAY CONCEIVED, DIRECTED AND CHOREOGRAPHED BY
JEROME ROBBINS
PRODUCTION DESIGNED BY BORIS LEVEN
FILMED IN PANAVISION 70/TECHNICOLOR
PRESENTED BY MIRISCH PICTURES, INC.
IN ASSOCIATION WITH SEVEN ARTS PRODUCTIONS, INC.
RELEASED THRU UNITED ARTISTS

SEATS NOW AT BOX OFFICE OR BY MAIL • ALL SEATS RESERVED

THE RIVOLI THEATRE
BROADWAY AND 49th STREET • Circle 7-1633

and heroic as her sweetheart and leader of the rival gang.

Excellent as young toughs (and dancers) in a variety of characterizations are Russ Tamblyn, Tucker Smith, Tony Mordente, Jose De Vega, Jay Norman and many more, and outstanding girls are Gina Trikonis, Yvonne Othon, Suzie Kaye and Sue Oakes.

Although the singing voices are, for the most part, dubbed by unspecified vocal performers, the device is not noticeable and detracts not one whit

from the beauty and eloquence of the songs.

In the end, of course, the moral of the tragedy comes through in the staggering sense of wastage of the energies of kids. It is screamed by the candy-store owner, played trenchantly by Ned Glass, when he flares, "You kids make this world lousy! When will you stop?"

It is a cry that should be heard by thoughtful people—sympathetic people—all over the land.

Richard Beymer, leader of the "Jets" and George Chakiris, leader of the rival street gang in a fight scene from *West Side Story*.

'White Christmas' Bows at the Music Hall

By BOSLEY CROWTHER

IT was twelve years ago that Bing Crosby was in a place and a film called "Holiday Inn," wherein he sang a little number tagged "White Christmas," written—as was all the music in that picture—by Irving Berlin. The occasion was happily historic, for a reason we scarcely need recall: "White Christmas" and Mr. Crosby became like "God Bless America" and Kate Smith—so much so, indeed, that the notion of starring Mr. Crosby in a film that would have the title "White Christmas" was broached as long as six years ago.

Various obstructions beset it, but the purpose was ultimately achieved. "White Christmas," with Mr. Crosby, opened yesterday at the Music Hall. What's more, it is in Technicolor and VistaVision, which is Paramount's new wide-screen

WHITE CHRISTMAS, written by Norman Krasna, Norman Panama and Melvin Frank; directed by Michael Curtiz; music and lyrics by Irving Berlin; produced by Robert E. Dolan for Paramount Pictures. At the Radio City Music Hall.

Bob Wallace	Bing Crosby
Phil Davis	Danny Kaye
Betty	Rosemary Clooney
Judy	Vera-Ellen
General Waverly	Dean Jagger
Emma	Mary Wickes
Joe	John Brascia
Susan	Anne Whitfield
Adjutant	Richard Shannon
General's Guest	Grady Sutton
Landlord	Sig Ruman
Albert	Robert Crossen

device, and it has Danny Kaye, Rosemary Clooney and Vera-Ellen in addition to its focal star. A new batch of Irving Berlin numbers comprises its musical score. Paramount, to put it simply, has done "White Christmas" up brown.

But, oddly enough, the confection is not so tasty as one might suppose. The flavoring is largely in the line-up and not in the output of the cooks. Everyone works hard at the business of singing, dancing and cracking jokes, but the stuff that they work with is minor. It doesn't have the old inspiration and spark.

For one thing, the credited scriptwriters—Norman Krasna, Norman Panama and Melvin Frank—have shown very little imagination in putting together what is sometimes called the "book." They have hacked out a way of getting two teams of entertainers—a pair of celebrated male hoofers and a singing sister act—to a ski lodge in New England (reminiscent of the Holiday Inn) which happens to be run by the good old general of the outfit the fellows were in during the war. And to show their appreciation of the good old general and the difficult circumstances he appears to be in, they provide free entertainment and call in a big rally of comrades for the Christmas holidays.

It is a routine accumulation of standard romance and sentiment, blessed by a few funny set-ups that are usually grabbed with most effect by Mr. Kaye. And the music of Mr. Berlin is a good bit less than inspired. Outside of the old "White Christmas," which is sung at the beginning and the end, there are only a couple of numbers that have a measure of charm. One of these is "Count Your Blessings," a song of re-assurance that Mr. Crosby and Miss Clooney chant, and another is "The Best Things Happen While You're Dancing," which Mr. Kaye sings and to which he and Vera-Ellen cavort.

Three numbers are given over to the admiration of generals and Army life, which seems not alone an extravagance but a reckless audacity. Even the sweetness of Dean Jagger as the old general does not justify the expense. Someone's nostalgia for the war years and the U. S. O. tours has taken the show awry.

Fortunately, the use of VistaVision, which is another process of projecting on a wide, flat screen, has made it possible to endow "White Christmas" with a fine pictorial quality. The colors on the big screen are rich and luminous, the images are clear and sharp, and rapid movements are got without blurring—or very little —such as sometimes is seen on other large screens. Director Michael Curtiz has made his picture look good. It is too bad that it doesn't hit the eardrums and the funnybone with equal force.

Danny Kaye, Vera-Ellen, Bing Crosby in Irving Berlin's *White Christmas.*

'The Wizard of Oz,' Produced by the Wizards of Hollywood, Works Its Magic on the Capitol's Screen

THE WIZARD OF OZ, screen play by Noel Langley, Florence Ryerson and Edgar Allan Woolf; adapted from the book by L. Frank Baum; musical adaptation by Herbert Stothart; lyrics by E. Y. Harburg and music by Harold Arlen; special effects by Arnold Gillespie; directed by Victor Fleming; produced by Mervyn LeRoy for Metro-Goldwyn-Mayer. At the Capitol.

Dorothy ....Judy Garland
Professor Marvel (the Wizard),
.....................Frank Morgan
Hunk (the Scarecrow).........Ray Bolger
Zeke (the Cowardly Lion)......Bert Lahr
Hickory (Tin Woodman)......Jack Haley
Glinda (the Good Witch)....Billie Burke
Miss Gulch (the Wicked Witch),
.................Margaret Hamilton
Uncle Henry ....Charles Grapewin
Auntie Em ....Clara Blandick
Nikko ....Pat Walshe
With the Singer Midgets as the Munchkins.

By FRANK S. NUGENT

By courtesy of the wizards of Hollywood, "The Wizard of Oz" reached the Capitol's screen yesterday as a delightful piece of wonder-working which had the youngsters' eyes shining and brought a quietly amused gleam to the wiser ones of the oldsters. Not since Disney's "Snow White" has anything quite so fantastic succeeded half so well. A fairybook tale has been told in the fairybook style, with witches, goblins, pixies and other wondrous things drawn in the brightest colors and set cavorting to a merry little score. It is all so well-intentioned, so genial and so gay that any reviewer who would look down his nose at the fun-making should be spanked and sent off, supperless, to bed.

Having too stout an appetite to chance so dire a punishment, we shall merely mention, and not dwell upon, the circumstance that even such great wizards as those who lurk in the concrete caverns of California are often tripped in their flights of fancy by trailing vines of piano wire and outcroppings of putty noses. With the best of will and ingenuity, they cannot make a Munchkin or a Flying Monkey that will not still suggest, however vaguely, a Singer's midget in a Jack Dawn masquerade. Nor can they, without a few betraying jolts and split-screen overlappings, bring down from the sky the great soap bubble in which the Good Witch rides and roll it smoothly into place. But then, of course, how can any one tell what a Munchkin, a Flying Monkey or a witch-bearing bubble would be like and how comport themselves under such remarkable circumstances?

And the circumstances of Dorothy's trip to Oz are so remarkable, indeed, that reason cannot deal with them at all. It blinks, and it must wink, too, at the cyclone that lifted Dorothy and her little dog, Toto, right out of Kansas and deposited them, not too gently, on the conical cap of the Wicked Witch of the East who had been holding Oz's Munchkins in thrall. Dorothy was quite a heroine, but she did want to get back to Kansas and her Aunt Em; and her only hope of that, said Glinda, the Good Witch of the North, was to see the Wizard of Oz who, as every one knows, was a whiz of a Wiz if ever a Wiz there was. So Dorothy sets off for the Emerald City, hexed by the broomstick-riding sister of the late Wicked Witch and accompanied, in due time, by three of Frank Baum's most enchanting creations, the Scarecrow, the Tin Woodman and the Cowardly Lion.

Judy Garland's Dorothy is a pert and fresh-faced miss with the wonder-lit eyes of a believer in fairy-tales, but the Baum fantasy is at its best when the Scarecrow, the Woodman and the Lion are on the move. The Scarecrow, with the elastic, dancing legs of Ray Bolger, joins the pilgrimage in search of brains; the Woodman, an armor-plated Jack Haley, wants a heart; the Cowardly Lion, comicalest of all, is Bert Lahr with an artistically curled mane, a threshing tail and a timid heart. As he mourns in one of his ballads, his Lion hasn't the prowess of a mow-ess; he can't sleep for brooding; he can't even count sheep because he's scared of sheep. And what he wants is courage to make him king of the forest so that even being afraid of a rhinocerus would be imposerus. Mr. Lahr's lion is fion.

There, in a few paragraphs, are most of the elements of the fantasy. We haven't time for the rest, but we must mention the talking trees that pelt the travelers with apples, the witch's sky-written warning to the Wizard, the enchanted poppy field, the magnificent humbuggery of Frank Morgan's whiz of a Wiz and the marvel of the chameleonlike "horse of another color." They are entertaining conceits all of them, presented with a naive relish for their absurdity and out of an obvious—and thoroughly natural—desire on the part of their fabricators to show what they could do. It is clear enough that Mr. Dawn, the make-up wizard, Victor Fleming, the director-wizard, Arnold Gillespie, the special effects wizard, and Mervyn LeRoy, the producing wizard, were pleased as Punches with the tricks they played. They have every reason to be.

The all star cast of *The Wizard of Oz*: Jack Haley (Tin Woodman), Ray Bolger (Scarecrow), Judy Garland (Dorothy) and Bert Lahr (Cowardly Lion).

We're off to see the Wizard—
The Wonderful Wizard of Oz.
We hear he is
A Whiz of a Wiz
If ever a Wiz there was.
If ever, if ever a Wiz there was,
The Wizard of Oz is one becoz—
Becoz, becoz, becoz, becoz, becoz,
Becoz of the wonderful things he doz.
We're off to see the Wizard
The Wonderful

WIZARD OF OZ

M·G·M's TECHNICOLOR PRODUCTION — 2 years in production with a cast of 9200, including Judy Garland as Dorothy, Frank Morgan as The Wizard, Ray Bolger as the Scarecrow, Bert Lahr as the Cowardly Lion, Jack Haley as the Tin Woodman, also Billie Burke as the Good Witch, Margaret Hamilton as the Bad Witch, Charley Grapewin as Uncle Henry, Toto as himself, and the Munchkins.

Screen Play by Noel Langley, Florence Ryerson and Edgar Allan Woolf. From the book by L. Frank Baum. A VICTOR FLEMING Production. Produced by MERVYN LE ROY. Directed by VICTOR FLEMING. Lyrics by E. Y. Harburg. Music by Harold Arlen.

A METRO-GOLDWYN-MAYER PICTURE IN TECHNICOLOR